UNDERGRADUATE TEXTS IN COMPUTER SCIENCE

Editors
David Gries
Fred B. Schneider

Springer
New York
Berlin
Heidelberg
Barcelona
Budapest
Hong Kong
London
Milan
Paris
Singapore
Tokyo

UNDERGRADUATE TEXTS IN COMPUTER SCIENCE

Beidler, Data Structures and Algorithms

Bergin, Data Structure Programming

Brooks, Problem Solving with Fortran 90

Grillmeyer, Exploring Computer Science with Scheme

Jalote, An Integrated Approach to Software Engineering, Second Edition

Kizza, Ethical and Social Issues in the Information Age

Kozen, Automata and Computability

Merritt and Stix, Migrating from Pascal to C++

Pearce, Programming and Meta-Programming in Scheme

Zeigler, Objects and Systems

Dexter C. Kozen

Automata and Computability

 Springer

Dexter C. Kozen
Department of Computer Science
Cornell University
Ithaca, NY 14853-7501
USA

Series Editors
David Gries
Fred B. Schneider
Department of Computer Science
Cornell University
Upson Hall
Ithaca, NY 14853-7501
USA

On the cover: Cover photo taken by John Still/Photonica.

With 1 figure.

Library of Congress Cataloging-in-Publication Data
Kozen, Dexter, 1951–
    Automata and computability/Dexter C. Kozen.
      p. cm. — (Undergraduate texts in computer science)
    Includes bibliographical references and index.
    ISBN 0-387-94907-0 (hardcover: alk. paper)
    1. Machine theory.   2. Computable functions.   I. Title.
  II. Series.
  QA267.K69   1997
  511.3 — dc21   96-37409

Printed on acid-free paper.

Production managed by Francine McNeill; manufacturing supervised by Jacqui Ashri.
Photocomposed copy prepared using Springer's LaTeX style macro.
Printed and bound by R.R. Donnelley and Sons, Harrisonburg, VA.
Printed in the United States of America.

9 8 7 6 5 4 3 2

ISBN 0-387-94907-0 Springer-Verlag New York Berlin Heidelberg SPIN 10681882

To Juris

Preface

These are my lecture notes from CS381/481: Automata and Computability Theory, a one-semester senior-level course I have taught at Cornell University for many years. I took this course myself in the fall of 1974 as a first-year Ph.D. student at Cornell from Juris Hartmanis and have been in love with the subject ever since.

The course is required for computer science majors at Cornell. It exists in two forms: CS481, an honors version; and CS381, a somewhat gentler-paced version. The syllabus is roughly the same, but CS481 goes deeper into the subject, covers more material, and is taught at a more abstract level. Students are encouraged to start off in one or the other, then switch within the first few weeks if they find the other version more suitable to their level of mathematical skill.

The purpose of the course is twofold: to introduce computer science students to the rich heritage of models and abstractions that have arisen over the years; and to develop the capacity to form abstractions of their own and reason in terms of them.

The course is quite mathematical in flavor, and a certain degree of previous mathematical experience is essential for survival. Students should already be conversant with elementary discrete mathematics, including the notions of set, function, relation, product, partial order, equivalence relation, graph, and tree. They should have a repertoire of basic proof techniques at their disposal, including a thorough understanding of the principle of mathematical induction.

The material covered in this text is somewhat more than can be covered in a one-semester course. It is also a mix of elementary and advanced topics. The basic course consists of the lectures numbered 1 through 39. Additionally, I have included several supplementary lectures numbered A through K on various more advanced topics. These can be included or omitted at the instructor's discretion or assigned as extra reading. They appear in roughly the order in which they should be covered.

At first these notes were meant to supplement and not supplant a textbook, but over the years they gradually took on a life of their own. In addition to the notes, I depended on various texts at one time or another: Cutland [30], Harrison [55], Hopcroft and Ullman [60], Lewis and Papadimitriou [79], Machtey and Young [81], and Manna [82]. In particular, the Hopcroft and Ullman text was the standard textbook for the course for many years, and for me it has been an indispensable source of knowledge and insight. All of these texts are excellent references, and I recommend them highly.

In addition to the lectures, I have included 12 homework sets and several miscellaneous exercises. Some of the exercises come with hints and/or solutions; these are indicated by the annotations "H" and "S," respectively. In addition, I have annotated exercises with zero to three stars to indicate relative difficulty.

I have stuck with the format of my previous textbook [72], in which the main text is divided into more or less self-contained lectures, each 4 to 8 pages. Although this format is rather unusual for a textbook, I have found it quite successful. Many readers have commented that they like it because it partitions the subject into bite-sized chunks that can be covered more or less independently.

I owe a supreme debt of gratitude to my wife Frances for her constant love, support, and superhuman patience, especially during the final throes of this project. I am also indebted to the many teachers, colleagues, teaching assistants, and students who over the years have shared the delights of this subject with me and from whom I have learned so much. I would expecially like to thank Rick Aaron, Arash Baratloo, Jim Baumgartner, Steve Bloom, Manuel Blum, Amy Briggs, Ashok Chandra, Wilfred Chen, Allan Cheng, Francis Chu, Bob Constable, Devdatt Dubhashi, Peter van Emde Boas, Allen Emerson, András Ferencz, Jeff Foster, Sophia Georgiakaki, David Gries, Joe Halpern, David Harel, Basil Hayek, Tom Henzinger, John Hopcroft, Nick Howe, Doug Ierardi, Tibor Janosi, Jim Jennings, Shyam Kapur, Steve Kautz, Nils Klarlund, Peter Kopke, Vladimir Kotlyar, Alan Kwan, Georges Lauri, Michael Leventon, Jake Levirne, David Liben-Nowell, Yvonne Lo, Steve Mahaney, Nikolay Mateev, Frank McSherry, Albert Meyer, Bob Milnikel, Francesmary Modugno, Anil Nerode, Damian Niwiński, David de la Nuez, Dan Oberlin, Jens Palsberg, Rohit

Parikh, David Pearson, Paul Pedersen, Vaughan Pratt, Zulfikar Ramzan, Jon Rosenberger, Jonathan Rynd, Erik Schmidt, Michael Schwartzbach, Amitabh Shah, Frederick Smith, Kjartan Stefánsson, Colin Stirling, Larry Stockmeyer, Aaron Stump, Jurek Tiuryn, Alex Tsow, Moshe Vardi, Igor Walukiewicz, Rafael Weinstein, Jim Wen, Dan Wineman, Thomas Yan, Paul Zimmons, and many others too numerous to mention. Of course, the greatest of these is Juris Hartmanis, whose boundless enthusiasm for the subject is the ultimate source of my own.

I would be most grateful for suggestions and criticism from readers.

Ithaca, New York   Dexter C. Kozen

Contents

Lectures

Lecture 1

Course Roadmap and Historical Perspective

The goal of this course is to understand the foundations of computation. We will ask some very basic questions, such as

- What does it mean for a function to be computable?

- Are there any noncomputable functions?

- How does computational power depend on programming constructs?

These questions may appear simple, but they are not. They have intrigued scientists for decades, and the subject is still far from closed.

In the quest for answers to these questions, we will encounter some fundamental and pervasive concepts along the way: *state, transition, nondeterminism, reduction,* and *undecidability,* to name a few. Some of the most important achievements in theoretical computer science have been the crystallization of these concepts. They have shown a remarkable persistence, even as technology changes from day to day. They are crucial for every good computer scientist to know, so that they can be recognized when they are encountered, as they surely will be.

Various models of computation have been proposed over the years, all of which capture some fundamental aspect of computation. We will concentrate on the following three classes of models, in order of increasing power:

(i) finite memory: finite automata, regular expressions;

(ii) finite memory with stack: pushdown automata;

(iii) unrestricted:

- Turing machines (Alan Turing [120]),

- Post systems (Emil Post [99, 100]),

- μ-recursive functions (Kurt Gödel [51], Jacques Herbrand),

- λ-calculus (Alonzo Church [23], Stephen C. Kleene [66]),

- combinatory logic (Moses Schönfinkel [111], Haskell B. Curry [29]).

These systems were developed long before computers existed. Nowadays one could add PASCAL, FORTRAN, BASIC, LISP, SCHEME, C++, JAVA, or any sufficiently powerful programming language to this list.

In parallel with and independent of the development of these models of computation, the linguist Noam Chomsky attempted to formalize the notion of *grammar* and *language*. This effort resulted in the definition of the *Chomsky hierarchy*, a hierarchy of language classes defined by grammars of increasing complexity:

(i) right-linear grammars;

(ii) context-free grammars;

(iii) unrestricted grammars.

Although grammars and machine models appear quite different on a superficial level, the process of parsing a sentence in a language bears a strong resemblance to computation. Upon closer inspection, it turns out that each of the grammar types (i), (ii), and (iii) are equivalent in computational power to the machine models (i), (ii), and (iii) above, respectively. There is even a fourth natural class called the *context-sensitive* grammars and languages, which fits in between (ii) and (iii) and which corresponds to a certain natural class of machine models called *linear bounded automata*.

It is quite surprising that a naturally defined hierarchy in one field should correspond so closely to a naturally defined hierarchy in a completely different field. Could this be mere coincidence?

Abstraction

The machine models mentioned above were first identified in the same way that theories in physics or any other scientific discipline arise. When studying real-world phenomena, one becomes aware of recurring patterns and themes that appear in various guises. These guises may differ substantially on a superficial level but may bear enough resemblance to one another to suggest that there are common underlying principles at work. When this happens, it makes sense to try to construct an abstract model that captures these underlying principles in the simplest possible way, devoid of the unimportant details of each particular manifestation. This is the process of *abstraction*. Abstraction is the essence of scientific progress, because it focuses attention on the important principles, unencumbered by irrelevant details.

Perhaps the most striking example of this phenomenon we will see is the formalization of the concept of *effective computability*. This quest started around the beginning of the twentieth century with the development of the *formalist* school of mathematics, championed by the philosopher Bertrand Russell and the mathematician David Hilbert. They wanted to reduce all of mathematics to the formal manipulation of symbols.

Of course, the formal manipulation of symbols is a form of computation, although there were no computers around at the time. However, there certainly existed an awareness of computation and algorithms. Mathematicians, logicians, and philosophers knew a constructive method when they saw it. There followed several attempts to come to grips with the general notion of *effective computability*. Several definitions emerged (Turing machines, Post systems, etc.), each with its own peculiarities and differing radically in appearance. However, it turned out that as different as all these formalisms appeared to be, they could all simulate one another, thus they were all computationally equivalent.

The formalist program was eventually shattered by Kurt Gödel's incompleteness theorem, which states that no matter how strong a deductive system for number theory you take, it will always be possible to construct simple statements that are true but unprovable. This theorem is widely regarded as one of the crowning intellectual achievements of twentieth century mathematics. It is essentially a statement about computability, and we will be in a position to give a full account of it by the end of the course.

The process of abstraction is inherently mathematical. It involves building models that capture observed behavior in the simplest possible way. Although we will consider plenty of concrete examples and applications of these models, we will work primarily in terms of their mathematical properties. We will always be as explicit as possible about these properties.

We will usually start with definitions, then subsequently reason purely in terms of those definitions. For some, this will undoubtedly be a new way of thinking, but it is a skill that is worth cultivating.

Keep in mind that a large intellectual effort often goes into coming up with just the right definition or model that captures the essence of the principle at hand with the least amount of extraneous baggage. After the fact, the reader often sees only the finished product and is not exposed to all the misguided false attempts and pitfalls that were encountered along the way. Remember that it took many years of intellectual struggle to arrive at the theory as it exists today. This is not to say that the book is closed—far from it!

Lecture 2

Strings and Sets

Decision Problems Versus Functions

A *decision problem* is a function with a one-bit output: "yes" or "no." To specify a decision problem, one must specify

- the set A of possible inputs, and

- the subset $B \subseteq A$ of "yes" instances.

For example, to decide if a given graph is connected, the set of possible inputs is the set of all (encodings of) graphs, and the "yes" instances are the connected graphs. To decide if a given number is a prime, the set of possible inputs is the set of all (binary encodings of) integers, and the "yes" instances are the primes.

In this course we will mostly consider decision problems as opposed to functions with more general outputs. We do this for mathematical simplicity and because the behavior we want to study is already present at this level.

Strings

Now to our first abstraction: we will always take the set of possible inputs to a decision problem to be the set of finite-length strings over some fixed finite alphabet (formal definitions below). We do this for uniformity and simplicity. Other types of data—graphs, the natural numbers $N = \{0, 1, 2, \ldots\}$, trees, even programs—can be encoded naturally as strings. By making this abstraction, we have to deal with only one data type and a few basic operations.

Definition 2.1

- An *alphabet* is any finite set. For example, we might use the alphabet $\{0, 1, 2, \ldots, 9\}$ if we are talking about decimal numbers; the set of all ASCII characters if talking about text; $\{0, 1\}$ if talking about bit strings. The only restriction is that the alphabet be finite. When speaking about an arbitrary finite alphabet abstractly, we usually denote it by the Greek letter Σ. We call elements of Σ *letters* or *symbols* and denote them by $a, b, c, \ldots$. We usually do not care at all about the nature of the elements of Σ, only that there are finitely many of them.

- A *string* over Σ is any finite-length sequence of elements of Σ. Example: if $\Sigma = \{a, b\}$, then $aabab$ is a string over Σ of length five. We use $x, y, z, \ldots$ to refer to strings.

- The *length* of a string x is the number of symbols in x. The length of x is denoted $|x|$. For example, $|aabab| = 5$.

- There is a unique string of length 0 over Σ called the *null string* or *empty string* and denoted by ϵ (Greek epsilon, not to be confused with the symbol for set containment $\in$). Thus $|\epsilon| = 0$.

- We write a^n for a string of a's of length n. For example, $a^5 = aaaaa$, $a^1 = a$, and $a^0 = \epsilon$. Formally, a^n is defined inductively:

$$a^0 \overset{\text{def}}{=} \epsilon,$$
$$a^{n+1} \overset{\text{def}}{=} a^n a.$$

- The set of all strings over alphabet Σ is denoted Σ^*. For example,

$$\{a, b\}^* = \{\epsilon, a, b, aa, ab, ba, bb, aaa, aab, \ldots\},$$
$$\{a\}^* = \{\epsilon, a, aa, aaa, aaaa, \ldots\}$$
$$= \{a^n \mid n \geq 0\}. \qquad \square$$

By convention, we take

$$\varnothing^* \overset{\text{def}}{=} \{\epsilon\},$$

where $\varnothing$ denotes the empty set. This may seem a bit strange, but there is good mathematical justification for it, which will become apparent shortly.

If Σ is nonempty, then Σ^* is an infinite set of finite-length strings. Be careful not to confuse strings and sets. We won't see any infinite strings until much later in the course. Here are some differences between strings and sets:

- $\{a, b\} = \{b, a\}$, but $ab \neq ba$;

- $\{a, a, b\} = \{a, b\}$, but $aab \neq ab$.

Note also that $\varnothing$, $\{\epsilon\}$, and ϵ are three different things. The first is a set with no elements; the second is a set with one element, namely ϵ; and the last is a string, not a set.

Operations on Strings

The operation of *concatenation* takes two strings x and y and makes a new string xy by putting them together end to end. The string xy is called the *concatenation* of x and y. Note that xy and yx are different in general. Here are some useful properties of concatenation.

- concatenation is *associative*: $(xy)z = x(yz)$;

- the null string ϵ is an *identity* for concatenation: $\epsilon x = x\epsilon = x$;

- $|xy| = |x| + |y|$.

A special case of the last equation is $a^m a^n = a^{m+n}$ for all $m, n \geq 0$.

A *monoid* is any algebraic structure consisting of a set with an associative binary operation and an identity for that operation. By our definitions above, the set Σ^* with string concatenation as the binary operation and ϵ as the identity is a monoid. We will see some other examples later in the course.

Definition 2.2
- We write x^n for the string obtained by concatenating n copies of x. For example, $(aab)^5 = aabaabaabaabaab$, $(aab)^1 = aab$, and $(aab)^0 = \epsilon$. Formally, x^n is defined inductively:

$$x^0 \stackrel{\text{def}}{=} \epsilon,$$
$$x^{n+1} \stackrel{\text{def}}{=} x^n x.$$

- If $a \in \Sigma$ and $x \in \Sigma^*$, we write $\#a(x)$ for the number of a's in x. For example, $\#0(001101001000) = 8$ and $\#1(00000) = 0$.

- A *prefix* of a string x is an initial substring of x; that is, a string y for which there exists a string z such that $x = yz$. For example, $abaab$ is a prefix of $abaababa$. The null string is a prefix of every string, and every string is a prefix of itself. A prefix y of x is a *proper* prefix of x if $y \neq \epsilon$ and $y \neq x$.   □

Operations on Sets

We usually denote sets of strings (subsets of Σ^*) by $A, B, C, \ldots$. The *cardinality* (number of elements) of set A is denoted $|A|$. The empty set $\varnothing$ is the unique set of cardinality 0.

Let's define some useful operations on sets. Some of these you have probably seen before, some probably not.

- *Set union:*

$$A \cup B \stackrel{\text{def}}{=} \{x \mid x \in A \text{ or } x \in B\}.$$

In other words, x is in the union of A and B iff[1] either x is in A or x is in B. For example, $\{a, ab\} \cup \{ab, aab\} = \{a, ab, aab\}$.

- *Set intersection:*

$$A \cap B \stackrel{\text{def}}{=} \{x \mid x \in A \text{ and } x \in B\}.$$

In other words, x is in the intersection of A and B iff x is in both A and B. For example, $\{a, ab\} \cap \{ab, aab\} = \{ab\}$.

- *Complement in Σ^*:*

$$\sim A \stackrel{\text{def}}{=} \{x \in \Sigma^* \mid x \notin A\}.$$

For example,

$$\sim \{\text{strings in } \Sigma^* \text{ of even length}\} = \{\text{strings in } \Sigma^* \text{ of odd length}\}.$$

Unlike $\cup$ and $\cap$, the definition of $\sim$ depends on Σ^*. The set $\sim A$ is sometimes denoted $\Sigma^* - A$ to emphasize this dependence.

- *Set concatenation:*

$$AB \stackrel{\text{def}}{=} \{xy \mid x \in A \text{ and } y \in B\}.$$

In other words, z is in AB iff z can be written as a concatenation of two strings x and y, where $x \in A$ and $y \in B$. For example, $\{a, ab\}\{b, ba\} = \{ab, aba, abb, abba\}$. When forming a set concatenation, you include *all* strings that can be obtained in this way. Note that AB and BA are different sets in general. For example, $\{b, ba\}\{a, ab\} = \{ba, bab, baa, baab\}$.

---

[1]iff = if and only if.

- The *powers* A^n of a set A are defined inductively as follows:

$$A^0 \overset{\text{def}}{=} \{\epsilon\},$$

$$A^{n+1} \overset{\text{def}}{=} AA^n.$$

In other words, A^n is formed by concatenating n copies of A together. Taking $A^0 = \{\epsilon\}$ makes the property $A^{m+n} = A^m A^n$ hold, even when one of m or n is 0. For example,

$$\{ab, aab\}^0 = \{\epsilon\},$$
$$\{ab, aab\}^1 = \{ab, aab\},$$
$$\{ab, aab\}^2 = \{abab, abaab, aabab, aabaab\},$$
$$\{ab, aab\}^3 = \{ababab, ababaab, abaabab, aababab,$$
$$abaabaab, aababaab, aabaabab, aabaabaab\}.$$

Also,

$$\{a, b\}^n = \{x \in \{a, b\}^* \mid |x| = n\}$$
$$= \{\text{strings over } \{a, b\} \text{ of length } n\}.$$

- The *asterate* A^* of a set A is the union of all finite powers of A:

$$A^* \overset{\text{def}}{=} \bigcup_{n \geq 0} A^n$$
$$= A^0 \cup A^1 \cup A^2 \cup A^3 \cup \cdots.$$

Another way to say this is

$$A^* = \{x_1 x_2 \cdots x_n \mid n \geq 0 \text{ and } x_i \in A, 1 \leq i \leq n\}.$$

Note that n can be 0; thus the null string ϵ is in A^* for any A.

We previously defined Σ^* to be the set of all finite-length strings over the alphabet Σ. This is exactly the asterate of the set Σ, so our notation is consistent.

- We define A^+ to be the union of all *nonzero* powers of A:

$$A^+ \overset{\text{def}}{=} AA^* = \bigcup_{n \geq 1} A^n.$$

Here are some useful properties of these set operations:

- Set union, set intersection, and set concatenation are *associative*:

$$(A \cup B) \cup C = A \cup (B \cup C),$$
$$(A \cap B) \cap C = A \cap (B \cap C),$$
$$(AB)C = A(BC).$$

- Set union and set intersection are *commutative*:

$$A \cup B = B \cup A,$$
$$A \cap B = B \cap A.$$

As noted above, set concatenation is not.

- The null set $\varnothing$ is an *identity* for $\cup$:

$$A \cup \varnothing = \varnothing \cup A = A.$$

- The set $\{\epsilon\}$ is an identity for set concatenation:

$$\{\epsilon\}A = A\{\epsilon\} = A.$$

- The null set $\varnothing$ is an *annihilator* for set concatenation:

$$A\varnothing = \varnothing A = \varnothing.$$

- Set union and intersection *distribute* over each other:

$$A \cup (B \cap C) = (A \cup B) \cap (A \cup C),$$
$$A \cap (B \cup C) = (A \cap B) \cup (A \cap C).$$

- Set concatenation distributes over union:

$$A(B \cup C) = AB \cup AC,$$
$$(A \cup B)C = AC \cup BC.$$

In fact, concatenation distributes over the union of any family of sets. If $\{B_i \mid i \in I\}$ is any family of sets indexed by another set I, finite or infinite, then

$$A(\bigcup_{i \in I} B_i) = \bigcup_{i \in I} AB_i,$$
$$(\bigcup_{i \in I} B_i)A = \bigcup_{i \in I} B_i A.$$

Here $\bigcup_{i \in I} B_i$ denotes the union of all the sets B_i for $i \in I$. An element x is in this union iff it is in one of the B_i.

Set concatenation does *not* distribute over intersection. For example, take $A = \{a, ab\}$, $B = \{b\}$, $C = \{\epsilon\}$, and see what you get when you compute $A(B \cap C)$ and $AB \cap AC$.

- The *De Morgan laws* hold:

$$\sim(A \cup B) = \sim A \cap \sim B,$$
$$\sim(A \cap B) = \sim A \cup \sim B.$$

- The asterate operation * satisfies the following properties:

$$A^*A^* = A^*,$$
$$A^{**} = A^*,$$
$$A^* = \{\epsilon\} \cup AA^* = \{\epsilon\} \cup A^*A,$$
$$\varnothing^* = \{\epsilon\}.$$

Lecture 3

Finite Automata and Regular Sets

States and Transitions

Intuitively, a *state* of a system is an instantaneous description of that system, a snapshot of reality frozen in time. A state gives all relevant information necessary to determine how the system can evolve from that point on. *Transitions* are changes of state; they can happen spontaneously or in response to external inputs.

We assume that state transitions are instantaneous. This is a mathematical abstraction. In reality, transitions usually take time. Clock cycles in digital computers enforce this abstraction and allow us to treat computers as digital instead of analog devices.

There are innumerable examples of state transition systems in the real world: electronic circuits, digital watches, elevators, Rubik's cube ($54!/9!^6$ states and 12 transitions, not counting peeling the little sticky squares off), the game of Life (2^k states on a screen with k cells, one transition).

A system that consists of only finitely many states and transitions among them is called a *finite-state transition system*. We model these abstractly by a mathematical model called a *finite automaton*.

Finite Automata

Formally, a *deterministic finite automaton* (DFA) is a structure

$$M = (Q, \Sigma, \delta, s, F),$$

where

- Q is a finite set; elements of Q are called *states*;

- Σ is a finite set, the *input alphabet*;

- $\delta : Q \times \Sigma \to Q$ is the *transition function* (recall that $Q \times \Sigma$ is the set of ordered pairs $\{(q, a) \mid q \in Q \text{ and } a \in \Sigma\}$). Intuitively, δ is a function that tells which state to move to in response to an input: if M is in state q and sees input a, it moves to state $\delta(q, a)$.

- $s \in Q$ is the *start state*;

- F is a subset of Q; elements of F are called *accept* or *final states*.

When you specify a finite automaton, you must give all five parts. Automata may be specified in this set-theoretic form or as a transition diagram or table as in the following example.

Example 3.1   Here is an example of a simple four-state finite automaton. We'll take the set of states to be $\{0, 1, 2, 3\}$; the input alphabet to be $\{a, b\}$; the start state to be 0; the set of accept states to be $\{3\}$; and the transition function to be

$$\delta(0, a) = 1,$$
$$\delta(1, a) = 2,$$
$$\delta(2, a) = \delta(3, a) = 3,$$
$$\delta(q, b) = q, \quad q \in \{0, 1, 2, 3\}.$$

All parts of the automaton are completely specified. We can also specify the automaton by means of a table

		a	b
$\to$	0	1	0
	1	2	1
	2	3	2
	$3F$	3	3

or transition diagram

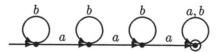

The final states are indicated by an F in the table and by a circle in the transition diagram. In both, the start state is indicated by $\to$. The states in the transition diagram from left to right correspond to the states $0, 1, 2, 3$ in the table. One advantage of transition diagrams is that you don't have to name the states.   □

Another convenient representation of finite automata is transition matrices; see Miscellaneous Exercise 7.

Informally, here is how a finite automaton operates. An input can be any string $x \in \Sigma^*$. Put a pebble down on the start state s. Scan the input string x from left to right, one symbol at a time, moving the pebble according to δ: if the next symbol of x is b and the pebble is on state q, move the pebble to $\delta(q, b)$. When we come to the end of the input string, the pebble is on some state p. The string x is said to be *accepted* by the machine M if $p \in F$ and *rejected* if $p \notin F$. There is no formal mechanism for scanning or moving the pebble; these are just intuitive devices.

For example, the automaton of Example 3.1, beginning in its start state 0, will be in state 3 after scanning the input string *baabbaab*, so that string is accepted; however, it will be in state 2 after scanning the string *babbbab*, so that string is rejected. For this automaton, a moment's thought reveals that when scanning any input string, the automaton will be in state 0 if it has seen no a's, state 1 if it has seen one a, state 2 if it has seen two a's, and state 3 if it has seen three or more a's.

This is how we do formally what we just described informally above. We first define a function

$$\widehat{\delta} : Q \times \Sigma^* \to Q$$

from δ by induction on the length of x:

$$\widehat{\delta}(q, \epsilon) \stackrel{\text{def}}{=} q, \tag{3.1}$$

$$\widehat{\delta}(q, xa) \stackrel{\text{def}}{=} \delta(\widehat{\delta}(q, x), a). \tag{3.2}$$

The function $\widehat{\delta}$ maps a state q and a string x to a new state $\widehat{\delta}(q, x)$. Intuitively, $\widehat{\delta}$ is the multistep version of δ. The state $\widehat{\delta}(q, x)$ is the state M ends up in when started in state q and fed the input x, moving in response to each symbol of x according to δ. Equation (3.1) is the basis of the inductive definition; it says that the machine doesn't move anywhere under the null input. Equation (3.2) is the induction step; it says that the state reachable from q under input string xa is the state reachable from p under input symbol a, where p is the state reachable from q under input string x.

Note that the second argument to $\widehat{\delta}$ can be any string in Σ^*, not just a string of length one as with δ; but $\widehat{\delta}$ and δ agree on strings of length one:

$$
\begin{aligned}
\widehat{\delta}(q, a) = \widehat{\delta}(q, \epsilon a) &\qquad \text{since } a = \epsilon a \\
= \delta(\widehat{\delta}(q, \epsilon), a) &\qquad \text{by (3.2), taking } x = \epsilon
\end{aligned}
$$

$$= \delta(q,a) \qquad \text{by (3.1).}$$

Formally, a string x is said to be *accepted* by the automaton M if

$$\widehat{\delta}(s,x) \in F$$

and *rejected* by the automaton M if

$$\widehat{\delta}(s,x) \notin F,$$

where s is the start state and F is the set of accept states. This captures formally the intuitive notion of acceptance and rejection described above.

The *set* or *language accepted by* M is the set of all strings accepted by M and is denoted $L(M)$:

$$L(M) \stackrel{\text{def}}{=} \{x \in \Sigma^* \mid \widehat{\delta}(s,x) \in F\}.$$

A subset $A \subseteq \Sigma^*$ is said to be *regular* if $A = L(M)$ for some finite automaton M. The set of strings accepted by the automaton of Example 3.1 is the set

$$\{x \in \{a,b\}^* \mid x \text{ contains at least three } a\text{'s}\},$$

so this is a regular set.

Example 3.2 Here is another example of a regular set and a finite automaton accepting it. Consider the set

$$\{xaaay \mid x,y \in \{a,b\}^*\}$$
$$= \{x \in \{a,b\}^* \mid x \text{ contains a substring of three consecutive } a\text{'s}\}.$$

For example, *baabaaaab* is in the set and should be accepted, whereas *babbabab* is not in the set and should be rejected (because the three a's are not consecutive). Here is an automaton for this set, specified in both table and transition diagram form:

		a	b
$\rightarrow$	0	1	0
	1	2	0
	2	3	0
	$3F$	3	3

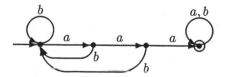

□

The idea here is that you use the states to count the number of consecutive a's you have seen. If you haven't seen three a's in a row and you see a b, you must go back to the start. Once you have seen three a's in a row, though, you stay in the accept state.

Lecture 4

More on Regular Sets

Here is another example of a regular set that is a little harder than the example given last time. Consider the set

$$\{x \in \{0,1\}^* \mid x \text{ represents a multiple of three in binary}\} \qquad (4.1)$$

(leading zeros permitted, ϵ represents the number 0). For example, the following binary strings represent multiples of three and should be accepted:

Binary	Decimal equivalent
0	0
11	3
110	6
1001	9
1100	12
1111	15
10010	18
$\vdots$	$\vdots$

Strings not representing multiples of three should be rejected. Here is an automaton accepting the set (4.1):

		0	1
$\rightarrow$	$0F$	0	1
	1	2	0
	2	1	2

The states **0**, **1**, **2** are written in boldface to distinguish them from the input symbols $0, 1$.

In the diagram, the states are **0**, **1**, **2** from left to right. We prove that this automaton accepts exactly the set (4.1) by induction on the length of the input string. First we associate a meaning to each state:

if the number represented by the string scanned so far is[1]	then the machine will be in state
$0 \bmod 3$	**0**
$1 \bmod 3$	**1**
$2 \bmod 3$	**2**

Let $\#x$ denote the number represented by string x in binary. For example,

$$\#\epsilon = 0,$$
$$\#0 = 0,$$
$$\#11 = 3,$$
$$\#100 = 4,$$

and so on. Formally, we want to show that for any string x in $\{0,1\}^*$,

$$\widehat{\delta}(\mathbf{0}, x) = \mathbf{0} \text{ iff } \#x \equiv 0 \bmod 3, \tag{4.2}$$
$$\widehat{\delta}(\mathbf{0}, x) = \mathbf{1} \text{ iff } \#x \equiv 1 \bmod 3,$$
$$\widehat{\delta}(\mathbf{0}, x) = \mathbf{2} \text{ iff } \#x \equiv 2 \bmod 3,$$

or in short,

$$\widehat{\delta}(\mathbf{0}, x) = \#x \bmod 3. \tag{4.3}$$

This will be our induction hypothesis. The final result we want, namely (4.2), is a weaker consequence of (4.3), but we need the more general statement (4.3) for the induction hypothesis.

We have by elementary number theory that

$$\#(x0) = 2(\#x) + 0,$$

---

[1] Here $a \bmod n$ denotes the remainder when dividing a by n using ordinary integer division. We also write $a \equiv b \bmod n$ (read: a is congruent to b modulo n) to mean that a and b have the same remainder when divided by n; in other words, that n divides $b - a$. Note that $a \equiv b \bmod n$ should be parsed $(a \equiv b) \bmod n$, and that in general $a \equiv b \bmod n$ and $a = b \bmod n$ mean different things. For example, $7 \equiv 2 \bmod 5$ but not $7 = 2 \bmod 5$.

$$\#(x1) = 2(\#x) + 1,$$

or in short,

$$\#(xc) = 2(\#x) + c \tag{4.4}$$

for $c \in \{0, 1\}$. From the machine above, we see that for any state $q \in \{0, 1, 2\}$ and input symbol $c \in \{0, 1\}$,

$$\delta(q, c) = (2q + c) \bmod 3. \tag{4.5}$$

This can be verified by checking all six cases corresponding to possible choices of q and c. (In fact, (4.5) would have been a great way to *define* the transition function formally—then we wouldn't have had to prove it!) Now we use the inductive definition of $\widehat{\delta}$ to show (4.3) by induction on $|x|$.

Basis

For $x = \epsilon$,

$$
\begin{aligned}
\widehat{\delta}(0, \epsilon) &= 0 && \text{by definition of } \widehat{\delta} \\
&= \#\epsilon && \text{since } \#\epsilon = 0 \\
&= \#\epsilon \bmod 3.
\end{aligned}
$$

Induction step

Assuming that (4.3) is true for $x \in \{0, 1\}^*$, we show that it is true for xc, where $c \in \{0, 1\}$.

$$
\begin{aligned}
\widehat{\delta}(0, xc) &= \delta(\widehat{\delta}(0, x), c) && \text{definition of } \widehat{\delta} \\
&= \delta(\#x \bmod 3, c) && \text{induction hypothesis} \\
&= (2(\#x \bmod 3) + c) \bmod 3 && \text{by (4.5)} \\
&= (2(\#x) + c) \bmod 3 && \text{elementary number theory} \\
&= \#xc \bmod 3 && \text{by (4.4).}
\end{aligned}
$$

Note that each step has its reason. We used the definition of δ, which is specific to this automaton; the definition of $\widehat{\delta}$ from δ, which is the same for all automata; and elementary properties of numbers and strings.

Some Closure Properties of Regular Sets

For $A, B \subseteq \Sigma^*$, recall the following definitions:

$$
\begin{aligned}
A \cup B &= \{x \mid x \in A \text{ or } x \in B\} && \text{union} \\
A \cap B &= \{x \mid x \in A \text{ and } x \in B\} && \text{intersection} \\
{\sim}A &= \{x \in \Sigma^* \mid x \notin A\} && \text{complement}
\end{aligned}
$$

$$AB = \{xy \mid x \in A \text{ and } y \in B\} \qquad\qquad \text{concatenation}$$
$$A^* = \{x_1 x_2 \cdots x_n \mid n \geq 0 \text{ and } x_i \in A,\, 1 \leq i \leq n\}$$
$$= A^0 \cup A^1 \cup A^2 \cup A^3 \cup \cdots \qquad\qquad \text{asterate.}$$

Do not confuse set concatenation with string concatenation. Sometimes $\sim A$ is written $\Sigma^* - A$.

We show below that if A and B are regular, then so are $A \cup B$, $A \cap B$, and $\sim A$. We'll show later that AB and A^* are also regular.

The Product Construction

Assume that A and B are regular. Then there are automata

$$M_1 = (Q_1,\ \Sigma,\ \delta_1,\ s_1,\ F_1),$$
$$M_2 = (Q_2,\ \Sigma,\ \delta_2,\ s_2,\ F_2)$$

with $L(M_1) = A$ and $L(M_2) = B$. To show that $A \cap B$ is regular, we will build an automaton M_3 such that $L(M_3) = A \cap B$.

Intuitively, M_3 will have the states of M_1 and M_2 encoded somehow in its states. On input $x \in \Sigma^*$, it will simulate M_1 and M_2 simultaneously on x, accepting iff both M_1 and M_2 would accept. Think about putting a pebble down on the start state of M_1 and another on the start state of M_2. As the input symbols come in, move both pebbles according to the rules of each machine. Accept if both pebbles occupy accept states in their respective machines when the end of the input string is reached.

Formally, let

$$M_3 = (Q_3,\ \Sigma,\ \delta_3,\ s_3,\ F_3),$$

where

$$Q_3 = Q_1 \times Q_2 = \{(p, q) \mid p \in Q_1 \text{ and } q \in Q_2\},$$
$$F_3 = F_1 \times F_2 = \{(p, q) \mid p \in F_1 \text{ and } q \in F_2\},$$
$$s_3 = (s_1, s_2),$$

and let

$$\delta_3 : Q_3 \times \Sigma \to Q_3$$

be the transition function defined by

$$\delta_3((p, q), a) = (\delta_1(p, a), \delta_2(q, a)).$$

The automaton M_3 is called the *product* of M_1 and M_2. A state (p, q) of M_3 encodes a configuration of pebbles on M_1 and M_2.

Recall the inductive definition (3.1) and (3.2) of the extended transition function $\widehat{\delta}$ from Lecture 2. Applied to δ_3, this gives

$$\widehat{\delta}_3((p,q),\epsilon) = (p,q),$$
$$\widehat{\delta}_3((p,q),xa) = \delta_3(\widehat{\delta}_3((p,q),x),a).$$

Lemma 4.1   *For all $x \in \Sigma^*$,*

$$\widehat{\delta}_3((p,q),x) = (\widehat{\delta}_1(p,x),\widehat{\delta}_2(q,x)).$$

Proof. By induction on $|x|$.

Basis

For $x = \epsilon$,

$$\widehat{\delta}_3((p,q),\epsilon) = (p,q) = (\widehat{\delta}_1(p,\epsilon),\widehat{\delta}_2(q,\epsilon)).$$

Induction step

Assuming the lemma holds for $x \in \Sigma^*$, we show that it holds for xa, where $a \in \Sigma$.

$$
\begin{aligned}
&\widehat{\delta}_3((p,q),xa) \\
&= \delta_3(\widehat{\delta}_3((p,q),x),a) && \text{definition of } \widehat{\delta}_3 \\
&= \delta_3((\widehat{\delta}_1(p,x),\widehat{\delta}_2(q,x)),a) && \text{induction hypothesis} \\
&= (\delta_1(\widehat{\delta}_1(p,x),a),\delta_2(\widehat{\delta}_2(q,x),a)) && \text{definition of } \delta_3 \\
&= (\widehat{\delta}_1(p,xa),\widehat{\delta}_2(q,xa)) && \text{definition of } \widehat{\delta}_1 \text{ and } \widehat{\delta}_2. \qquad \square
\end{aligned}
$$

Theorem 4.2 $L(M_3) = L(M_1) \cap L(M_2)$.

Proof. For all $x \in \Sigma^*$,

$$
\begin{aligned}
&x \in L(M_3) \\
&\iff \widehat{\delta}_3(s_3,x) \in F_3 && \text{definition of acceptance} \\
&\iff \widehat{\delta}_3((s_1,s_2),x) \in F_1 \times F_2 && \text{definition of } s_3 \text{ and } F_3 \\
&\iff (\widehat{\delta}_1(s_1,x),\widehat{\delta}_2(s_2,x)) \in F_1 \times F_2 && \text{Lemma 4.1} \\
&\iff \widehat{\delta}_1(s_1,x) \in F_1 \text{ and } \widehat{\delta}_2(s_2,x) \in F_2 && \text{definition of set product} \\
&\iff x \in L(M_1) \text{ and } x \in L(M_2) && \text{definition of acceptance} \\
&\iff x \in L(M_1) \cap L(M_2) && \text{definition of intersection.} \quad \square
\end{aligned}
$$

To show that regular sets are closed under complement, take a deterministic automaton accepting A and interchange the set of accept and nonaccept states. The resulting automaton accepts exactly when the original automaton would reject, so the set accepted is $\sim A$.

Once we know regular sets are closed under $\cap$ and $\sim$, it follows that they are closed under $\cup$ by one of the De Morgan laws:

$$A \cup B = \sim(\sim A \cap \sim B).$$

If you use the constructions for $\cap$ and $\sim$ given above, this gives an automaton for $A \cup B$ that looks exactly like the product automaton for $A \cap B$, except that the accept states are

$$F_3 = \{(p,q) \mid p \in F_1 \text{ or } q \in F_2\} = (F_1 \times Q_2) \cup (Q_1 \times F_2)$$

instead of $F_1 \times F_2$.

Historical Notes

Finite-state transition systems were introduced by McCulloch and Pitts in 1943 [84]. Deterministic finite automata in the form presented here were studied by Kleene [70]. Our notation is borrowed from Hopcroft and Ullman [60].

Lecture 5

Nondeterministic Finite Automata

Nondeterminism

Nondeterminism is an important abstraction in computer science. It refers to situations in which the next state of a computation is not uniquely determined by the current state. Nondeterminism arises in real life when there is incomplete information about the state or when there are external forces at work that can affect the course of a computation. For example, the behavior of a process in a distributed system might depend on messages from other processes that arrive at unpredictable times with unpredictable contents.

Nondeterminism is also important in the design of efficient algorithms. There are many instances of important combinatorial problems with efficient nondeterministic solutions but no known efficient deterministic solution. The famous $P = NP$ problem—whether all problems solvable in nondeterministic polynomial time can be solved in deterministic polynomial time—is a major open problem in computer science and arguably one of the most important open problems in all of mathematics.

In nondeterministic situations, we may not know how a computation will evolve, but we may have some idea of the range of possibilities. This is modeled formally by allowing automata to have multiple-valued transition functions.

In this lecture and the next, we will show how nondeterminism is incorporated naturally in the context of finite automata. One might think that adding nondeterminism might increase expressive power, but in fact for finite automata it does not: in terms of the sets accepted, nondeterministic finite automata are no more powerful than deterministic ones. In other words, for every nondeterministic finite automaton, there is a deterministic one accepting the same set. However, nondeterministic machines may be exponentially more succinct.

Nondeterministic Finite Automata

A *nondeterministic finite automaton* (NFA) is one for which the next state is not necessarily uniquely determined by the current state and input symbol. In a deterministic automaton, there is exactly one start state and exactly one transition out of each state for each symbol in Σ. In a nondeterministic automaton, there may be one, more than one, or zero. The set of *possible* next states that the automaton may move to from a particular state q in response to a particular input symbol a is part of the specification of the automaton, but there is no mechanism for deciding which one will actually be taken. Formally, we won't be able to represent this with a function $\delta : Q \times \Sigma \rightarrow Q$ anymore; we will have to use something more general. Also, a nondeterministic automaton may have many start states and may start in any one of them.

Informally, a nondeterministic automaton is said to *accept* its input x if it is possible to start in some start state and scan x, moving according to the transition rules and making choices along the way whenever the next state is not uniquely determined, such that when the end of x is reached, the machine is in an accept state. Because the start state is not determined and because of the choices along the way, there may be several possible paths through the automaton in response to the input x; some may lead to accept states while others may lead to reject states. The automaton is said to *accept* x if *at least one* computation path on input x starting from *at least one* start state leads to an accept state. The automaton is said to *reject* x if *no* computation path on input x from *any* start state leads to an accept state. Another way of saying this is that x is accepted iff there exists a path with label x from some start state to some accept state. Again, there is no mechanism for determining which state to start in or which of the possible next moves to take in response to an input symbol.

It is helpful to think about this process in terms of *guessing* and *verifying*. On a given input, imagine the automaton *guessing* a successful computation or proof that the input is a "yes" instance of the decision problem, then *verifying* that its guess was indeed correct.

For example, consider the set

$$A = \{x \in \{0,1\}^* \mid \text{the fifth symbol from the right is } 1\}.$$

Thus $11010010 \in A$ but $11000010 \notin A$.

Here is a six-state nondeterministic automaton accepting A:

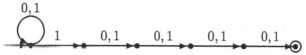

There is only one start state, namely the leftmost, and only one accept state, namely the rightmost. The automaton is not deterministic, because there are two transitions from the leftmost state labeled 1 (one back to itself and one to the second state) and no transitions from the rightmost state. This automaton accepts the set A, because for any string x whose fifth symbol from the right is 1, *there exists* a sequence of legal transitions leading from the start state to the accept state (it moves from the first state to the second when it scans the fifth symbol from the right); and for any string x whose fifth symbol from the right is 0, there is *no possible* sequence of legal transitions leading to the accept state, no matter what choices it makes (recall that to accept, the machine must be in an accept state when the end of the input string is reached).

Intuitively, we can think of the machine in the leftmost state as *guessing*, every time it sees a 1, whether that 1 is the fifth letter from the right. It might be and it might not be—the machine doesn't know, and there is no way for it to tell at that point. If it guesses that it is not, then it goes around the loop again. If it guesses that it is, then it commits to that guess by moving to the second state, an irrevocable decision. Now it must *verify* that its guess was correct; this is the purpose of the tail of the automaton leading to the accept state. If the 1 that it guessed was fifth from the right really is fifth from the right, then the machine will be in its accept state exactly when it comes to the end of the input string, therefore it will accept the string. If not, then maybe the symbol fifth from the right is a 0, and *no* guess would have worked; or maybe the symbol fifth from the right was a 1, but the machine just guessed the wrong 1.

Note, however, that for any string $x \in A$ (that is, for any string with a 1 fifth from the right), *there is* a lucky guess that leads to acceptance; whereas for any string $x \notin A$ (that is, for any string with a 0 fifth from the right), *no* guess can possibly lead to acceptance, no matter how lucky the automaton is.

In general, to show that a nondeterministic machine accepts a set B, we must argue that for any string $x \in B$, there is a lucky sequence of guesses that leads from a start state to an accept state when the end of x is reached;

but for any string $x \notin B$, *no* sequence of guesses leads to an accept state when the end of x is reached, no matter how lucky the automaton is.

Keep in mind that this process of *guessing and verifying* is just an intuitive aid. The formal definition of nondeterministic acceptance will be given in Lecture 6.

There does exist a deterministic automaton accepting the set A, but any such automaton must have at least $2^5 = 32$ states, since a deterministic machine essentially has to remember the last five symbols seen.

The Subset Construction

We will prove a rather remarkable fact: in terms of the sets accepted, nondeterministic finite automata are no more powerful than deterministic ones. In other words, for every nondeterministic finite automaton, there is a deterministic one accepting the same set. The deterministic automaton, however, may require more states.

This theorem can be proved using the *subset construction*. Here is the intuitive idea; we will give a formal treatment in Lecture 6. Given a nondeterministic machine N, think of putting pebbles on the states to keep track of all the states N could possibly be in after scanning a prefix of the input. We start with pebbles on all the start states of the nondeterministic machine. Say after scanning some prefix y of the input string, we have pebbles on some set P of states, and say P is the set of all states N could possibly be in after scanning y, depending on the nondeterministic choices that N could have made so far. If input symbol b comes in, pick the pebbles up off the states of P and put a pebble down on each state reachable from a state in P under input symbol b. Let P' be the new set of states covered by pebbles. Then P' is the set of states that N could possibly be in after scanning yb.

Although for a state q of N, there may be many possible next states after scanning b, note that the set P' is uniquely determined by b and the set P. We will thus build a deterministic automaton M *whose states are these sets*. That is, a state of M will be a *set* of states of N. The start state of M will be the *set* of start states of N, indicating that we start with one pebble on each of the start states of N. A final state of M will be any set P containing a final state of N, since we want to accept x if it is possible for N to have made choices while scanning x that lead to an accept state of N.

It takes a stretch of the imagination to regard a set of states of N as a single state of M. Let's illustrate the construction with a shortened version of the example above.

Example 5.1   Consider the set

$$A = \{x \in \{0,1\}^* \mid \text{the second symbol from the right is } 1\}.$$

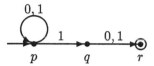

Label the states p, q, r from left to right, as illustrated. The states of M will be *subsets* of the set of states of N. In this example there are eight such subsets:

$$\varnothing, \{p\}, \{q\}, \{r\}, \{p,q\}, \{p,r\}, \{q,r\}, \{p,q,r\}.$$

Here is the deterministic automaton M:

	0	1
$\varnothing$	$\varnothing$	$\varnothing$
$\rightarrow \{p\}$	$\{p\}$	$\{p,q\}$
$\{q\}$	$\{r\}$	$\{r\}$
$\{r\}F$	$\varnothing$	$\varnothing$
$\{p,q\}$	$\{p,r\}$	$\{p,q,r\}$
$\{p,r\}F$	$\{p\}$	$\{p,q\}$
$\{q,r\}F$	$\{r\}$	$\{r\}$
$\{p,q,r\}F$	$\{p,r\}$	$\{p,q,r\}$

For example, if we have pebbles on p and q (the fifth row of the table), and if we see input symbol 0 (first column), then in the next step there will be pebbles on p and r. This is because in the automaton N, p is reachable from p under input 0 and r is reachable from q under input 0, and these are the only states reachable from p and q under input 0. The accept states of M (marked F in the table) are those sets containing an accept state of N. The start state of M is $\{p\}$, the set of all start states of N.

Following 0 and 1 transitions from the start state $\{p\}$ of M, one can see that states $\{q,r\}, \{q\}, \{r\}, \varnothing$ of M can never be reached. These states of M are *inaccessible*, and we might as well throw them out. This leaves

	0	1
$\rightarrow \{p\}$	$\{p\}$	$\{p,q\}$
$\{p,q\}$	$\{p,r\}$	$\{p,q,r\}$
$\{p,r\}F$	$\{p\}$	$\{p,q\}$
$\{p,q,r\}F$	$\{p,r\}$	$\{p,q,r\}$

This four-state automaton is exactly the one you would have come up with if you had built a deterministic automaton directly to remember the last two bits seen and accept if the next-to-last bit is a 1:

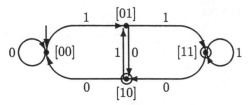

Here the state labels [*bc*] indicate the last two bits seen (for our purposes the null string is as good as having just seen two 0's). Note that these two automata are isomorphic (i.e., they are the same automaton up to the renaming of states):

$$\{p\} \approx [00],$$
$$\{p,q\} \approx [01],$$
$$\{p,r\} \approx [10],$$
$$\{p,q,r\} \approx [11].$$ □

Example 5.2   Consider the set

$$\{x \in \{a\}^* \mid |x| \text{ is divisible by 3 or 5}\}. \tag{5.1}$$

Here is an eight-state nondeterministic automaton N with two start states accepting this set (labels a on transitions are omitted since there is only one input symbol).

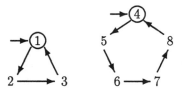

The only nondeterminism is in the choice of start state. The machine guesses at the outset whether to check for divisibility by 3 or 5. After that, the computation is deterministic.

Let Q be the states of N. We will build a deterministic machine M whose states are subsets of Q. There are $2^8 = 256$ of these in all, but most will be inaccessible (not reachable from the start state of M under any input). Think about moving pebbles—for this particular automaton, if you start with pebbles on the start states and move pebbles to mark all states the machine could possibly be in, you always have exactly two pebbles on N. This says that only subsets of Q with two elements will be accessible as states of M.

The subset construction gives the following deterministic automaton M with 15 accessible states:

$$\{3,8\} \leftarrow \{2,7\} \leftarrow (\{1,6\}) \leftarrow \{3,5\} \leftarrow (\{2,4\}) \leftarrow (\{1,8\}) \leftarrow \{3,7\} \leftarrow \{2,6\}$$

$$\rightarrow (\{1,4\}) \rightarrow \{2,5\} \rightarrow \{3,6\} \rightarrow (\{1,7\}) \rightarrow \{2,8\} \rightarrow (\{3,4\}) \rightarrow (\{1,5\})$$

□

In the next lecture we will give a formal definition of nondeterministic finite automata and a general account of the subset construction.

Lecture 6

The Subset Construction

Formal Definition of Nondeterministic Finite Automata

A *nondeterministic finite automaton (NFA)* is a five-tuple

$$N = (Q,\ \Sigma,\ \Delta,\ S,\ F),$$

where everything is the same as in a deterministic automaton, except for the following two differences.

- S is a *set* of states, that is, $S \subseteq Q$, instead of a single state. The elements of S are called *start states*.

- Δ is a function

$$\Delta : Q \times \Sigma \to 2^Q,$$

  where 2^Q denotes the *power set* of Q or the set of all subsets of Q:

$$2^Q \overset{\text{def}}{=} \{A \mid A \subseteq Q\}.$$

Intuitively, $\Delta(p, a)$ gives the set of all states that N is allowed to move to from p in one step under input symbol a. We often write

$$p \xrightarrow{a} q$$

if $q \in \Delta(p, q)$. The set $\Delta(p, a)$ can be the empty set $\varnothing$. The function Δ is called the *transition function*.

Now we define acceptance for NFAs. The function Δ extends in a natural way by induction to a function

$$\widehat{\Delta} : 2^Q \times \Sigma^* \to 2^Q$$

according to the rules

$$\widehat{\Delta}(A, \epsilon) \stackrel{\text{def}}{=} A, \tag{6.1}$$

$$\widehat{\Delta}(A, xa) \stackrel{\text{def}}{=} \bigcup_{q \in \widehat{\Delta}(A, x)} \Delta(q, a). \tag{6.2}$$

Intuitively, for $A \subseteq Q$ and $x \in \Sigma^*$, $\widehat{\Delta}(A, x)$ is the set of all states reachable under input string x from *some* state in A. Note that Δ takes a single state as its first argument and a single symbol as its second argument, whereas $\widehat{\Delta}$ takes a *set* of states as its first argument and a *string* of symbols as its second argument.

Equation (6.1) says that the set of all states reachable from a state in A under the null input is just A. In (6.2), the notation on the right-hand side means the union of all the sets $\Delta(q, a)$ for $q \in \widehat{\Delta}(A, x)$; in other words, $r \in \widehat{\Delta}(A, xa)$ if there exists $q \in \widehat{\Delta}(A, x)$ such that $r \in \Delta(q, a)$.

$$p \;-\!-\!-\!-\!-\!-\!-\!-\!\overset{x}{-\!-}\!-\!-\!-\!-\!-\!-\!-\!\to\; q \;\overset{a}{\longrightarrow}\; r$$

Thus $q \in \widehat{\Delta}(A, x)$ if N can move from some state $p \in A$ to state q under input x. This is the nondeterministic analog of the construction of $\widehat{\delta}$ for deterministic automata we have already seen.

Note that for $a \in \Sigma$,

$$\begin{aligned}
\widehat{\Delta}(A, a) &= \bigcup_{p \in \widehat{\Delta}(A, \epsilon)} \Delta(p, a) \\
&= \bigcup_{p \in A} \Delta(p, a).
\end{aligned}$$

The automaton N is said to *accept* $x \in \Sigma^*$ if

$$\widehat{\Delta}(S, x) \cap F \neq \varnothing.$$

In other words, N accepts x if there exists an accept state q (i.e., $q \in F$) such that q is reachable from a start state under input string x (i.e., $q \in \widehat{\Delta}(S, x)$).

We define $L(N)$ to be the set of all strings accepted by N:

$$L(N) = \{x \in \Sigma^* \mid N \text{ accepts } x\}.$$

Under this definition, every DFA

$$(Q, \Sigma, \delta, s, F)$$

is equivalent to an NFA

$$(Q, \Sigma, \Delta, \{s\}, F),$$

where $\Delta(p, a) \stackrel{\text{def}}{=} \{\delta(p, a)\}$. Below we will show that the converse holds as well: every NFA is equivalent to some DFA.

Here are some basic lemmas that we will find useful when dealing with NFAs. The first corresponds to Exercise 3 of Homework 1 for deterministic automata.

Lemma 6.1 *For any $x, y \in \Sigma^*$ and $A \subseteq Q$,*

$$\widehat{\Delta}(A, xy) = \widehat{\Delta}(\widehat{\Delta}(A, x), y).$$

Proof. The proof is by induction on $|y|$.

Basis

For $y = \epsilon$,

$$\begin{aligned}
\widehat{\Delta}(A, x\epsilon) &= \widehat{\Delta}(A, x) \\
&= \widehat{\Delta}(\widehat{\Delta}(A, x), \epsilon) \quad \text{by (6.1).}
\end{aligned}$$

Induction step

For any $y \in \Sigma^*$ and $a \in \Sigma$,

$$\begin{aligned}
\widehat{\Delta}(A, xya) &= \bigcup_{q \in \widehat{\Delta}(A, xy)} \Delta(q, a) \quad\quad \text{by (6.2)} \\
&= \bigcup_{q \in \widehat{\Delta}(\widehat{\Delta}(A, x), y)} \Delta(q, a) \quad \text{induction hypothesis} \\
&= \widehat{\Delta}(\widehat{\Delta}(A, x), ya) \quad\quad \text{by (6.2).} \qquad\qquad \square
\end{aligned}$$

Lemma 6.2 *The function $\widehat{\Delta}$ commutes with set union: for any indexed family A_i of subsets of Q and $x \in \Sigma^*$,*

$$\widehat{\Delta}(\bigcup_i A_i, x) = \bigcup_i \widehat{\Delta}(A_i, x).$$

Proof. By induction on $|x|$.

Basis

By (6.1),

$$\widehat{\Delta}(\bigcup_i A_i, \epsilon) = \bigcup_i A_i = \bigcup_i \widehat{\Delta}(A_i, \epsilon).$$

Induction step

$$
\begin{aligned}
\widehat{\Delta}(\bigcup_i A_i, xa) &= \bigcup_{p \in \widehat{\Delta}(\bigcup_i A_i, x)} \Delta(p, a) \quad &\text{by (6.2)} \\
&= \bigcup_{p \in \bigcup_i \widehat{\Delta}(A_i, x)} \Delta(p, a) \quad &\text{induction hypothesis} \\
&= \bigcup_i \bigcup_{p \in \widehat{\Delta}(A_i, x)} \Delta(p, a) \quad &\text{basic set theory} \\
&= \bigcup_i \widehat{\Delta}(A_i, xa) \quad &\text{by (6.2).} \qquad \square
\end{aligned}
$$

In particular, expressing a set as the union of its singleton subsets,

$$\widehat{\Delta}(A, x) = \bigcup_{p \in A} \widehat{\Delta}(\{p\}, x). \tag{6.3}$$

The Subset Construction: General Account

The subset construction works in general. Let

$$N = (Q_N, \Sigma, \Delta_N, S_N, F_N)$$

be an arbitrary NFA. We will use the subset construction to produce an equivalent DFA. Let M be the DFA

$$M = (Q_M, \Sigma, \delta_M, s_M, F_M),$$

where

$$
\begin{aligned}
Q_M &\stackrel{\text{def}}{=} 2^{Q_N}, \\
\delta_M(A, a) &\stackrel{\text{def}}{=} \widehat{\Delta}_N(A, a), \\
s_M &\stackrel{\text{def}}{=} S_N, \\
F_M &\stackrel{\text{def}}{=} \{A \subseteq Q_N \mid A \cap F_N \neq \varnothing\}.
\end{aligned}
$$

Note that δ_M is a function from states of M and input symbols to states of M, as it should be, because states of M are *sets* of states of N.

Lemma 6.3 *For any $A \subseteq Q_N$ and $x \in \Sigma^*$,*

$$\widehat{\delta}_M(A, x) = \widehat{\Delta}_N(A, x).$$

Proof. Induction on $|x|$.

Basis

For $x = \epsilon$, we want to show

$$\widehat{\delta}_M(A, \epsilon) = \widehat{\Delta}_N(A, \epsilon).$$

But both of these are A, by definition of $\widehat{\delta}_M$ and $\widehat{\Delta}_N$.

Induction step

Assume that

$$\widehat{\delta}_M(A, x) = \widehat{\Delta}_N(A, x).$$

We want to show the same is true for xa, $a \in \Sigma$.

$$
\begin{aligned}
\widehat{\delta}_M(A, xa) &= \delta_M(\widehat{\delta}_M(A, x), a) && \text{definition of } \widehat{\delta}_M \\
&= \delta_M(\widehat{\Delta}_N(A, x), a) && \text{induction hypothesis} \\
&= \widehat{\Delta}_N(\widehat{\Delta}_N(A, x), a) && \text{definition of } \delta_M \\
&= \widehat{\Delta}_N(A, xa) && \text{Lemma 6.1.} \qquad \square
\end{aligned}
$$

Theorem 6.4 *The automata M and N accept the same set.*

Proof. For any $x \in \Sigma^*$,

$$
\begin{aligned}
&x \in L(M) \\
&\iff \widehat{\delta}_M(s_M, x) \in F_M && \text{definition of acceptance for } M \\
&\iff \widehat{\Delta}_N(S_N, x) \cap F_N \neq \varnothing && \text{definition of } s_M \text{ and } F_M, \text{ Lemma 6.3} \\
&\iff x \in L(N) && \text{definition of acceptance for } N. \qquad \square
\end{aligned}
$$

ϵ-Transitions

Here is another extension of finite automata that turns out to be quite useful but really adds no more power.

An ϵ-*transition* is a transition with label ϵ, a letter that stands for the null string ϵ:

$$p \xrightarrow{\epsilon} q.$$

The automaton can take such a transition anytime without reading an input symbol.

Example 6.5

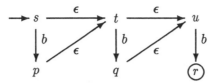

If the machine is in state s and the next input symbol is b, it can nonde-terministically decide to do one of three things:

- read the b and move to state p;

- slide to t without reading an input symbol, then read the b and move to state q; or

- slide to t without reading an input symbol, then slide to u without reading an input symbol, then read the b and move to state r.

The set of strings accepted by this automaton is $\{b, bb, bbb\}$.   □

Example 6.6   Here is a nondeterministic automaton with ϵ-transitions accepting the set $\{x \in \{a\}^* \mid |x| \text{ is divisible by 3 or 5}\}$:

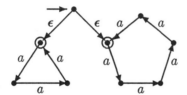

The automaton chooses at the outset which of the two conditions to check for (divisibility by 3 or 5) and slides to one of the two loops accordingly without reading an input symbol.   □

The main benefit of ϵ-transitions is convenience. They do not really add any power: a modified subset construction involving the notion of ϵ-*closure* can be used to show that every NFA with ϵ-transitions can be simulated by a DFA without ϵ-transitions (Miscellaneous Exercise 10); thus all sets accepted by nondeterministic automata with ϵ-transitions are regular. We will also give an alternative treatment in Lecture 10 using homomorphisms.

More Closure Properties

Recall that the concatenation of sets A and B is the set

$$AB = \{xy \mid x \in A \text{ and } y \in B\}.$$

For example,

$$\{a, ab\}\{b, ba\} = \{ab, aba, abb, abba\}.$$

If A and B are regular, then so is AB. To see this, let M be an automaton for A and N an automaton for B. Make a new automaton P whose states are the union of the state sets of M and N, and take all the transitions of M and N as transitions of P. Make the start states of M the start states of P and the final states of N the final states of P. Finally, put ϵ-transitions from all the final states of M to all the start states of N. Then $L(P) = AB$.

Example 6.7   Let $A = \{aa\}$, $B = \{bb\}$. Here are automata for A and B:

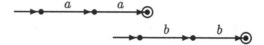

Here is the automaton you get by the construction above for AB:

If A is regular, then so is its asterate:

$$A^* = \{\epsilon\} \cup A \cup A^2 \cup A^3 \cup \cdots$$
$$= \{x_1 x_2 \cdots x_n \mid n \geq 0 \text{ and } x_i \in A, 1 \leq i \leq n\}.$$

To see this, take an automaton M for A. Build an automaton P for A^* as follows. Start with all the states and transitions of M. Add a new state s. Add ϵ-transitions from s to all the start states of M and from all the final states of M to s. Make s the only start state of P and also the only final state of P (thus the start and final states of M are *not* start and final states of P). Then P accepts exactly the set A^*.

Example 6.8   Let $A = \{aa\}$. Consider the three-state automaton for A in Example 6.7. Here is the automaton you get for A^* by the construction above:

In this construction, you must add the new start/final state s. You might think that it suffices to put in ϵ-transitions from the old final states back to the old start states and make the old start states final states, but this doesn't always work. Here's a counterexample:

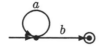

The set accepted is $\{a^n b \mid n \geq 0\}$. The asterate of this set is

$$\{\epsilon\} \cup \{\text{strings ending with } b\},$$

but if you put in an ϵ-transition from the final state back to the start state and made the start state a final state, then the set accepted would be $\{a, b\}^*$.

Historical Notes

Rabin and Scott [102] introduced nondeterministic finite automata and showed using the subset construction that they were no more powerful than deterministic finite automata.

Closure properties of regular sets were studied by Ginsburg and Rose [46, 48], Ginsburg [43], McNaughton and Yamada [85], and Rabin and Scott [102], among others.

Lecture 7

Pattern Matching

What happens when one types `rm *` in UNIX? (If you don't know, don't try it to find out!) What if the current directory contains the files

```
a.tex   bc.tex   a.dvi   bc.dvi
```

and one types `rm *.dvi`? What would happen if there were a file named `.dvi`?

What is going on here is *pattern matching*. The * in UNIX is a pattern that matches any string of symbols, including the null string.

Pattern matching is an important application of finite automata. The UNIX commands `grep`, `fgrep`, and `egrep` are basic pattern-matching utilities that use finite automata in their implementation.

Let Σ be a finite alphabet. A *pattern* is a string of symbols of a certain form representing a (possibly infinite) set of strings in Σ^*. The set of patterns is defined formally by induction below. They are either *atomic patterns* or *compound patterns* built up inductively from atomic patterns using certain *operators*. We'll denote patterns by Greek letters α, β, γ, ...

As we define patterns, we will tell which strings $x \in \Sigma^*$ *match* them. The set of strings in Σ^* matching a given pattern α will be denoted $L(\alpha)$. Thus

$$L(\alpha) = \{x \in \Sigma^* \mid x \text{ matches } \alpha\}.$$

In the following, forget the UNIX definition of $*$. We will use the symbol $*$ for something else.

The *atomic patterns* are

- a for each $a \in \Sigma$, matched by the symbol a only; in symbols, $L(a) = \{a\}$;

- ϵ, matched only by ϵ, the null string; in symbols, $L(\epsilon) = \{\epsilon\}$;

- $\emptyset$, matched by nothing; in symbols, $L(\emptyset) = \emptyset$, the empty set;

- $\#$, matched by any symbol in Σ; in symbols, $L(\#) = \Sigma$;

- $@$, matched by any string in Σ^*; in symbols, $L(@) = \Sigma^*$.

Compound patterns are formed inductively using binary operators $+$, $\cap$, and $\cdot$ (usually not written) and unary operators $^+$, *, and $\sim$. If α and β are patterns, then so are $\alpha + \beta$, $\alpha \cap \beta$, α^*, α^+, $\sim\alpha$, and $\alpha\beta$. The last of these is short for $\alpha \cdot \beta$.

We also define inductively which strings match each pattern. We have already said which strings match the atomic patterns. This is the basis of the inductive definition. Now suppose we have already defined the sets of strings $L(\alpha)$ and $L(\beta)$ matching α and β, respectively. Then we'll say that

- x matches $\alpha + \beta$ if x matches either α or β:
$$L(\alpha + \beta) = L(\alpha) \cup L(\beta);$$

- x matches $\alpha \cap \beta$ if x matches both α and β:
$$L(\alpha \cap \beta) = L(\alpha) \cap L(\beta);$$

- x matches $\alpha\beta$ if x can be broken down as $x = yz$ such that y matches α and z matches β:
$$L(\alpha\beta) = L(\alpha)L(\beta)$$
$$= \{yz \mid y \in L(\alpha) \text{ and } z \in L(\beta)\};$$

- x matches $\sim\alpha$ if x does not match α:
$$L(\sim\alpha) = \sim L(\alpha)$$
$$= \Sigma^* - L(\alpha);$$

- x matches α^* if x can be expressed as a concatenation of zero or more strings, all of which match α:
$$L(\alpha^*) = \{x_1 x_2 \cdots x_n \mid n \geq 0 \text{ and } x_i \in L(\alpha), 1 \leq i \leq n\}$$
$$= L(\alpha)^0 \cup L(\alpha)^1 \cup L(\alpha)^2 \cup \cdots$$

$$= L(\alpha)^*.$$

The null string ϵ always matches α^*, since ϵ is a concatenation of zero strings, all of which (vacuously) match α.

- x matches α^+ if x can be expressed as a concatenation of one or more strings, all of which match α:

$$L(\alpha^+) = \{x_1 x_2 \cdots x_n \mid n \geq 1 \text{ and } x_i \in L(\alpha), 1 \leq i \leq n\}$$
$$= L(\alpha)^1 \cup L(\alpha)^2 \cup L(\alpha)^3 \cup \cdots$$
$$= L(\alpha)^+.$$

Note that patterns are just certain strings of symbols over the alphabet

$$\Sigma \cup \{\epsilon, \emptyset, \#, @, +, \cap, \sim, {}^*, {}^+, (,)\}.$$

Note also that the meanings of $\#$, $@$, and $\sim$ depend on Σ. For example, if $\Sigma = \{a, b, c\}$ then $L(\#) = \{a, b, c\}$, but if $\Sigma = \{a\}$ then $L(\#) = \{a\}$.

Example 7.1
- $\Sigma^* = L(@) = L(\#^*)$.

- Singleton sets: if $x \in \Sigma^*$, then x itself is a pattern and is matched only by the string x; i.e., $\{x\} = L(x)$.

- Finite sets: if $x_1, \ldots, x_m \in \Sigma^*$, then

$$\{x_1, x_2, \ldots, x_m\} = L(x_1 + x_2 + \cdots + x_m). \qquad \square$$

Note that we can write the last pattern $x_1 + x_2 + \cdots + x_m$ without parentheses, since the two patterns $(\alpha + \beta) + \gamma$ and $\alpha + (\beta + \gamma)$ are matched by the same set of strings; i.e.,

$$L((\alpha + \beta) + \gamma) = L(\alpha + (\beta + \gamma)).$$

Mathematically speaking, the operator $+$ is *associative*. The concatenation operator $\cdot$ is associative, too. Hence we can also unambiguously write $\alpha\beta\gamma$ without parentheses.

Example 7.2
- strings containing at least three occurrences of a:

    $@a@a@a@$;

- strings containing an a followed later by a b; that is, strings of the form $xaybz$ for some x, y, z:

    $@a@b@$;

- all single letters except a:

    $\# \cap \sim a$;

- strings with no occurrence of the letter a:

  $$(\# \cap \sim a)^*;$$

- strings in which every occurrence of a is followed sometime later by an occurrence of b; in other words, strings in which there are either no occurrences of a, or there is an occurrence of b followed by no occurrence of a; for example, aab matches but bba doesn't:

  $$(\# \cap \sim a)^* + @b(\# \cap \sim a)^*.$$

  If the alphabet is $\{a, b\}$, then this takes a much simpler form:

  $$\epsilon + @b. \qquad\qquad\qquad\qquad\qquad\qquad\qquad \square$$

Before we go too much further, there is a subtlety that needs to be mentioned. Note the slight difference in appearance between $\boldsymbol{\epsilon}$ and ϵ and between $\boldsymbol{\emptyset}$ and $\varnothing$. The objects $\boldsymbol{\epsilon}$ and $\boldsymbol{\emptyset}$ are *symbols* in the language of patterns, whereas ϵ and $\varnothing$ are *metasymbols* that we are using to name the null string and the empty set, respectively. These are different sorts of things: $\boldsymbol{\epsilon}$ and $\boldsymbol{\emptyset}$ are symbols, that is, strings of length one, whereas ϵ is a string of length zero and $\varnothing$ isn't even a string.

We'll maintain the distinction for a few lectures until we get used to the idea, but at some point in the near future we'll drop the boldface and use ϵ and $\varnothing$ exclusively. We'll always be able to infer from context whether we mean the symbols or the metasymbols. This is a little more convenient and conforms to standard usage, but bear in mind that they are still different things.

While we're on the subject of abuse of notation, we should also mention that very often you will see things like $x \in a^*b^*$ in texts and articles. Strictly speaking, one should write $x \in L(a^*b^*)$, since a^*b^* is a pattern, not a set of strings. But as long as you know what you really mean and can stand the guilt, it is okay to write $x \in a^*b^*$.

Lecture 8

Pattern Matching and Regular Expressions

Here are some interesting and important questions:

- How hard is it to determine whether a given string x matches a given pattern α? This is an important practical question. There are very efficient algorithms, as we will see.

- Is every set represented by some pattern? Answer: no. For example, the set

$$\{a^n b^n \mid n \geq 0\}$$

is not represented by any pattern. We'll prove this later.

- Patterns α and β are *equivalent* if $L(\alpha) = L(\beta)$. How do you tell whether α and β are equivalent? Sometimes it is obvious and sometimes not.

- Which operators are redundant? For example, we can get rid of ϵ since it is equivalent to $\sim(\#@)$ and also to $\emptyset^*$. We can get rid of @ since it is equivalent to $\#^*$. We can get rid of unary $+$ since α^+ is equivalent to $\alpha\alpha^*$. We can get rid of #, since if $\Sigma = \{a_1, \ldots, a_n\}$ then # is equivalent to the pattern

$$a_1 + a_2 + \cdots + a_n.$$

The operator $\cap$ is also redundant, by one of the De Morgan laws:

$\alpha \cap \beta$ is equivalent to $\sim(\sim\alpha + \sim\beta)$.

Redundancy is an important question. From a user's point of view, we would like to have a lot of operators since this lets us write more succinct patterns; but from a programmer's point of view, we would like to have as few as possible since there is less code to write. Also, from a theoretical point of view, fewer operators mean fewer cases we have to treat in giving formal semantics and proofs of correctness.

An amazing and difficult-to-prove fact is that the operator $\sim$ is redundant. Thus every pattern is equivalent to one using only atomic patterns $a \in \Sigma$, ϵ, $\emptyset$, and operators $+$, $\cdot$, and $*$. Patterns using only these symbols are called *regular expressions*. Actually, as we have observed, even ϵ is redundant, but we include it in the definition of regular expressions because it occurs so often.

Our goal for this lecture and the next will be to show that the family of subsets of Σ^* represented by patterns is exactly the family of regular sets. Thus as a way of describing subsets of Σ^*, finite automata, patterns, and regular expressions are equally expressive.

Some Notational Conveniences

Since the binary operators $+$ and $\cdot$ are associative, that is,

$$L(\alpha + (\beta + \gamma)) = L((\alpha + \beta) + \gamma),$$
$$L(\alpha(\beta\gamma)) = L((\alpha\beta)\gamma),$$

we can write

$$\alpha + \beta + \gamma \quad \text{and} \quad \alpha\beta\gamma$$

without ambiguity. To resolve ambiguity in other situations, we assign precedence to operators. For example,

$$\alpha + \beta\gamma$$

could be interpreted as either

$$\alpha + (\beta\gamma) \quad \text{or} \quad (\alpha + \beta)\gamma,$$

which are not equivalent. We adopt the convention that the concatenation operator $\cdot$ has higher precedence than $+$, so that we would prefer the former interpretation. Similarly, we assign $*$ higher precedence than $+$ or $\cdot$, so that

$$\alpha + \beta^*$$

is interpreted as

$$\alpha + (\beta^*)$$

and not as

$$(\alpha + \beta)^*.$$

All else failing, use parentheses.

Equivalence of Patterns, Regular Expressions, and Finite Automata

Patterns, regular expressions (patterns built from atomic patterns $a \in \Sigma$, ϵ, $\emptyset$, and operators $+$, *, and $\cdot$ only), and finite automata are all equivalent in expressive power: they all represent the regular sets.

Theorem 8.1   *Let $A \subseteq \Sigma^*$. The following three statements are equivalent:*

(i) A is regular; that is, $A = L(M)$ for some finite automaton M;

(ii) $A = L(\alpha)$ for some pattern α;

(iii) $A = L(\alpha)$ for some regular expression α.

Proof. The implication (iii) $\Rightarrow$ (ii) is trivial, since every regular expression is a pattern. We prove (ii) $\Rightarrow$ (i) here and (i) $\Rightarrow$ (iii) in Lecture 9.

The heart of the proof (ii) $\Rightarrow$ (i) involves showing that certain basic sets (corresponding to atomic patterns) are regular, and the regular sets are closed under certain closure operations corresponding to the operators used to build patterns. Note that

- the singleton set $\{a\}$ is regular, $a \in \Sigma$,

- the singleton set $\{\epsilon\}$ is regular, and

- the empty set $\emptyset$ is regular,

since each of these sets is the set accepted by some automaton. Here are nondeterministic automata for these three sets, respectively:

Also, we have previously shown that the regular sets are closed under the set operations $\cup$, $\cap$, $\sim$, $\cdot$, *, and $^+$; that is, if A and B are regular sets, then so are $A \cup B$, $A \cap B$, $\sim A = \Sigma^* - A$, AB, A^*, and A^+.

These facts can be used to prove inductively that (ii) $\Rightarrow$ (i). Let α be a given pattern. We wish to show that $L(\alpha)$ is a regular set. We proceed by induction on the structure of α. The pattern α is of one of the following forms:

(i) a, where $a \in \Sigma$;   (vi) $\beta + \gamma$;

(ii) ϵ;   (vii) $\beta \cap \gamma$;

(iii) $\emptyset$;   (viii) $\beta\gamma$;

(iv)   #;   (ix) $\sim\beta$;

(v)   @;   (x) β^*;

                                                      (xi) β^+.

There are five base cases (i) through (v) corresponding to the atomic patterns and six induction cases (vi) through (xi) corresponding to compound patterns. Each of these cases uses a closure property of the regular sets previously observed.

For (i), (ii), and (iii), we have $L(a) = \{a\}$ for $a \in \Sigma$, $L(\epsilon) = \{\epsilon\}$, and $L(\emptyset) = \emptyset$, and these are regular sets.

For (iv), (v), and (xi), we observed earlier that the operators #, @, and $^+$ were redundant, so we may disregard these cases since they are already covered by the other cases.

For (vi), recall that $L(\beta+\gamma) = L(\beta) \cup L(\gamma)$ by definition of the + operator. By the induction hypothesis, $L(\beta)$ and $L(\gamma)$ are regular. Since the regular sets are closed under union, $L(\beta + \gamma) = L(\beta) \cup L(\gamma)$ is also regular.

The arguments for the remaining cases (vii) through (x) are similar to the argument for (vi). Each of these cases uses a closure property of the regular sets that we have observed previously in Lectures 4 and 6.   □

Example 8.2   Let's convert the regular expression

$$(aaa)^* + (aaaaa)^*$$

for the set

$$\{x \in \{a\}^* \mid |x| \text{ is divisible by either 3 or 5}\}$$

to an equivalent NFA. First we show how to construct an automaton for $(aaa)^*$. We take an automaton accepting only the string aaa, say

Applying the construction of Lecture 6, we add a new start state and ϵ-transitions from the new start state to all the old start states and from all the old accept states to the new start state. We let the new start state be the only accept state of the new automaton. This gives

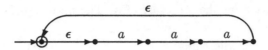

The construction for $(aaaaa)^*$ is similar, giving

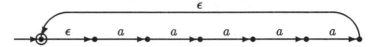

To get an NFA for $(aaa)^* + (aaaaa)^*$, we can simply take the disjoint union of these two automata:

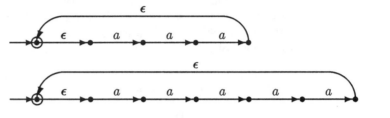

□

Lecture 9

Regular Expressions and Finite Automata

Simplification of Expressions

For small regular expressions, one can often see how to construct an equivalent automaton directly without going through the mechanical procedure of the previous lecture. It is therefore useful to try to simplify the expression first.

For regular expressions α, β, if $L(\alpha) = L(\beta)$, we write $\alpha \equiv \beta$ and say that α and β are *equivalent*. The relation $\equiv$ on regular expressions is an equivalence relation; that is, it is

- reflexive: $\alpha \equiv \alpha$ for all α;

- symmetric: if $\alpha \equiv \beta$, then $\beta \equiv \alpha$; and

- transitive: if $\alpha \equiv \beta$ and $\beta \equiv \gamma$, then $\alpha \equiv \gamma$.

If $\alpha \equiv \beta$, one can substitute α for β (or vice versa) in any regular expression, and the resulting expression will be equivalent to the original.

Here are a few laws that can be used to simplify regular expressions.

$$\alpha + (\beta + \gamma) \equiv (\alpha + \beta) + \gamma \tag{9.1}$$
$$\alpha + \beta \equiv \beta + \alpha \tag{9.2}$$

$$\alpha + \emptyset \equiv \alpha \tag{9.3}$$

$$\alpha + \alpha \equiv \alpha \tag{9.4}$$

$$\alpha(\beta\gamma) \equiv (\alpha\beta)\gamma \tag{9.5}$$

$$\epsilon\alpha \equiv \alpha\epsilon \equiv \alpha \tag{9.6}$$

$$\alpha(\beta + \gamma) \equiv \alpha\beta + \alpha\gamma \tag{9.7}$$

$$(\alpha + \beta)\gamma \equiv \alpha\gamma + \beta\gamma \tag{9.8}$$

$$\emptyset\alpha \equiv \alpha\emptyset \equiv \emptyset \tag{9.9}$$

$$\epsilon + \alpha\alpha^* \equiv \alpha^* \tag{9.10}$$

$$\epsilon + \alpha^*\alpha \equiv \alpha^* \tag{9.11}$$

$$\beta + \alpha\gamma \leq \gamma \Rightarrow \alpha^*\beta \leq \gamma \tag{9.12}$$

$$\beta + \gamma\alpha \leq \gamma \Rightarrow \beta\alpha^* \leq \gamma \tag{9.13}$$

In (9.12) and (9.13), $\leq$ refers to the subset order:

$$\alpha \leq \beta \stackrel{\text{def}}{\iff} L(\alpha) \subseteq L(\beta)$$
$$\iff L(\alpha + \beta) = L(\beta)$$
$$\iff \alpha + \beta \equiv \beta.$$

Laws (9.12) and (9.13) are not equations but rules from which one can derive equations from other equations. Laws (9.1) through (9.13) can be justified by replacing each expression by its definition and reasoning set theoretically.

Here are some useful equations that follow from (9.1) through (9.13) that you can use to simplify expressions.

$$(\alpha\beta)^*\alpha \equiv \alpha(\beta\alpha)^* \tag{9.14}$$

$$(\alpha^*\beta)^*\alpha^* \equiv (\alpha + \beta)^* \tag{9.15}$$

$$\alpha^*(\beta\alpha^*)^* \equiv (\alpha + \beta)^* \tag{9.16}$$

$$(\epsilon + \alpha)^* \equiv \alpha^* \tag{9.17}$$

$$\alpha\alpha^* \equiv \alpha^*\alpha \tag{9.18}$$

An interesting fact that is beyond the scope of this course is that all true equations between regular expressions can be proved purely algebraically from the axioms and rules (9.1) through (9.13) plus the laws of equational logic [73].

To illustrate, let's convert some regular expressions to finite automata.

Example 9.1 $(11+0)^*(00+1)^*$

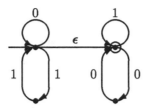

This expression is simple enough that the easiest thing to do is eyeball it. The mechanical method described in Lecture 8 would give more states and ϵ-transitions than shown here. The two states connected by an ϵ-transition cannot be collapsed into one state, since then 10 would be accepted, which does not match the regular expression.   □

Example 9.2 $(1+01+001)^*(\epsilon+0+00)$

Using the algebraic laws above, we can rewrite the expression:

$$(1+01+001)^*(\epsilon+0+00) \equiv ((\epsilon+0+00)1)^*(\epsilon+0+00)$$
$$\equiv ((\epsilon+0)(\epsilon+0)1)^*(\epsilon+0)(\epsilon+0).$$

It is now easier to see that the set represented is the set of all strings over $\{0,1\}$ with no substring of more than two adjacent 0's.

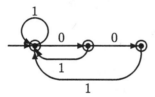

□

Just because all states of an NFA are accept states doesn't mean that all strings are accepted! Note that in Example 9.2, 000 is not accepted.

Converting Automata to Regular Expressions

To finish the proof of Theorem 8.1, it remains to show how to convert a given finite automaton M to an equivalent regular expression.

Given an NFA

$$M = (Q,\ \Sigma,\ \Delta,\ S,\ F),$$

a subset $X \subseteq Q$, and states $u, v \in Q$, we show how to construct a regular expression

$$\alpha_{uv}^X$$

representing the set of all strings x such that there is a path from u to v in M labeled x (i.e., such that $v \in \widehat{\Delta}(\{u\}, x)$) and all states along that path, with the possible exception of u and v, lie in X.

The expressions are constructed inductively on the size of X. For the basis $X = \varnothing$, let $a_1, \ldots, a_k$ be all the symbols in Σ such that $v \in \Delta(u, a_i)$. For $u \neq v$, take

$$\alpha_{uv}^{\varnothing} \stackrel{\text{def}}{=} \begin{cases} a_1 + \cdots + a_k & \text{if } k \geq 1, \\ \varnothing & \text{if } k = 0; \end{cases}$$

and for $u = v$, take

$$\alpha_{uv}^{\varnothing} \stackrel{\text{def}}{=} \begin{cases} a_1 + \cdots + a_k + \epsilon & \text{if } k \geq 1, \\ \epsilon & \text{if } k = 0. \end{cases}$$

For nonempty X, we can choose any element $q \in X$ and take

$$\alpha_{uv}^{X} \stackrel{\text{def}}{=} \alpha_{uv}^{X-\{q\}} + \alpha_{uq}^{X-\{q\}} (\alpha_{qq}^{X-\{q\}})^* \alpha_{qv}^{X-\{q\}}. \tag{9.19}$$

To justify the definition (9.19), note that any path from u to v with all intermediate states in X either (i) never visits q, hence the expression

$$\alpha_{uv}^{X-\{q\}}$$

on the right-hand side of (9.19); or (ii) visits q for the first time, hence the expression

$$\alpha_{uq}^{X-\{q\}},$$

followed by a finite number (possibly zero) of loops from q back to itself without visiting q in between and staying in X, hence the expression

$$(\alpha_{qq}^{X-\{q\}})^*,$$

followed by a path from q to v after leaving q for the last time, hence the expression

$$\alpha_{qv}^{X-\{q\}}.$$

The sum of all expressions of the form

$$\alpha_{sf}^{Q},$$

where s is a start state and f is a final state, represents the set of strings accepted by M.

As a practical rule of thumb when doing homework exercises, when choosing the $q \in X$ to drop out in (9.19), it is best to try to choose one that disconnects the automaton as much as possible.

Example 9.3   Let's convert the automaton

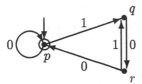

to an equivalent regular expression. The set accepted by this automaton will be represented by the inductively defined regular expression

$$\alpha_{pp}^{\{p,q,r\}},$$

since p is the only start and the only accept state. Removing the state q (we can choose any state we like here), we can take

$$\alpha_{pp}^{\{p,q,r\}} = \alpha_{pp}^{\{p,r\}} + \alpha_{pq}^{\{p,r\}}(\alpha_{qq}^{\{p,r\}})^*\alpha_{qp}^{\{p,r\}}.$$

Looking at the automaton, the only paths going from p to p and staying in the states $\{p,r\}$ are paths going around the single loop labeled 0 from p to p some finite number of times; thus we can take

$$\alpha_{pp}^{\{p,r\}} = 0^*.$$

By similar informal reasoning, we can take

$$\alpha_{pq}^{\{p,r\}} = 0^*1,$$
$$\alpha_{qq}^{\{p,r\}} = \epsilon + 01 + 000^*1$$
$$\equiv \epsilon + 0(\epsilon + 00^*)1$$
$$\equiv \epsilon + 00^*1,$$
$$\alpha_{qp}^{\{p,r\}} = 000^*.$$

Thus we can take

$$\alpha_{pp}^{\{p,q,r\}} = 0^* + 0^*1(\epsilon + 00^*1)^*000^*.$$

This is matched by the set of all strings accepted by the automaton. We can further simplify the expression using the algebraic laws (9.1) through (9.18):

$$0^* + 0^*1(\epsilon + 00^*1)^*000^*$$
$$\equiv 0^* + 0^*1(00^*1)^*000^* \qquad \text{by (9.17)}$$
$$\equiv \epsilon + 00^* + 0^*10(0^*10)^*00^* \qquad \text{by (9.10) and (9.14)}$$
$$\equiv \epsilon + (\epsilon + 0^*10(0^*10)^*)00^* \qquad \text{by (9.8)}$$
$$\equiv \epsilon + (0^*10)^*00^* \qquad \text{by (9.10)}$$
$$\equiv \epsilon + (0^*10)^*0^*0 \qquad \text{by (9.18)}$$
$$\equiv \epsilon + (0 + 10)^*0 \qquad \text{by (9.15).} \qquad \square$$

Historical Notes

Kleene [70] proved that deterministic finite automata and regular expressions are equivalent. A shorter proof was given by McNaughton and Yamada [85].

The relationship between right- and left-linear grammars and regular sets (Homework 5, Exercise 1) was observed by Chomsky and Miller [21].

Supplementary Lecture A

Kleene Algebra and Regular Expressions

In Lecture 9, we gave a combinatorial proof that every finite automaton has an equivalent regular expression. Here is an algebraic proof that generalizes that argument. It is worth looking at because it introduces the notion of *Kleene algebra* and the use of matrices. We will show how to use matrices and Kleene algebra to solve systems of linear equations involving sets of strings.

Kleene algebra is named after Stephen C. Kleene, who invented the regular sets [70].

Kleene Algebra

We have already observed in Lecture 9 that the set operations $\cup$, $\cdot$, and * on subsets of Σ^*, along with the distinguished subsets $\varnothing$ and $\{\epsilon\}$, satisfy certain important algebraic properties. These were listed in Lecture 9, axioms (9.1) through (9.13). Let us call any algebraic structure satisfying these properties a *Kleene algebra*. In general, a Kleene algebra $\mathcal{K}$ consists of a nonempty set with two distinguished constants 0 and 1, two binary operations $+$ and $\cdot$ (usually omitted in expressions), and a unary operation * satisfying the following axioms.

$$a + (b + c) = (a + b) + c \qquad \text{associativity of } + \qquad (A.1)$$

$$a + b = b + a \qquad \text{commutativity of } + \qquad (A.2)$$

$$a + a = a \qquad \text{idempotence of } + \qquad \text{(A.3)}$$

$$a + 0 = a \qquad \text{0 is an identity for } + \qquad \text{(A.4)}$$

$$a(bc) = (ab)c \qquad \text{associativity of } \cdot \qquad \text{(A.5)}$$

$$a1 = 1a = a \qquad \text{1 is an identity for } \cdot \qquad \text{(A.6)}$$

$$a0 = 0a = 0 \qquad \text{0 is an annihilator for } \cdot \qquad \text{(A.7)}$$

$$a(b + c) = ab + ac \qquad \text{distributivity} \qquad \text{(A.8)}$$

$$(a + b)c = ac + bc \qquad \text{distributivity} \qquad \text{(A.9)}$$

$$1 + aa^* = a^* \qquad \text{(A.10)}$$

$$1 + a^*a = a^* \qquad \text{(A.11)}$$

$$b + ac \le c \Rightarrow a^*b \le c \qquad \text{(A.12)}$$

$$b + ca \le c \Rightarrow ba^* \le c \qquad \text{(A.13)}$$

In (A.12) and (A.13), $\le$ refers to the naturally defined order

$$a \le b \overset{\text{def}}{\Longleftrightarrow} a + b = b.$$

In 2^{Σ^*}, $\le$ is just set inclusion $\subseteq$.

Axioms (A.1) through (A.9) discuss the properties of addition and multiplication in a Kleene algebra. These properties are the same as those of ordinary addition and multiplication, with the addition of the idempotence axiom (A.3). These axioms can be summed up briefly by saying that $\mathcal{K}$ is an *idempotent semiring*. The remaining axioms (A.10) through (A.13) discuss the properties of the operator *. They say essentially that * behaves like the asterate operator on sets of strings or the reflexive transitive closure operator on binary relations.

It follows quite easily from the axioms that $\le$ is a partial order; that is, it is reflexive ($a \le a$), transitive ($a \le b$ and $b \le c$ imply $a \le c$), and antisymmetric ($a \le b$ and $b \le a$ imply $a = b$). Moreover, $a + b$ is the least upper bound of a and b with respect to $\le$. All the operators are monotone with respect to $\le$; in other words, if $a \le b$, then $ac \le bc$, $ca \le cb$, $a + c \le b + c$, and $a^* \le b^*$.

By (A.10) and distributivity, we have

$$b + aa^*b \le a^*b,$$

which says that a^*b satisfies the inequality $b + ac \le c$ when substituted for c. The implication (A.12) says that a^*b is the $\le$-least element of $\mathcal{K}$ for which this is true. It follows that

Lemma A.1   *In any Kleene algebra, a^*b is the $\le$-least solution of the equation $x = ax + b$.*

Proof. Miscellaneous Exercise 21.   □

Instead of (A.12) and (A.13), we might take the equivalent axioms

$$ac \leq c \Rightarrow a^*c \leq c, \qquad\qquad\qquad\qquad\qquad \text{(A.14)}$$
$$ca \leq c \Rightarrow ca^* \leq c \qquad\qquad\qquad\qquad\qquad \text{(A.15)}$$

(see Miscellaneous Exercise 22).

Here are some typical theorems of Kleene algebra. These can be derived by purely equational reasoning from the axioms above (Miscellaneous Exercise 20).

$$a^*a^* = a^*$$
$$a^{**} = a^*$$
$$(a^*b)^*a^* = (a+b)^* \qquad\qquad \text{denesting rule} \qquad\qquad \text{(A.16)}$$
$$a(ba)^* = (ab)^*a \qquad\qquad \text{shifting rule} \qquad\qquad \text{(A.17)}$$
$$a^* = (aa)^* + a(aa)^*$$

Equations (A.16) and (A.17), the *denesting rule* and the *shifting rule*, respectively, turn out to be particularly useful in simplifying regular expressions.

The family 2^{Σ^*} of all subsets of Σ^* with constants $\varnothing$ and $\{\epsilon\}$ and operations $\cup, \cdot,$ and * forms a Kleene algebra, as does the family of all regular subsets of Σ^* with the same operations. As mentioned in Lecture 9, it can be shown that an equation $\alpha = \beta$ is a theorem of Kleene algebra, that is, is derivable from axioms (A.1) through (A.13), if and only if α and β are equivalent as regular expressions [73].

Another example of a Kleene algebra is the family of all binary relations on a set X with the empty relation for 0, the identity relation

$$\iota \stackrel{\text{def}}{=} \{(u,u) \mid u \in X\}$$

for 1, $\cup$ for +, relational composition

$$R \circ S \stackrel{\text{def}}{=} \{(u,w) \mid \exists v \in X \ (u,v) \in R \text{ and } (v,w) \in S\}$$

for $\cdot$, and reflexive transitive closure for *:

$$R^* \stackrel{\text{def}}{=} \bigcup_{n \geq 0} R^n,$$

where

$$R^0 \stackrel{\text{def}}{=} \iota,$$
$$R^{n+1} \stackrel{\text{def}}{=} R^n \circ R.$$

Still another example is the family of $n \times n$ Boolean matrices with the zero matrix for 0, the identity matrix for 1, componentwise Boolean matrix addition and multiplication for $+$ and $\cdot$, respectively, and reflexive transitive closure for $*$. This is really the same as the previous example, where the set X has n elements.

Matrices

Given an arbitrary Kleene algebra $\mathcal{K}$, the set of $n \times n$ matrices over $\mathcal{K}$, which we will denote by $\mathcal{M}(n, \mathcal{K})$, also forms a Kleene algebra. In $\mathcal{M}(2, \mathcal{K})$, for example, the identity elements for $+$ and $\cdot$ are

$$\begin{bmatrix} 0 & 0 \\ 0 & 0 \end{bmatrix} \text{ and } \begin{bmatrix} 1 & 0 \\ 0 & 1 \end{bmatrix},$$

respectively, and the operations $+$, $\cdot$, and $*$ are given by

$$\begin{bmatrix} a & b \\ c & d \end{bmatrix} + \begin{bmatrix} e & f \\ g & h \end{bmatrix} \overset{\text{def}}{=} \begin{bmatrix} a+e & b+f \\ c+g & d+h \end{bmatrix},$$

$$\begin{bmatrix} a & b \\ c & d \end{bmatrix} \cdot \begin{bmatrix} e & f \\ g & h \end{bmatrix} \overset{\text{def}}{=} \begin{bmatrix} ae+bg & af+bh \\ ce+dg & cf+dh \end{bmatrix}, \text{ and}$$

$$\begin{bmatrix} a & b \\ c & d \end{bmatrix}^* \overset{\text{def}}{=} \begin{bmatrix} (a+bd^*c)^* & (a+bd^*c)^*bd^* \\ (d+ca^*b)^*ca^* & (d+ca^*b)^* \end{bmatrix}, \tag{A.18}$$

respectively. In general, $+$ and $\cdot$ in $\mathcal{M}(n, \mathcal{K})$ are ordinary matrix addition and multiplication, respectively, the identity for $+$ is the zero matrix, and the identity for $\cdot$ is the identity matrix.

To define E^* for a given $n \times n$ matrix E over $\mathcal{K}$, we proceed by induction on n. If $n = 1$, the structure $\mathcal{M}(n, \mathcal{K})$ is just $\mathcal{K}$, so we are done. For $n > 1$, break E up into four submatrices

$$E = \left[\begin{array}{c|c} A & B \\ \hline C & D \end{array} \right]$$

such that A and D are square, say $m \times m$ and $(n - m) \times (n - m)$, respectively. By the induction hypothesis, $\mathcal{M}(m, \mathcal{K})$ and $\mathcal{M}(n - m, \mathcal{K})$ are Kleene algebras, so it makes sense to form the asterates of any $m \times m$ or $(n - m) \times (n - m)$ matrix over $\mathcal{K}$, and these matrices will satisfy all the axioms for $*$. This allows us to define

$$E^* \overset{\text{def}}{=} \left[\begin{array}{c|c} (A + BD^*C)^* & (A + BD^*C)^*BD^* \\ \hline (D + CA^*B)^*CA^* & (D + CA^*B)^* \end{array} \right]. \tag{A.19}$$

Compare this definition to (A.18).

The expressions on the right-hand sides of (A.18) and (A.19) may look like they were pulled out of thin air. Where did we get them from? The answer will come to you if you stare really hard at the following mandala:

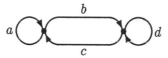

It can be shown that $\mathcal{M}(n, \mathcal{K})$ is a Kleene algebra under these definitions:

Lemma A.2   *If $\mathcal{K}$ is a Kleene algebra, then so is $\mathcal{M}(n, \mathcal{K})$.*

Proof. Miscellaneous Exercise 24. We must verify that $\mathcal{M}(n, \mathcal{K})$ satisfies the axioms (A.1) through (A.13) of Kleene algebra assuming only that $\mathcal{K}$ does.   □

If E is a matrix of indeterminates, and if the inductive construction of E^* given in (A.19) is carried out *symbolically*, then the entries of the resulting matrix E^* will be regular expressions in those indeterminates. This construction generalizes the construction of Lecture 9, which corresponds to the case $m = 1$.

Systems of Linear Equations

It is possible to solve systems of linear equations over a Kleene algebra $\mathcal{K}$. Suppose we are given a set of n variables $x_1, \ldots, x_n$ ranging over $\mathcal{K}$ and a system of n equations of the form

$$x_i = a_{i1}x_1 + \cdots + a_{in}x_n + b_i, \quad 1 \leq i \leq n,$$

where the a_{ij} and b_i are elements of $\mathcal{K}$. Arranging the a_{ij} in an $n \times n$ matrix A, the b_i in a vector b of length n, and the x_i in a vector x of length n, we obtain the matrix-vector equation

$$x = Ax + b. \tag{A.20}$$

It is now not hard to show

Theorem A.3   *The vector A^*b is a solution to (A.20); moreover, it is the $\leq$-least solution in $\mathcal{K}^n$.*

Proof. Miscellaneous Exercise 25.   □

Now we use this to give a regular expression equivalent to an arbitrarily given deterministic finite automaton

$$M = (Q, \Sigma, \delta, s, F).$$

Assume without loss of generality that $Q = \{1, 2, \ldots, n\}$. For each $q \in Q$, let X_q denote the set of strings in Σ^* that would be accepted by M if q were the start state; that is,

$$X_q \stackrel{\text{def}}{=} \{x \in \Sigma^* \mid \widehat{\delta}(q, x) \in F\}.$$

The X_q satisfy the following system of equations:

$$X_q = \left\{ \begin{array}{ll} \sum_{a \in \Sigma} a X_{\delta(q,a)} & \text{if } q \notin F, \\ \sum_{a \in \Sigma} a X_{\delta(q,a)} + 1 & \text{if } q \in F. \end{array} \right.$$

Moreover, the X_q give the least solution with respect to $\subseteq$. As above, these equations can be arranged in a single matrix-vector equation of the form

$$X = AX + b, \tag{A.21}$$

where A is an $n \times n$ matrix containing sums of elements of Σ, b is a 0-1 vector of length n, and X is a vector consisting of $X_1, \ldots, X_n$. The vector X is the least solution of (A.21). By Theorem A.3,

$$X = A^* b.$$

Compute the matrix A^* symbolically according to (A.19), so that its entries are regular expressions, then multiply by b. A regular expression for $L(M)$ can then be read off from the sth entry of $A^* b$, where s is the start state of M.

Historical Notes

Salomaa [108] gave the first complete axiomatization of the algebra of regular sets. The algebraic theory was developed extensively in the monograph of Conway [27]. Many others have contributed to the theory, including Redko [103], Backhouse [6], Bloom and Ésik [10], Boffa [11, 12], Gécseg and Peák [41], Krob [74], Kuich and Salomaa [76], and Salomaa and Soittola [109]. The definition of Kleene algebra and the complete axiomatization given here is from Kozen [73].

Lecture 10

Homomorphisms

A *homomorphism* is a map $h : \Sigma^* \to \Gamma^*$ such that for all $x, y \in \Sigma^*$,

$$h(xy) = h(x)h(y), \qquad (10.1)$$
$$h(\epsilon) = \epsilon. \qquad (10.2)$$

Actually, (10.2) is a consequence of (10.1):

$$|h(\epsilon)| = |h(\epsilon\epsilon)|$$
$$= |h(\epsilon)h(\epsilon)|$$
$$= |h(\epsilon)| + |h(\epsilon)|;$$

subtracting $|h(\epsilon)|$ from both sides, we have $|h(\epsilon)| = 0$, therefore $h(\epsilon) = \epsilon$.

It follows from these properties that any homomorphism defined on Σ^* is uniquely determined by its values on Σ. For example, if $h(a) = ccc$ and $h(b) = dd$, then

$$h(abaab) = h(a)h(b)h(a)h(a)h(b) = cccddcccccccdd.$$

Moreover, any map $h : \Sigma \to \Gamma^*$ extends uniquely by induction to a homomorphism defined on all of Σ^*. Therefore, in order to specify a homomorphism completely, we need only say what values it takes on elements of Σ.

If $A \subseteq \Sigma^*$, define

$$h(A) \stackrel{\text{def}}{=} \{h(x) \mid x \in A\} \subseteq \Gamma^*,$$

and if $B \subseteq \Gamma^*$, define

$$h^{-1}(B) \stackrel{\text{def}}{=} \{x \mid h(x) \in B\} \subseteq \Sigma^*.$$

The set $h(A)$ is called the *image* of A under h, and the set $h^{-1}(B)$ is called the *preimage* of B under h.

We will show two useful closure properties of the regular sets: any homomorphic image or homomorphic preimage of a regular set is regular.

Theorem 10.1   *Let $h : \Sigma^* \to \Gamma^*$ be a homomorphism. If $B \subseteq \Gamma^*$ is regular, then so is its preimage $h^{-1}(B)$ under h.*

Proof. Let $M = (Q, \Gamma, \delta, s, F)$ be a DFA such that $L(M) = B$. Create a new DFA $M' = (Q, \Sigma, \delta', s, F)$ for $h^{-1}(B)$ as follows. The set of states, start state, and final states of M' are the same as in M. The input alphabet is Σ instead of Γ. The transition function δ' is defined by

$$\delta'(q, a) \stackrel{\text{def}}{=} \widehat{\delta}(q, h(a)).$$

Note that we have to use $\widehat{\delta}$ on the right-hand side, since $h(a)$ need not be a single letter.

Now it follows by induction on $|x|$ that for all $x \in \Sigma^*$,

$$\widehat{\delta}'(q, x) = \widehat{\delta}(q, h(x)). \tag{10.3}$$

For the basis $x = \epsilon$, using (10.1),

$$\widehat{\delta}'(q, \epsilon) = q = \widehat{\delta}(q, \epsilon) = \widehat{\delta}(q, h(\epsilon)).$$

For the induction step, assume that $\widehat{\delta}'(q, x) = \widehat{\delta}(q, h(x))$. Then

$$
\begin{aligned}
\widehat{\delta}'(q, xa) &= \delta'(\widehat{\delta}'(q, x), a) && \text{definition of } \widehat{\delta}' \\
&= \delta'(\widehat{\delta}(q, h(x)), a) && \text{induction hypothesis} \\
&= \widehat{\delta}(\widehat{\delta}(q, h(x)), h(a)) && \text{definition of } \delta' \\
&= \widehat{\delta}(q, h(x)h(a)) && \text{Homework 1, Exercise 3} \\
&= \widehat{\delta}(q, h(xa)) && \text{property (10.2) of homomorphisms.}
\end{aligned}
$$

Now we can use (10.3) to prove that $L(M') = h^{-1}(L(M))$. For any $x \in \Sigma^*$,

$$
\begin{aligned}
x \in L(M') &\iff \widehat{\delta}'(s, x) \in F && \text{definition of acceptance} \\
&\iff \widehat{\delta}(s, h(x)) \in F && \text{by (10.3)} \\
&\iff h(x) \in L(M) && \text{definition of acceptance} \\
&\iff x \in h^{-1}(L(M)) && \text{definition of } h^{-1}(L(M)). \qquad \square
\end{aligned}
$$

Theorem 10.2   *Let $h : \Sigma^* \to \Gamma^*$ be a homomorphism. If $A \subseteq \Sigma^*$ is regular, then so is its image $h(A)$ under h.*

Proof. For this proof, we will use regular expressions. Let α be a regular expression over Σ such that $L(\alpha) = A$. Let α' be the regular expression obtained by replacing each letter $a \in \Sigma$ appearing in α with the string $h(a) \in \Gamma^*$. For example, if $h(a) = ccc$ and $h(b) = dd$, then

$$((a + b)^* ab)' = (ccc + dd)^* cccdd.$$

Formally, α' is defined by induction:

$$a' = h(a), \quad a \in \Sigma,$$
$$\emptyset' = \emptyset,$$
$$(\beta + \gamma)' = \beta' + \gamma',$$
$$(\beta\gamma)' = \beta'\gamma',$$
$$\beta^{*\prime} = \beta'^*.$$

We claim that for any regular expression β over Σ,

$$L(\beta') = h(L(\beta)); \tag{10.4}$$

in particular, $L(\alpha') = h(A)$. This can be proved by induction on the structure of β. To do this, we will need two facts about homomorphisms: for any pair of subsets $C, D \subseteq \Sigma^*$ and any family of subsets $C_i \subseteq \Sigma^*, i \in I$,

$$h(CD) = h(C)h(D), \tag{10.5}$$
$$h(\bigcup_{i \in I} C_i) = \bigcup_{i \in I} h(C_i). \tag{10.6}$$

To prove (10.5),

$$
\begin{aligned}
h(CD) &= \{h(w) \mid w \in CD\} \\
&= \{h(yz) \mid y \in C,\ z \in D\} \\
&= \{h(y)h(z) \mid y \in C,\ z \in D\} \\
&= \{uv \mid u \in h(C),\ v \in h(D)\} \\
&= h(C)h(D).
\end{aligned}
$$

To prove (10.6),

$$
\begin{aligned}
h(\bigcup_i C_i) &= \{h(w) \mid w \in \bigcup_i C_i\} \\
&= \{h(w) \mid \exists i\ w \in C_i\} \\
&= \bigcup_i \{h(w) \mid w \in C_i\} \\
&= \bigcup_i h(C_i).
\end{aligned}
$$

Now we prove (10.4) by induction. There are two base cases:

$$L(a') = L(h(a)) = \{h(a)\} = h(\{a\}) = h(L(a))$$

and

$$L(\emptyset') = L(\emptyset) = \emptyset = h(\emptyset) = h(L(\emptyset)).$$

The case of ϵ is covered by the other cases, since $\epsilon = \emptyset^*$.

There are three induction cases, one for each of the operators $+$, $\cdot$, and $*$. For $+$,

$$
\begin{aligned}
L((\beta + \gamma)') &= L(\beta' + \gamma') && \text{definition of } ' \\
&= L(\beta') \cup L(\gamma') && \text{definition of } + \\
&= h(L(\beta)) \cup h(L(\gamma)) && \text{induction hypothesis} \\
&= h(L(\beta) \cup L(\gamma)) && \text{property (10.6)} \\
&= h(L(\beta + \gamma)) && \text{definition of } +.
\end{aligned}
$$

The proof for $\cdot$ is similar, using property (10.5) instead of (10.6). Finally, for $*$,

$$
\begin{aligned}
L(\beta^{*'}) & \\
&= L(\beta'^*) && \text{definition of } ' \\
&= L(\beta')^* && \text{definition of regular expression operator } * \\
&= h(L(\beta))^* && \text{induction hypothesis} \\
&= \bigcup_{n \geq 0} h(L(\beta))^n && \text{definition of set operator } * \\
&= \bigcup_{n \geq 0} h(L(\beta)^n) && \text{property (10.5)} \\
&= h\left(\bigcup_{n \geq 0} L(\beta)^n\right) && \text{property (10.6)} \\
&= h(L(\beta)^*) && \text{definition of set operator } * \\
&= h(L(\beta^*)) && \text{definition of regular expression operator } *. \quad \square
\end{aligned}
$$

Warning: It is *not* true that A is regular whenever $h(A)$ is. This is not what Theorem 10.1 says. We will show later that the set $\{a^n b^n \mid n \geq 0\}$ is not regular, but the image of this set under the homomorphism $h(a) = h(b) = a$ is the regular set $\{a^n \mid n \text{ is even}\}$. The preimage $h^{-1}(\{a^n \mid n \text{ is even}\})$ is not $\{a^n b^n \mid n \geq 0\}$, but $\{x \in \{a, b\}^* \mid |x| \text{ is even}\}$, which is regular.

Automata with ϵ-transitions

Here is an example of how to use homomorphisms to give a clean treatment of ϵ-transitions. Define an *NFA with ϵ-transitions* to be a structure

$$M = (Q,\ \Sigma,\ \epsilon,\ \Delta,\ S,\ F)$$

such that ϵ is a special symbol not in Σ and

$$M_\epsilon = (Q,\ \Sigma \cup \{\epsilon\},\ \Delta,\ S,\ F)$$

is an ordinary NFA over the alphabet $\Sigma \cup \{\epsilon\}$. We define acceptance for automata with ϵ-transitions as follows: for any $x \in \Sigma^*$, M *accepts* x if there exists $y \in (\Sigma \cup \{\epsilon\})^*$ such that

- M_ϵ accepts y under the ordinary definition of acceptance for NFAs, and

- x is obtained from y by erasing all occurrences of the symbol ϵ; that is, $x = h(y)$, where

  $$h : (\Sigma \cup \{\epsilon\})^* \to \Sigma^*$$

  is the homomorphism defined by

  $$h(a) \overset{\text{def}}{=} a, \quad a \in \Sigma,$$
  $$h(\epsilon) \overset{\text{def}}{=} \epsilon.$$

In other words,

$$L(M) \overset{\text{def}}{=} h(L(M_\epsilon)).$$

This definition and the definition involving ϵ-closure described in Lecture 6 are equivalent (Miscellaneous Exercise 10). It is immediate from this definition and Theorem 10.2 that the set accepted by any finite automaton with ϵ-transitions is regular.

Hamming Distance

Here is another example of the use of homomorphisms. We can use them to give slick solutions to Exercise 3 of Homework 2 and Miscellaneous Exercise 8, the problems involving Hamming distance. Let $\Sigma = \{0, 1\}$ and consider the alphabet

$$\Sigma \times \Sigma = \left\{ \begin{array}{|c|}\hline 0 \\\hline 0 \\\hline\end{array},\ \begin{array}{|c|}\hline 0 \\\hline 1 \\\hline\end{array},\ \begin{array}{|c|}\hline 1 \\\hline 0 \\\hline\end{array},\ \begin{array}{|c|}\hline 1 \\\hline 1 \\\hline\end{array} \right\}.$$

The elements of $\Sigma \times \Sigma$ are ordered pairs, but we write the components one on top of the other. Let **top** : $\Sigma \times \Sigma \to \Sigma$ and **bottom** : $\Sigma \times \Sigma \to \Sigma$ be the two projections

$$\mathbf{top}\left(\boxed{\begin{array}{c} a \\ \hline b \end{array}}\right) = a,$$

$$\mathbf{bottom}\left(\boxed{\begin{array}{c} a \\ \hline b \end{array}}\right) = b.$$

These maps extend uniquely to homomorphisms $(\Sigma \times \Sigma)^* \to \Sigma^*$, which we also denote by **top** and **bottom**. For example,

$$\mathbf{top}\left(\boxed{\begin{array}{c|c|c|c} 0 & 0 & 1 & 0 \\ \hline 0 & 1 & 1 & 1 \end{array}}\right) = 0010,$$

$$\mathbf{bottom}\left(\boxed{\begin{array}{c|c|c|c} 0 & 0 & 1 & 0 \\ \hline 0 & 1 & 1 & 1 \end{array}}\right) = 0111.$$

Thus we can think of strings in $(\Sigma \times \Sigma)^*$ as consisting of two tracks, and the homomorphisms **top** and **bottom** give the contents of the top and bottom track, respectively.

For fixed k, let D_k be the set of all strings in $(\Sigma \times \Sigma)^*$ containing no more than k occurrences of

$$\boxed{\begin{array}{c} 0 \\ \hline 1 \end{array}} \text{ or } \boxed{\begin{array}{c} 1 \\ \hline 0 \end{array}}.$$

This is certainly a regular set. Note also that

$$D_k = \{x \in (\Sigma \times \Sigma)^* \mid H(\mathbf{top}(x), \mathbf{bottom}(x)) \le k\},$$

where H is the Hamming distance function. Now take any regular set $A \subseteq \Sigma^*$, and consider the set

$$\mathbf{top}(\mathbf{bottom}^{-1}(A) \cap D_k). \tag{10.7}$$

Believe it or not, this set is exactly $N_k(A)$, the set of strings in Σ^* of Hamming distance at most k from some string in A. The set $\mathbf{bottom}^{-1}(A)$ is the set of strings whose bottom track is in A; the set $\mathbf{bottom}^{-1}(A) \cap D_k$ is the set of strings whose bottom track is in A and whose top track is of Hamming distance at most k from the bottom track; and the set (10.7) is the set of top tracks of all such strings.

Moreover, the set (10.7) is a regular set, because the regular sets are closed under intersection, homomorphic image, and homomorphic preimage.

Lecture 11

Limitations of Finite Automata

We have studied what finite automata can do; let's see what they cannot do. The canonical example of a nonregular set (one accepted by no finite automaton) is

$$B = \{a^n b^n \mid n \geq 0\} = \{\epsilon, ab, aabb, aaabbb, aaaabbbb, \ldots\},$$

the set of all strings of the form $a^* b^*$ with equally many a's and b's.

Intuitively, in order to accept the set B, an automaton scanning a string of the form $a^* b^*$ would have to remember when passing the center point between the a's and b's how many a's it has seen, since it would have to compare that with the number of b's and accept iff the two numbers are the same.

$$aaaaaaaaaaaaaaaaaaaaaaaaaaaaaab\,bbbb\,bbbbbbbbbbbbbbbbbbbbbbbbbb$$
$$\uparrow$$
$$q$$

Moreover, it would have to do this for arbitrarily long strings of a's and b's, much longer than the number of states. This is an unbounded amount of information, and there is no way it can remember this with only finite memory. All it "knows" at that point is represented in the state q it is in, which is only a finite amount of information. You might at first think there may be some clever strategy, such as counting mod 3, 5, and 7, or something similar. But any such attempt is doomed to failure: you cannot distinguish between infinitely many different cases with only finitely many states.

This is just an informal argument. But we can easily give a formal proof by contradiction that B is not regular. Assuming that B were regular, there would be a DFA M such that $L(M) = B$. Let k be the number of states of this alleged M. Consider the action of M on input $a^n b^n$, where $n \gg k$. It starts in its start state s. Since the string $a^n b^n$ is in B, M must accept it, thus M must be in some final state r after scanning $a^n b^n$.

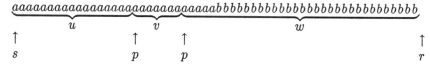

Since $n \gg k$, by the pigeonhole principle there must be some state p that the automaton enters more than once while scanning the initial sequence of a's. Break up the string $a^n b^n$ into three pieces u, v, w, where v is the string of a's scanned between two occurrences of the state p, as illustrated in the following picture:

$$\underbrace{aaaaaaaaaaaaaaaa}_{u}\underbrace{aaaaaaaa}_{v}\underbrace{aaaab\,bbbbbbbbbbbbbbbbbbbbbbbbbbb}_{w}$$

$\quad\uparrow\qquad\qquad\qquad\uparrow\quad\uparrow\qquad\qquad\qquad\qquad\qquad\uparrow$
$\quad s\qquad\qquad\qquad p\quad p\qquad\qquad\qquad\qquad\qquad r$

Let $j = |v| > 0$. In this example, $j = 7$. Then

$$\widehat{\delta}(s, u) = p,$$
$$\widehat{\delta}(p, v) = p,$$
$$\widehat{\delta}(p, w) = r \in F.$$

The string v could be deleted and the resulting string would be erroneously accepted:

$$\widehat{\delta}(s, uw) = \widehat{\delta}(\widehat{\delta}(s, u), w)$$
$$= \widehat{\delta}(p, w)$$
$$= r \in F.$$

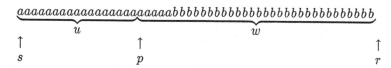

It's erroneous because after deleting v, the number of a's is strictly less than the number of b's: $uw = a^{n-j} b^n \in L(M)$, but $uw \notin B$. This contradicts our assumption that $L(M) = B$.

We could also insert extra copies of v and the resulting string would be erroneously accepted. For example, $uv^3w = a^{n+2j}b^n$ is erroneously accepted:

$$\begin{aligned}
\widehat{\delta}(s, uvvvw) &= \widehat{\delta}(\widehat{\delta}(\widehat{\delta}(\widehat{\delta}(\widehat{\delta}(s, u), v), v), v), w) \\
&= \widehat{\delta}(\widehat{\delta}(\widehat{\delta}(\widehat{\delta}(p, v), v), v), w) \\
&= \widehat{\delta}(\widehat{\delta}(\widehat{\delta}(p, v), v), w) \\
&= \widehat{\delta}(\widehat{\delta}(p, v), w) \\
&= \widehat{\delta}(p, w) \\
&= r \in F.
\end{aligned}$$

For another example of a nonregular set, consider

$$\begin{aligned}
C &= \{a^{2^n} \mid n \geq 0\} \\
&= \{x \in \{a\}^* \mid |x| \text{ is a power of 2}\} \\
&= \{a, a^2, a^4, a^8, a^{16}, \ldots\}.
\end{aligned}$$

This set is also nonregular. Suppose (again for a contradiction) that $L(M) = C$ for some DFA M. Let k be the number of states of M. Let $n \gg k$ and consider the action of M on input $a^{2^n} \in C$. Since $n \gg k$, by the pigeonhole principle the automaton must repeat a state p while scanning the first n symbols of a^{2^n}. Thus $2^n = i + j + m$ for some i, j, m with $0 < j \leq n$ and

$$\begin{aligned}
\widehat{\delta}(s, a^i) &= p, \\
\widehat{\delta}(p, a^j) &= p, \\
\widehat{\delta}(p, a^m) &= r \in F.
\end{aligned}$$

As above, we could insert an extra a^j to get a^{2^n+j}, and this string would be erroneously accepted:

$$\begin{aligned}
\widehat{\delta}(s, a^{2^n+j}) &= \widehat{\delta}(s, a^i a^j a^j a^m) \\
&= \widehat{\delta}(\widehat{\delta}(\widehat{\delta}(\widehat{\delta}(s, a^i), a^j), a^j), a^m) \\
&= \widehat{\delta}(\widehat{\delta}(\widehat{\delta}(p, a^j), a^j), a^m) \\
&= \widehat{\delta}(\widehat{\delta}(p, a^j), a^m) \\
&= \widehat{\delta}(p, a^m) \\
&= r \in F.
\end{aligned}$$

This is erroneous because $2^n + j$ is not a power of 2:

$$2^n + j \leq 2^n + n$$

$$< 2^n + 2^n$$
$$= 2^{n+1}$$

and 2^{n+1} is the next power of 2 greater than 2^n.

The Pumping Lemma

We can encapsulate the arguments above in a general theorem called the *pumping lemma*. This lemma is very useful in proving sets nonregular. The idea is that whenever an automaton scans a long string (longer than the number of states) and accepts, there must be a repeated state, and extra copies of the segment of the input between the two occurrences of that state can be inserted and the resulting string is still accepted.

Theorem 11.1 **(Pumping lemma)**   *Let A be a regular set. Then the following property holds of A:*

(P) *There exists $k \geq 0$ such that for any strings x, y, z with $xyz \in A$ and $|y| \geq k$, there exist strings u, v, w such that $y = uvw$, $v \neq \epsilon$, and for all $i \geq 0$, the string $xuv^i wz \in A$.*

Informally, if A is regular, then for any string in A and any sufficiently long substring y of that string, y has a nonnull substring v of which you can pump in as many copies as you like and the resulting string is still in A.

We have essentially already proved this theorem. Think of k as the number of states of a DFA accepting A. Since y is at least as long as the number of states, there must be a repeated state while scanning y. The string v is the substring between the two occurrences of that state. We can pump in as many copies of v as we want (or delete v—this would be the case $i = 0$), and the resulting string is still accepted.

Games with the Demon

The pumping lemma is often used to show that certain sets are nonregular. For this purpose we usually use it in its contrapositive form:

Theorem 11.2 **(Pumping lemma, contrapositive form)**   *Let A be a set of strings. Suppose that the following property holds of A.*

($\neg$P) *For all $k \geq 0$ there exist strings x, y, z such that $xyz \in A$, $|y| \geq k$, and for all u, v, w with $y = uvw$ and $v \neq \epsilon$, there exists an $i \geq 0$ such that $xuv^i wz \notin A$.*

Then A is not regular.

To use the pumping lemma to prove that a given set A is nonregular, we need to establish that $(\neg P)$ holds of A. Because of the alternating "for all/there exists" form of $(\neg P)$, we can think of this as a game between you and a demon. You want to show that A is nonregular, and the demon wants to show that A is regular. The game proceeds as follows:

1. The demon picks k. (If A really is regular, the demon's best strategy here is to pick k to be the number of states of a DFA for A.)

2. You pick x, y, z such that $xyz \in A$ and $|y| \geq k$.

3. The demon picks u, v, w such that $y = uvw$ and $v \neq \epsilon$.

4. You pick $i \geq 0$.

You win if $xuv^i wz \notin A$, and the demon wins if $xuv^i wz \in A$.

The property $(\neg P)$ for A is equivalent to saying that you have a *winning strategy* in this game. This means that by playing optimally, you can always win no matter what the demon does in steps 1 and 3.

If you can show that you have a winning strategy, you have essentially shown that the condition $(\neg P)$ holds for A, therefore by Theorem 11.2, A is not regular.

We have thus reduced the problem of showing that a given set is non-regular to the puzzle of finding a winning strategy in the corresponding demon game. Each nonregular set gives a different game. We'll give several examples in Lecture 12.

Warning: Although there do exist stronger versions that give necessary and sufficient conditions for regularity (Miscellaneous Exercise 44), the version of the pumping lemma given here gives only a necessary condition; there exist sets satisfying (P) that are nonregular (Miscellaneous Exercise 43). You cannot show that a set *is* regular by showing that it satisfies (P). To show a given set *is* regular, you should construct a finite automaton or regular expression for it.

Historical Notes

The pumping lemma for regular sets is due to Bar-Hillel, Perles, and Shamir [8]. This version gives only a necessary condition for regularity. Necessary and sufficient conditions are given by Stanat and Weiss [117], Jaffe [62], and Ehrenfeucht, Parikh, and Rozenberg [33].

Lecture 12

Using the Pumping Lemma

Example 12.1 Let's use the pumping lemma in the form of the demon game to show that the set

$$A = \{a^n b^m \mid n \geq m\}$$

is not regular. The set A is the set of strings in $a^* b^*$ with no more b's than a's. The demon, who is betting that A is regular, picks some number k. A good response for you is to pick $x = a^k$, $y = b^k$, and $z = \epsilon$. Then $xyz = a^k b^k \in A$ and $|y| = k$; so far you have followed the rules. The demon must now pick u, v, w such that $y = uvw$ and $v \neq \epsilon$. Say the demon picks u, v, w of length j, m, n, respectively, with $k = j + m + n$ and $m > 0$. No matter what the demon picks, you can take $i = 2$ and you win:

$$
\begin{aligned}
xuv^2 wz &= a^k b^j b^m b^m b^n \\
&= a^k b^{j+2m+n} \\
&= a^k b^{k+m},
\end{aligned}
$$

which is not in A, because the number of b's is strictly larger than the number of a's.

This strategy always leads to victory for you in the demon game associated with the set A. As we argued in Lecture 11, this is tantamount to showing that A is nonregular. □

Example 12.2   For another example, take the set

$$C = \{a^{n!} \mid n \geq 0\}.$$

We would like to show that this set is not regular. This one is a little harder. It is an example of a nonregular set over a single-letter alphabet. Intuitively, it is not regular because the differences in the lengths of the successive elements of the set grow too fast.

Suppose the demon chooses k. A good choice for you is $x = z = \epsilon$ and $y = a^{k!}$. Then $xyz = a^{k!} \in C$ and $|y| = k! \geq k$, so you have not cheated. The demon must now choose u, v, w such that $y = uvw$ and $v \neq \epsilon$. Say the demon chooses u, v, w of length j, m, n, respectively, with $k! = j + m + n$ and $m > 0$. You now need to find i such that $xuv^iwz \notin C$; in other words, $|xuv^iwz| \neq p!$ for any p. Note that for any i,

$$|xuv^iwz| = j + im + n = k! + (i-1)m,$$

so you will win if you can choose i such that $k! + (i-1)m \neq p!$ for any p. Take $i = (k+1)! + 1$. Then

$$k! + (i-1)m = k! + (k+1)!m = k!(1 + m(k+1)),$$

and we want to show that this cannot be $p!$ for any p. But if

$$p! = k!(1 + m(k+1)),$$

then we could divide both sides by $k!$ to get

$$p(p-1)(p-2)\cdots(k+2)(k+1) = 1 + m(k+1),$$

which is impossible, because the left-hand side is divisible by $k+1$ and the right-hand side is not. $\qquad\square$

A Trick

When trying to show that a set is nonregular, one can often simplify the problem by using one of the closure properties of regular sets. This often allows us to reduce a complicated set to a simpler set that is already known to be nonregular, thereby avoiding the use of the pumping lemma.

To illustrate, consider the set

$$D = \{x \in \{a, b\}^* \mid \#a(x) = \#b(x)\}.$$

To show that this set is nonregular, suppose for a contradiction that it were regular. Then the set

$$D \cap a^*b^*$$

would also be regular, since the intersection of two regular sets is always regular (the product construction, remember?). But

$$D \cap L(a^*b^*) = \{a^n b^n \mid n \geq 0\},$$

which we have already shown to be nonregular. This is a contradiction.

For another illustration of this trick, consider the set A of Example 12.1 above:

$$A = \{a^n b^m \mid n \geq m\},$$

the set of strings $x \in L(a^*b^*)$ with no more b's than a's. By Exercise 2 of Homework 2, if A were regular, then so would be the set

$$\mathbf{rev}\, A = \{b^m a^n \mid n \geq m\},$$

and by interchanging a and b, we would get that the set

$$A' = \{a^m b^n \mid n \geq m\}$$

is also regular. Formally, "interchanging a and b" means applying the homomorphism $a \mapsto b$, $b \mapsto a$. But then the intersection

$$A \cap A' = \{a^n b^n \mid n \geq 0\}$$

would be regular. But we have already shown using the pumping lemma that this set is nonregular. This is a contradiction.

Ultimate Periodicity

Let U be a subset of $\mathbb{N} = \{0, 1, 2, 3, \ldots\}$, the natural numbers.

The set U is said to be *ultimately periodic* if there exist numbers $n \geq 0$ and $p > 0$ such that for all $m \geq n$, $m \in U$ if and only if $m + p \in U$. The number p is called a *period* of U.

In other words, except for a finite initial part (the numbers less than n), numbers are in or out of the set U according to a repeating pattern. For example, consider the set

$$\{0, 3, 7, 11, 19, 20, 23, 26, 29, 32, 35, 38, 41, 44, 47, 50, \ldots\}.$$

Starting at 20, every third element is in the set, therefore this set is ultimately periodic with $n = 20$ and $p = 3$. Note that neither n nor p is unique; for example, for this set we could also have taken $n = 21$ and $p = 6$, or $n = 100$ and $p = 33$.

Regular sets over a single-letter alphabet $\{a\}$ and ultimately periodic subsets of $\mathbb{N}$ are strongly related:

Theorem 12.3 *Let $A \subseteq \{a\}^*$. Then A is regular if and only if the set $\{m \mid a^m \in A\}$, the set of lengths of strings in A, is ultimately periodic.*

Proof. If A is regular, then any DFA for it consists of a finite tail of some length, say $n \geq 0$, followed by a loop of length $p > 0$ (plus possibly some inaccessible states, which can be thrown out).

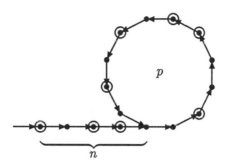

To see this, consider any DFA for A. Since the alphabet is $\{a\}$ and the machine is deterministic, there is exactly one edge out of each state, and it has label a. Thus there is a unique path through the automaton starting at the start state. Follow this path until the first time you see a state that you have seen before. Since the collection of states is finite, eventually this must happen. The first time this happens, we have discovered a loop. Let p be the length of the loop, and let n be the length of the initial tail preceding the first time we enter the loop. For all strings a^m with $m \geq n$, the automaton is in the loop part after scanning a^m. Then a^m is accepted iff a^{m+p} is, since the automaton moves around the loop once under the last p a's of a^{m+p}. Thus it is in the same state after scanning both strings. Therefore, the set of lengths of accepted strings is ultimately periodic.

Conversely, given any ultimately periodic set U, let p be the period and let n be the starting point of the periodic behavior. Then one can build an automaton with a tail of length n and loop of length p accepting exactly the set of strings in $\{a\}^*$ whose lengths are in U. For example, for the ultimately periodic set

$$\{0, 3, 7, 11, 19, 20, 23, 26, 29, 32, 35, 38, 41, 44, 47, 50, \ldots\}$$

mentioned above, the automaton would be

$\square$

Corollary 12.4 *Let A be any regular set over any finite alphabet Σ, not necessarily consisting of a single letter. Then the set*

$$\textbf{lengths } A = \{|x| \mid x \in A\}$$

of lengths of strings in A is ultimately periodic.

Proof. Define the homomorphism $h : \Sigma \rightarrow \{a\}$ by $h(b) = a$ for all $b \in \Sigma$. Then $h(x) = a^{|x|}$. Since h preserves length, we have that **lengths A = lengths $h(A)$**. But $h(A)$ is a regular subset of $\{a\}^*$, since the regular sets are closed under homomorphic image; therefore, by Theorem 12.3, **lengths $h(A)$** is ultimately periodic.   □

Historical Notes

A general treatment of ultimate periodicity and regularity-preserving functions is given in Seiferas and McNaughton [113]; see Miscellaneous Exercise 34.

Lecture 13

DFA State Minimization

By now you have probably come across several situations in which you have observed that some automaton could be simplified either by deleting states inaccessible from the start state or by collapsing states that were equivalent in some sense. For example, if you were to apply the subset construction to the NFA

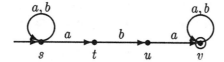

accepting the set of all strings containing the substring aba, you would obtain a DFA with $2^4 = 16$ states. However, all except six of these states are inaccessible. Deleting them, you would obtain the DFA

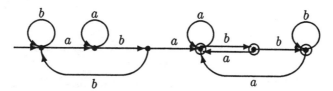

From left to right, the states of this DFA correspond to the subsets $\{s\}$, $\{s,t\}$, $\{s,u\}$, $\{s,t,v\}$, $\{s,u,v\}$, $\{s,v\}$.

Now, note that the rightmost three states of this DFA might as well be collapsed into a single state, since they are all accept states, and once the machine enters one of them it cannot escape. Thus this DFA is equivalent to

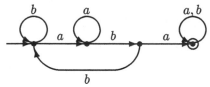

This is a simple example in which the equivalence of states is obvious, but sometimes it is not so obvious. In this and the next lecture we will develop a mechanical method to find all equivalent states of any given DFA and collapse them. This will give a DFA for any given regular set A that has as few states as possible. An amazing fact is that every regular set has a minimal DFA that is unique up to isomorphism, and there is a purely mechanical method for constructing it from any given DFA for A.

Say we are given a DFA $M = (Q, \Sigma, \delta, s, F)$ for A. The minimization process consists of two stages:

1. Get rid of inaccessible states; that is, states q for which there exists no string $x \in \Sigma^*$ such that $\widehat{\delta}(s, x) = q$.

2. Collapse "equivalent" states.

Removing inaccessible states surely does not change the set accepted. It is quite straightforward to see how to do this mechanically using depth-first search on the transition graph. Let us then assume that this has been done. For stage 2, we need to say what we mean by "equivalent" and how we do the collapsing. Let's look at some examples before giving a formal definition.

Example 13.1

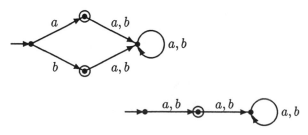

These automata both accept the set $\{a, b\}$. The automaton with four states goes to different states depending on the first input symbol, but there's really no reason for the states to be separate. They are equivalent and can be collapsed into one state, giving the automaton with three states. □

Example 13.2

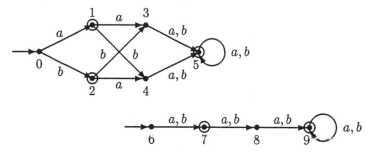

This example is a little more complicated. The automata both accept the set $\{a, b\} \cup \{\text{strings of length 3 or greater}\}$. In the first automaton, states 3 and 4 are equivalent, since they both go to state 5 under both input symbols, so there's no reason to keep them separate. Once we collapse them, we can collapse 1 and 2 for the same reason, giving the second automaton. State 0 becomes state 6; states 1 and 2 collapse to become state 7; states 3 and 4 collapse to become state 8; and state 5 becomes state 9.   □

Example 13.3

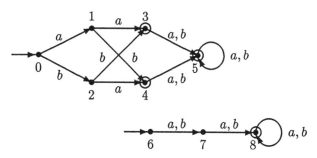

Here we have modified the first automaton by making states 3, 4 accept states instead of 1, 2. Now states 3, 4, 5 are equivalent and can be collapsed. These become state 8 of the second automaton. The set accepted is the set of all strings of length at least two.   □

Example 13.4

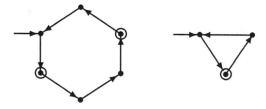

These automata both accept the set $\{a^m \mid m \equiv 1 \bmod 3\}$ (edge labels are omitted). In the left automaton, diametrically opposed states are equivalent and can be collapsed, giving the automaton on the right.   □

The Quotient Construction

How do we know in general when two states can be collapsed safely without changing the set accepted? How do we do the collapsing formally? Is there a fast algorithm for doing it? How can we determine whether any further collapsing is possible?

Surely we never want to collapse an accept state p and a reject state q, because if $p = \widehat{\delta}(s, x) \in F$ and $q = \widehat{\delta}(s, y) \notin F$, then x must be accepted and y must be rejected even after collapsing, so there is no way to declare the collapsed state to be an accept or reject state without error. Also, if we collapse p and q, then we had better also collapse $\delta(p, a)$ and $\delta(q, a)$ to maintain determinism. These two observations together imply inductively that we cannot collapse p and q if $\widehat{\delta}(p, x) \in F$ and $\widehat{\delta}(q, x) \notin F$ for some string x.

It turns out that this criterion is necessary and sufficient for deciding whether a pair of states can be collapsed. That is, if there exists a string x such that $\widehat{\delta}(p, x) \in F$ and $\widehat{\delta}(q, x) \notin F$ or vice versa, then p and q cannot be safely collapsed; and if no such x exists, then they can.

Here's how we show this formally. We first define an equivalence relation $\approx$ on Q by

$$p \approx q \overset{\text{def}}{\Longleftrightarrow} \forall x \in \Sigma^* \ (\widehat{\delta}(p, x) \in F \Longleftrightarrow \widehat{\delta}(q, x) \in F).$$

This definition is just a formal restatement of the collapsing criterion. It is not hard to argue that the relation $\approx$ is indeed an equivalence relation: it is

- *reflexive*: $p \approx p$ for all p;

- *symmetric*: if $p \approx q$, then $q \approx p$; and

- *transitive*: if $p \approx q$ and $q \approx r$, then $p \approx r$.

As with all equivalence relations, $\approx$ partitions the set on which it is defined into disjoint *equivalence classes*:

$$[p] \overset{\text{def}}{=} \{q \mid q \approx p\}.$$

Every element $p \in Q$ is contained in exactly one equivalence class $[p]$, and

$$p \approx q \Longleftrightarrow [p] = [q].$$

We now define a DFA $M/\approx$ called the *quotient automaton*, whose states correspond to the equivalence classes of $\approx$. This construction is called a *quotient construction* and is quite common in algebra. We will see a more general account of it in Supplementary Lectures C and D.

There is one state of $M/\approx$ for each $\approx$-equivalence class. In fact, formally, the states of $M/\approx$ *are* the equivalence classes; this is the mathematical way of "collapsing" equivalent states.

Define

$$M/\approx \stackrel{\text{def}}{=} (Q', \Sigma, \delta', s', F'),$$

where

$$Q' \stackrel{\text{def}}{=} \{[p] \mid p \in Q\},$$
$$\delta'([p], a) \stackrel{\text{def}}{=} [\delta(p, a)], \tag{13.1}$$
$$s' \stackrel{\text{def}}{=} [s],$$
$$F' \stackrel{\text{def}}{=} \{[p] \mid p \in F\}.$$

There is a subtle but important point involving the definition of δ' in (13.1): we need to show that it is *well-defined*. Note that the action of δ' on the equivalence class $[p]$ is defined in terms of p. It is conceivable that a different choice of representative of the class $[p]$ (i.e., some q such that $q \approx p$) might lead to a different right-hand side in (13.1). Lemma 13.5 says exactly that this does not happen.

Lemma 13.5   *If $p \approx q$, then $\delta(p, a) \approx \delta(q, a)$. Equivalently, if $[p] = [q]$, then $[\delta(p, a)] = [\delta(q, a)]$.*

Proof. Suppose $p \approx q$. Let $a \in \Sigma$ and $y \in \Sigma^*$.

$$\widehat{\delta}(\delta(p, a), y) \in F \iff \widehat{\delta}(p, ay) \in F$$
$$\iff \widehat{\delta}(q, ay) \in F \qquad \text{since } p \approx q$$
$$\iff \widehat{\delta}(\delta(q, a), y) \in F.$$

Since y was arbitrary, $\delta(p, a) \approx \delta(q, a)$ by definition of $\approx$. $\square$

Lemma 13.6 $p \in F \iff [p] \in F'$.

Proof. The direction $\Rightarrow$ is immediate from the definition of F'. For the direction $\Leftarrow$, we need to show that if $p \approx q$ and $p \in F$, then $q \in F$. In other words, every $\approx$-equivalence class is either a subset of F or disjoint from F. This follows immediately by taking $x = \epsilon$ in the definition of $p \approx q$. $\square$

Lemma 13.7   *For all $x \in \Sigma^*$, $\widehat{\delta}'([p], x) = [\widehat{\delta}(p, x)]$.*

Proof. By induction on $|x|$.

Basis

For $x = \epsilon$,

$$\widehat{\delta}'([p], \epsilon) = [p] \qquad \text{definition of } \widehat{\delta}'$$
$$= [\widehat{\delta}(p, \epsilon)] \quad \text{definition of } \widehat{\delta}.$$

Induction step

Assume $\widehat{\delta}'([p], x) = [\widehat{\delta}(p, x)]$, and let $a \in \Sigma$.

$$\widehat{\delta}'([p], xa) = \delta'(\widehat{\delta}'([p], x), a) \quad \text{definition of } \widehat{\delta}'$$
$$= \delta'([\widehat{\delta}(p, x)], a) \quad \text{induction hypothesis}$$
$$= [\delta(\widehat{\delta}(p, x), a)] \quad \text{definition of } \delta'$$
$$= [\widehat{\delta}(p, xa)] \quad \text{definition of } \widehat{\delta}. \qquad \square$$

Theorem 13.8 $L(M/\approx) = L(M)$.

Proof. For $x \in \Sigma^*$,

$$x \in L(M/\approx) \iff \widehat{\delta}'(s', x) \in F' \quad \text{definition of acceptance}$$
$$\iff \widehat{\delta}'([s], x) \in F' \quad \text{definition of } s'$$
$$\iff [\widehat{\delta}(s, x)] \in F' \quad \text{Lemma 13.7}$$
$$\iff \widehat{\delta}(s, x) \in F \quad \text{Lemma 13.6}$$
$$\iff x \in L(M) \quad \text{definition of acceptance.} \qquad \square$$

$M/\approx$ Cannot Be Collapsed Further

It is conceivable that after doing the quotient construction once, we might be able to collapse even further by doing it again. It turns out that once is enough. To see this, let's do the quotient construction a second time. Define

$$[p] \sim [q] \overset{\text{def}}{\iff} \forall x \in \Sigma^* \ (\widehat{\delta}'([p], x) \in F' \iff \widehat{\delta}'([q], x) \in F').$$

This is exactly the same definition as $\approx$ above, only applied to the quotient automaton $M/\approx$. We use the notation $\sim$ for the equivalence relation on Q' to distinguish it from the relation $\approx$ on Q. Now

$$[p] \sim [q]$$
$$\Rightarrow \forall x \ (\widehat{\delta}'([p], x) \in F' \iff \widehat{\delta}'([q], x) \in F') \quad \text{definition of } \sim$$
$$\Rightarrow \forall x \ ([\widehat{\delta}(p, x)] \in F' \iff [\widehat{\delta}(q, x)] \in F') \quad \text{Lemma 13.7}$$

$$\Rightarrow \forall x \ (\widehat{\delta}(p, x) \in F \iff \widehat{\delta}(q, x) \in F) \qquad \text{Lemma 13.6}$$

$$\Rightarrow p \approx q \qquad \text{definition of } \approx$$

$$\Rightarrow [p] = [q].$$

Thus any two equivalent states of $M/\approx$ are in fact equal, and the collapsing relation $\sim$ on Q' is just the identity relation $=$.

Lecture 14

A Minimization Algorithm

Here is an algorithm for computing the collapsing relation $\approx$ for a given DFA M with no inaccessible states. Our algorithm will mark (unordered) pairs of states $\{p, q\}$. A pair $\{p, q\}$ will be marked as soon as a reason is discovered why p and q are *not* equivalent.

1. Write down a table of all pairs $\{p, q\}$, initially unmarked.

2. Mark $\{p, q\}$ if $p \in F$ and $q \notin F$ or vice versa.

3. Repeat the following until no more changes occur: if there exists an unmarked pair $\{p, q\}$ such that $\{\delta(p, a), \delta(q, a)\}$ is marked for some $a \in \Sigma$, then mark $\{p, q\}$.

4. When done, $p \approx q$ iff $\{p, q\}$ is not marked.

Here are some things to note about this algorithm:

- If $\{p, q\}$ is marked in step 2, then p and q are surely not equivalent: take $x = \epsilon$ in the definition of $\approx$.

- We may have to look at the same pair $\{p, q\}$ many times in step 3, since any change in the table may suddenly allow $\{p, q\}$ to be marked. We stop only after we make an entire pass through the table with no new marks.

- The algorithm runs for only a finite number of steps, since there are only $\binom{n}{2}$ possible marks that can be made,[1] and we have to make at least one new mark in each pass to keep going.

- Step 4 is really a statement of the theorem that the algorithm correctly computes $\approx$. This requires proof, which we defer until later.

Example 14.1   Let's minimize the automaton of Example 13.2 of Lecture 13.

$$
\begin{array}{c|cc}
 & a & b \\
\hline
\rightarrow \quad 0 & 1 & 2 \\
1F & 3 & 4 \\
2F & 4 & 3 \\
3 & 5 & 5 \\
4 & 5 & 5 \\
5F & 5 & 5 \\
\end{array}
$$

Here is the table built in step 1. Initially all pairs are unmarked.

```
0
-  1
-  -  2
-  -  -  3
-  -  -  -  4
-  -  -  -  -  5
```

After step 2, all pairs consisting of one accept state and one nonaccept state have been marked.

```
0
✓  1
✓  -  2
-  ✓  ✓  3
-  ✓  ✓  -  4
✓  -  -  ✓  ✓  5
```

Now look at an unmarked pair, say $\{0,3\}$. Under input a, 0 and 3 go to 1 and 5, respectively (write: $\{0,3\} \rightarrow \{1,5\}$). The pair $\{1,5\}$ is not marked, so we don't mark $\{0,3\}$, at least not yet. Under input b, $\{0,3\} \rightarrow \{2,5\}$, which is not marked, so we still don't mark $\{0,3\}$. We then look at unmarked pairs $\{0,4\}$ and $\{1,2\}$ and find out we cannot mark them yet for the same reasons. But for $\{1,5\}$, under input a, $\{1,5\} \rightarrow \{3,5\}$, and $\{3,5\}$ is marked, so we mark $\{1,5\}$. Similarly, under input a, $\{2,5\} \rightarrow \{4,5\}$ which is marked, so we mark $\{2,5\}$. Under both inputs a and b, $\{3,4\} \rightarrow \{5,5\}$, which is never marked (it's not even in the table), so we do not mark $\{3,4\}$. After the first

---

[1] $\binom{n}{k} \stackrel{\text{def}}{=} \frac{n!}{k!(n-k)!}$, the number of subsets of size k in a set of size n.

pass of step 3, the table looks like

```
0
✓   1
✓   –   2
–   ✓   ✓   3
–   ✓   ✓   –   4
✓   ✓   ✓   ✓   ✓   5
```

Now we make another pass through the table. As before, $\{0,3\} \to \{1,5\}$ under input a, but this time $\{1,5\}$ is marked, so we mark $\{0,3\}$. Similarly, $\{0,4\} \to \{2,5\}$ under input b, and $\{2,5\}$ is marked, so we mark $\{0,4\}$. This gives

```
0
✓   1
✓   –   2
✓   ✓   ✓   3
✓   ✓   ✓   –   4
✓   ✓   ✓   ✓   ✓   5
```

Now we check the remaining unmarked pairs and find out that $\{1,2\} \to \{3,4\}$ and $\{3,4\} \to \{5,5\}$ under both a and b, and neither $\{3,4\}$ nor $\{5,5\}$ is marked, so there are no new marks. We are left with unmarked pairs $\{1,2\}$ and $\{3,4\}$, indicating that $1 \approx 2$ and $3 \approx 4$.   □

Example 14.2   Now let's do Example 13.4 of Lecture 13.

		a
$\to$	0	1
	1F	2
	2	3
	3	4
	4F	5
	5	0

Here is the table after step 2.

```
0
✓   1
–   ✓   2
–   ✓   –   3
✓   –   ✓   ✓   4
–   ✓   –   –   ✓   5
```

Then:

- $\{0,2\} \to \{1,3\}$, which is marked, so mark $\{0,2\}$.

- $\{0,3\} \to \{1,4\}$, which is not marked, so do not mark $\{0,3\}$.

- $\{0,5\} \to \{0,1\}$, which is marked, so mark $\{0,5\}$.

- $\{1,4\} \to \{2,5\}$, which is not marked, so do not mark $\{1,4\}$.

- $\{2,3\} \to \{3,4\}$, which is marked, so mark $\{2,3\}$.

- $\{2,5\} \to \{0,3\}$, which is not marked, so do not mark $\{2,5\}$.

- $\{3,5\} \to \{0,4\}$, which is marked, so mark $\{3,5\}$.

After the first pass, the table looks like this:

```
0
✓   1
✓   ✓   2
−   ✓   ✓   3
✓   −   ✓   ✓   4
✓   ✓   −   ✓   ✓   5
```

Now do another pass. We discover that $\{0,3\} \to \{1,4\} \to \{2,5\} \to \{0,3\}$ and none of these are marked, so we are done. Thus $0 \approx 3$, $1 \approx 4$, and $2 \approx 5$. □

Correctness of the Collapsing Algorithm

Theorem 14.3 *The pair $\{p,q\}$ is marked by the above algorithm if and only if there exists $x \in \Sigma^*$ such that $\widehat{\delta}(p,x) \in F$ and $\widehat{\delta}(q,x) \notin F$ or vice versa; i.e., if and only if $p \not\approx q$.*

Proof. This is easily proved by induction. We leave the proof as an exercise (Miscellaneous Exercise 49). □

A nice way to look at the algorithm is as a finite automaton itself. Let

$$\mathcal{Q} = \{\{p,q\} \mid p,q \in Q,\ p \neq q\}.$$

There are $\binom{n}{2}$ elements of $\mathcal{Q}$, where n is the size of Q. Define a nondeterministic "transition function"

$$\Delta : \mathcal{Q} \to 2^{\mathcal{Q}}$$

on $\mathcal{Q}$ as follows:

$$\Delta(\{p,q\},a) = \{\{p',q'\} \mid p = \delta(p',a),\ q = \delta(q',a)\}.$$

Define a set of "start states" $\mathcal{S} \subseteq \mathcal{Q}$ as follows:

$$\mathcal{S} = \{\{p,q\} \mid p \in F,\ q \notin F\}.$$

(We don't need to write "...or vice versa" because $\{p, q\}$ is an unordered pair.) Step 2 of the algorithm marks the elements of $\mathcal{S}$, and step 3 marks pairs in $\Delta(\{p, q\}, a)$ when $\{p, q\}$ is marked for any $a \in \Sigma$. In these terms, Theorem 14.3 says that $p \not\approx q$ iff $\{p, q\}$ is accessible in this automaton.

Lecture 15

Myhill–Nerode Relations

Two deterministic finite automata

$$M = (Q_M, \ \Sigma, \ \delta_M, \ s_M, \ F_M),$$
$$N = (Q_N, \ \Sigma, \ \delta_N, \ s_N, \ F_N)$$

are said to be *isomorphic* (Greek for "same form") if there is a one-to-one and onto mapping $f : Q_M \to Q_N$ such that

- $f(s_M) = s_N$,
- $f(\delta_M(p, a)) = \delta_N(f(p), a)$ for all $p \in Q_M$, $a \in \Sigma$, and
- $p \in F_M$ iff $f(p) \in F_N$.

That is, they are essentially the same automaton up to renaming of states. It is easily argued that isomorphic automata accept the same set.

In this lecture and the next we will show that if M and N are any two automata with no inaccessible states accepting the same set, then the quotient automata $M/\approx$ and $N/\approx$ obtained by the collapsing algorithm of Lecture 14 are isomorphic. Thus the DFA obtained by the collapsing algorithm is the minimal DFA for the set it accepts, and this automaton is unique up to isomorphism.

We will do this by exploiting a profound and beautiful correspondence between finite automata with input alphabet Σ and certain equivalence relations on Σ^*. We will show that the unique minimal DFA for a regular set R can be defined in a natural way *directly from R*, and that any minimal automaton for R is isomorphic to this automaton.

Myhill–Nerode Relations

Let $R \subseteq \Sigma^*$ be a regular set, and let $M = (Q, \Sigma, \delta, s, F)$ be a DFA for R with no inaccessible states. The automaton M induces an equivalence relation $\equiv_M$ on Σ^* defined by

$$x \equiv_M y \overset{\text{def}}{\Longleftrightarrow} \widehat{\delta}(s, x) = \widehat{\delta}(s, y).$$

(Don't confuse this relation with the collapsing relation $\approx$ of Lecture 13—that relation was defined on Q, whereas $\equiv_M$ is defined on Σ^*.)

One can easily show that the relation $\equiv_M$ is an equivalence relation; that is, that it is reflexive, symmetric, and transitive. In addition, $\equiv_M$ satisfies a few other useful properties:

(i) It is a *right congruence*: for any $x, y \in \Sigma^*$ and $a \in \Sigma$,

$$x \equiv_M y \Rightarrow xa \equiv_M ya.$$

To see this, assume that $x \equiv_M y$. Then

$$
\begin{aligned}
\widehat{\delta}(s, xa) &= \delta(\widehat{\delta}(s, x), a) \\
&= \delta(\widehat{\delta}(s, y), a) \quad \text{by assumption} \\
&= \widehat{\delta}(s, ya).
\end{aligned}
$$

(ii) It *refines R*: for any $x, y \in \Sigma^*$,

$$x \equiv_M y \Rightarrow (x \in R \Longleftrightarrow y \in R).$$

This is because $\widehat{\delta}(s, x) = \widehat{\delta}(s, y)$, and this is either an accept or a reject state, so either both x and y are accepted or both are rejected. Another way to say this is that every $\equiv_M$-class has either all its elements in R or none of its elements in R; in other words, R is a union of $\equiv_M$-classes.

(iii) It is of *finite index*; that is, it has only finitely many equivalence classes. This is because there is exactly one equivalence class

$$\{x \in \Sigma^* \mid \widehat{\delta}(s, x) = q\}$$

corresponding to each state q of M.

Let us call an equivalence relation $\equiv$ on Σ^* a *Myhill–Nerode relation for R* if it satisfies properties (i), (ii), and (iii); that is, if it is a right congruence of finite index refining R.

The interesting thing about this definition is that it characterizes exactly the relations on Σ^* that are $\equiv_M$ for some automaton M. In other words, we can reconstruct M from $\equiv_M$ using only the fact that $\equiv_M$ is Myhill–Nerode. To see this, we will show how to construct an automaton $M_\equiv$ for R from any given Myhill–Nerode relation $\equiv$ for R. We will show later that the two constructions

$$M \mapsto \equiv_M,$$
$$\equiv \mapsto M_\equiv$$

are inverses up to isomorphism of automata.

Let $R \subseteq \Sigma^*$, and let $\equiv$ be an arbitrary Myhill–Nerode relation for R. Right now we're not assuming that R is regular, only that the relation $\equiv$ satisfies (i), (ii), and (iii). The $\equiv$-class of the string x is

$$[x] \stackrel{\text{def}}{=} \{y \mid y \equiv x\}.$$

Although there are infinitely many strings, there are only finitely many $\equiv$-classes, by property (iii).

Now define the DFA $M_\equiv = (Q, \Sigma, \delta, s, F)$, where

$$Q \stackrel{\text{def}}{=} \{[x] \mid x \in \Sigma^*\},$$
$$s \stackrel{\text{def}}{=} [\epsilon],$$
$$F \stackrel{\text{def}}{=} \{[x] \mid x \subset R\},$$
$$\delta([x], a) \stackrel{\text{def}}{=} [xa].$$

It follows from property (i) of Myhill–Nerode relations that δ is well defined. In other words, we have defined the action of δ on an equivalence class $[x]$ in terms of an element x chosen from that class, and it is conceivable that we could have gotten something different had we chosen another $y \in [x]$ such that $[xa] \neq [ya]$. The property of right congruence says exactly that this cannot happen.

Finally, observe that

$$x \in R \Longleftrightarrow [x] \in F. \tag{15.1}$$

The implication ($\Rightarrow$) is from the definition of F, and ($\Leftarrow$) follows from the definition of F and property (ii) of Myhill–Nerode relations.

Now we are ready to prove that $L(M_\equiv) = R$.

Lemma 15.1 $\widehat{\delta}([x], y) = [xy]$.

Proof. Induction on $|y|$.

Basis

$$\widehat{\delta}([x], \epsilon) = [x] = [x\epsilon].$$

Induction step

$$\begin{aligned}
\widehat{\delta}([x], ya) &= \delta(\widehat{\delta}([x], y), a) &&\text{definition of } \widehat{\delta} \\
&= \delta([xy], a) &&\text{induction hypothesis} \\
&= [xya] &&\text{definition of } \delta. \qquad \square
\end{aligned}$$

Theorem 15.2 $L(M_\equiv) = R.$

Proof.

$$\begin{aligned}
x \in L(M_\equiv) &\Longleftrightarrow \widehat{\delta}([\epsilon], x) \in F &&\text{definition of acceptance} \\
&\Longleftrightarrow [x] \in F &&\text{Lemma 15.1} \\
&\Longleftrightarrow x \in R &&\text{property (15.1).} \qquad \square
\end{aligned}$$

$M \mapsto {\equiv_M}$ and ${\equiv} \mapsto M_\equiv$ Are Inverses

We have described two natural constructions, one taking a given automaton M for R with no inaccessible states to a corresponding Myhill–Nerode relation $\equiv_M$ for R, and one taking a given Myhill–Nerode relation $\equiv$ for R to a DFA $M_\equiv$ for R. We now wish to show that these two operations are inverses up to isomorphism.

Lemma 15.3   (i) *If $\equiv$ is a Myhill–Nerode relation for R, and if we apply the construction ${\equiv} \mapsto M_\equiv$ and then apply the construction $M \mapsto {\equiv_M}$ to the result, the resulting relation $\equiv_{M_\equiv}$ is identical to $\equiv$.*

(ii) *If M is a DFA for R with no inaccessible states, and if we apply the construction $M \mapsto {\equiv_M}$ and then apply the construction ${\equiv} \mapsto M_\equiv$ to the result, the resulting DFA $M_{\equiv_M}$ is isomorphic to M.*

Proof. (i) Let $M_\equiv = (Q, \Sigma, \delta, s, F)$ be the automaton constructed from $\equiv$ as described above. Then for any $x, y \in \Sigma^*$,

$$\begin{aligned}
x \equiv_{M_\equiv} y &\Longleftrightarrow \widehat{\delta}(s, x) = \widehat{\delta}(s, y) &&\text{definition of } \equiv_{M_\equiv} \\
&\Longleftrightarrow \widehat{\delta}([\epsilon], x) = \widehat{\delta}([\epsilon], y) &&\text{definition of } s \\
&\Longleftrightarrow [x] = [y] &&\text{Lemma 15.1} \\
&\Longleftrightarrow x \equiv y.
\end{aligned}$$

(ii) Let $M = (Q, \Sigma, \delta, s, F)$ and let $M_{\equiv_M} = (Q', \Sigma, \delta', s', F')$. Recall from the construction that

$$[x] = \{y \mid y \equiv_M x\} = \{y \mid \widehat{\delta}(s, y) = \widehat{\delta}(s, x)\},$$
$$Q' = \{[x] \mid x \in \Sigma^*\},$$
$$s' = [\epsilon],$$
$$F' = \{[x] \mid x \in R\},$$
$$\delta'([x], a) = [xa].$$

We will show that $M_{\equiv_M}$ and M are isomorphic under the map

$$f : Q' \to Q,$$
$$f([x]) = \widehat{\delta}(s, x).$$

By the definition of $\equiv_M$, $[x] = [y]$ iff $\widehat{\delta}(s, x) = \widehat{\delta}(s, y)$, so the map f is well defined on $\equiv_M$-classes and is one-to-one. Since M has no inaccessible states, f is onto.

To show that f is an isomorphism of automata, we need to show that f preserves all automata-theoretic structure: the start state, transition function, and final states. That is, we need to show

- $f(s') = s$,

- $f(\delta'([x], a)) = \delta(f([x]), a)$,

- $[x] \in F' \iff f([x]) \in F$.

These are argued as follows:

$$\begin{aligned}
f(s') &= f([\epsilon]) &&\text{definition of } s' \\
&= \widehat{\delta}(s, \epsilon) &&\text{definition of } f \\
&= s &&\text{definition of } \widehat{\delta};
\end{aligned}$$

$$\begin{aligned}
f(\delta'([x], a)) &= f([xa]) &&\text{definition of } \delta' \\
&= \widehat{\delta}(s, xa) &&\text{definition of } f \\
&= \delta(\widehat{\delta}(s, x), a) &&\text{definition of } \widehat{\delta} \\
&= \delta(f([x]), a) &&\text{definition of } f;
\end{aligned}$$

$$\begin{aligned}
[x] \in F' &\iff x \in R &&\text{definition of } F \text{ and property (ii)} \\
&\iff \widehat{\delta}(s, x) \in F &&\text{since } L(M) = R \\
&\iff f([x]) \in F &&\text{definition of } f.
\end{aligned}$$

$\square$

We have shown:

Theorem 15.4 *Let Σ be a finite alphabet. Up to isomorphism of automata, there is a one-to-one correspondence between deterministic finite automata over Σ with no inaccessible states accepting R and Myhill–Nerode relations for R on Σ^*.*

Lecture 16

The Myhill–Nerode Theorem

Let $R \subseteq \Sigma^*$ be a regular set. Recall from Lecture 15 that a *Myhill–Nerode relation for* R is an equivalence relation $\equiv$ on Σ^* satisfying the following three properties:

(i) $\equiv$ is a *right congruence*: for any $x, y \in \Sigma^*$ and $a \in \Sigma$,

$$x \equiv y \Rightarrow xa \equiv ya;$$

(ii) $\equiv$ *refines* R: for any $x, y \in \Sigma^*$,

$$x \equiv y \Rightarrow (x \in R \Longleftrightarrow y \in R);$$

(iii) $\equiv$ is of *finite index*; that is, $\equiv$ has only finitely many equivalence classes.

We showed that there was a natural one-to-one correspondence (up to isomorphism of automata) between

- deterministic finite automata for R with input alphabet Σ and with no inaccessible states, and

- Myhill–Nerode relations for R on Σ^*.

This is interesting, because it says we can deal with regular sets and finite automata in terms of a few simple, purely algebraic properties.

In this lecture we will show that there exists a *coarsest* Myhill–Nerode relation $\equiv_R$ for any given regular set R; that is, one that every other Myhill–Nerode relation for R refines. The notions of *coarsest* and *refinement* will be defined below. The relation $\equiv_R$ corresponds to the unique minimal DFA for R.

Recall from Lecture 15 the two constructions

- $M \mapsto \equiv_M$, which takes an arbitrary DFA $M = (Q, \Sigma, \delta, s, F)$ with no inaccessible states accepting R and produces a Myhill–Nerode relation $\equiv_M$ for R:

$$x \equiv_M y \overset{\text{def}}{\Longleftrightarrow} \widehat{\delta}(s, x) = \widehat{\delta}(s, y);$$

- $\equiv \mapsto M_\equiv$, which takes an arbitrary Myhill–Nerode relation $\equiv$ on Σ^* for R and produces a DFA $M_\equiv = (Q, \Sigma, \delta, s, F)$ accepting R:

$$[x] \overset{\text{def}}{=} \{y \mid y \equiv x\},$$
$$Q \overset{\text{def}}{=} \{[x] \mid x \in \Sigma^*\},$$
$$s \overset{\text{def}}{=} [\epsilon],$$
$$\delta([x], a) \overset{\text{def}}{=} [xa],$$
$$F \overset{\text{def}}{=} \{[x] \mid x \in R\}.$$

We showed that these two constructions are inverses up to isomorphism.

Definition 16.1   A relation $\equiv_1$ is said to *refine* another relation $\equiv_2$ if $\equiv_1 \subseteq \equiv_2$, considered as sets of ordered pairs. In other words, $\equiv_1$ *refines* $\equiv_2$ if for all x and y, $x \equiv_1 y$ implies $x \equiv_2 y$. For equivalence relations $\equiv_1$ and $\equiv_2$, this is the same as saying that for every x, the $\equiv_1$-class of x is included in the $\equiv_2$-class of x.   □

For example, the equivalence relation $x \equiv y \bmod 6$ on the integers refines the equivalence relation $x \equiv y \bmod 3$. For another example, clause (ii) of the definition of Myhill–Nerode relations says that a Myhill–Nerode relation $\equiv$ for R refines the equivalence relation with equivalence classes R and $\Sigma^* - R$.

The relation of *refinement* between equivalence relations is a partial order: it is reflexive (every relation refines itself), transitive (if $\equiv_1$ refines $\equiv_2$ and $\equiv_2$ refines $\equiv_3$, then $\equiv_1$ refines $\equiv_3$), and antisymmetric (if $\equiv_1$ refines $\equiv_2$ and $\equiv_2$ refines $\equiv_1$, then $\equiv_1$ and $\equiv_2$ are the same relation).

If $\equiv_1$ refines $\equiv_2$, then $\equiv_1$ is the *finer* and $\equiv_2$ is the *coarser* of the two relations. There is always a finest and a coarsest equivalence relation on any set U, namely the *identity relation* $\{(x, x) \mid x \in U\}$ and the *universal relation* $\{(x, y) \mid x, y \in U\}$, respectively.

Now let $R \subseteq \Sigma^*$, regular or not. We define an equivalence relation $\equiv_R$ on Σ^* in terms of R as follows:

$$x \equiv_R y \stackrel{\text{def}}{\Longleftrightarrow} \forall z \in \Sigma^* \ (xz \in R \Longleftrightarrow yz \in R). \qquad (16.1)$$

In other words, two strings are equivalent under $\equiv_R$ if, whenever you append the same string to both of them, the resulting two strings are either both in R or both not in R. It is not hard to show that this is an equivalence relation for any R.

We show that for any set R, regular or not, the relation $\equiv_R$ satisfies the first two properties (i) and (ii) of Myhill–Nerode relations and is the coarsest such relation on Σ^*. In case R is regular, this relation is also of finite index, therefore a Myhill–Nerode relation for R. In fact, it is the coarsest possible Myhill–Nerode relation for R and corresponds to the unique minimal finite automaton for R.

Lemma 16.2   *Let $R \subseteq \Sigma^*$, regular or not. The relation $\equiv_R$ defined by (16.1) is a right congruence refining R and is the coarsest such relation on Σ^*.*

Proof. To show that $\equiv_R$ is a right congruence, take $z = aw$ in the definition of $\equiv_R$:

$$x \equiv_R y \Rightarrow \forall a \in \Sigma \ \forall w \in \Sigma^* (xaw \in R \Longleftrightarrow yaw \in R)$$
$$\Rightarrow \forall a \in \Sigma \ (xa \equiv_R ya).$$

To show that $\equiv_R$ refines R, take $z = \epsilon$ in the definition of $\equiv_R$:

$$x \equiv_R y \Rightarrow (x \in R \Longleftrightarrow y \in R).$$

Moreover, $\equiv_R$ is the coarsest such relation, because any other equivalence relation $\equiv$ satisfying (i) and (ii) refines $\equiv_R$:

$$x \equiv y$$
$$\Rightarrow \forall z \ (xz \equiv yz) \qquad \text{by induction on } |z|, \text{ using property (i)}$$
$$\Rightarrow \forall z \ (xz \in R \Longleftrightarrow yz \in R) \qquad \text{property (ii)}$$
$$\Rightarrow x \equiv_R y \qquad \text{definition of } \equiv_R. \qquad \square$$

At this point all the hard work is done. We can now state and prove the *Myhill–Nerode theorem*:

Theorem 16.3   **(Myhill–Nerode theorem)**   *Let $R \subseteq \Sigma^*$. The following statements are equivalent:*

(a) R is regular;

(b) there exists a Myhill–Nerode relation for R;

(c) the relation $\equiv_R$ is of finite index.

Proof. (a) $\Rightarrow$ (b)   Given a DFA M for R, the construction $M \mapsto\ \equiv_M$ produces a Myhill–Nerode relation for R.

(b) $\Rightarrow$ (c)   By Lemma 16.2, any Myhill–Nerode relation for R is of finite index and refines $\equiv_R$; therefore $\equiv_R$ is of finite index.

(c) $\Rightarrow$ (a)   If $\equiv_R$ is of finite index, then it is a Myhill–Nerode relation for R, and the construction $\equiv\ \mapsto M_\equiv$ produces a DFA for R. $\square$

Since $\equiv_R$ is the unique coarsest Myhill–Nerode relation for a regular set R, it corresponds to the DFA for R with the fewest states among all DFAs for R.

The collapsing algorithm of Lecture 14 actually gives this automaton. Suppose $M = (Q,\ \Sigma,\ \delta,\ s,\ F)$ is a DFA for R that is already collapsed; that is, there are no inaccessible states, and the collapsing relation

$$p \approx q \overset{\text{def}}{\Longleftrightarrow} \forall x \in \Sigma^*\ (\widehat{\delta}(p, x) \in F \Longleftrightarrow \widehat{\delta}(q, x) \in F)$$

is the identity relation on Q. Then the Myhill–Nerode relation $\equiv_M$ corresponding to M is exactly $\equiv_R$:

$x \equiv_R y$

$\Longleftrightarrow \forall z \in \Sigma^*\ (xz \in R \Longleftrightarrow yz \in R)$ definition of $\equiv_R$

$\Longleftrightarrow \forall z \in \Sigma^*\ (\widehat{\delta}(s, xz) \in F \Longleftrightarrow \widehat{\delta}(s, yz) \in F)$ definition of acceptance

$\Longleftrightarrow \forall z \in \Sigma^*\ (\widehat{\delta}(\widehat{\delta}(s, x), z) \in F \Longleftrightarrow \widehat{\delta}(\widehat{\delta}(s, y), z) \in F)$

   Homework 1, Exercise 3

$\Longleftrightarrow \widehat{\delta}(s, x) \approx \widehat{\delta}(s, y)$ definition of $\approx$

$\Longleftrightarrow \widehat{\delta}(s, x) = \widehat{\delta}(s, y)$ since M is collapsed

$\Longleftrightarrow x \equiv_M y$ definition of $\equiv_M$.

An Application

The Myhill–Nerode theorem can be used to determine whether a set R is regular or nonregular by determining the number of $\equiv_R$-classes. For example, consider the set

$$A = \{a^n b^n \mid n \geq 0\}.$$

If $k \neq m$, then $a^k \not\equiv_A a^m$, since $a^k b^k \in A$ but $a^m b^k \notin A$. Therefore, there are infinitely many $\equiv_A$-classes, at least one for each a^k, $k \geq 0$. By the Myhill–Nerode theorem, A is not regular.

In fact, one can show that the $\equiv_A$-classes are exactly

$$G_k = \{a^k\}, \quad k \geq 0,$$

$$H_k = \{a^{n+k}b^n \mid 1 \leq n\}, \quad k \geq 0,$$
$$E = \Sigma^* - \bigcup_{k \geq 0} G_k \cup H_k = \Sigma^* - \{a^m b^n \mid 0 \leq n \leq m\}.$$

For strings in G_k, all and only strings in $\{a^n b^{n+k} \mid n \geq 0\}$ can be appended to obtain a string in A; for strings in H_k, only the string b^k can be appended to obtain a string in A; and no string can be appended to a string in E to obtain a string in A.

We will see another application of the Myhill–Nerode theorem involving two-way finite automata in Lectures 17 and 18.

Historical Notes

Minimization of DFAs was studied by Huffman [61], Moore [90], Nerode [94], and Hopcroft [59], among others. The Myhill–Nerode theorem is due independently to Myhill [91] and Nerode [94] in slightly different forms.

Supplementary Lecture B

Collapsing Nondeterministic Automata

With respect to minimization, the situation for nondeterministic automata is not as satisfactory as that for deterministic automata. For example, minimal NFAs are not necessarily unique up to isomorphism (Miscellaneous Exercise 60). However, part of the Myhill–Nerode theory developed in Lectures 13 through 16 does generalize to NFAs. The generalization is based on the notion of *bisimulation*, an important concept in the theory of concurrency [87]. In this lecture we briefly investigate this connection.

The version of bisimulation we consider here is called *strong bisimulation* in the concurrency literature. There are weaker forms that apply too. We show that bisimulation relations between nondeterministic automata and collapsing relations on deterministic automata are strongly related. The former generalize the latter in two significant ways: they work for nondeterministic automata, and they can relate two different automata.

Bisimulation

Let

$$M = (Q_M, \Sigma, \Delta_M, S_M, F_M),$$
$$N = (Q_N, \Sigma, \Delta_N, S_N, F_N)$$

be two NFAs. Recall that for NFAs, $\Delta(p, a)$ is a set of states.

Let $\approx$ be a binary relation relating states of M with states of N; that is, $\approx$ is a subset of $Q_M \times Q_N$. For $B \subseteq Q_N$, define

$$C_\approx(B) \stackrel{\text{def}}{=} \{p \in Q_M \mid \exists q \in B \; p \approx q\},$$

the set of all states of M that are related via $\approx$ to some state in B. Similarly, for $A \subseteq Q_M$, define

$$C_\approx(A) \stackrel{\text{def}}{=} \{q \in Q_N \mid \exists p \in A \; p \approx q\}.$$

The relation $\approx$ can be extended in a natural way to *subsets* of Q_M and Q_N: for $A \subseteq Q_M$ and $B \subseteq Q_N$,

$$A \approx B \stackrel{\text{def}}{\Longleftrightarrow} A \subseteq C_\approx(B) \text{ and } B \subseteq C_\approx(A) \qquad \text{(B.1)}$$
$$\Longleftrightarrow \forall p \in A \; \exists q \in B \; p \approx q \text{ and } \forall q \in B \; \exists p \in A \; p \approx q.$$

Note that $\{p\} \approx \{q\}$ iff $p \approx q$ and that $B \subseteq B'$ implies $C_\approx(B) \subseteq C_\approx(B')$.

Definition B.1   The relation $\approx$ is called a *bisimulation* if the following three conditions are met:

(i) $S_M \approx S_N$;

(ii) if $p \approx q$, then for all $a \in \Sigma$, $\Delta_M(p, a) \approx \Delta_N(q, a)$; and

(iii) if $p \approx q$, then $p \in F_M$ iff $q \in F_N$. $\square$

Note the similarity of these conditions to the defining conditions of collapsing relations on DFAs from Lecture 13.

We say that M and N are *bisimilar* if there exists a bisimulation between them. The *bisimilarity class* of M is the family of all NFAs that are bisimilar to M. We will show that bisimilar automata accept the same set and that every bisimilarity class contains a unique minimal NFA that can be obtained by a collapsing construction.

First let's establish some basic consequences of Definition B.1.

Lemma B.2   *(i) Bisimulation is symmetric: if $\approx$ is a bisimulation between M and N, then its reverse*

$$\{(q, p) \mid p \approx q\}$$

is a bisimulation between N and M.

(ii) Bisimulation is transitive: if $\approx_1$ is a bisimulation between M and N and $\approx_2$ is a bisimulation between N and P, then their composition

$$\approx_1 \circ \approx_2 \stackrel{\text{def}}{=} \{(p,r) \mid \exists q \ p \approx_1 q \ \text{and} \ q \approx_2 r\}$$

is a bisimulation between M and P.

(iii) The union of any nonempty family of bisimulations between M and N is a bisimulation between M and N.

Proof. All three properties follow quite easily from the definition of bisimulation. We argue (iii) explicitly.

Let $\{\approx_i \mid i \in I\}$ be a nonempty indexed set of bisimulations between M and N. Define

$$\approx \stackrel{\text{def}}{=} \bigcup_{i \in I} \approx_i .$$

Thus

$$p \approx q \iff \exists i \in I \ p \approx_i q.$$

Since I is nonempty, $S_M \approx_i S_N$ for some $i \in I$, therefore $S_M \approx S_N$. If $p \approx q$, then for some $i \in I$, $p \approx_i q$. Therefore, $\Delta(p,a) \approx_i \Delta(q,a)$ and $\Delta(p,a) \approx \Delta(q,a)$. Finally, if $p \approx q$, then $p \approx_i q$ for some $i \in I$, whence $p \in F_M$ iff $q \in F_N$.   □

Lemma B.3   *Let $\approx$ be a bisimulation between M and N. If $A \approx B$, then for all $x \in \Sigma^*$, $\widehat{\Delta}_M(A,x) \approx \widehat{\Delta}_N(B,x)$.*

Proof. Suppose $A \approx B$. For $x = \epsilon$,

$$\widehat{\Delta}_M(A,\epsilon) = A \approx B = \widehat{\Delta}_M(B,\epsilon).$$

For $x = a \in \Sigma$, since $A \subseteq C_{\approx}(B)$, if $p \in A$ then there exists $q \in B$ such that $p \approx q$. By Definition B.1(ii),

$$\Delta_M(p,a) \subseteq C_{\approx}(\Delta_N(q,a)) \subseteq C_{\approx}(\widehat{\Delta}_N(B,a)).$$

Therefore,

$$\widehat{\Delta}_M(A,a) = \bigcup_{p \in A} \Delta_M(p,a) \subseteq C_{\approx}(\widehat{\Delta}_N(B,a)).$$

By a symmetric argument, $\widehat{\Delta}_N(B,a) \subseteq C_{\approx}(\widehat{\Delta}_M(A,a))$. Therefore,

$$\widehat{\Delta}_M(A,a) \approx \widehat{\Delta}_N(B,a). \tag{B.2}$$

Proceeding by induction, suppose that $\widehat{\Delta}_M(A,x) \approx \widehat{\Delta}_N(B,x)$. By (B.2) and Lemma 6.1,

$$\begin{aligned}
\widehat{\Delta}_M(A,xa) &= \widehat{\Delta}_M(\widehat{\Delta}_M(A,x),a) \\
&\approx \widehat{\Delta}_N(\widehat{\Delta}_N(B,x),a) \\
&= \widehat{\Delta}_N(B,xa).
\end{aligned}$$

□

Theorem B.4   *Bisimilar automata accept the same set.*

Proof. Suppose $\approx$ is a bisimulation between M and N. By Definition B.1(i) and Lemma B.3, for any $x \in \Sigma^*$, $\hat{\Delta}_M(S_M, x) \approx \hat{\Delta}_N(S_N, x)$. By Definition B.1(iii), $\hat{\Delta}_M(S_M, x) \cap F_M \neq \varnothing$ iff $\hat{\Delta}_N(S_N, x) \cap F_N \neq \varnothing$. By definition of acceptance for nondeterministic automata, $x \in L(M)$ iff $x \in L(N)$. Since x is arbitrary, $L(M) = L(N)$.   □

In fact, one can show that if M and N are bisimilar, then (B.1) is a bisimulation between the deterministic automata obtained from M and N by the subset construction (Miscellaneous Exercise 64).

As with the deterministic theory, minimization involves elimination of inaccessible states and collapsing. Here's how we deal with accessibility. Let $\approx$ be a bisimulation between M and N. The *support* of $\approx$ in M is the set $C_\approx(Q_N)$, the set of states of M that are related by $\approx$ to some state of N.

Lemma B.5   *A state of M is in the support of all bisimulations involving M if and only if it is accessible.*

Proof. Let $\approx$ be an arbitrary bisimulation between M and another automaton. By Definition B.1(i), every start state of M is in the support of $\approx$; and by Definition B.1(ii), if p is in the support of $\approx$, then every element of $\Delta(p, a)$ is in the support of $\approx$ for every $a \in \Sigma$. It follows inductively that every accessible state of M is in the support of $\approx$.

Conversely, it is not difficult to check that the relation

$$\{(p, p) \mid p \text{ is accessible}\} \tag{B.3}$$

is a bisimulation between M and itself. If a state is in the support of all bisimulations, then it must be in the support of (B.3), therefore accessible.   □

Autobisimulation

Definition B.6   An *autobisimulation* is a bisimulation between an automaton and itself.   □

Theorem B.7   *Any nondeterministic automaton M has a coarsest autobisimulation $\equiv_M$. The relation $\equiv_M$ is an equivalence relation.*

Proof. Let B be the set of all autobisimulations on M. The set B is nonempty, since it contains the identity relation at least. Let $\equiv_M$ be the union of all the relations in B. By Lemma B.2(iii), $\equiv_M$ is itself in B and is refined by every element of B. The relation $\equiv_M$ is reflexive, since the identity relation is in B, and is symmetric and transitive by Lemma B.2(i) and (ii).   □

We can now remove inaccessible states and collapse by the maximal auto-bisimulation to get a minimal NFA bisimilar to the original NFA. Let

$$M = (Q, \Sigma, \Delta, S, F).$$

We have already observed that the accessible subautomaton of M is bisim-ilar to M under the bisimulation (B.3), so we can assume without loss of generality that M has no inaccessible states. Let $\equiv$ be $\equiv_M$, the maximal autobisimulation on M. For $p \in Q$, let $[p]$ denote the $\equiv$-equivalence class of p, and let $\gtrsim$ be the relation relating p to its $\equiv$-equivalence class:

$$[p] \overset{\text{def}}{=} \{q \mid p \equiv q\},$$
$$\gtrsim \overset{\text{def}}{=} \{(p, [p]) \mid p \in Q\}.$$

For any $A \subseteq Q$, define

$$A' \overset{\text{def}}{=} \{[p] \mid p \in A\}. \tag{B.4}$$

Lemma B.8   *For all $A, B \subseteq Q$,*

(i) $A \subseteq C_\equiv(B) \Longleftrightarrow A' \subseteq B'$,

(ii) $A \equiv B \Longleftrightarrow A' = B'$, *and*

(iii) $A \gtrsim A'$.

These properties are straightforward consequences of the definitions and are left as exercises (Miscellaneous Exercise 62).

Now define the quotient automaton

$$M' \overset{\text{def}}{=} (Q', \Sigma, \Delta', S', F'),$$

where Q', S', and F' refer to (B.4) and

$$\Delta'([p], a) \overset{\text{def}}{=} \Delta(p, a)'.$$

The function Δ' is well defined, because

$$[p] = [q] \Rightarrow p \equiv q$$
$$\Rightarrow \Delta(p, a) \equiv \Delta(q, a) \qquad \text{Definition B.1(ii)}$$
$$\Rightarrow \Delta(p, a)' = \Delta(q, a)' \qquad \text{Lemma B.8(ii)}.$$

Lemma B.9   *The relation $\gtrsim$ is a bisimulation between M and M'.*

Proof. By Lemma B.8(iii), we have $S \gtrsim S'$, and if $p \gtrsim [q]$, then $p \equiv q$. Therefore,

$$\Delta(p, a) \gtrsim \Delta(p, a)' = \Delta'([p], a) = \Delta'([q], a).$$

This takes care of start states and transitions. For the final states, if $p \in F$, then $[p] \in F'$. Conversely, if $[p] \in F'$, there exists $q \in [p]$ such that $q \in F$; then $p \equiv q$, therefore $p \in F$. $\qquad\qquad\qquad\qquad\qquad\qquad$ $\square$

By Theorem B.4, M and M' accept the same set.

Lemma B.10 *The only autobisimulation on M' is the identity relation $=$.*

Proof. Let $\sim$ be an autobisimulation on M'. If $\sim$ related two distinct states, then the composition

$$\gtrsim \circ \sim \circ \lesssim, \tag{B.5}$$

where $\lesssim$ is the reverse of $\gtrsim$, would relate two non-$\equiv_M$-equivalent states of M, contradicting the maximality of $\equiv_M$. Thus $\sim$ is a subset of the identity relation.

On the other hand, if there is a state $[p]$ of M' that is not related to itself by $\sim$, then the state p of M is not related to any state of M under (B.5), contradicting Lemma B.5 and the assumption that all states of M are accessible. $\qquad\qquad\qquad\qquad\qquad\qquad\qquad\qquad\qquad\qquad\qquad\qquad$ $\square$

Theorem B.11 *Let M be an NFA with no inaccessible states and let $\equiv_M$ be the maximal autobisimulation on M. The quotient automaton M' is the minimal automaton bisimilar to M and is unique up to isomorphism.*

Proof. To show this, it will suffice to show that for any automaton N bisimilar to M, if we remove inaccessible states and then collapse the resulting NFA by its maximal autobisimulation, we obtain an automaton isomorphic to M'.

Using (B.3), we can assume without loss of generality that N has no inaccessible states. Let $\equiv_N$ be the maximal autobisimulation on N, and let N' be the quotient automaton.

By Lemmas B.2 and B.9, M' and N' are bisimilar. We will show that any bisimulation between M' and N' gives a one-to-one correspondence between the states of M' and N'. This establishes the result, since a bisimulation that is a one-to-one correspondence constitutes an isomorphism (Miscellaneous Exercise 63).

Let $\approx$ be a bisimulation between M' and N'. Under $\approx$, every state of M' is related to at least one state of N', and every state of N' is related to at most one state of M'; otherwise the composition of $\approx$ with its reverse would not be the identity on M', contradicting Lemma B.10. Therefore, $\approx$ embeds M' into N' injectively (i.e., in a one-to-one fashion). By a symmetric argument, the reverse of $\approx$ embeds N' into M' injectively. Therefore, $\approx$ gives a one-to-one correspondence between the states of M' and N'. $\qquad$ $\square$

An Algorithm

Here is an algorithm for computing the maximal bisimulation between any given pair of NFAs M and N. There may exist no bisimulation between M and N, in which case the algorithm halts and reports failure. For the case $M = N$, the algorithm computes the maximal autobisimulation. The algorithm is a direct generalization of the algorithm of Lecture 14.

As in Lecture 14, the algorithm will mark pairs of states (p, q), where $p \in Q_M$ and $q \in Q_N$. A pair (p, q) will be marked when a proof is discovered that p and q cannot be related by any bisimulation.

1. Write down a table of all pairs (p, q), initially unmarked.

2. Mark (p, q) if $p \in F_M$ and $q \notin F_N$ or vice versa.

3. Repeat the following until no more changes occur: if (p, q) is unmarked, and if for some $a \in \Sigma$, either

    - there exists $p' \in \Delta_M(p, a)$ such that for all $q' \in \Delta_N(q, a)$, (p', q') is marked, or

    - there exists $q' \in \Delta_N(q, a)$ such that for all $p' \in \Delta_M(p, a)$, (p', q') is marked,

    then mark (p, q).

4. Define $p \equiv q$ iff (p, q) is never marked. Check whether $S_M \equiv S_N$. If so, then $\equiv$ is the maximal bisimulation between M and N. If not, then no bisimulation between M and N exists.

One can easily prove by induction on the stages of this algorithm that if the pair (p, q) is ever marked, then $p \not\approx q$ for any bisimulation $\approx$ between M and N, because we only mark pairs that violate some condition in the definition of bisimulation. Therefore, any bisimulation $\approx$ is a refinement of $\equiv$. In particular, the maximal bisimulation between M and N, if it exists, is a refinement of $\equiv$. If $S_M \not\equiv S_N$, then the same is true for any refinement of $\equiv$; in this case, no bisimulation exists.

On the other hand, suppose $S_M \equiv S_N$. To show that the algorithm is correct, we need only show that $\equiv$ is a bisimulation; then it must be the maximal one. We have $S_M \equiv S_N$ by assumption. Also, $\equiv$ respects the transition functions of M and N because of step 3 of the algorithm and respects final states of M and N because of step 2 of the algorithm.

We have shown:

Theorem B.12   *The algorithm above correctly computes the maximal bisimulation between two NFAs if a bisimulation exists. If no bisimulation exists, the algorithm halts and reports failure. If both automata are the same, the algorithm computes the maximal autobisimulation.*

Supplementary Lecture C

Automata on Terms

The theory of finite automata has many interesting and useful generalizations that allow more general types of inputs, such as infinite strings and finite and infinite trees. In this lecture and the next we will study one such generalization: finite automata on *terms*, also known as *finite labeled trees*. This generalization is quite natural and has a decidedly algebraic flavor. In particular, we will show that the entire Myhill–Nerode theory developed in Lectures 13 through 16 is really a consequence of basic results in *universal algebra*, a branch of algebra that deals with general algebraic concepts such as direct product, homomorphism, homomorphic image, and quotient algebra.

Signatures and Terms

A *signature* is an alphabet Σ consisting of various *function* and *relation symbols* in which each symbol is assigned a natural number, called its *arity*. An element of Σ is called *constant, unary, binary, ternary,* or *n-ary* if its arity is 0, 1, 2, 3, or n, respectively. We regard an n-ary function or relation symbol as denoting some (as yet unspecified) function or relation of n inputs on some (as yet unspecified) domain.

For example, the signature of monoids consists of two function symbols, a binary multiplication symbol $\cdot$ and a constant 1 for the multiplicative identity. The signature of groups consists of the symbols for monoids plus a unary function symbol $^{-1}$ for multiplicative inverse. The signature of Kleene algebra consists of two binary function symbols $+$ and $\cdot$, one unary function symbol $*$, and two constants 0 and 1.

Informally, a *ground term* over Σ is an expression built from the function symbols of Σ that respects the arities of all the symbols. The set of ground terms over Σ is denoted T_Σ. Formally,

(i) any constant function symbol $c \in \Sigma$ is in T_Σ; and

(ii) if $t_1, \ldots, t_n \in T_\Sigma$ and f is an n-ary function symbol of Σ, then $ft_1 \cdots t_n \in T_\Sigma$. We can picture the term $ft_1 \cdots t_n$ as a labeled tree

Actually, (i) is a special case of (ii): the precondition "if $t_1, \ldots, t_n \in T_\Sigma$" is vacuously true when $n = 0$.

For example, if f is binary, g is unary, and a, b are constants, then the following are examples of terms:

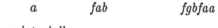

or pictorially,

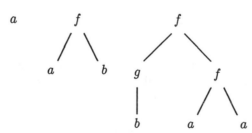

The term $ft_1 \cdots t_n$ is an expression representing the result of applying an n-ary function denoted by f to n inputs denoted by $t_1, \ldots, t_n$, although we have not yet said what the function denoted by f is. So far, f is just an uninterpreted symbol, and a term is just a syntactic expression with no further meaning.

Even though we don't use parentheses, the terms $t_1, \ldots, t_n$ are uniquely determined by the term $ft_1 \cdots t_n$ and the fact that f is n-ary. In other words, there is one and only one way to parse the string $ft_1 \cdots t_n$ as a ground term. A formal proof of this fact is given as an exercise (Miscellaneous Exercise 94), but is better left until after the study of context-free languages.

Note that if there are no constants in Σ, then T_Σ is empty. If there are only finitely many constants and no other function symbols, then T_Σ is finite. In all other cases, T_Σ is infinite.

Σ-algebras

A Σ-*algebra* is a structure $\mathcal{A}$ consisting of a set A, called the *carrier* of $\mathcal{A}$, along with a map that assigns a function $f^{\mathcal{A}}$ or relation $R^{\mathcal{A}}$ of the appropriate arity to each function symbol $f \in \Sigma$ or relation symbol $R \in \Sigma$. If f is an n-ary function symbol, then the function associated with f must be an n-ary function $f^{\mathcal{A}} : A^n \to A$. If R is an n-ary relation symbol, then the relation $R^{\mathcal{A}}$ must be an n-ary relation $R^{\mathcal{A}} \subseteq A^n$. Constant function symbols c are interpreted as 0-ary functions (functions with no inputs), which are just elements $c^{\mathcal{A}}$ of A. A unary relation is just a subset of A.

This interpretation of symbols of Σ extends in a natural way by induction to all ground terms. Each ground term t is naturally associated with an element $t^{\mathcal{A}} \in A$, defined inductively as follows:

$$ f t_1 \cdots t_n{}^{\mathcal{A}} \stackrel{\text{def}}{=} f^{\mathcal{A}}(t_1^{\mathcal{A}}, \dots, t_n^{\mathcal{A}}). $$

This includes the base case: the interpretation of a constant c as an element $c^{\mathcal{A}} \in A$ is part of the specification of $\mathcal{A}$.

Example C.1   Let Γ be a finite alphabet. The monoid Γ^* is an algebra of signature $\cdot, 1$. The carrier of this algebra is the set Γ^*, the binary function symbol $\cdot$ is interpreted as string concatenation, and the constant 1 is interpreted as the null string ϵ. □

Example C.2   The family of regular sets over an alphabet Γ is a Kleene algebra in which $+$ is interpreted as set union, $\cdot$ as set concatenation, * as asterate, 0 as the null set, and 1 as the set $\{\epsilon\}$. □

Example C.3   The family of binary relations on a set X is also a Kleene algebra in which $+$ is interpreted as set union, $\cdot$ as relational composition, * as reflexive transitive closure, 0 as the null relation, and 1 as the identity relation. □

Term Algebras

Example C.4   Let Σ be an arbitrary signature. The set T_Σ of ground terms over Σ gives a family of Σ-algebras under the following natural interpretation: for n-ary f,

$$ f^{T_\Sigma}(t_1, \dots, t_n) \stackrel{\text{def}}{=} f t_1 \cdots t_n. $$

This definition includes constants

$$c^{T_\Sigma} \stackrel{\text{def}}{=} c.$$

The particular algebra depends on the interpretation of the relation symbols of Σ as relations on T_Σ. In such algebras, each ground term t denotes itself: $t^{T_\Sigma} = t$. These algebras are called *syntactic* or *term algebras*.   □

Automata on Terms

Now here's something interesting.

Definition C.5   Let Σ be a signature consisting of finitely many function symbols and a single unary relation symbol R. A *(deterministic) term automaton* over Σ is a finite Σ-algebra.   □

Let $\mathcal{A}$ be a term automaton over Σ with carrier A. We'll call elements of A *states*. The states satisfying the unary relation $R^{\mathcal{A}}$ will be called *final* or *accept states*. Since a unary relation on A is just a subset of A, we can write $R^{\mathcal{A}}(q)$ or $q \in R^{\mathcal{A}}$ interchangeably. Inputs to $\mathcal{A}$ are ground terms over Σ; that is, elements of T_Σ.

Definition C.6   A ground term t is said to be *accepted* by $\mathcal{A}$ if $t^{\mathcal{A}} \in R^{\mathcal{A}}$. The set of terms accepted by $\mathcal{A}$ is denoted $L(\mathcal{A})$. A set of terms is called *regular* if it is $L(\mathcal{A})$ for some $\mathcal{A}$.   □

To understand what is going on here, think of a ground term t as a labeled tree. The automaton $\mathcal{A}$, given t as input, starts at the leaves of t and works upward, associating a state with each subterm inductively. If there is a constant $c \in \Sigma$ labeling a particular leaf of t, the state that is associated with that leaf is $c^{\mathcal{A}}$. If the immediate subterms $t_1, \ldots, t_n$ of the term $f t_1 \cdots t_n$ are labeled with states $q_1, \ldots, q_n$, respectively, then the term $f t_1 \cdots t_n$ is labeled with the state $f^{\mathcal{A}}(q_1, \ldots, q_n)$. A term is accepted if the state labeling the root is in $R^{\mathcal{A}}$; that is, if it is an accept state. There is no need for a start state; this role is played by the elements $c^{\mathcal{A}}$ associated with the constants $c \in \Sigma$.

Now let's describe the relationship of this new definition of automata to our previous definition and explain how the old one is a special case of the new one. Given an ordinary DFA over strings

$$M = (Q, \Sigma', \delta, s, F),$$

where Σ' is a finite alphabet, let

$$\Sigma \stackrel{\text{def}}{=} \Sigma' \cup \{\square, R\},$$

where $\square, R \notin \Sigma'$. We make Σ into a signature by declaring all elements of Σ' to be unary function symbols, $\square$ a constant, and R a unary relation symbol. There is a one-to-one correspondence between ground terms over Σ and strings in Σ'^*: the string $a_1 a_2 \cdots a_{n-1} a_n \in \Sigma'^*$ corresponds to the ground term $a_n a_{n-1} \cdots a_2 a_1 \Box \in T_\Sigma$. In particular, the empty string $\epsilon \in \Sigma'^*$ corresponds to the ground term $\Box \in T_\Sigma$.

Now we make a Σ-algebra out of M, which we will denote by $\mathcal{M}$. The carrier of $\mathcal{M}$ is Q. The symbols of Σ are interpreted as follows:

$$\Box^\mathcal{M} \stackrel{\text{def}}{=} s,$$

$$a^\mathcal{M}(q) \stackrel{\text{def}}{=} \delta(q, a),$$

$$R^\mathcal{M} \stackrel{\text{def}}{=} F.$$

In other words, the constant $\Box$ is interpreted as the start state of M; the symbol $a \in \Sigma'$ is interpreted as the unary function $q \mapsto \delta(q, a)$; and the relation symbol R is interpreted as the set of final states F. It is not difficult to show by induction that

$$\widehat{\delta}(s, a_1 a_2 \cdots a_{n-1} a_n) = a_n a_{n-1} \cdots a_2 a_1 \Box^\mathcal{M}.$$

Therefore,

$$a_1 a_2 \cdots a_{n-1} a_n \in L(M) \iff \widehat{\delta}(s, a_1 a_2 \cdots a_{n-1} a_n) \in F$$
$$\iff a_n a_{n-1} \cdots a_2 a_1 \Box^\mathcal{M} \in R^\mathcal{M}$$
$$\iff a_n a_{n-1} \cdots a_2 a_1 \Box \in L(\mathcal{M}).$$

It should be pretty apparent by now that much of automata theory is just algebra. What is the value of this alternative point of view? Let's develop the connection a little further to find out.

Homomorphisms

A central concept of universal algebra is the notion of *homomorphism*. Intuitively, a Σ-*algebra homomorphism* is a map between two Σ-algebras that preserves all algebraic structure as specified by Σ. Formally,

Definition C.7 Let $\mathcal{A}$ and $\mathcal{B}$ be two Σ-algebras with carriers A and B, respectively. A Σ-*algebra homomorphism* from $\mathcal{A}$ to $\mathcal{B}$ is a map $\sigma : A \to B$ such that

(i) for all n-ary function symbols $f \in \Sigma$ and all $a_1, \ldots, a_n \in A$,

$$\sigma(f^\mathcal{A}(a_1, \ldots, a_n)) = f^\mathcal{B}(\sigma(a_1), \ldots, \sigma(a_n));$$

(ii) for all n-ary relation symbols $R \in \Sigma$ and all $a_1, \ldots, a_n \in A$,

$$R^\mathcal{A}(a_1, \ldots, a_n) \iff R^\mathcal{B}(\sigma(a_1), \ldots, \sigma(a_n)). \qquad \Box$$

Condition (i) of Definition C.7 says that for any function symbol $f \in \Sigma$, we can apply $f^\mathcal{A}$ to $a_1, \ldots, a_n$ in A and then apply the homomorphism σ to the result to get an element of B, or we can apply σ to each of $a_1, \ldots, a_n$, then apply f^B to the resulting elements of B, and we get to the same place. Condition (ii) says that the distinguished relation R holds before applying the homomorphism if and only if it holds after.

Example C.8   The homomorphisms described in Lecture 10 are monoid homomorphisms. Conditions (10.1) and (10.2) are exactly Definition C.7(i) for the signature $\cdot, 1$ of monoids.   □

Example C.9   Let $\mathcal{A}$ be any Σ-algebra. The function $t \mapsto t^{\mathcal{A}}$ mapping a ground term $t \in T_\Sigma$ to its interpretation $t^{\mathcal{A}}$ in $\mathcal{A}$ satisfies Definition C.7(i), because for all n-ary $f \in \Sigma$ and $t_1, \ldots, t_n \in T_\Sigma$,

$$f^{T_\Sigma}(t_1, \ldots, t_n)^{\mathcal{A}} = f t_1 \cdots t_n{}^{\mathcal{A}}$$
$$= f^{\mathcal{A}}(t_1^{\mathcal{A}}, \ldots, t_n^{\mathcal{A}}).$$

Moreover, it is the only function $T_\Sigma \to \mathcal{A}$ that does so.   □

For a term automaton $\mathcal{M}$, whether or not the map $t \mapsto t^{\mathcal{M}}$ satisfies Definition C.7(ii) depends on the interpretation of the unary relation symbol R in the term algebra T_Σ. There is only one interpretation that works: $L(\mathcal{M})$. Thus we might have defined $L(\mathcal{M})$ to be the unique interpretation of R in T_Σ making the map $t \mapsto t^{\mathcal{M}}$ a homomorphism.

Definition C.10   A homomorphism $\sigma : \mathcal{A} \to \mathcal{B}$ that is onto (for all $b \in \mathcal{B}$, there exists $a \in \mathcal{A}$ such that $\sigma(a) = b$) is called an *epimorphism*. A homomorphism $\sigma : \mathcal{A} \to \mathcal{B}$ that is one-to-one (for all $a, b \in \mathcal{A}$, if $\sigma(a) = \sigma(b)$, then $a = b$) is called a *monomorphism*. A homomorphism that is both an epimorphism and a monomorphism is called an *isomorphism*. If $\sigma : \mathcal{A} \to \mathcal{B}$ is an epimorphism, then the algebra $\mathcal{B}$ is called a *homomorphic image* of $\mathcal{A}$.   □

Let Σ be a signature consisting of finitely many function symbols and a single unary relation symbol R. Let $A \subseteq T_\Sigma$ be an arbitrary set of ground terms, and let $T_\Sigma(A)$ denote the term algebra obtained by interpreting R as the set A; that is, $R^{T_\Sigma(A)} = A$.

Lemma C.11   *The set A is regular if and only if the algebra $T_\Sigma(A)$ has a finite homomorphic image.*

Proof. Once we have stated this, it's easy to prove. A finite homomorphic image $\mathcal{A}$ of $T_\Sigma(A)$ is just a term automaton for A. The homomorphism is the interpretation map $t \mapsto t^{\mathcal{A}}$. The inductive definition of this map corresponds to a run of the automaton. We leave the details as an exercise (Miscellaneous Exercise 66).   □

In the next lecture, Supplementary Lecture D, we will give an account of the Myhill–Nerode theorem in this more general setting.

Supplementary Lecture D

The Myhill–Nerode Theorem for Term Automata

In the last lecture we generalized DFAs on strings to term automata over a signature Σ and demonstrated that automata-theoretic concepts such as "final states" and "run" were really more general algebraic concepts in disguise. In this lecture we continue to develop this correspondence, leading finally to a fuller understanding of the Myhill–Nerode theorem.

Congruence

First we need to introduce the important algebraic concept of *congruence*. Congruences and homomorphisms go hand-in-hand. Recall from Supplementary Lecture C that a *homomorphism* between two Σ-algebras is a map that preserves all algebraic structure (Definition C.7). Every homomorphism $\sigma : \mathcal{A} \to \mathcal{B}$ induces a certain natural binary relation on $\mathcal{A}$:

$$u \equiv_\sigma v \overset{\text{def}}{\Longleftrightarrow} \sigma(u) = \sigma(v).$$

The relation $\equiv_\sigma$ is called the *kernel*[1] of σ.

---

[1]If you have taken algebra, you may have seen the word *kernel* used differently: normal subgroups of groups, ideals of rings, null spaces of linear transformations. These concepts are closely allied and serve the same purpose. The definition of *kernel* as a binary relation is more broadly applicable.

The kernel of any homomorphism defined on $\mathcal{A}$ is an equivalence relation on $\mathcal{A}$ (reflexive, symmetric, transitive). It also respects all algebraic structure in the following sense:

(i) for all n-ary function symbols $f \in \Sigma$, if $u_i \equiv_\sigma v_i$, $1 \leq i \leq n$, then
$$f^{\mathcal{A}}(u_1, \ldots, u_n) \equiv_\sigma f^{\mathcal{A}}(v_1, \ldots, v_n);$$

(ii) for all n-ary relation symbols $R \in \Sigma$, if $u_i \equiv_\sigma v_i$, $1 \leq i \leq n$, then
$$R^{\mathcal{A}}(u_1, \ldots, u_n) \iff R^{\mathcal{A}}(v_1, \ldots, v_n).$$

These properties follow immediately from the properties of homomorphisms and the definition of $\equiv_\sigma$.

In general, a *congruence* on $\mathcal{A}$ is any equivalence relation on $\mathcal{A}$ satisfying properties (i) and (ii):

Definition D.1   Let $\mathcal{A}$ be a Σ-algebra with carrier A. A *congruence* on $\mathcal{A}$ is an equivalence relation $\equiv$ on A such that

(i) for all n-ary function symbols $f \in \Sigma$, if $u_i \equiv v_i$, $1 \leq i \leq n$, then
$$f^{\mathcal{A}}(u_1, \ldots, u_n) \equiv f^{\mathcal{A}}(v_1, \ldots, v_n);$$

(ii) for all n-ary relation symbols $R \in \Sigma$, if $u_i \equiv v_i$, $1 \leq i \leq n$, then
$$R^{\mathcal{A}}(u_1, \ldots, u_n) \iff R^{\mathcal{A}}(v_1, \ldots, v_n). \qquad \square$$

Thus the kernel of every homomorphism is a congruence. Now, the interesting thing about this definition is that it goes the other way as well: every congruence is the kernel of some homomorphism. In other words, given an arbitrary congruence $\equiv$, we can construct a homomorphism σ such that $\equiv_\sigma$ is $\equiv$. In fact, we can make the homomorphism σ an epimorphism. We will prove this using a general algebraic construction called the *quotient construction*.

We saw an example of the quotient construction in Lecture 13, where we used it to collapse a DFA. We saw it again in Lecture 15, where we constructed an automaton for a set A from a given Myhill–Nerode relation for A. By now you have probably figured out where we are going with this: the collapsing relations $\approx$ of Lecture 13, the Myhill–Nerode relations $\equiv$ of Lecture 15, and the maximal Myhill–Nerode relation $\equiv_R$ of Lecture 16 are all congruences on Σ-algebras! We warned you not to confuse these different kinds of relations, because some were defined on automata and others on strings; but now we can roll them all into a single concept. This is the power and beauty of abstraction.

Lemma D.2   *(i) The kernel of any homomorphism is a congruence.*

(ii) Any congruence is the kernel of an epimorphism.

Proof. For (ii), build a quotient algebra whose elements are the congruence classes $[u]$. There is a unique interpretation of the function and relation symbols in the quotient making the map $u \mapsto [u]$ an epimorphism. We'll leave the details as an exercise (Miscellaneous Exercise 67). □

In fact, if the map $t \mapsto t^{\mathcal{A}}$ is onto (i.e., if each element of $\mathcal{A}$ is named by a term), then the congruences on $\mathcal{A}$ and homomorphic images of $\mathcal{A}$ are in one-to-one correspondence up to isomorphism. This is true of term algebras, since the map $t \mapsto t^{T_\Sigma}$ is the identity. This is completely analogous to Lemma 15.3, which for the case of automata over strings gives a one-to-one correspondence up to isomorphism between the Myhill–Nerode relations for A (i.e., the right congruences of finite index refining A) and the DFAs with no inaccessible states accepting A. Here "no inaccessible states" just means that the map $t \mapsto t^{\mathcal{A}}$ is onto.

The Myhill–Nerode Theorem

Recall from Lecture 16 the statement of the Myhill–Nerode theorem: for a set A of strings over a finite alphabet Σ, the following three conditions are equivalent:

(i) A is regular;

(ii) there exists a Myhill–Nerode relation for A;

(iii) the relation $\equiv_A$ is of finite index, where

$$x \equiv_A y \stackrel{\text{def}}{\Longleftrightarrow} \forall z \in \Sigma^* \ (xz \in A \Longleftrightarrow yz \in A).$$

Recall that *finite index* means finitely many equivalence classes, and a relation is *Myhill–Nerode for A* if it is a right congruence of finite index refining A.

This theorem generalizes in a natural way to automata over terms. Define a *context* to be a term in $T_{\Sigma \cup \{x\}}$, where x is a new symbol of arity 0. For a context u and ground term $t \in T_\Sigma$, denote by $\mathbf{s}_t^x(u)$ the term in T_Σ obtained by substituting t for all occurrences of x in u. Formally,

$$\mathbf{s}_t^x(x) \stackrel{\text{def}}{=} t,$$
$$\mathbf{s}_t^x(ft_1 \cdots t_n) \stackrel{\text{def}}{=} f\mathbf{s}_t^x(t_1) \cdots \mathbf{s}_t^x(t_n).$$

As usual, the last line includes the case of constants:

$$\mathbf{s}_t^x(c) \stackrel{\text{def}}{=} c.$$

Let Σ be a signature consisting of finitely many function symbols and a single unary relation symbol R. For a given $A \subseteq T_\Sigma$ and ground terms $s, t \in T_\Sigma$, define

$$s \equiv_A t \overset{\text{def}}{\Longleftrightarrow} \text{ for all contexts } u, \; \mathbf{s}_s^x(u) \in A \Longleftrightarrow \mathbf{s}_t^x(u) \in A.$$

It is not difficult to argue that $\equiv_A$ is a congruence on $T_\Sigma(A)$ (Miscellaneous Exercise 68).

Theorem D.3   **(Myhill–Nerode theorem for term automata)**   *Let $A \subseteq T_\Sigma$. Let $T_\Sigma(A)$ denote the term algebra over Σ in which R is interpreted as the unary relation A. The following statements are equivalent:*

(i) A is regular;

(i′) $T_\Sigma(A)$ has a finite homomorphic image;

(ii) there exists a congruence of finite index on $T_\Sigma(A)$;

(iii) the relation $\equiv_A$ is of finite index.

Proof. We have already observed (Lemma C.11) that to say A is regular (i.e., accepted by a term automaton) is just another way of saying that $T_\Sigma(A)$ has a finite homomorphic image. Thus (i) and (i′) are equivalent.

(i′) $\Rightarrow$ (ii)   If $T_\Sigma(A)$ has a finite homomorphic image under epimorphism σ, then the kernel of σ is of finite index, since its congruence classes are in one-to-one correspondence with the elements of the homomorphic image.

(ii) $\Rightarrow$ (iii)   Let $\equiv$ be any congruence on $T_\Sigma(A)$. We show that $\equiv$ refines $\equiv_A$; therefore, $\equiv_A$ is of finite index if $\equiv$ is. Suppose $s \equiv t$. It follows by a straightforward inductive argument using Definition D.1(i) that for any context u, $\mathbf{s}_s^x(u) \equiv \mathbf{s}_t^x(u)$; then by Definition D.1(ii), $\mathbf{s}_s^x(u) \in A$ iff $\mathbf{s}_t^x(u) \in A$. Since the context u was arbitrary, $s \equiv_A t$.

(iii) $\Rightarrow$ (i′)   Since $\equiv_A$ is a congruence, it is the kernel of an epimorphism obtained by the quotient construction. Since $\equiv_A$ is of finite index, the quotient algebra is finite and therefore a finite homomorphic image of $T_\Sigma(A)$.   □

As in Lecture 16, the quotient of $T_\Sigma(A)$ by $\equiv_A$ gives the minimal homomorphic image of $T_\Sigma(A)$; and for any other homomorphic image $\mathcal{B}$, there is a unique homomorphism $\mathcal{B} \to T_\Sigma(A)/{\equiv_A}$.

Historical Notes

Thatcher and Wright [119] generalized finite automata on strings to finite automata on terms and developed the algebraic connection. The more general version of the Myhill–Nerode theorem (Theorem D.3) is in some sense an inevitable consequence of Myhill and Nerode's work [91, 94] since according to Thatcher and Wright, "conventional finite automata theory goes through for the generalization—and it goes through quite neatly" [119]. The first explicit mention of the equivalence of the term analogs of (i) and (ii) in the statement of the Myhill–Nerode theorem seems to be by Brainerd [13, 14] and Eilenberg and Wright [34], although the latter claim that their paper "contains nothing that is essentially new, except perhaps for a point of view" [34]. A relation on terms analogous to $\equiv_A$ was defined and clause (iii) added explicitly by Arbib and Give'on [5, Definition 2.13], although it is also essentially implicit in work of Brainerd [13, 14].

Good general references are Gécseg and Steinby [42] and Englefriet [35].

Lecture 17

Two-Way Finite Automata

Two-way finite automata are similar to the machines we have been studying, except that they can read the input string in either direction. We think of them as having a *read head*, which can move left or right over the input string. Like ordinary finite automata, they have a finite set Q of *states* and can be either deterministic (2DFA) or nondeterministic (2NFA).

Although these automata appear much more powerful than one-way finite automata, in reality they are equivalent in the sense that they only accept regular sets. We will prove this result using the Myhill–Nerode theorem.

We think of the symbols of the input string as occupying cells of a finite tape, one symbol per cell. The input string is enclosed in left and right endmarkers $\vdash$ and $\dashv$, which are not elements of the input alphabet Σ. The read head may not move outside of the endmarkers.

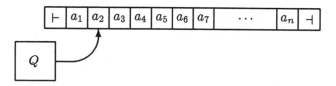

Informally, the machine starts in its start state s with its read head pointing to the left endmarker. At any point in time, the machine is in some state q with its read head scanning some tape cell containing an input symbol a_i or one of the endmarkers. Based on its current state and the symbol occupying the tape cell it is currently scanning, it moves its read head either left or right one cell and enters a new state. It *accepts* by entering a special accept state t and *rejects* by entering a special reject state r. The machine's action on a particular state and symbol is determined by a transition function δ that is part of the specification of the machine.

Example 17.1   Here is an informal description of a 2DFA accepting the set

$$A = \{x \in \{a, b\}^* \mid \#a(x) \text{ is a multiple of 3 and } \#b(x) \text{ is even}\}.$$

The machine starts in its start state scanning the left endmarker. It scans left to right over the input, counting the number of a's mod 3 and ignoring the b's. When it reaches the right endmarker $\dashv$, if the number of a's it has seen is not a multiple of 3, it enters its reject state, thereby rejecting the input—the input string x is not in the set A, since the first condition is not satisfied. Otherwise it scans right to left over the input, counting the number of b's mod 2 and ignoring the a's. When it reaches the left endmarker $\vdash$ again, if the number of b's it has seen is odd, it enters its reject state; otherwise, it enters its accept state.   □

Unlike ordinary finite automata, a 2DFA needs only a single accept state and a single reject state. We can think of it as halting immediately when it enters one of these two states, although formally it keeps running but remains in the accept or reject state. The machine need not read the entire input before accepting or rejecting. Indeed, it need not ever accept or reject at all, but may loop infinitely without ever entering its accept or reject state.

Formal Definition of 2DFA

Formally, a 2DFA is an octuple

$$M = (Q, \Sigma, \vdash, \dashv, \delta, s, t, r),$$

where

- Q is a finite set (the *states*),

- Σ is a finite set (the *input alphabet*),

- $\vdash$ is the *left endmarker*, $\vdash \notin \Sigma$,

- $\dashv$ is the *right endmarker*, $\dashv \notin \Sigma$,

- $\delta : Q \times (\Sigma \cup \{\vdash, \dashv\}) \to (Q \times \{L, R\})$ is the *transition function* (L, R stand for left and right, respectively),

- $s \in Q$ is the *start state*,

- $t \in Q$ is the *accept state*, and

- $r \in Q$ is the *reject state*, $r \neq t$,

such that for all states q,

$$\begin{aligned}
\delta(q, \vdash) &= (u, R) \quad \text{for some } u \in Q, \\
\delta(q, \dashv) &= (v, L) \quad \text{for some } v \in Q,
\end{aligned} \tag{17.1}$$

and for all symbols $b \in \Sigma \cup \{\vdash\}$,

$$\begin{aligned}
\delta(t, b) &= (t, R), & \delta(r, b) &= (r, R), \\
\delta(t, \dashv) &= (t, L), & \delta(r, \dashv) &= (r, L).
\end{aligned} \tag{17.2}$$

Intuitively, the function δ takes a state and a symbol as arguments and returns a new state and a direction to move the head. If $\delta(p, b) = (q, d)$, then whenever the machine is in state p and scanning a tape cell containing symbol b, it moves its head one cell in the direction d and enters state q. The restrictions (17.1) prevent the machine from ever moving outside the input area. The restrictions (17.2) say that once the machine enters its accept or reject state, it stays in that state and moves its head all the way to the right of the tape. The octuple is not a legal 2DFA if its transition function δ does not satisfy these conditions.

Example 17.2   Here is a formal description of the 2DFA described informally in Example 17.1 above.

$$\begin{aligned}
Q &= \{q_0, q_1, q_2, p_0, p_1, t, r\}, \\
\Sigma &= \{a, b\}.
\end{aligned}$$

The start, accept, and reject states are q_0, t, and r, respectively. The transition function δ is given by the following table:

	$\vdash$	a	b	$\dashv$
q_0	(q_0, R)	(q_1, R)	(q_0, R)	(p_0, L)
q_1	$-$	(q_2, R)	(q_1, R)	(r, L)
q_2	$-$	(q_0, R)	(q_2, R)	(r, L)
p_0	(t, R)	(p_0, L)	(p_1, L)	$-$
p_1	(r, R)	(p_1, L)	(p_0, L)	$-$
t	(t, R)	(t, R)	(t, R)	(t, L)
r	(r, R)	(r, R)	(r, R)	(r, L)

The entries marked $-$ will never occur in any computation, so it doesn't matter what we put here. The machine is in states q_0, q_1, or q_2 on the first pass over the input from left to right; it is in state q_i if the number of a's it has seen so far is i mod 3. The machine is in state p_0 or p_1 on the second pass over the input from right to left, the index indicating the parity of the number of b's it has seen so far.   □

Configurations and Acceptance

Fix an input $x \in \Sigma^*$, say $x = a_1 a_2 \cdots a_n$. Let $a_0 = \vdash$ and $a_{n+1} = \dashv$. Then

$$a_0 a_1 a_2 \cdots a_n a_{n+1} = \vdash x \dashv.$$

A *configuration* of the machine on input x is a pair (q, i) such that $q \in Q$ and $0 \le i \le n + 1$. Informally, the pair (q, i) gives a current state and current position of the read head. The *start configuration* is $(s, 0)$, meaning that the machine is in its start state s and scanning the left endmarker.

A binary relation $\xrightarrow[x]{1}$, the *next configuration relation*, is defined on configurations as follows:

$$\delta(p, a_i) = (q, L) \Rightarrow (p, i) \xrightarrow[x]{1} (q, i - 1),$$
$$\delta(p, a_i) = (q, R) \Rightarrow (p, i) \xrightarrow[x]{1} (q, i + 1).$$

The relation $\xrightarrow[x]{1}$ describes one step of the machine on input x. We define the relations $\xrightarrow[x]{n}$ inductively, $n \ge 0$:

- $(p, i) \xrightarrow[x]{0} (p, i)$; and

- if $(p, i) \xrightarrow[x]{n} (q, j)$ and $(q, j) \xrightarrow[x]{1} (u, k)$, then $(p, i) \xrightarrow[x]{n+1} (u, k)$.

The relation $\xrightarrow[x]{n}$ is just the n-fold composition of $\xrightarrow[x]{1}$. The relations $\xrightarrow[x]{n}$ are functions; that is, for any configuration (p, i), there is exactly one configuration (q, j) such that $(p, i) \xrightarrow[x]{n} (q, j)$. Now define

$$(p, i) \xrightarrow[x]{*} (q, j) \stackrel{\text{def}}{\Longleftrightarrow} \exists n \ge 0 \ (p, i) \xrightarrow[x]{n} (q, j).$$

Note that the definitions of these relations depend on the input x. The machine is said to *accept* the input x if

$$(s, 0) \xrightarrow[x]{*} (t, i) \quad \text{for some } i.$$

In other words, the machine enters its accept state at some point. The machine is said to *reject* the input x if

$$(s, 0) \xrightarrow[x]{*} (r, i) \quad \text{for some } i.$$

In other words, the machine enters its reject state at some point. It cannot both accept and reject input x by our assumption that $t \ne r$ and by properties (17.2). The machine is said to *halt* on input x if it either accepts x or rejects x. Note that this is a purely mathematical definition—the machine doesn't really grind to a halt! It is possible that the machine neither accepts nor rejects x, in which case it is said to *loop* on x. The set $L(M)$ is defined to be the set of strings accepted by M.

Example 17.3 The 2DFA described in Example 17.2 goes through the following sequence of configurations on input *aababbb*, leading to acceptance:

$$(q_0, 0),\ (q_0, 1),\ (q_1, 2),\ (q_2, 3),\ (q_2, 4),\ (q_0, 5),\ (q_0, 6),\ (q_0, 7),\ (q_0, 8),$$
$$(p_0, 7),\ (p_1, 6),\ (p_0, 5),\ (p_1, 4),\ (p_1, 3),\ (p_0, 2),\ (p_0, 1),\ (p_0, 0),\ (t, 1).$$

It goes through the following sequence of configurations on input *aababa*, leading to rejection:

$$(q_0, 0),\ (q_0, 1),\ (q_1, 2),\ (q_2, 3),\ (q_2, 4),\ (q_0, 5),\ (q_0, 6),\ (q_1, 7),\ (r, 6).$$

It goes through the following sequence of configurations on input *aababb*, leading to rejection:

$$(q_0, 0),\ (q_0, 1),\ (q_1, 2),\ (q_2, 3),\ (q_2, 4),\ (q_0, 5),\ (q_0, 6),\ (q_0, 7),$$
$$(p_0, 6),\ (p_1, 5),\ (p_0, 4),\ (p_0, 3),\ (p_1, 2),\ (p_1, 1),\ (p_1, 0),\ (r, 1). \qquad \square$$

Lecture 18

2DFAs and Regular Sets

In this lecture we show that 2DFAs are no more powerful than ordinary DFAs. Here is the idea. Consider a long input string broken up in an arbitrary place into two substrings xz. How much information about x can the machine carry across the boundary from x into z? Since the machine is two-way, it can cross the boundary between x and z several times. Each time it crosses the boundary moving from right to left, that is, from z into x, it does so in some state q. When it crosses the boundary again moving from left to right (if ever), it comes out of x in some state, say p. Now if it ever goes into x in the future in state q again, it will emerge again in state p, because its future action is completely determined by its current configuration (state and head position). Moreover, the state p depends only on q and x. We will write $T_x(q) = p$ to denote this relationship. We can keep track of all such information by means of a finite table

$$T_x : (Q \cup \{\bullet\}) \to (Q \cup \{\perp\}),$$

where Q is the set of states of the 2DFA M, and $\bullet$ and $\perp$ are two other objects not in Q whose purpose is described below.

On input xz, the machine M starts in its start state scanning the left endmarker. As it computes, it moves its read head. The head may eventually cross the boundary moving left to right from x into z. The first time it does so (if ever), it is in some state, which we will call $T_x(\bullet)$ (this is the purpose of $\bullet$). The machine may *never* emerge from x; in this case we write $T_x(\bullet) = \perp$

(this is the purpose of $\perp$). The state $T_x(\bullet)$ gives some information about x, but only a finite amount of information, since there are only finitely many possibilities for $T_x(\bullet)$. Note also that $T_x(\bullet)$ depends only on x and not on z: if the input were xw instead of xz, the first time the machine passed the boundary from x into w, it would also be in state $T_x(\bullet)$, because its action up to that point is determined only by x; it hasn't seen anything to the right of the boundary yet.

If $T_x(\bullet) = \perp$, M must be in an infinite loop inside x and will never accept or reject, by our assumption about moving all the way to the right endmarker whenever it accepts or rejects.

Suppose that the machine does emerge from x into z. It may wander around in z for a while, then later may move back into x from right to left in state q. If this happens, then it will either

- eventually emerge from x again in some state p, in which case we define $T_x(q) = p$; or

- never emerge, in which case we define $T_x(q) = \perp$.

Again, note that $T_x(q)$ depends only on x and q and not on z. If the machine entered x from the right on input xw in state q, then it would emerge again in state $T_x(q)$ (or never emerge, if $T_x(q) = \perp$), because M is deterministic, and its behavior while inside x is completely determined by x and the state it entered x in.

If we write down $T_x(q)$ for every state q along with $T_x(\bullet)$, this gives all the information about x one could ever hope to carry across the boundary from x to z. One can imagine an agent sitting to the right of the boundary between x and z, trying to obtain information about x. All it is allowed to do is observe the state $T_x(\bullet)$ the first time the machine emerges from x (if ever) and later send probes into x in various states q to see what state $T_x(q)$ the machine comes out in (if at all). If y is another string such that $T_y = T_x$, then x and y will be indistinguishable from the agent's point of view.

Now note that there are only finitely many possible tables

$$T : (Q \cup \{\bullet\}) \to (Q \cup \{\perp\}),$$

namely $(k+1)^{k+1}$, where k is the size of Q. Thus there is only a finite amount of information about x that can be passed across the boundary to the right of x, and it is all encoded in the table T_x.

Note also that if $T_x = T_y$ and M accepts xz, then M accepts yz. This is because the sequence of states the machine is in as it passes the boundary between x and z (or between y and z) in either direction is completely determined by the table $T_x = T_y$ and z. To accept xz, the machine must at some point be scanning the right endmarker in its accept state t. Since the sequence of states along the boundary is the same and the action when the machine is scanning z is the same, this also must happen on input yz.

Now we can use the Myhill–Nerode theorem to show that $L(M)$ is regular. We have just argued that

$$T_x = T_y \implies \forall z \ (M \text{ accepts } xz \iff M \text{ accepts } yz)$$
$$\iff \forall z \ (xz \in L(M) \iff yz \in L(M))$$
$$\iff x \equiv_{L(M)} y,$$

where $\equiv_{L(M)}$ is the relation first defined in Eq. (16.1) of Lecture 16. Thus if two strings have the same table, then they are equivalent under $\equiv_{L(M)}$. Since there are only finitely many tables, the relation $\equiv_{L(M)}$ has only finitely many equivalence classes, at most one for each table; therefore, $\equiv_{L(M)}$ is of finite index. By the Myhill–Nerode theorem, $L(M)$ is a regular set.

Constructing a DFA

The argument above may be a bit unsatisfying, since it does not explicitly construct a DFA equivalent to a given 2DFA M. We can easily do so, however. Intuitively, we can build a DFA whose states correspond to the tables.

Formally, define

$$x \equiv y \stackrel{\text{def}}{\iff} T_x = T_y.$$

That is, call two strings in Σ^* equivalent if they have the same table. There are only finitely many equivalence classes, at most one for each table; thus $\equiv$ is of finite index. We can also show the following:

(i) The table T_{xa} is uniquely determined by T_x and a; that is, if $T_x = T_y$, then $T_{xa} = T_{ya}$. This says that $\equiv$ is a right congruence.

(ii) Whether or not x is accepted by M is completely determined by T_x; that is, if $T_x = T_y$, then either both x and y are accepted by M or neither is. This says that $\equiv$ refines $L(M)$.

These observations together say that $\equiv$ is a Myhill–Nerode relation for $L(M)$. Using the construction $\equiv \mapsto M_\equiv$ described in Lecture 15, we can obtain a DFA for $L(M)$ explicitly.

To show (i), we show how to construct T_{xa} from T_x and a.

- If $p_0, p_1, \ldots, p_k, q_0, q_1, \ldots, q_k \in Q$ such that $\delta(p_i, a) = (q_i, L)$ and $T_x(q_i) = p_{i+1}, 0 \le i \le k-1$, and $\delta(p_k, a) = (q_k, R)$, then $T_{xa}(p_0) = q_k$.

- If $p_0, p_1, \ldots, p_k, q_0, q_1, \ldots, q_{k-1} \in Q$ such that $\delta(p_i, a) = (q_i, L)$ and $T_x(q_i) = p_{i+1}, 0 \le i \le k-1$, and $p_k = p_i, i < k$, then $T_{xa}(p_0) = \bot$.

- If $p_0, p_1, \ldots, p_k, q_0, q_1, \ldots, q_k \in Q$ such that $\delta(p_i, a) = (q_i, L), 0 < i \le k$, $T_x(q_i) = p_{i+1}, 0 \le i \le k-1$, and $T_x(q_k) = \bot$, then $T_{xa}(p_0) = \bot$.

- If $T_x(\bullet) = \bot$, then $T_{xa}(\bullet) = \bot$.

- If $T_x(\bullet) = p$, then $T_{xa}(\bullet) = T_{xa}(p)$.

For (ii), suppose $T_x = T_y$ and consider the sequence of states M is in as it crosses the boundary in either direction between the input string and the right endmarker $\dashv$. This sequence is the same on input x as it is on input y, since it is completely determined by the table. Both strings x and y are accepted iff this sequence contains the accept state t.

We have shown that the relation $\equiv$ is a Myhill–Nerode relation for $L(M)$, where M is an arbitrary 2DFA. The construction $\equiv \mapsto M_\equiv$ of Lecture 15 gives a DFA equivalent to M. Recall that in that construction, the states of the DFA correspond in a one-to-one fashion with the $\equiv$-classes; and here, each $\equiv$-class $[x]$ corresponds to a table $T_x : (Q \cup \{\bullet\}) \to (Q \cup \{\bot\})$.

If we wanted to, we could build a DFA M' directly from the tables:

$$Q' \stackrel{\text{def}}{=} \{T : (Q \cup \{\bullet\}) \to (Q \cup \{\bot\})\},$$
$$s' \stackrel{\text{def}}{=} T_\epsilon,$$
$$\delta'(T_x, a) \stackrel{\text{def}}{=} T_{xa},$$
$$F' \stackrel{\text{def}}{=} \{T_x \mid x \in L(M)\}.$$

The transition function δ' is well defined because of property (i), and $T_x \in F'$ iff $x \in L(M)$ by property (ii). As usual, one can prove by induction on $|y|$ that

$$\widehat{\delta}'(T_x, y) = T_{xy};$$

then

$$x \in L(M') \iff \widehat{\delta}'(s', x) \in F'$$
$$\iff \widehat{\delta}'(T_\epsilon, x) \in F'$$
$$\iff T_x \in F'$$
$$\iff x \in L(M).$$

Thus $L(M') = L(M)$.

Another proof, due to Vardi [122], is given in Miscellaneous Exercise 61.

Historical Notes

Two-way finite automata were first studied by Rabin and Scott [102] and Shepherdson [114]. Vardi [122] gave a shorter proof of equivalence to DFAs (Miscellaneous Exercise 61).

Lecture 19

Context-Free Grammars and Languages

You may have seen something like the following used to give a formal definition of a language. This notation is sometimes called BNF for *Backus–Naur form*.

$$\text{<stmt>} ::= \text{<if-stmt>} \mid \text{<while-stmt>} \mid \text{<begin-stmt>} \mid \text{<assg-stmt>}$$

$$\text{<if-stmt>} ::= \textbf{if } \text{<bool-expr>} \textbf{ then } \text{<stmt>} \textbf{ else } \text{<stmt>}$$

$$\text{<while-stmt>} ::= \textbf{while } \text{<bool-expr>} \textbf{ do } \text{<stmt>}$$

$$\text{<begin-stmt>} ::= \textbf{begin } \text{<stmt-list>} \textbf{ end}$$

$$\text{<stmt-list>} ::= \text{<stmt>} \mid \text{<stmt>} \text{ ; <stmt-list>}$$

$$\text{<assg-stmt>} ::= \text{<var>} := \text{<arith-expr>}$$

$$\text{<bool-expr>} ::= \text{<arith-expr><compare-op><arith-expr>}$$

$$\text{<compare-op>} ::= \; < \mid > \mid \leq \mid \geq \mid = \mid \neq$$

$$\text{<arith-expr>} ::= \text{<var>} \mid \text{<const>} \mid (\text{<arith-expr><arith-op><arith-expr>})$$

$$\text{<arith-op>} ::= + \mid - \mid * \mid /$$

$$\text{<const>} ::= 0 \mid 1 \mid 2 \mid 3 \mid 4 \mid 5 \mid 6 \mid 7 \mid 8 \mid 9$$

$$\text{<var>} ::= a \mid b \mid c \mid \cdots \mid x \mid y \mid z$$

This is an example of a *context-free grammar*. It consists of a finite set of rules defining the set of well-formed expressions in some language; in this example, the syntactically correct programs of a simple PASCAL-like programming language.

For example, the first rule above says that a *statement* is either an *if statement*, a *while statement*, a *begin statement*, or an *assignment statement*. If statements, while statements, begin statements, and assignment statements are described formally by other rules further down. The third rule says that a *while statement* consists of the word **while**, followed by a Boolean expression, followed by the word **do**, followed by a statement.

The objects <xxx> are called *nonterminal symbols*. Each nonterminal symbol generates a set of strings over a finite alphabet Σ in a systematic way described formally below. For example, the nonterminal <arith-expr> above generates the set of syntactically correct arithmetic expressions in this language. The strings corresponding to the nonterminal <xxx> are generated using rules with <xxx> on the left-hand side. The alternatives on the right-hand side, separated by vertical bars |, describe different ways strings corresponding to <xxx> can be generated. These alternatives may involve other nonterminals <yyy>, which must be further eliminated by applying rules with <yyy> on the left-hand side. The rules can be recursive; for example, the rule above for <stmt-list> says that a statement list is either a statement or a statement followed by a semicolon (;) followed by a statement list.

The string

$$\textbf{while } x \leq y \textbf{ do begin } x := (x+1)\,; y := (y-1) \textbf{ end} \qquad (19.1)$$

is generated by the nonterminal <stmt> in the grammar above. To show this, we can give a sequence of expressions called *sentential forms* starting from <stmt> and ending with the string (19.1) such that each sentential form is derived from the previous by an application of one of the rules. Each application consists of replacing some nonterminal symbol <xxx> in the sentential form with one of the alternatives on the right-hand side of a rule for <xxx>. Here are the first few sentential forms in a derivation of (19.1):

<stmt>

<while-stmt>

while <bool-expr> **do** <stmt>

while <arith-expr><compare-op><arith-expr> **do** <stmt>

while <var><compare-op><arith-expr> **do** <stmt>

while <var> $\leq$ <arith-expr> **do** <stmt>

while <var> $\leq$ <var> **do** <stmt>

while $x \leq$ <var> **do** <stmt>

while $x \leq y$ **do** <stmt>

while $x \leq y$ **do** <begin-stmt>

. . .

Applying different rules will yield different results. For example, the string

begin if $z = (x + 3)$ **then** $y := z$ **else** $y := x$ **end**

can also be generated. The set of all strings not containing any nonterminals generated by the grammar is called the *language* generated by the grammar. In general, this set of strings may be infinite, even if the set of rules is finite.

There may also be several different derivations of the same string. A grammar is said to be *unambiguous* if this cannot happen. The grammar given above is unambiguous.

We will give a general definition of context-free grammars (CFGs) and the languages they generate. The language (subset of Σ^*) generated by the context-free grammar G is denoted $L(G)$. A subset of Σ^* is called a *context-free language* (CFL) if it is $L(G)$ for some CFG G.

CFLs are good for describing infinite sets of strings in a finite way. They are particularly useful in computer science for describing the syntax of programming languages, well-formed arithmetic expressions, well-nested begin-end blocks, strings of balanced parentheses, and so on.

All regular sets are CFLs (Homework 5, Exercise 1), but not necessarily vice versa. The following are examples of CFLs that are not regular:

- $\{a^n b^n \mid n \geq 0\}$;

- $\{$palindromes over $\{a, b\}\} = \{x \in \{a, b\}^* \mid x = \mathbf{rev}\ x\}$; and

- $\{$balanced strings of parentheses$\}$.

Not all sets are CFLs; for example, the set $\{a^n b^n a^n \mid n \geq 0\}$ is not. We can prove this formally using a pumping lemma for CFLs analogous to the pumping lemma for regular sets. We will discuss the pumping lemma for CFLs in Lecture 22.

Pushdown Automata (PDAs): A Preview

A *pushdown automaton* (PDA) is like a finite automaton, except that in addition to its finite control, it has a *stack* or *pushdown store*, which it can use to record a potentially unbounded amount of information.

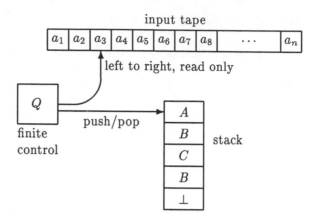

The input head is read-only and may only move right. The machine can store information on the stack in a last-in-first-out (LIFO) fashion. It can *push* symbols onto the top of the stack or *pop* them off the top of the stack. It may not read down into the stack without popping the top symbols off, in which case they are lost.

We will define these machines formally in Lecture 23 and prove that the class of languages accepted by nondeterministic PDAs is exactly the class of CFLs.

Formal Definition of CFGs and CFLs

Formally, a *context-free grammar* (CFG) is a quadruple

$$G = (N, \Sigma, P, S),$$

where

- N is a finite set (the *nonterminal symbols*),

- Σ is a finite set (the *terminal symbols*) disjoint from N,

- P is a finite subset of $N \times (N \cup \Sigma)^*$ (the *productions*), and

- $S \in N$ (the *start symbol*).

We use capital letters $A, B, C, \ldots$ for nonterminals and $a, b, c, \ldots$ for terminal symbols. Strings in $(N \cup \Sigma)^*$ are denoted $\alpha, \beta, \gamma, \ldots$. Instead of writing productions as (A, α), we write $A \to \alpha$. We often use the vertical bar | as in the example above to abbreviate a set of productions with the same left-hand side. For example, instead of writing

$$A \to \alpha_1, \qquad A \to \alpha_2, \qquad A \to \alpha_3,$$

we might write

$$A \to \alpha_1 \mid \alpha_2 \mid \alpha_3.$$

If $\alpha, \beta \in (N \cup \Sigma)^*$, we say that β *is derivable from α in one step* and write

$$\alpha \xrightarrow[G]{1} \beta$$

if β can be obtained from α by replacing some occurrence of a nonterminal A in α with γ, where $A \to \gamma$ is in P; that is, if there exist $\alpha_1, \alpha_2 \in (N \cup \Sigma)^*$ and production $A \to \gamma$ such that

$$\alpha = \alpha_1 A \alpha_2 \quad \text{and} \quad \beta = \alpha_1 \gamma \alpha_2.$$

Let $\xrightarrow[G]{*}$ be the reflexive transitive closure of the relation $\xrightarrow[G]{1}$; that is, define

- $\alpha \xrightarrow[G]{0} \alpha$ for any α,

- $\alpha \xrightarrow[G]{n+1} \beta$ if there exists γ such that $\alpha \xrightarrow[G]{n} \gamma$ and $\gamma \xrightarrow[G]{1} \beta$, and

- $\alpha \xrightarrow[G]{*} \beta$ if $\alpha \xrightarrow[G]{n} \beta$ for some $n \geq 0$.

A string in $(N \cup \Sigma)^*$ derivable from the start symbol S is called a *sentential form*. A sentential form is called a *sentence* if it consists only of terminal symbols; that is, if it is in Σ^*. The *language generated by G*, denoted $L(G)$, is the set of all sentences:

$$L(G) = \{x \in \Sigma^* \mid S \xrightarrow[G]{*} x\}.$$

A subset $B \subseteq \Sigma^*$ is a *context-free language* (CFL) if $B = L(G)$ for some context-free grammar G.

Example 19.1 The nonregular set $\{a^n b^n \mid n \geq 0\}$ is a CFL. It is generated by the grammar

$$S \to aSb \mid \epsilon,$$

where ϵ is the null string. More precisely, $G = (N, \Sigma, P, S)$, where

$$N = \{S\},$$
$$\Sigma = \{a, b\},$$
$$P = \{S \to aSb, \ S \to \epsilon\}.$$

Here is a derivation of $a^3 b^3$ in G:

$$S \xrightarrow[G]{1} aSb \xrightarrow[G]{1} aaSbb \xrightarrow[G]{1} aaaSbbb \xrightarrow[G]{1} aaabbb.$$

The first three steps apply the production $S \to aSb$ and the last applies the production $S \to \epsilon$. Thus

$$S \xrightarrow[G]{4} aaabbb.$$

One can show by induction on n that

$$S \xrightarrow[G]{n+1} a^n b^n,$$

so all strings of the form $a^n b^n$ are in $L(G)$; conversely, the only strings in $L(G)$ are of the form $a^n b^n$, as can be shown by induction on the length of the derivation.   □

Example 19.2   The nonregular set

$$\{\text{palindromes over } \{a,b\}^*\} = \{x \in \{a,b\}^* \mid x = \mathbf{rev}\, x\}$$

is a CFL generated by the grammar

$$S \rightarrow aSa \mid bSb \mid a \mid b \mid \epsilon.$$

The first two productions generate any number of balanced a's or b's at the outer ends of the string, working from the outside in. The last three productions are used to finish the derivation. The productions $S \rightarrow a$ and $S \rightarrow b$ are used to generate an odd-length palindrome with an a or b, respectively, as the middle symbol; and the production $S \rightarrow \epsilon$ is used to generate an even-length palindrome.   □

Historical Notes

Context-free grammars and languages were introduced by Chomsky [17, 18, 20], although they were foreshadowed by the systems of Post [100] and Markov [83]. Backus–Naur form was used to specify the syntax of programming languages by Backus [7] and Naur [93].

Lecture 20

Balanced Parentheses

Intuitively, a string of parentheses is *balanced* if each left parenthesis has a matching right parenthesis and the matched pairs are well nested. The set PAREN of balanced strings of parentheses [ ] is the prototypical context-free language and plays a pivotal role in the theory of CFLs.

The set PAREN is generated by the grammar

$$S \rightarrow [S] \mid SS \mid \epsilon.$$

This is not obvious, so let's give a proof. First we need a formal characterization of *balanced*. To avoid confusing notation, we'll use

$$L(x) \overset{\text{def}}{=} \#[(x) = \text{the number of left parentheses in } x,$$

$$R(x) \overset{\text{def}}{=} \#](x) = \text{the number of right parentheses in } x.$$

We will define a string x of parentheses to be *balanced* if and only if

(i) $L(x) = R(x)$, and

(ii) for all prefixes y of x, $L(y) \geq R(y)$.

(Recall that a *prefix* of x is a string y such that $x = yz$ for some z.) To see that this definition correctly captures the intuitive notion of *balanced*, note that property (i) says that there must be the same number of left parentheses as right parentheses, which must certainly be true if x is balanced; and property (ii) says that for any way of partitioning x into yz, there cannot be more right parentheses in y than left parentheses, because right parentheses can only match left parentheses to the left of them. Thus (i) and (ii) are certainly necessary conditions for a string to be balanced. To see that they are sufficient, draw the graph of the function $L(y) - R(y)$ as y ranges over prefixes of x:

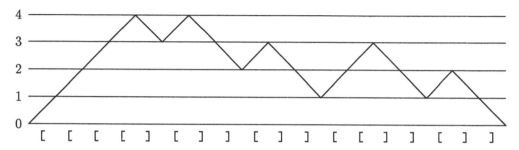

Property (i) says that the graph ends with value 0 (i.e., $L(x) - R(x) = 0$), and (ii) says that it never dips below 0 on the way across. If the graph satisfies these two properties, then given any parenthesis in the string, one can find the matching parenthesis by shooting upward and ricocheting off the graph twice.

Thus we will take (i) and (ii) as our formal definition of balanced strings of parentheses and prove that the given grammar generates exactly the set of such strings, no more and no less.

Theorem 20.1 *Let G be the CFG*

$$S \rightarrow [S] \mid SS \mid \epsilon.$$

Then

$$L(G) = \{x \in \{[,]\}^* \mid x \text{ satisfies (i) and (ii)}\}.$$

Proof. We show the inclusion in both directions. Both arguments will be by induction, but induction on different things.

First we show the forward inclusion: if $S \xrightarrow[G]{*} x$, then x satisfies (i) and (ii). Thus any string generated by G is balanced.

We would like to use induction on the length of the derivation of x from S, but since the intermediate sentential forms in this derivation will contain nonterminals, we need to strengthen our induction hypothesis to allow nonterminals. Thus we will actually show that for any $\alpha \in (N \cup \Sigma)^*$, if $S \xrightarrow[G]{*} \alpha$, then α satisfies (i) and (ii). This will be proved by induction on the length of the derivation $S \xrightarrow[G]{*} \alpha$.

Basis

If $S \xrightarrow[G]{0} \alpha$, then $\alpha = S$ by definition of the relation $\xrightarrow[G]{0}$. But the sentential form S satisfies (i) and (ii) trivially.

Induction step

Suppose $S \xrightarrow[G]{n+1} \alpha$. Let β be the sentential form immediately preceding α in the derivation. Then

$$S \xrightarrow[G]{n} \beta \xrightarrow[G]{1} \alpha.$$

By the induction hypothesis, β satisfies (i) and (ii). There are now three cases, corresponding to the three productions in the grammar that could have been applied in the last step to derive α from β. We will show in each case that properties (i) and (ii) are preserved.

The first two cases, corresponding to productions $S \rightarrow \epsilon$ and $S \rightarrow SS$, are easy because neither production changes the number or order of parentheses. In either case there exist $\beta_1, \beta_2 \in (N \cup \Sigma)^*$ such that

$$\beta = \beta_1 S \beta_2 \quad \text{and} \quad \alpha = \begin{cases} \beta_1 \beta_2 & \text{if } S \rightarrow \epsilon \text{ was applied,} \\ \beta_1 SS \beta_2 & \text{if } S \rightarrow SS \text{ was applied;} \end{cases}$$

and in either case α satisfies (i) and (ii) iff β does.

If the last production applied was $S \rightarrow [S]$, then there exist $\beta_1, \beta_2 \in (N \cup \Sigma)^*$ such that

$$\beta = \beta_1 S \beta_2 \quad \text{and} \quad \alpha = \beta_1 [S] \beta_2,$$

and by the induction hypothesis (i) and (ii) hold of β. Then

$$\begin{aligned} L(\alpha) &= L(\beta) + 1 \\ &= R(\beta) + 1 \quad \text{since } \beta \text{ satisfies (i)} \\ &= R(\alpha), \end{aligned}$$

thus (i) holds of α. To show that (ii) holds of α, let γ be an arbitrary prefix of α. We want to show that $L(\gamma) \geq R(\gamma)$. Either

- γ is a prefix of β_1, in which case γ is a prefix of β, so (ii) holds for the prefix γ by the induction hypothesis; or

- γ is a prefix of $\beta_1 [S$ but not of β_1, in which case

$$L(\gamma) = L(\beta_1) + 1$$
$$\geq R(\beta_1) + 1 \quad \text{induction hypothesis, since } \beta_1 \text{ is a prefix of } \beta$$
$$> R(\beta_1)$$
$$= R(\gamma); \quad \text{or}$$

- $\gamma = \beta_1 [S] \delta$, where δ is a prefix of β_2, in which case

$$L(\gamma) = L(\beta_1 S \delta) + 1$$
$$\geq R(\beta_1 S \delta) + 1 \quad \text{induction hypothesis}$$
$$= R(\gamma).$$

Thus in all cases $L(\gamma) \geq R(\gamma)$. Since γ was arbitrary, (ii) holds of α. This concludes the inductive proof that if $S \xrightarrow[G]{*} x$, then x is balanced.

Now we wish to show the other direction: if x is balanced, then $S \xrightarrow[G]{*} x$. This is done by induction on $|x|$. Assume that x satisfies (i) and (ii).

Basis

If $|x| = 0$, we have $x = \epsilon$ and $S \xrightarrow[G]{*} x$ in one step using the production $S \to \epsilon$.

Induction step

If $|x| > 0$, we break the argument into two cases: either

(a) there exists a *proper* prefix y of x (one such that $0 < |y| < |x|$) satisfying (i) and (ii), or

(b) no such prefix exists.

In case (a), we have $x = yz$ for some z, $0 < |z| < |x|$, and z satisfies (i) and (ii) as well:

$$L(z) = L(x) - L(y) = R(x) - R(y) = R(z),$$

and for any prefix w of z,

$$L(w) = L(yw) - L(y)$$
$$\geq R(yw) - R(y) \quad \text{since } yw \text{ is a prefix of } x \text{ and } L(y) = R(y)$$
$$= R(w).$$

By the induction hypothesis, $S \xrightarrow[G]{*} y$ and $S \xrightarrow[G]{*} z$. Then we can derive x by starting with the production $S \to SS$, then deriving y from the first S, then deriving z from the second S:

$$S \xrightarrow[G]{1} SS \xrightarrow[G]{*} yS \xrightarrow[G]{*} yz = x.$$

In case (b), no such y exists. Then $x = [z]$ for some z, and z satisfies (i) and (ii). It satisfies (i) since

$$L(z) = L(x) - 1 = R(x) - 1 = R(z),$$

and it satisfies (ii) since for all nonnull prefixes u of z,

$$L(u) - R(u) = L([u) - 1 - R([u) \geq 0$$

since $L([u) - R([u) \geq 1$ because we are in case (b). By the induction hypothesis, $S \xrightarrow[G]{*} z$. Combining this derivation with the production $S \to [S]$, we get a derivation of x:

$$S \xrightarrow[G]{1} [S] \xrightarrow[G]{*} [z] = x.$$

Thus every string satisfying (i) and (ii) can be derived. $\square$

Lecture 21

Normal Forms

For many applications, it is often helpful to assume that CFGs are in one or another special restricted form. Two of the most useful such forms are *Chomsky normal form* (CNF) and *Greibach normal form* (GNF).

Definition 21.1   A CFG is in *Chomsky normal form* (CNF) if all productions are of the form

$$A \to BC \text{ or } A \to a,$$

where $A, B, C \in N$ and $a \in \Sigma$. A CFG is in *Greibach normal form* (GNF) if all productions are of the form

$$A \to a B_1 B_2 \cdots B_k$$

for some $k \geq 0$, where $A, B_1, \ldots, B_k \in N$ and $a \in \Sigma$. Note that $k = 0$ is allowed, giving productions of the form $A \to a$.   □

For example, the two grammars

$$S \to AB \mid AC \mid SS, \quad C \to SB, \quad A \to [, \quad B \to], \qquad (21.1)$$
$$S \to [B \mid [SB \mid [BS \mid [SBS, \quad B \to] \qquad (21.2)$$

are grammars in Chomsky and Greibach normal form, respectively, for the set of all nonnull strings of balanced parentheses [ ].

No grammar in Chomsky or Greibach form can generate the null string ϵ (Why not?). Apart from this one exception, they are completely general:

Theorem 21.2 *For any CFG G, there is a CFG G' in Chomsky normal form and a CFG G'' in Greibach normal form such that*

$$L(G'') = L(G') = L(G) - \{\epsilon\}.$$

Getting Rid of ϵ- and Unit Productions

To prove Theorem 21.2, we must first show how to get rid of all ϵ-*productions* $A \to \epsilon$ and *unit productions* $A \to B$. These productions are bothersome because they make it hard to determine whether applying a production makes any progress toward deriving a string of terminals. For instance, with unit productions, there can be loops in the derivation, and with ϵ-productions, one can generate very long strings of nonterminals and then erase them all. Without ϵ- or unit productions, every step in the derivation makes demonstrable progress toward the terminal string in the sense that either the sentential form gets strictly longer or a new terminal symbol appears.

We cannot simply throw out the ϵ- and unit productions, because they may be needed to generate some strings in $L(G)$; so before we throw them out, we had better throw in some other productions we can use instead.

Lemma 21.3 *For any CFG $G = (N, \Sigma, P, S)$, there is a CFG G' with no ϵ- or unit productions such that $L(G') = L(G) - \{\epsilon\}$.*

Proof. Let $\widehat{P}$ be the smallest set of productions containing P and closed under the two rules

(a) if $A \to \alpha B \beta$ and $B \to \epsilon$ are in $\widehat{P}$, then $A \to \alpha\beta$ is in $\widehat{P}$; and

(b) if $A \to B$ and $B \to \gamma$ are in $\widehat{P}$, then $A \to \gamma$ is in $\widehat{P}$.

We can construct $\widehat{P}$ inductively from P by adding productions as required to satisfy (a) and (b). Note that only finitely many productions ever get added, since each new right-hand side is a substring of an old right-hand side. Thus $\widehat{P}$ is still finite.

Now let $\widehat{G}$ be the grammar

$$\widehat{G} = (N, \Sigma, \widehat{P}, S).$$

Since $P \subseteq \widehat{P}$, every derivation of G is a derivation of $\widehat{G}$; thus $L(G) \subseteq L(\widehat{G})$. But $L(G) = L(\widehat{G})$, since each new production that was thrown in because of rule (a) or (b) can be simulated in two steps by the two productions that caused it to be thrown in.

Now we show that for nonnull $x \in \Sigma^*$, any derivation $S \xrightarrow[\widehat{G}]{*} x$ of minimum length does not use any ϵ- or unit productions. Thus the ϵ- and unit productions are superfluous and can be deleted from $\widehat{G}$ with impunity.

Let $x \neq \epsilon$ and consider a minimum-length derivation $S \xrightarrow[\widehat{G}]{*} x$. Suppose for a contradiction that an ϵ-production $B \to \epsilon$ is used at some point in the derivation, say

$$S \xrightarrow[\widehat{G}]{*} \gamma B \delta \xrightarrow[\widehat{G}]{1} \gamma \delta \xrightarrow[\widehat{G}]{*} x.$$

One of γ, δ is nonnull, otherwise x would be null, contradicting the assumption that it isn't. Thus that occurrence of B must first have appeared earlier in the derivation when a production of the form $A \to \alpha B \beta$ was applied:

$$S \xrightarrow[\widehat{G}]{m} \eta A \theta \xrightarrow[\widehat{G}]{1} \eta \alpha B \beta \theta \xrightarrow[\widehat{G}]{n} \gamma B \delta \xrightarrow[\widehat{G}]{1} \gamma \delta \xrightarrow[\widehat{G}]{k} x$$

for some $m, n, k \geq 0$. But by rule (a), $A \to \alpha \beta$ is also in $\widehat{P}$, and this production could have been applied at that point instead, giving a strictly shorter derivation of x:

$$S \xrightarrow[\widehat{G}]{m} \eta A \theta \xrightarrow[\widehat{G}]{1} \eta \alpha \beta \theta \xrightarrow[\widehat{G}]{n} \gamma \delta \xrightarrow[\widehat{G}]{k} x.$$

This contradicts our assumption that the derivation was of minimum length.

A similar argument shows that unit productions do not appear in minimum-length derivations in $\widehat{G}$. Let $x \neq \epsilon$ and consider a derivation $S \xrightarrow[\widehat{G}]{*} x$ of minimum length. Suppose a unit production $A \to B$ is used at some point, say

$$S \xrightarrow[\widehat{G}]{*} \alpha A \beta \xrightarrow[\widehat{G}]{1} \alpha B \beta \xrightarrow[\widehat{G}]{*} x.$$

We must eventually dispose of that occurrence of B, say by applying a production $B \to \gamma$ later on.

$$S \xrightarrow[\widehat{G}]{m} \alpha A \beta \xrightarrow[\widehat{G}]{1} \alpha B \beta \xrightarrow[\widehat{G}]{n} \eta B \theta \xrightarrow[\widehat{G}]{1} \eta \gamma \theta \xrightarrow[\widehat{G}]{k} x.$$

But by rule (b), $A \to \gamma$ is also in $\widehat{P}$, and this could have been applied instead, giving a strictly shorter derivation of x:

$$S \xrightarrow[\widehat{G}]{m} \alpha A \beta \xrightarrow[\widehat{G}]{1} \alpha \gamma \beta \xrightarrow[\widehat{G}]{n} \eta \gamma \theta \xrightarrow[\widehat{G}]{k} x.$$

Again, this contradicts the minimality of the length of the derivation.

Thus we do not need ϵ-productions or unit productions to generate nonnull strings. If we discard them from $\widehat{G}$, we obtain a grammar G' generating $L(G) - \{\epsilon\}$. $\qquad \square$

Chomsky Normal Form

Once we are rid of ϵ- and unit productions, it is a simple matter to put the resulting grammar into Chomsky normal form. For each terminal $a \in \Sigma$, introduce a new nonterminal A_a and production $A_a \rightarrow a$, and replace all occurrences of a on the right-hand sides of old productions (except productions of the form $B \rightarrow a$) with A_a. Then all productions are of the form

$$A \rightarrow a \text{ or } A \rightarrow B_1 B_2 \cdots B_k, \quad k \geq 2,$$

where the B_i are nonterminals. The set of terminal strings generated is not changed; it just takes one more step than before to generate a terminal symbol. For any production

$$A \rightarrow B_1 B_2 \cdots B_k$$

with $k \geq 3$, introduce a new nonterminal C and replace this production with the two productions

$$A \rightarrow B_1 C \quad \text{and} \quad C \rightarrow B_2 B_3 \cdots B_k.$$

Keep doing this until all right-hand sides are of length at most 2.

Example 21.4   Let's derive a CNF grammar for the set

$$\{a^n b^n \mid n \geq 0\} - \{\epsilon\} = \{a^n b^n \mid n \geq 1\}.$$

Starting with the grammar

$$S \rightarrow aSb \mid \epsilon$$

for $\{a^n b^n \mid n \geq 0\}$, we remove the ϵ-production as described in Lemma 21.3 to get

$$S \rightarrow aSb \mid ab,$$

which generates $\{a^n b^n \mid n \geq 1\}$. Then we add nonterminals A, B and replace these productions with

$$S \rightarrow ASB \mid AB, \qquad A \rightarrow a, \qquad B \rightarrow b.$$

Finally, we add a nonterminal C and replace $S \rightarrow ASB$ with

$$S \rightarrow AC \quad \text{and} \quad C \rightarrow SB.$$

The final grammar in Chomsky form is

$$S \rightarrow AB \mid AC, \qquad C \rightarrow SB, \qquad A \rightarrow a, \qquad B \rightarrow b. \qquad \square$$

Example 21.5   We derive a CNF grammar for the set of nonnull strings of balanced parentheses [ ]. Start with the grammar

$$S \rightarrow [S] \mid SS \mid \epsilon$$

for all balanced strings of parentheses. Applying the construction of Lemma 21.3 to get rid of the ϵ- and unit productions, we get

$$S \rightarrow [S] \mid SS \mid [\ ].$$

Next we add new nonterminals A, B and replace these productions with

$$S \rightarrow ASB \mid SS \mid AB, \qquad A \rightarrow [, \qquad B \rightarrow].$$

Finally, we add a new nonterminal C and replace $S \rightarrow ASB$ with

$$S \rightarrow AC \quad \text{and} \quad C \rightarrow SB.$$

The resulting grammar in Chomsky form is exactly (21.1). $\square$

Greibach Normal Form

Now we show how to convert an arbitrary grammar to an equivalent one (except possibly for ϵ) in Greibach normal form.

We start with a grammar $G = (N, \Sigma, P, S)$ in Chomsky normal form. This assumption is mainly for ease of presentation; we could easily modify the construction to apply more generally. The construction as given here produces a Greibach grammar with at most two nonterminals on the right-hand side (cf. [60, Exercise 4.16, p. 104]).

For $\alpha, \beta \in (N \cup \Sigma)^*$, write

$$\alpha \xrightarrow[G]{L} \beta$$

if β can be derived from α by a sequence of steps in which productions are applied only to the leftmost symbol in the sentential form (which must therefore be a nonterminal). For $A \in N$ and $a \in \Sigma$, define

$$R_{A,a} = \{\beta \in N^* \mid A \xrightarrow[G]{L} a\beta\}.$$

For example, in the CNF grammar (21.1), we would have

$$C \xrightarrow[G]{L} SB \xrightarrow[G]{L} SSB \xrightarrow[G]{L} SSSB \xrightarrow[G]{L} ACSSB \xrightarrow[G]{L} [CSSB,$$

so $CSSB \in R_{C,[}$.

The set $R_{A,a}$ is a regular set over the alphabet N, because the grammar with nonterminals $\{A' \mid A \in N\}$, terminals N, start symbol S', and productions

$$\{A' \rightarrow B'C \mid A \rightarrow BC \in P\} \cup \{A' \rightarrow \epsilon \mid A \rightarrow a \in P\}$$

is a strongly left-linear grammar for it.[1] This may seem slightly bizarre, since the terminals of this grammar are the nonterminals N of G, but a moment's thought will convince you that it makes perfect sense.

Since $R_{A,a}$ is regular, by Homework 5, Exercise 1 it also has a strongly right-linear grammar $G_{A,a}$; that is, one in which all productions are of the form $X \rightarrow BY$ or $X \rightarrow \epsilon$, where X, Y are nonterminals of $G_{A,a}$ and $B \in N$. Let $T_{A,a}$ be the start symbol of $G_{A,a}$.

Assume without loss of generality that the sets of nonterminals of the grammars $G_{A,a}$ and G are pairwise disjoint. This assumption can be enforced by renaming if necessary. Form the grammar G_1 by adding all the nonterminals and productions of all the $G_{A,a}$ to G. Take the start symbol of G_1 to be S. Productions of G_1 are of the following three forms:

$$X \rightarrow b, \qquad X \rightarrow \epsilon, \qquad X \rightarrow BY,$$

where $b \in \Sigma$ and $B \in N$. Note that G_1 is trivially equivalent to G, since none of the new nonterminals can be derived from S.

Now let G_2 be the grammar obtained from G_1 by removing any production of the form

$$X \rightarrow BY$$

and replacing it with the productions

$$X \rightarrow bT_{B,b}Y$$

for all $b \in \Sigma$. Productions of G_2 are of the form

$$X \rightarrow b, \qquad X \rightarrow \epsilon, \qquad X \rightarrow bT_{B,b}Y,$$

where $b \in \Sigma$.

Finally, get rid of the ϵ-productions in G_2 using the construction of Lemma 21.3. This construction does not introduce any unit productions, since every non-ϵ-production has a terminal symbol on the right-hand side. Thus the resulting grammar G_3 is in Greibach form with at most two nonterminals on the right-hand side of any production.

Before we prove that $L(G_3) = L(G)$, let's pause and illustrate the construction with an example.

Example 21.6 Consider the balanced parentheses of Example 21.5. Starting with the Chomsky grammar

$$S \rightarrow AB \mid AC \mid SS, \qquad C \rightarrow SB, \qquad A \rightarrow [, \qquad B \rightarrow],$$

---

[1] See Homework 5, Exercise 1.

first compute the regular sets $R_{D,d}$:

$$R_{S,[} = (B + C)S^*,$$
$$R_{C,[} = (B + C)S^*B,$$
$$R_{A,[} = R_{B,]} = \{\epsilon\},$$

and all others are $\varnothing$. Here are strongly right-linear grammars for these sets:

$$
\begin{aligned}
&T_{S,[} \to BX \mid CX, && X \to SX \mid \epsilon, \\
&T_{C,[} \to BY \mid CY, && Y \to SY \mid BZ, && Z \to \epsilon, \\
&T_{A,[} \to \epsilon, \\
&T_{B,]} \to \epsilon.
\end{aligned}
$$

Combining these grammars with G and making the substitutions as described above, we obtain the grammar G_2:

$$
\begin{aligned}
&S \to [T_{A,[}B \mid [T_{A,[}C \mid [T_{S,[}S, && C \to [T_{S,[}B, && A \to [, \\
&T_{S,[} \to]T_{B,]}X \mid [T_{C,[}X, && X \to [T_{S,[}X \mid \epsilon, && B \to], \\
&T_{C,[} \to]T_{B,]}Y \mid [T_{C,[}Y, && Y \to [T_{S,[}Y \mid]T_{B,]}Z, && Z \to \epsilon, \\
&T_{A,[} \to \epsilon, && T_{B,]} \to \epsilon.
\end{aligned}
$$

Removing ϵ-transitions, we get the Greibach grammar G_3:

$$
\begin{aligned}
&S \to [B \mid [C \mid [T_{S,[}S, && C \to [T_{S,[}B, && A \to [, \\
&T_{S,[} \to]X \mid [T_{C,[}X \mid b \mid [T_{C,[}, && X \to [T_{S,[}X \mid [T_{S,[}, && B \to], \\
&T_{C,[} \to]Y \mid [T_{C,[}Y, && Y \to [T_{S,[}Y \mid].
\end{aligned}
$$

The Greibach grammar produced by this construction is by no means the simplest possible, as can be seen by comparing it to the somewhat simpler (21.2). □

Now we prove that $L(G) = L(G_3)$. Surely $L(G) = L(G_1)$, since none of the new nonterminals added in the construction of G_1 can be derived from any nonterminal of G, including the start symbol S of G_1. Also, $L(G_2) = L(G_3)$ by Lemma 21.3. Thus the heart of the proof is showing that $L(G_1) = L(G_2)$.

Lemma 21.7   *For any nonterminal X and $x \in \Sigma^*$,*

$$X \xrightarrow[G_1]{*} x \iff X \xrightarrow[G_2]{*} x.$$

Proof. The proof is by induction on the length of derivations. If x can be derived in one step from X in either grammar, then it must be by a production of the form $X \to b$ or $X \to \epsilon$, and these productions are the same in both grammars.

For the induction step, we show that

$$X \xrightarrow[G_1]{*} x \text{ starting with the production } X \to BY$$

if and only if

$$X \xrightarrow[G_2]{*} x \text{ starting with the production } X \to bT_{B,b}Y,$$

where b is the first symbol of x. Note that x must have a first symbol, since derivations in G_1 starting with $X \to BY$ cannot generate ϵ, because B is a nonterminal of the original CNF grammar G, therefore can generate only nonnull strings.

Any leftmost derivation

$$X \xrightarrow[G_1]{1} BY \xrightarrow[G_1]{*} bz$$

is of the form

$$X \xrightarrow[G_1]{1} BY \xrightarrow[G_1]{k+1} bB_1B_2 \cdots B_kY \xrightarrow[G_1]{m} bz,$$

where $bB_1B_2 \cdots B_kY$ is the first sentential form in the sequence in which the terminal b appears, and $B_1B_2 \cdots B_k \in R_{B,b}$. By definition of the grammar $G_{B,b}$, this occurs if and only if

$$X \xrightarrow[G_2]{1} bT_{B,b}Y \xrightarrow[G_1]{k+1} bB_1B_2 \cdots B_kY \xrightarrow[G_1]{m} bz,$$

where the subderivation

$$T_{B,b} \xrightarrow[G_1]{k+1} B_1B_2 \cdots B_k$$

is a leftmost derivation in $G_{B,b}$. By the induction hypothesis, this occurs iff

$$X \xrightarrow[G_2]{1} bT_{B,b}Y \xrightarrow[G_2]{*} bz. \qquad \square$$

It follows from Lemma 21.7 by taking $X = S$ that $L(G_1) = L(G_2)$, therefore $L(G) = L(G_3)$.

Historical Notes

Bar-Hillel, Perles, and Shamir [8] showed how to get rid of ϵ- and unit productions. Chomsky and Greibach normal forms are due to Chomsky [18] and Greibach [53], respectively.

Lecture 22

The Pumping Lemma for CFLs

There is a pumping lemma for CFLs similar to the one for regular sets. It can be used in the same way to show that certain sets are not context-free. Here is the official version; there will also be a corresponding game with the demon that will be useful in practice.

Theorem 22.1 **(Pumping lemma for CFLs)** *For every CFL A, there exists $k \geq 0$ such that every $z \in A$ of length at least k can be broken up into five substrings $z = uvwxy$ such that $vx \neq \epsilon$, $|vwx| \leq k$, and for all $i \geq 0$, $uv^i wx^i y \in A$.*

Informally, for every CFL A, every sufficiently long string in A can be subdivided into five segments such that the middle three segments are not too long, the second and fourth are not both null, and no matter how many extra copies of the second and fourth you pump in simultaneously, the string stays in A.

Note that this differs from the pumping lemma for regular sets in that we pump simultaneously on two substrings v and x separated by a substring w.

The key insight that gives this theorem is that for a grammar in Chomsky normal form, any parse tree for a very long string must have a very long path, and any very long path must have at least two occurrences of some nonterminal. A *parse tree* or *derivation tree* of a string z is a tree representing the productions applied in a derivation of z from the start symbol S independent of the order of application. For example, consider the Chomsky grammar

$$S \to AC \mid AB, \qquad A \to a, \qquad B \to b, \qquad C \to SB$$

for $\{a^n b^n \mid n \geq 1\}$. Here is a parse tree for the string $a^4 b^4$ in this grammar:

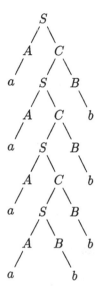

The productions can be applied in any order. For example, a leftmost derivation of $a^4 b^4$ (always applying a production to the leftmost remaining nonterminal) would give

$$S \to AC \to aC \to aSB \to aACB \to aaCB \to aaSBB \to aaACBB$$
$$\to aaaCBB \to aaaSBBB \to aaaABBBB \to aaaaBBBB$$
$$\to aaaabBBB \to aaaabbBB \to aaaabbbB \to aaaabbbb,$$

and a rightmost derivation would give

$$S \to AC \to ASB \to ASb \to AACb \to AASBb \to AASbb \to AAACbb$$
$$\to AAASBbb \to AAASbbb \to AAAABbbb \to AAAAbbbb$$
$$\to AAAabbbb \to AAaabbbb \to Aaaabbbb \to aaaabbbb,$$

but these two derivations have the same parse tree, namely the one pictured above.

Parse trees of Chomsky grammars for long strings must have long paths, because the number of symbols can at most double when you go down a level. This is because the right-hand sides of productions contain at most two symbols. For example, take the tree above and duplicate the terminals generated at each level on all lower levels, just to keep track of the symbols that have been generated so far:

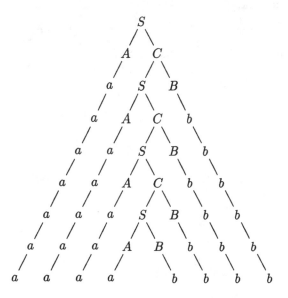

The number of symbols at each level is at most twice the number on the level immediately above. Thus at the very most, we can have one symbol at the top level (level 0), 2 at level 1, 4 at level 2, ..., 2^i at level i. In order to have at least 2^n symbols at the bottom level, the tree must be of depth[1] at least n; that is, it must have at least $n + 1$ levels.

Proof of the pumping lemma. Let G be a grammar for A in Chomsky normal form. Take $k = 2^{n+1}$, where n is the number of nonterminals of G. Suppose $z \in A$ and $|z| \geq k$. By the argument above, any parse tree in G for z must be of depth at least $n + 1$. Consider the longest path in the tree. (In the example above, the path from S at the root down to the leftmost b in the terminal string is such a path.) That path is of length at least $n + 1$, therefore must contain at least $n + 1$ occurrences of nonterminals. By the pigeonhole principle, some nonterminal occurs more than once along the path. Take the first pair of occurrences of the same nonterminal along the path, reading from bottom to top. In the example above, we would take the two circled occurrences of S:

---

[1] The *depth* is the number of edges on the longest path from the root to a leaf.

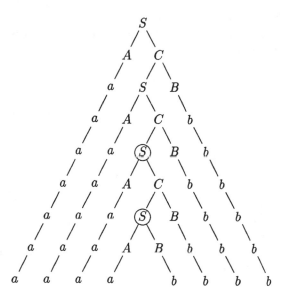

Say X is the nonterminal with two occurrences. Break z up into substrings $uvwxy$ such that w is the string of terminals generated by the lower occurrence of X and vwx is the string generated by the upper occurrence of X. In our running example, $w = ab$ is the string generated by the lower occurrence of S and $vwx = aabb$ is the string generated by the upper occurrence of S:

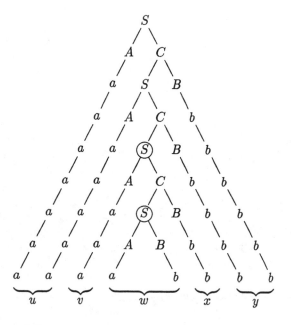

Thus in this example we have $u = aa$, $v = a$, $w = ab$, $x = b$, and $y = bb$. Let T be the subtree rooted at the upper occurrence of X and let t be the subtree rooted at the lower occurrence of X. In our example,

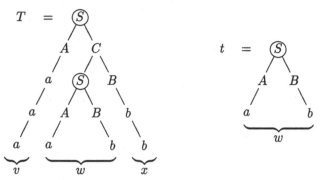

By removing t from the original tree and replacing it with a copy of T, we get a valid parse tree of uv^2wx^2y:

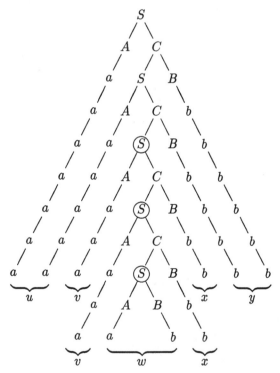

We can repeat this cutting out of t and replacing it with a copy of T as many times as we like to get a valid parse tree for uv^iwx^iy for any $i \geq 1$. We can even cut T out of the original tree and replace it with t to get a parse tree for $uv^0wx^0y = uwy$:

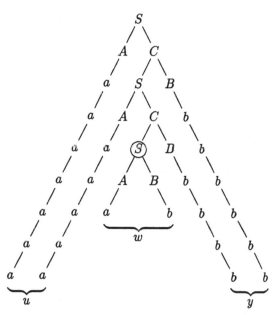

Note that $vx \neq \epsilon$; that is, v and x are not both null.

We also have $|vwx| \leq k$, since we chose the first repeated occurrence of a nonterminal reading from the bottom, and we must see such a repetition by the time we get up to height $n+1$. Since we took the longest path in the tree, the depth of the subtree under the upper occurrence of the repeated nonterminal X is at most $n+1$, therefore can have no more than $2^{n+1} = k$ terminals.   □

Games with the Demon

Like its regular cousin, the pumping lemma for CFLs is most useful in its contrapositive form. In this form, it states that in order to conclude that A is *not* context-free, it suffices to establish the following property:

Property 22.2   *For all $k \geq 0$, there exists $z \in A$ of length at least k such that for all ways of breaking z up into substrings $z = uvwxy$ with $vx \neq \epsilon$ and $|vwx| \leq k$, there exists an $i \geq 0$ such that $uv^iwx^iy \notin A$.*

Property 22.2 is equivalent to saying that you have a winning strategy in the following game with the demon:

1. The demon picks $k \geq 0$.

2. You pick $z \in A$ of length at least k.

3. The demon picks strings u, v, w, x, y such that $z = uvwxy$, $|vx| > 0$, and $|vwx| \leq k$.

4. You pick $i \geq 0$. If $uv^iwx^iy \notin A$, then you win.

If you want to show that a given set A is not context-free, it suffices to show that you have a winning strategy in this game; that is, no matter what the demon does in steps 1 and 3, you have moves in steps 2 and 4 that can beat him.

Example 22.3 Let's use the pumping lemma to show that the set

$$A = \{a^n b^n a^n \mid n \geq 0\}$$

is not context-free. We'll do this by showing that we can always win the game with the demon.

Say the demon picks k in step 1. You have to argue that you can win no matter what k is. A good choice for you in step 2 is to pick $z = a^k b^k a^k$. Then $z \in A$ and $|z| = 3k \geq k$. Then in step 3, say the demon picks u, v, w, x, y such that $z = uvwxy$, $vx \neq \epsilon$, and $|vwx| \leq k$. You pick $i = 2$. In every case, you win: if the demon picked either v or x to contain at least one a and at least one b, then uv^2wx^2y is not of the form $a^*b^*a^*$, hence certainly not in A; if the demon picked v and x to contain only a's, then uv^2wx^2y has more than twice as many a's as b's, hence is not in A; if the demon picked v and x to contain only b's, then uv^2wx^2y has fewer than twice as many a's as b's, hence is not in A; and finally, if one of v or x contains only a's and the other contains only b's, then uv^2wx^2y cannot be of the form $a^m b^m a^m$, hence is not in A. In all cases you can ensure $uv^2wx^2y \notin A$, so you have a winning strategy. By the pumping lemma, A is not context-free. □

Example 22.4 Let's use the pumping lemma to show that the set

$$A = \{ww \mid w \in \{a, b\}^*\}$$

is not context-free. Since the family of CFLs is closed under intersection with regular sets (Homework 7, Exercise 2), it suffices to show that the set

$$A' = A \cap L(a^*b^*a^*b^*)$$
$$= \{a^n b^m a^n b^m \mid m, n \geq 0\}$$

is not context-free.

Say the demon picks k. You pick $z = a^k b^k a^k b^k$. Call each of the four substrings of the form a^k or b^k a *block*. Then $z \in A'$ and $|z| \geq k$. Say the demon picks u, v, w, x, y such that $z = uvwxy$, $vx \neq \epsilon$, and $|vwx| < k$. No matter what the demon does, you can win by picking $i = 2$:

- If one of v or x contains both a's and b's (i.e., if one of v or x straddles a block boundary), then uv^2wx^2y is not of the form $a^*b^*a^*b^*$, thus is not in A'.

- If v and x are both from the same block, then uv^2wx^2y has one block longer than the other three, therefore is not in A'.

- If v and x are in different blocks, then the blocks must be adjacent; otherwise $|vwx|$ would be greater than k. Thus one of the blocks containing v or x must be a block of a's and the other a block of b's. Then uv^2wx^2y has either two blocks of a's of different size (if vx contains an a) or two blocks of b's of different size (if vx contains a b) or both. In any case, uv^2wx^2y is not of the form $a^nb^ma^nb^m$.

Since you can always ensure a win by playing this strategy, A' (and therefore A) is not a CFL by the pumping lemma.

Surprisingly, the complement of A, namely

$$\{a,b\}^* - \{ww \mid w \in \{a,b\}^*\},$$

is a CFL. Here is a CFG for it:

$$S \rightarrow AB \mid BA \mid A \mid B,$$
$$A \rightarrow CAC \mid a,$$
$$B \rightarrow CBC \mid b,$$
$$C \rightarrow a \mid b.$$

This grammar generates

(i) all strings of odd length (starting with productions $S \rightarrow A$ and $S \rightarrow B$); or

(ii) strings of the form $xayubv$ or $ubvxay$, where $x,y,u,v \in \{a,b\}^*$, $|x| = |y|$, and $|u| = |v|$.

The nonterminal A generates all strings of the form xay, $|x| = |y|$. The nonterminal B generates all strings of the form ubv, $|u| = |v|$. No string of the form (i) can be of the form ww, since ww is always of even length. No string of the form (ii) can be of the form ww, since there are occurrences of a and b separated by a distance of $n/2$, where n is the length of the string.

This example shows that the family of CFLs is not closed under complement.   □

Note that in both these examples, your choice of $i = 2$ in step 4 was independent of the demon's move in step 3. This may not always be possible! However, keep in mind that you have the freedom to pick i in step 4 *after* you have seen what the demon did in step 3.

Historical Notes

The pumping lemma for CFLs is due to Bar-Hillel, Perles, and Shamir [8]. A somewhat stronger version was given by Ogden [96].

Lecture 23

Pushdown Automata

A *nondeterministic pushdown automaton* (NPDA) is like a nondeterministic finite automaton, except it has a *stack* or *pushdown store* that it can use to record a potentially unbounded amount of information.

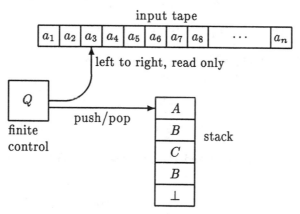

The input head is read-only and may only move from left to right. The machine can store information on the stack in a last-in-first-out (LIFO) fashion. In each step, the machine pops the top symbol off the stack; based on this symbol, the input symbol it is currently reading, and its current state, it can push a sequence of symbols onto the stack, move its read head one cell to the right, and enter a new state, according to the transition rules of the machine. We also allow ϵ-*transitions* in which it can pop and push without reading the next input symbol or moving its read head.

Although it can store an unbounded amount of information on the stack, it may not read down into the stack without popping the top elements off, in which case they are lost. Thus its access to the information on the stack is limited.

Formally, a nondeterministic PDA is a 7-tuple

$$M = (Q, \Sigma, \Gamma, \delta, s, \bot, F),$$

where

- Q is a finite set (the *states*),

- Σ is a finite set (the *input alphabet*),

- Γ is a finite set (the *stack alphabet*),

- $\delta \subseteq (Q \times (\Sigma \cup \{\epsilon\}) \times \Gamma) \times (Q \times \Gamma^*)$, δ finite (the *transition relation*),

- $s \in Q$ (the *start state*),

- $\bot \in \Gamma$ (the *initial stack symbol*), and

- $F \subseteq Q$ (the *final* or *accept states*).

If

$$((p, a, A), (q, B_1 B_2 \cdots B_k)) \in \delta,$$

this means intuitively that whenever the machine is in state p reading input symbol a on the input tape and A on the top of the stack, it can pop A off the stack, push $B_1 B_2 \cdots B_k$ onto the stack (B_k first and B_1 last), move its read head right one cell past the a, and enter state q. If

$$((p, \epsilon, A), (q, B_1 B_2 \cdots B_k)) \in \delta,$$

this means intuitively that whenever the machine is in state p with A on the top of the stack, it can pop A off the stack, push $B_1 B_2 \cdots B_k$ onto the stack (B_k first and B_1 last), leave its read head where it is, and enter state q.

The machine is nondeterministic, so there may be several transitions that are possible.

Configurations

A *configuration* of the machine M is an element of $Q \times \Sigma^* \times \Gamma^*$ describing the current state, the portion of the input yet unread (i.e., under and to the right of the read head), and the current stack contents. A configuration gives complete information about the global state of M at some point during a computation. For example, the configuration

$$(p, baaabba, ABAC\bot)$$

might describe the situation

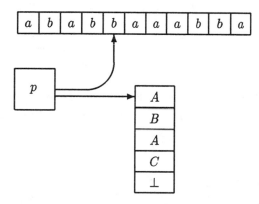

The portion of the input to the left of the input head need not be represented in the configuration, because it cannot affect the computation from that point on. In general, the set of configurations is infinite.

The *start configuration* on input x is $(s, x, \bot)$. That is, the machine always starts in its start state s with its read head pointing to the leftmost input symbol and the stack containing only the symbol $\bot$.

The *next configuration relation* $\xrightarrow[M]{1}$ describes how the machine can move from one configuration to another in one step. It is defined formally as follows: if

$$((p, a, A), (q, \gamma)) \in \delta,$$

then for any $y \in \Sigma^*$ and $\beta \in \Gamma^*$,

$$(p, ay, A\beta) \xrightarrow[M]{1} (q, y, \gamma\beta); \tag{23.1}$$

and if

$$((p, \epsilon, A), (q, \gamma)) \in \delta,$$

then for any $y \in \Sigma^*$ and $\beta \in \Gamma^*$,

$$(p, y, A\beta) \xrightarrow[M]{1} (q, y, \gamma\beta). \tag{23.2}$$

In (23.1), the ay changed to y, indicating that the input symbol a was eaten; the $A\beta$ changed to $\gamma\beta$, indicating that the A was popped and γ was pushed; and the p changed to q, indicating the change of state. In (23.2), everything is the same except that the y does not change, indicating that no input symbol was eaten. No two configurations are related by $\xrightarrow[M]{1}$ unless required by (23.1) or (23.2).

Define the relations $\xrightarrow[M]{n}$ and $\xrightarrow[M]{*}$ as follows:

$$C \xrightarrow[M]{0} D \overset{\text{def}}{\iff} C = D,$$

$$C \xrightarrow[M]{n+1} D \overset{\text{def}}{\iff} \exists E \; C \xrightarrow[M]{n} E \text{ and } E \xrightarrow[M]{1} D,$$

$$C \xrightarrow[M]{*} D \overset{\text{def}}{\iff} \exists n \geq 0 \; C \xrightarrow[M]{n} D.$$

Then $\xrightarrow[M]{*}$ is the reflexive transitive closure of $\xrightarrow[M]{1}$. In other words, $C \xrightarrow[M]{*} D$ if the configuration D follows from the configuration C in zero or more steps of the next configuration relation $\xrightarrow[M]{1}$.

Acceptance

There are two alternative definitions of acceptance in common use: by *empty stack* and by *final state*. It turns out that it doesn't matter which definition we use, since each kind of machine can simulate the other.

Let's consider acceptance by final state first. Informally, the machine M is said to *accept its input x by final state* if it ever enters a state in F after scanning its entire input, starting in the start configuration on input x. Formally, M *accepts x by final state* if

$$(s, x, \bot) \xrightarrow[M]{*} (q, \epsilon, \gamma)$$

for some $q \in F$ and $\gamma \in \Gamma^*$. In the right-hand configuration, ϵ is the null string, signifying that the entire input has been read, and γ is junk left on the stack.

Informally, M is said to *accept its input x by empty stack* if it ever pops the last element off the stack without pushing anything back on after reading the entire input, starting in the start configuration on input x. Formally, M *accepts x by empty stack* if

$$(s, x, \bot) \xrightarrow[M]{*} (q, \epsilon, \epsilon)$$

for some $q \in Q$. In this definition, the q in the right-hand configuration can be any state whatsoever, and the ϵ in the second and third positions indicate that the entire input has been read and the stack is empty, respectively. Note that F is irrelevant in the definition of acceptance by empty stack.

The two different forms of automata can simulate each other (see Lecture E); thus it doesn't matter which one we work with.

In either definition of acceptance, the entire input string has to be read. Because of ϵ-transitions, it is possible that a PDA can get into an infinite loop without reading the entire input.

Example 23.1   Here is a nondeterministic pushdown automaton that accepts the set of balanced strings of parentheses [ ] by empty stack. It has just one state q. Informally, the machine will scan its input from left to right; whenever it sees a [, it will push the [onto the stack, and whenever it sees a] and the top stack symbol is [, it will pop the [off the stack. (If you matched up the parentheses, you would see that the] it is currently reading is the one matching the [on top of the stack that was pushed earlier.) Formally, let

$$Q = \{q\},$$
$$\Sigma = \{[,]\},$$
$$\Gamma = \{\bot, [\},$$
$$\text{start state} = q,$$
$$\text{initial stack symbol} = \bot,$$

and let δ consist of the following transitions:

(i) $((q, [, \bot), (q, [\bot));$

(ii) $((q, [, [), (q, [[));$

(iii) $((q,], [), (q,\epsilon));$

(iv) $((q,\epsilon, \bot), (q,\epsilon)).$

Informally, transitions (i) and (ii) say that whenever the next input symbol is [, the [is pushed onto the stack on top of the symbol currently there (actually, the symbol currently there is popped but then immediately pushed back on). Transition (iii) says that whenever the next input symbol is] and there is a [on top of the stack, the [is popped and nothing else is pushed. Transition (iv) is taken when the end of the input string is reached in order to dump the $\bot$ off the stack and accept.

Here is a sequence of configurations leading to the acceptance of the balanced string [[[ ]] [ ]] [ ].

	Configuration			Transition applied
	$(q,$ [[[ ]] [ ]] [ ],	$\perp)$		start configuration
$\rightarrow$	$(q,$ [[ ]] [ ]] [ ],	[$\perp)$		transition (i)
$\rightarrow$	$(q,$ [ ]] [ ]] [ ],	[[$\perp)$		transition (ii)
$\rightarrow$	$(q,$]] [ ]] [ ],	[[[$\perp)$		transition (ii)
$\rightarrow$	$(q,$] [ ]] [ ],	[[$\perp)$		transition (iii)
$\rightarrow$	$(q,$ [ ]] [ ],	[$\perp)$		transition (iii)
$\rightarrow$	$(q,$]] [ ],	[[$\perp)$		transition (ii)
$\rightarrow$	$(q,$] [ ],	[$\perp)$		transition (iii)
$\rightarrow$	$(q,$ [ ],	$\perp)$		transition (iii)
$\rightarrow$	$(q,$],	[$\perp)$		transition (i)
$\rightarrow$	$(q,$ $\epsilon,$	$\perp)$		transition (iii)
$\rightarrow$	$(q,$ $\epsilon,$	$\epsilon)$		transition (iv)

The machine could well have taken transition (iv) prematurely at a couple of places; for example, in its very first step. This would have led to the configuration

$$(q, \text{[[[ ]] [ ]] [ ]}, \epsilon),$$

and the machine would have been stuck, since no transition is possible from a configuration with an empty stack. Moreover, this is not an accept configuration, since there is a nonnull portion of the input yet unread. However, this is not a problem, since the machine is nondeterministic and the usual rules for nondeterminism apply: the machine is said to accept the input if *some* sequence of transitions leads to an accept configuration. If it does take transition (iv) prematurely, then this was just a bad guess where the end of the input string was.

To prove that this machine is correct, one must argue that for every balanced string x, there is a sequence of transitions leading to an accept configuration from the start configuration on input x; and for every unbalanced string x, *no* sequence of transitions leads to an accept configuration from the start configuration on input x.   □

Example 23.2   We showed in Lecture 22 using the pumping lemma that the set

$$\{ww \mid w \in \{a, b\}^*\}$$

is not a CFL (and therefore, as we will show in Lecture 25, not accepted by any NPDA) but that its complement

$$\{a, b\}^* - \{ww \mid w \in \{a, b\}^*\} \tag{23.3}$$

is. The set (23.3) can be accepted by a nondeterministic pushdown automaton as follows. Initially guess whether to check for an odd number of input symbols or for an even number of the form $xayubv$ or $ubvxay$ with $|x| = |y|$ and $|u| = |v|$. To check for the former condition, we do not need the stack at all—we can just count mod 2 with a finite automaton encoded in the finite control of the PDA. To check for the latter, we scan the input for a nondeterministically chosen length of time, pushing the input symbols onto the stack. We use the stack as an integer counter. At some nondeterministically chosen time, we remember the current input symbol in the finite control—this is the a or b that is guessed to be the symbol in the first half not matching the corresponding symbol in the second half—then continue to scan, popping one symbol off the stack for each input symbol read. When the initial stack symbol $\perp$ is on top of the stack, we start pushing symbols again. At some point we nondeterministically guess where the corresponding symbol in the second half is. If it is the same symbol as the one remembered from the first half, reject. Otherwise we scan the rest of the input, popping the stack as we go. If the stack contains only $\perp$ when the end of the input is reached, we accept by popping the $\perp$, leaving an empty stack. □

We close with a few technical remarks about NPDAs:

1. In *deterministic* PDAs (Supplementary Lecture F), we will need an endmarker on the input so that the machine knows when it is at the end of the input string. In NPDAs, the endmarker is unnecessary, since the machine can guess nondeterministically where the end of the string is. If it guesses wrong and empties its stack before scanning the entire input, then that was just a bad guess.

2. We distinguish the initial stack symbol $\perp$ only because we need it to define the start configuration. Other than that, it is treated like any other stack symbol and can be pushed and popped at any time. In particular, it need not stay on the bottom of the stack after the start configuration; it can be popped in the first move and something else pushed in its place if desired.

3. A transition $((p, a, A), (q, \beta))$ or $((p, \epsilon, A), (q, \beta))$ does not apply unless A is on top of the stack. In particular, *no* transition applies if the stack is empty. In that case the machine is stuck.

4. In acceptance by empty stack, the stack must be empty *in a configuration*, that is, *after* applying a transition. In our intuitive description above, when a transition such as $((p, \epsilon, A), (q, BC))$ is taken with only A on the stack, the stack is momentarily empty between the time A is popped and BC is pushed. This does not count in the definition of acceptance by empty stack. To accept by empty stack, everything must be popped and nothing pushed back on.

Supplementary Lecture E

Final State Versus Empty Stack

It doesn't matter whether we take NPDAs to accept by empty stack or by final state; the two methods of acceptance are equivalent in the sense that each type of machine can simulate the other. Given an arbitrary NPDA M that accepts by final state or empty stack, we will show how to construct an equivalent NPDA M' with a single accept state for which acceptance by empty stack and by final state coincide.

The construction of M' differs slightly, depending on whether M accepts by final state or by empty stack, but there is enough in common between the two constructions that we will do them together, pointing out where they differ.

We have not discussed deterministic PDAs yet—we will do so in Supplementary Lecture F—but for future reference, the construction we are about to give can be made to preserve determinism.

Let

$$M = (Q, \Sigma, \Gamma, \delta, s, \perp, F)$$

be an NPDA that accepts by empty stack or by final state. Let u, t be two new states not in Q, and let $\perp\!\!\!\perp$ be a new stack symbol not in Γ. Define

$$G \stackrel{\text{def}}{=} \begin{cases} Q & \text{if } M \text{ accepts by empty stack,} \\ F & \text{if } M \text{ accepts by final state;} \end{cases}$$

$$\Delta \stackrel{\text{def}}{=} \begin{cases} \{\bot\!\!\bot\} & \text{if } M \text{ accepts by empty stack,} \\ \Gamma \cup \{\bot\!\!\bot\} & \text{if } M \text{ accepts by final state.} \end{cases}$$

Consider the NPDA

$$M' = (Q \cup \{u, t\}, \ \Sigma, \ \Gamma \cup \{\bot\!\!\bot\}, \ \delta', \ u, \ \bot\!\!\bot, \ \{t\}),$$

where δ' contains all the transitions of δ, as well as the transitions

$$((u, \epsilon, \bot\!\!\bot), (s, \bot\bot\!\!\bot)), \tag{E.1}$$
$$((q, \epsilon, A), (t, A)), \quad q \in G, \quad A \in \Delta, \tag{E.2}$$
$$((t, \epsilon, A), (t, \epsilon)), \quad A \in \Gamma \cup \{\bot\!\!\bot\}. \tag{E.3}$$

Thus the new automaton M' has a new start state u, a new initial stack symbol $\bot\!\!\bot$, and a new single final state t. In the first step, by transition (E.1), it pushes the old initial stack symbol $\bot$ on top of $\bot\!\!\bot$, then enters the old start state s. It can then run as M would, since it contains all the transitions of M. At some point it might enter state t according to (E.2). Once it enters state t, it can dump everything off its stack using transitions (E.3). Moreover, this is the *only* way it can empty its stack, since it cannot pop $\bot\!\!\bot$ except in state t. Thus acceptance by empty stack and by final state coincide for M'.

Now we show that $L(M') = L(M)$. Suppose first that M accepts by empty stack. If M accepts x, then

$$(s, x, \bot) \xrightarrow[M]{n} (q, \epsilon, \epsilon)$$

for some n. But then

$$(u, x, \bot\!\!\bot) \xrightarrow[M']{1} (s, x, \bot\bot\!\!\bot) \xrightarrow[M']{n} (q, \epsilon, \bot\!\!\bot) \xrightarrow[M']{1} (t, \epsilon, \bot\!\!\bot) \xrightarrow[M']{1} (t, \epsilon, \epsilon).$$

Now suppose M accepts by final state. If M accepts x, then

$$(s, x, \bot) \xrightarrow[M]{n} (q, \epsilon, \gamma), \quad q \in F.$$

Then

$$(u, x, \bot\!\!\bot) \xrightarrow[M']{1} (s, x, \bot\bot\!\!\bot) \xrightarrow[M']{n} (q, \epsilon, \gamma\bot\!\!\bot) \xrightarrow[M']{1} (t, \epsilon, \gamma\bot\!\!\bot) \xrightarrow[M']{*} (t, \epsilon, \epsilon).$$

Thus in either case, M' accepts x. Since x was arbitrary, $L(M) \subseteq L(M')$.

Conversely, suppose M' accepts x. Then

$$(u, x, \bot\!\!\bot) \xrightarrow[M']{1} (s, x, \bot\bot\!\!\bot) \xrightarrow[M']{n} (q, y, \gamma\bot\!\!\bot) \xrightarrow[M']{1} (t, y, \gamma\bot\!\!\bot) \xrightarrow[M']{*} (t, \epsilon, \epsilon)$$

for some $q \in G$. But $y = \epsilon$, since M' cannot read any input symbols once it enters state t; therefore,

$$(s, x, \bot) \xrightarrow[M]{n} (q, \epsilon, \gamma). \tag{E.4}$$

Now let's consider the definitions of G and Δ and transitions (E.2) governing the first move into state t, and ask how the transition

$$(q, \epsilon, \gamma \perp\!\!\!\perp) \xrightarrow[M']{1} (t, \epsilon, \gamma \perp\!\!\!\perp)$$

could come about. If M accepts by empty stack, then we must have $\gamma = \epsilon$. On the other hand, if M accepts by final state, then we must have $q \in F$. In either case, (E.4) says that M accepts x. Since x was arbitrary, $L(M') \subseteq L(M)$.

Lecture 24

PDAs and CFGs

In this lecture and the next we will show that nondeterministic pushdown automata and context-free grammars are equivalent in expressive power: the languages accepted by NPDAs are exactly the context-free languages. In this lecture we will show how to convert a given CFG to an equivalent NPDA. We will do the other direction in Lecture 25.

Suppose we are given a CFG $G = (N, \Sigma, P, S)$. We wish to construct an NPDA M such that $L(M) = L(G)$. By a simple construction from Lecture 21, we can assume without loss of generality that all productions of G are of the form

$$A \rightarrow cB_1 B_2 \cdots B_k,$$

where $c \in \Sigma \cup \{\epsilon\}$ and $k \geq 0$.

We construct from G an equivalent NPDA M with only one state that accepts by empty stack. Let

$$M = (\{q\}, \Sigma, N, \delta, q, S, \varnothing),$$

where

- q is the only state,

- Σ, the set of terminals of G, is the input alphabet of M,

- N, the set of nonterminals of G, is the stack alphabet of M,

- δ is the transition relation defined below,

- q is the start state,

- S, the start symbol of G, is the initial stack symbol of M,

- $\varnothing$, the null set, is the set of final states (actually, this is irrelevant, since M accepts by empty stack).

The transition relation δ is defined as follows. For each production

$$A \rightarrow cB_1 B_2 \cdots B_k$$

in P, let δ contain the transition

$$((q, c, A), (q, B_1 B_2 \cdots B_k)).$$

Thus δ has one transition for each production of G. Recall that for $c \in \Sigma$, this says, "When in state q scanning input symbol c with A on top of the stack, scan past the c, pop A off the stack, push $B_1 B_2 \cdots B_k$ onto the stack (B_k first), and enter state q," and for $c = \epsilon$, "When in state q with A on top of the stack, without scanning an input symbol, pop A off the stack, push $B_1 B_2 \cdots B_k$ onto the stack (B_k first), and enter state q."

That completes the description of M. Before we prove $L(M) = L(G)$, let's look at an example.

Consider the set of nonnull balanced strings of parentheses [ ]. Below we give a list of productions of a grammar in Greibach normal form for this set. Beside each production, we give the corresponding transition of the NPDA as specified by the construction above.

(i) $S \rightarrow [BS$ $((q, [, S), (q, BS))$

(ii) $S \rightarrow [B$ $((q, [, S), (q, B))$

(iii) $S \rightarrow [SB$ $((q, [, S), (q, SB))$

(iv) $S \rightarrow [SBS$ $((q, [, S), (q, SBS))$

(v) $B \rightarrow]$ $((q,], B), (q, \epsilon))$

Recall that a *leftmost derivation* is one in which productions are always applied to the leftmost nonterminal in the sentential form. We will show that a leftmost derivation in G of a terminal string x corresponds exactly to an accepting computation of M on input x. The sequence of sentential forms in the leftmost derivation corresponds to the sequence of configurations of M in the computation.

For example, consider the input $x = $ [[[ ]] [ ]]. In the middle column below is a sequence of sentential forms in a leftmost derivation of x in G. In the right column is the corresponding sequence of configurations of M. In the left column is the number of the production or transition applied.

Rule applied	Sentential forms in a leftmost derivation of x in G	Configurations of M in an accepting computation of M on input x
	S	$(q,$ [[[ ]] [ ]], $\quad S)$
(iii)	$[SB$	$(q,$ [[ ]] [ ]], $\quad SB)$
(iv)	$[\,[SBSB$	$(q,$ [ ]] [ ]], $SBSB)$
(ii)	$[\,[\,[BBSB$	$(q,$]] [ ]], $BBSB)$
(v)	$[\,[\,[\,]BSB$	$(q,$] [ ]], $\quad BSB)$
(v)	$[\,[\,[\,]\,]SB$	$(q,$ [ ]], $\quad SB)$
(ii)	$[\,[\,[\,]\,]\,[BB$	$(q,$]], $\quad BB)$
(v)	$[\,[\,[\,]\,]\,[\,]B$	$(q,$], $\quad B)$
(v)	$[\,[\,[\,]\,]\,[\,]\,]$	$(q,$ $\epsilon,$ $\quad \epsilon)$

In the middle column, the first sentential form is the start symbol of G and the last sentential form is the terminal string x. In the right column the first configuration is the start configuration of M on input x and the last configuration is an accept configuration (the two ϵ's denote that the entire input has been read and the stack is empty).

One can see from this example the correspondence between the sentential forms and the configurations. In the sentential forms, the terminal string x is generated from left to right, one terminal in each step, just like the input string x in the automaton is scanned off from left to right, one symbol in each step. Thus the two strings of terminals appearing in each row always concatenate to give x. Moreover, the string of nonterminals in each sentential form is exactly the contents of the stack in the corresponding configuration of the PDA.

We can formalize this observation in a general lemma that relates the sentential forms in leftmost derivations of $x \in G$ and the configurations of M in accepting computations of M on input x. This lemma holds not just for the example above but in general.

Lemma 24.1 *For any $z, y \in \Sigma^*$, $\gamma \in N^*$, and $A \in N$, $A \xrightarrow[G]{n} z\gamma$ via a leftmost derivation if and only if $(q, zy, A) \xrightarrow[M]{n} (q, y, \gamma)$.*

For example, in the fourth row of the table above, we would have $z = $ [[[, $y = $]] [ ]], $\gamma = BBSB$, $A = S$, and $n = 3$.

Proof. The proof is by induction on n.

Basis

For $n = 0$, we have

$$A \xrightarrow[G]{0} z\gamma \iff A = z\gamma$$
$$\iff z = \epsilon \text{ and } \gamma = A$$
$$\iff (q, zy, A) = (q, y, \gamma)$$
$$\iff (q, zy, A) \xrightarrow[M]{0} (q, y, \gamma).$$

Induction step

We do the two implications $\Rightarrow$ and $\Leftarrow$ separately for clarity.

First suppose $A \xrightarrow[G]{n+1} z\gamma$ via a leftmost derivation. Suppose that $B \to c\beta$ was the last production applied, where $c \in \Sigma \cup \{\epsilon\}$ and $\beta \in N^*$. Then

$$A \xrightarrow[G]{n} uB\alpha \xrightarrow[G]{1} uc\beta\alpha = z\gamma,$$

where $z = uc$ and $\gamma = \beta\alpha$. By the induction hypothesis,

$$(q, ucy, A) \xrightarrow[M]{n} (q, cy, B\alpha). \tag{24.1}$$

By the definition of M,

$$((q, c, B), (q, \beta)) \in \delta,$$

thus

$$(q, cy, B\alpha) \xrightarrow[M]{1} (q, y, \beta\alpha). \tag{24.2}$$

Combining (24.1) and (24.2), we have

$$(q, zy, A) = (q, ucy, A) \xrightarrow[M]{n+1} (q, y, \beta\alpha) = (q, y, \gamma).$$

Conversely, suppose

$$(q, zy, A) \xrightarrow[M]{n+1} (q, y, \gamma),$$

and let

$$((q, c, B), (q, \beta)) \in \delta$$

be the last transition taken. Then $z = uc$ for some $u \in \Sigma^*$, $\gamma = \beta\alpha$ for some $\alpha \in \Gamma^*$, and

$$(q, ucy, A) \xrightarrow[M]{n} (q, cy, B\alpha) \xrightarrow[M]{1} (q, y, \beta\alpha).$$

By the induction hypothesis,

$$A \xrightarrow[G]{n} uB\alpha$$

via a leftmost derivation in G, and by construction of M,

$$B \to c\beta$$

is a production of G. Applying this production to the sentential form $uB\alpha$, we get

$$A \xrightarrow[G]{n} uB\alpha \xrightarrow[G]{1} uc\beta\alpha = z\gamma$$

via a leftmost derivation.   □

Theorem 24.2 $L(M) = L(G)$.

Proof.

$$x \in L(G)$$

$\Longleftrightarrow S \xrightarrow[G]{*} x$ by a leftmost derivation   definition of $L(G)$

$\Longleftrightarrow (q, x, S) \xrightarrow[M]{*} (q, \epsilon, \epsilon)$ Lemma 24.1

$\Longleftrightarrow x \in L(M)$ definition of $L(M)$.   □

Lecture 25

Simulating NPDAs by CFGs

We have shown that every CFL is accepted by some NPDA. Now we show conversely that NPDAs accept only CFLs. Thus NPDAs and CFGs are equivalent in expressive power. We will do this in two steps by showing that

(i) every NPDA can be simulated by an NPDA with one state; and

(ii) every NPDA with one state has an equivalent CFG.

Actually, step (ii) is the easier of the two, since we have already done all the work in Lecture 24. In that lecture, given a grammar in which all productions were of the form

$$A \rightarrow cB_1 B_2 \cdots B_k$$

for some $k \geq 0$ and $c \in \Sigma \cup \{\epsilon\}$, we constructed an equivalent NPDA with one state. That construction is invertible. Suppose we have an NPDA with one state

$$M = (\{q\}, \Sigma, \Gamma, \delta, q, \perp, \varnothing)$$

that accepts by empty stack. Define the grammar

$$G = (\Gamma, \Sigma, P, \perp),$$

where P contains a production

$$A \to cB_1 B_2 \cdots B_k$$

for every transition

$$((q, c, A), (q, B_1 B_2 \cdots B_k)) \in \delta,$$

where $c \in \Sigma \cup \{\epsilon\}$. Then Lemma 24.1 and Theorem 24.2 apply verbatim, thus $L(G) = L(M)$.

It remains to show how to simulate an arbitrary NPDA by an NPDA with one state. Essentially, we will maintain all state information on the stack. By the construction of Supplementary Lecture E, we can assume without loss of generality that M is of the form

$$M = (Q, \Sigma, \Gamma, \delta, s, \perp, \{t\});$$

that is, M has a single final state t, and M can empty its stack after it enters state t.

Let

$$\Gamma' \overset{\text{def}}{=} Q \times \Gamma \times Q.$$

Elements of Γ' are written $\langle p\ A\ q \rangle$, where $p, q \in Q$ and $A \in \Gamma$. We will construct a new NPDA

$$M' = (\{*\}, \Sigma, \Gamma', \delta', *, \langle s \perp t \rangle, \varnothing)$$

with one state $*$ that accepts by empty stack. The new machine M' will be able to scan a string x starting with only $\langle p\ A\ q \rangle$ on its stack and end up with an empty stack iff M can scan x starting in state p with only A on its stack and end up in state q with an empty stack.

The transition relation δ' of M' is defined as follows: for each transition

$$((p, c, A), (q_0, B_1 B_2 \cdots B_k)) \in \delta,$$

where $c \in \Sigma \cup \{\epsilon\}$, include in δ' the transitions

$$((*, c, \langle p\ A\ q_k \rangle), (*, \langle q_0\ B_1\ q_1 \rangle \langle q_1\ B_2\ q_2 \rangle \cdots \langle q_{k-1}\ B_k\ q_k \rangle))$$

for all possible choices of $q_1, q_2, \ldots, q_k$. For $k = 0$, this reduces to: if

$$((p, c, A), (q_0, \epsilon)) \in \delta,$$

include in δ' the transition

$$((*, c, \langle p\ A\ q_0 \rangle), (*, \epsilon)).$$

Intuitively, M' simulates M, guessing nondeterministically what states M will be in at certain future points in the computation, saving those guesses on the stack, and then verifying later that those guesses were correct.

The following lemma formalizes the intuitive relationship between computations of M and M'.

Lemma 25.1   *Let M' be the NPDA constructed from M as above. Then*

$$(p, x, B_1 B_2 \cdots B_k) \xrightarrow[M]{n} (q, \epsilon, \epsilon)$$

if and only if there exist $q_0, q_1, \ldots, q_k$ such that $p = q_0$, $q = q_k$, and

$$(*, x, \langle q_0\, B_1\, q_1 \rangle \langle q_1\, B_2\, q_2 \rangle \cdots \langle q_{k-1}\, B_k\, q_k \rangle) \xrightarrow[M']{n} (*, \epsilon, \epsilon).$$

In particular,

$$(p, x, B) \xrightarrow[M]{n} (q, \epsilon, \epsilon) \iff (*, x, \langle p\, B\, q \rangle) \xrightarrow[M']{n} (*, \epsilon, \epsilon).$$

Proof. By induction on n (What else?). For $n = 0$, both sides are equivalent to the assertion that $p = q$, $x = \epsilon$, and $k = 0$.

Now suppose that $(p, x, B_1 B_2 \cdots B_k) \xrightarrow[M]{n+1} (q, \epsilon, \epsilon)$. Let

$$((p, c, B_1), (r, C_1 C_2 \cdots C_m))$$

be the first transition applied, where $c \in \Sigma \cup \{\epsilon\}$ and $m \geq 0$. Then $x = cy$ and

$$(p, x, B_1 B_2 \cdots B_k) \xrightarrow[M]{1} (r, y, C_1 C_2 \cdots C_m B_2 \cdots B_k)$$
$$\xrightarrow[M]{n} (q, \epsilon, \epsilon).$$

By the induction hypothesis, there exist $r_0, r_1, \ldots, r_{m-1}, q_1, \ldots, q_{k-1}, q_k$ such that $r = r_0$, $q = q_k$, and

$$(*, y, \langle r_0\, C_1\, r_1 \rangle \langle r_1\, C_2\, r_2 \rangle \cdots \langle r_{m-1}\, C_m\, q_1 \rangle \langle q_1\, B_2\, q_2 \rangle \cdots \langle q_{k-1}\, B_k\, q_k \rangle)$$
$$\xrightarrow[M']{n} (*, \epsilon, \epsilon).$$

Also, by construction of M',

$$((*, c, \langle p\, B_1\, q_1 \rangle), (*, \langle r_0\, C_1\, r_1 \rangle \langle r_1\, C_2\, r_2 \rangle \cdots \langle r_{m-1}\, C_m\, q_1 \rangle))$$

is a transition of M'. Combining these, we get

$$(*, x, \langle p\, B_1\, q_1 \rangle \langle q_1\, B_2\, q_2 \rangle \cdots \langle q_{k-1}\, B_k\, q_k \rangle)$$
$$\xrightarrow[M']{1} (*, y, \langle r_0\, C_1\, r_1 \rangle \langle r_1\, C_2\, r_2 \rangle \cdots \langle r_{m-1}\, C_m\, q_1 \rangle \langle q_1\, B_2\, q_2 \rangle \cdots \langle q_{k-1}\, B_k\, q_k \rangle)$$
$$\xrightarrow[M']{n} (*, \epsilon, \epsilon).$$

Conversely, suppose

$$(*, x, \langle q_0\, B_1\, q_1 \rangle \langle q_1\, B_2\, q_2 \rangle \cdots \langle q_{k-1}\, B_k\, q_k \rangle) \xrightarrow[M']{n} (*, \epsilon, \epsilon).$$

Let

$$((*, c, \langle q_0\, B_1\, q_1 \rangle), (*, \langle r_0\, C_1\, r_1 \rangle \langle r_1\, C_2\, r_2 \rangle \cdots \langle r_{m-1}\, C_m\, q_1 \rangle))$$

be the first transition applied, where $c \in \Sigma \cup \{\epsilon\}$ and $m \geq 0$. Then $x = cy$ and

$$(*, x, \langle q_0 \ B_1 \ q_1 \rangle \langle q_1 \ B_2 \ q_2 \rangle \cdots \langle q_{k-1} \ B_k \ q_k \rangle)$$
$$\xrightarrow[M']{1} (*, y, \langle r_0 \ C_1 \ r_1 \rangle \langle r_1 \ C_2 \ r_2 \rangle \cdots \langle r_{m-1} \ C_m \ q_1 \rangle \langle q_1 \ B_2 \ q_2 \rangle \cdots \langle q_{k-1} \ B_k \ q_k \rangle)$$
$$\xrightarrow[M']{n} (*, \epsilon, \epsilon).$$

By the induction hypothesis,

$$(r_0, y, C_1 C_2 \cdots C_m B_2 \cdots B_k) \xrightarrow[M]{n} (q_k, \epsilon, \epsilon).$$

Also, by construction of M',

$$((q_0, c, B_1), (r_0, C_1 C_2 \cdots C_m))$$

is a transition of M. Combining these, we get

$$(q_0, x, B_1 B_2 \cdots B_k) \xrightarrow[M]{1} (r_0, y, C_1 C_2 \cdots C_m B_2 \cdots B_k)$$
$$\xrightarrow[M]{n} (q_k, \epsilon, \epsilon). \qquad \square$$

Theorem 25.2 $L(M') = L(M)$.

Proof. For all $x \in \Sigma^*$,

$$x \in L(M') \iff (*, x, \langle s \perp t \rangle) \xrightarrow[M']{*} (*, \epsilon, \epsilon)$$
$$\iff (s, x, \perp) \xrightarrow[M]{*} (t, \epsilon, \epsilon) \qquad \text{Lemma 25.1}$$
$$\iff x \in L(M). \qquad \square$$

Historical Notes

Pushdown automata were introduced by Oettinger [95]. The equivalence of PDAs and CFGs was established by Chomsky [19], Schützenberger [112], and Evey [36].

Supplementary Lecture F

Deterministic Pushdown Automata

A *deterministic pushdown automaton* (DPDA) is an octuple

$$M = (Q, \Sigma, \Gamma, \delta, \bot, \dashv, s, F),$$

where everything is the same as with NPDAs, except:

(i) $\dashv$ is a special symbol not in Σ, called the *right endmarker*, and

$$\delta \subseteq (Q \times (\Sigma \cup \{\dashv\} \cup \{\epsilon\}) \times \Gamma) \times (Q \times \Gamma^*).$$

(ii) δ is *deterministic* in the sense that exactly one transition applies in any given situation. This means that for any $p \in Q$, $a \in \Sigma \cup \{\dashv\}$, and $A \in \Gamma$, δ contains exactly one transition of the form $((p, a, A), (q, \beta))$ or $((p, \epsilon, A), (q, \beta))$.

(iii) δ is restricted so that $\bot$ is always on the bottom of the stack. The machine may pop $\bot$ off momentarily, but must push it directly back on. In other words, all transitions involving $\bot$ must be of the form $((p, a, \bot), (q, \beta\bot))$.

The right endmarker $\dashv$ delimits the input string and is a necessary addition. With NPDAs, we could guess where the end of the input string was, but with DPDAs we have no such luxury.

The restriction in (iii) is so that the machine never deadlocks by emptying its stack. This assumption is without loss of generality; even if the machine did not obey it, we could make it do so by a construction involving a new stack symbol $\perp\!\!\perp$, as in Supplementary Lecture E. In that construction, we must modify the transitions (E.2) to read the symbol $\dashv$.

We consider only acceptance by final state. One can define acceptance by empty stack and prove that such machines are equivalent. The assumption (iii) would have to be modified accordingly.

The definitions of configurations and acceptance by final state are the same as with NPDAs. The start configuration on input $x \in \Sigma^*$ is $(s, x \dashv, \perp)$, and x is accepted iff

$$(s, x \dashv, \perp) \xrightarrow[M]{*} (q, \epsilon, \beta)$$

for some $q \in F$ and $\beta \in \Gamma^*$.

A language accepted by a DPDA is called a *deterministic context-free language* (DCFL). Surely every DCFL is a CFL, since every DPDA can be simulated by an NPDA. In this lecture we will show that the family of DCFLs is closed under complement. We know that there exist CFLs whose complements are not CFLs; for example,

$$\{a, b\}^* - \{ww \mid w \in \{a, b\}^*\}.$$

These CFLs cannot be DCFLs. Thus, unlike finite automata, nondeterminism in PDAs gives strictly more power.

To show that the DCFLs are closed under complement, we will construct, given any DPDA M with input alphabet Σ, a new DPDA M' such that $L(M') = \Sigma^* - L(M)$.

We would like to build M' to simulate M and accept iff M does not accept. Unfortunately, we cannot just switch accept and nonaccept states like we did with DFAs. The main difficulty here is that unlike finite automata, DPDAs need not scan all of their input; they may loop infinitely on inputs they do not accept without reading the entire input string. The machine M' will have to detect any such pathological behavior in M, since M' will have to scan the entire input and enter an accept state on all those inputs that are not accepted by M, including those inputs on which M loops prematurely.

We solve this problem by showing how to modify M to detect such spurious looping and deal with it gracefully. After each modification step, we will argue that the resulting machine still accepts the same set as M and is still deterministic.

Checking for End of Input

It will be useful to include one bit of information in the finite control of M to remember whether or not M has seen the endmarker $\dashv$ yet. Formally, we duplicate the finite control Q to get a new copy $Q' = \{q' \mid q \in Q\}$ disjoint from Q and add a new transition

$$((p', a, A), (q', \beta))$$

for each transition $((p, a, A), (q, \beta)) \in \delta$. We remove any transition of the form $((p, \dashv, A), (q, \beta))$ and replace it with $((p, \dashv, A), (q', \beta))$. The primed states thus behave exactly like the unprimed original states, except that we jump from an unprimed state to a primed state when we scan the endmarker. The start state will still be s, but we will take as final states all primed states corresponding to final states in the old machine M; that is, the new set of final states will be

$$F' = \{q' \mid q \in F\}.$$

The new machine is still deterministic, since there is still exactly one transition that applies in any configuration. It accepts the same set, since if

$$(s, x \dashv, \bot) \xrightarrow[M]{*} (q, \epsilon, \gamma), \quad q \in F$$

in the old machine, then there must be some intermediate transition that reads the $\dashv$:

$$(s, x \dashv, \bot) \xrightarrow[M]{*} (p, \dashv, A\beta) \xrightarrow[M]{1} (r, \epsilon, \alpha\beta) \xrightarrow[M]{*} (q, \epsilon, \gamma).$$

Then in the new machine,

$$(s, x \dashv, \bot) \xrightarrow[M']{*} (p, \dashv, A\beta) \xrightarrow[M']{1} (r', \epsilon, \alpha\beta) \xrightarrow[M']{*} (q', \epsilon, \gamma).$$

Conversely, if

$$(s, x \dashv, \bot) \xrightarrow[M']{*} (q', \epsilon, \gamma), \quad q' \in F'$$

in the new machine, then removing the primes gives a valid accepting computation sequence

$$(s, x \dashv, \bot) \xrightarrow[M]{*} (q, \epsilon, \gamma), \quad q \in F$$

in the old machine.

Now we can tell from information in the state whether we have seen $\dashv$ or not. With this information, we can make the machine remain in an accept state if it has already scanned the $\dashv$ and accepted. This is done by deleting every primed transition $((p', \epsilon, A), (q', \beta))$ with $p' \in F'$ and replacing it with $((p', \epsilon, A), (p', A))$.

Getting Rid of Spurious Loops

We include two new nonaccept states r and r' and transitions

$$((r, a, A), (r, A)), \quad a \in \Sigma, \; A \in \Gamma,$$
$$((r, \dashv, A), (r', A)), \quad A \in \Gamma,$$
$$((r', \epsilon, A), (r', A)), \quad A \in \Gamma.$$

We can think of r' as a reject state. If the machine is in state r, it will always scan to the end of the input and enter state r', leaving the stack intact. Once the machine is in state r', it stays there. (So far there is no way for the machine to reach state r or r', but just wait ...)

We will now show how to modify the machine so that for all inputs, the machine scans the entire input and enters either an accept state or the state r'. Let x be any input. Because of determinism, there is a unique infinite sequence of configurations the machine goes through on input x. Let γ_i denote the stack contents at time $i \in \{0, 1, 2, \ldots\}$. There exists an infinite sequence of times $i_0 < i_1 < i_2 < \cdots$ such that for all i_k,

$$|\gamma_{i_k}| \leq |\gamma_i|, \quad i \geq i_k. \tag{F.1}$$

We can take $i_0 = 0$, since $\gamma_0 = \perp$ and $|\gamma_0| = 1$, and the machine never empties its stack. Proceeding inductively, we can take i_{k+1} to be the earliest time after i_k such that $|\gamma_{i_{k+1}}|$ is minimum among all $|\gamma_i|$, $i > i_k$.

Now we pick an infinite subsequence $j_0 < j_1 < j_2 < \cdots$ of $i_0 < i_1 < i_2 < \cdots$ such that the same transition, say $((p, \epsilon, A), (q, \beta))$, is applied at times $j_0, j_1, j_2, \ldots$. Such a subsequence exists by the pigeonhole principle: there are only finitely many transitions in δ, so at least one must be applied infinitely often. The states p, q can be primed or unprimed. The transition must be an ϵ-transition, since it is applied infinitely often, and there are only finitely many input symbols to scan.

By (F.1), the machine never sees any stack symbol below the top symbol of γ_{j_k} after time j_k, and the top symbol is A. Thus the only stack symbols it sees after time j_k are those it pushes after time j_k. Since the machine is deterministic, once it applies transition $((p, \epsilon, A), (q, \beta))$, it is in a loop and will go through the same periodic sequence of ϵ-transitions repeated forever, since it sees nothing that can force it to do anything different. Moreover, this behavior is independent of the input. Thus if p is not an accept state, then the input is not accepted. We might as well remove the transition $((p, \epsilon, A), (q, \beta))$ from δ and replace it with the transition $((p, \epsilon, A), (r, A))$ if p is an unprimed state or $((p, \epsilon, A), (r', A))$ if p is a primed state. The language accepted by the automaton is not changed.

If this is done for all transitions $((p, \epsilon, A), (q, \beta))$ causing such spurious loops, we obtain a machine equivalent to M that on any input scans the entire input string and the endmarker ⊣ and enters either an accept state or the state r'. To get a machine M' accepting the complement of $L(M)$, make r' the unique accept state of M'.

Historical Notes

Deterministic PDAs were first studied by Fischer [37], Schützenberger [112], Haines [54], and Ginsburg and Greibach [44].

Lecture 26

Parsing

One of the most important applications of context-free languages and pushdown automata is in compilers. The input to a PASCAL compiler is a PASCAL program, but it is presented to the compiler as a string of ASCII characters. Before it can do anything else, the compiler has to scan this string and determine the syntactic structure of the program. This process is called *parsing*.

The syntax of the programming language (or at least big parts of it) is often specified in terms of a context-free grammar. The process of parsing is essentially determining a parse tree or derivation tree of the program in that grammar. This tree provides the structure the compiler needs to know in order to generate code.

The subroutine of the compiler that parses the input is called the *parser*. Many parsers use a single stack and resemble deterministic PDAs. By now the theory of deterministic PDAs and parsing is so well developed that in many instances a parser for a given grammar can be generated automatically. This technology is used in what we call *compiler compilers*.

Example 26.1   Consider well-parenthesized expressions of propositional logic. There are propositional variables P, Q, R, ..., constants $\bot, \top$ (for *false* and *true*, respectively), binary operators $\wedge$ (*and*), $\vee$ (*or*), $\rightarrow$ (*implication* or *if-then*), and $\leftrightarrow$ (*if and only if* or *biconditional*), and unary operator $\neg$ (*not*), as well as parentheses. The following grammar generates the well-parenthesized propositional expressions (we've used $\Rightarrow$ instead of the usual $\rightarrow$ for productions to avoid confusion with the propositional implication operator):

$$
\begin{aligned}
E &\Rightarrow (EBE) \mid (UE) \mid C \mid V, \\
B &\Rightarrow \vee \mid \wedge \mid \rightarrow \mid \leftrightarrow, \\
U &\Rightarrow \neg, \\
C &\Rightarrow \bot \mid \top, \\
V &\Rightarrow P \mid Q \mid R \mid \ldots \; .
\end{aligned}
\tag{26.1}
$$

The words "well-parenthesized" mean that there must be parentheses around any compound expression. (We'll show how to get rid of them later using *operator precedence*.) The presence of the parentheses ensures that the grammar is unambiguous—that is, each expression in the language has a *unique* parse tree, so that there is one and only one way to parse the expression. A typical expression in this language is

$$
(((P \vee Q) \wedge R) \vee (Q \wedge (\neg P))). \tag{26.2}
$$

Each expression represents an *expression tree* that gives the order of evaluation. The expression tree corresponding to the propositional expression (26.2) is

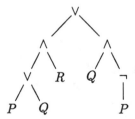

In order to generate code to evaluate the expression, the compiler needs to know this expression tree. The expression tree and the unique parse tree for the expression in the grammar (26.1) above contain the same information; in fact, the expression tree can be read off immediately from the parse tree. Thus parsing is essentially equivalent to producing the expression tree, which can then be used to generate code to evaluate the expression.

Here's an example of a parser for propositional expressions that produces the expression tree directly. This is a typical parser you might see in a real compiler.

Start with only the initial stack symbol $\bot$ on the stack. Scan the expression from left to right, performing one of the following actions depending on each symbol:

(i) If the symbol is a (, push it onto the stack.

(ii) If the symbol is an operator, either unary or binary, push it onto the stack.

(iii) If the symbol is a constant, push a pointer to it onto the stack.

(iv) If the symbol is a variable, look it up in the symbol table and push a pointer to the symbol table entry onto the stack. The symbol table is a dictionary containing the name of every variable used in the program and a pointer to a memory location where its value will be stored. If the variable has never been seen before, a new symbol table entry is created.

(v) If the symbol is a), do a *reduce*. This is where all the action takes place. A reduce step consists of the following sequence of actions:

(a) Allocate a block of storage for a new node in the expression tree. The block has space for the name of an operator and pointers to left and right operands.

(b) Pop the top object off the stack. It had better be a pointer to an operand (either a constant, variable, or node in the expression tree created previously). If not, give a syntax error. If so, save the pointer in the newly allocated node as the right operand.

(c) Pop the top object off the stack. It had better be an operator. If not, give a syntax error. If so, save the operator name in the newly allocated node. If the operator is unary, skip the next step (d) and go directly to (e).

(d) Pop the top object off the stack. It had better be a pointer to an operand. If not, give a syntax error. If so, save the pointer in the newly allocated node as the left operand.

(e) Pop the top object off the stack. It had better be a (. This is the left parenthesis matching the right parenthesis we just scanned. If not, give a syntax error.

(f) Push a pointer to the newly allocated node onto the stack.

Let's illustrate this algorithm on the input string

$$(((P \vee Q) \wedge R) \vee (Q \wedge (\neg P))).$$

We start with the stack containing only an initial stack symbol $\perp$. We scan the first three ('s and push them according to (i). We scan P and push a pointer to its symbol table entry according to (iv). We push the operator $\vee$ according to (ii), then push a pointer to Q according to (iv). At this point the stack looks like

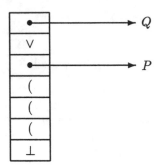

We now scan the) and do a reduce step (v). We allocate a block of storage for a new node in the expression tree, pop the operands and operator on top of the stack and save them in the node, pop the matching (, and push a pointer to the new node. Now we have

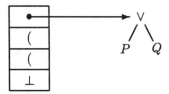

on the stack, and we are scanning

$$(((P \lor Q) \land R) \lor (Q \land (\neg P)))$$
$$\uparrow$$

We push the $\land$ and a pointer to R. At that point we have

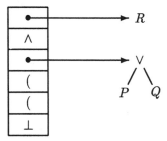

and we scan the next), so we reduce, giving

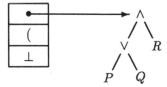

and we are left scanning

$$(((P \lor Q) \land R) \lor (Q \land (\neg P)))$$
$$\uparrow$$

Now we scan and push everything up to the next). This gives

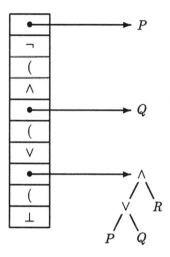

We scan the first of the final three)'s and reduce. This gives

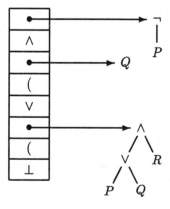

We scan the next) and reduce, giving

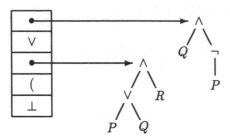

Finally, we scan the last) and reduce, giving

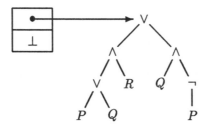

When we come to the end of the expression, we are left with nothing on the stack but a pointer to the entire expression tree and the initial stack symbol.   □

Operator Precedence

The grammar of the preceding example is *unambiguous* in the sense that there is one and only one parse tree (and hence only one possible expression tree) for every expression in the language. If we don't want to write all those parentheses, we can change the language to allow us to omit them if we like:

$$E \Rightarrow EBE \mid UE \mid C \mid V \mid (E),$$
$$B \Rightarrow \vee \mid \wedge \mid \rightarrow \mid \leftrightarrow,$$
$$U \Rightarrow \neg,$$
$$C \Rightarrow 0 \mid 1,$$
$$V \Rightarrow P \mid Q \mid R \mid \dots .$$

But the problem with this is that the grammar is now ambiguous. For example, there are two possible trees corresponding to the expression

$$P \vee Q \wedge R,$$

namely

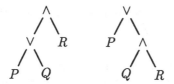

with very different semantics. We need a way of resolving the ambiguity. This is often done by giving a *precedence relation* on operators that specifies which operators are to be evaluated first in case of ambiguity. The precedence relation is just a partial order on the operators. To resolve ambiguity among operators of equal precedence, we will perform the operations from left to right. (The left-to-right convention corresponds to common informal usage, but some programming languages, such as APL, use the opposite convention.) Under these conventions, we only need parentheses when we want to depart from the default parse tree.

For example, consider the following grammar for well-formed arithmetic expressions over constants $0, 1$, variables a, b, c, and operator symbols $+$ (addition), binary $-$ (subtraction), unary $-$ (negation), $\cdot$ (multiplication), and $/$ (division):

$$
\begin{aligned}
E &\rightarrow E + E \mid E - E \mid E \cdot E \mid E/E \mid -E \mid C \mid V \mid (E), \\
C &\rightarrow 0 \mid 1, \\
V &\rightarrow a \mid b \mid c.
\end{aligned}
\tag{26.3}
$$

This grammar is ambiguous. For example, there are five different parse trees for the expression

$$
a + b \cdot c + d
\tag{26.4}
$$

corresponding to the five expression trees

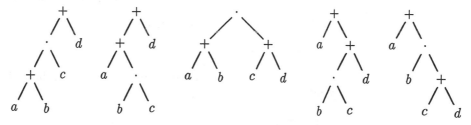

The usual precedence relation on the arithmetic operators gives unary minus highest precedence, followed by $\cdot$ and $/$, which have equal precedence, followed by $+$ and binary $-$, which have equal and lowest precedence. Thus for the arithmetic expression (26.4), the preferred expression tree is the second from the left. This is because the $\cdot$ wants to be performed before either of the $+$'s, and between the $+$'s the leftmost wants to be performed first. If we want the expression evaluated differently, say according to the middle expression tree, then we need to use parentheses:

$$(a + b) \cdot (c + d).$$

The operators $+$ and binary $-$ have equal precedence, since common usage would evaluate both $a - b + c$ and $a + b - c$ from left to right.

One can modify the grammar (26.3) so as to obtain an equivalent unambiguous grammar. The same set of strings is generated, but the precedence of the operators is accounted for. In the modified grammar, each generated string again has a unique parse tree, and this parse tree correctly reflects the precedence of the operators. Such a grammar equivalent to (26.3) would be

$$E \rightarrow E + F \mid E - F \mid F,$$
$$F \rightarrow F \cdot G \mid F/G \mid G,$$
$$G \rightarrow -G \mid H,$$
$$H \rightarrow C \mid V \mid (E),$$
$$C \rightarrow 0 \mid 1,$$
$$V \rightarrow a \mid b \mid c.$$

Given a precedence relation on the operators, the parsing algorithm above can be modified to handle expressions that are not fully parenthesized as follows. Whenever we are about to scan a binary operator B, we check to make sure there is an operand on top of the stack, then we look at the stack symbol A immediately below it. If A is a symbol of lower precedence than B (and for this purpose the left parenthesis and the initial stack symbol have lower precedence than any operator), we push B. If A is a symbol of higher or equal precedence, then we reduce and repeat the process.

Let's illustrate with the expression

$$a + b \cdot c + d.$$

We start with the stack containing only $\bot$. We scan the variable a and push a pointer to it.

At this point we are about to scan the $+$ (we don't actually scan past it yet, we just look at it). We check under the operand on top of the stack and see the initial stack symbol $\bot$, which has lower precedence than $+$, so we scan and push the $+$. We then scan and push the b, giving

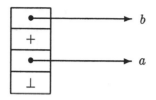

At this point we are about to scan the ·. We check under the operand on top of the stack and see the +, which has lower precedence than ·, so we scan and push the ·. We then scan and push the c, giving

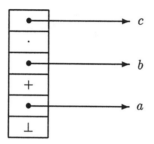

Now we are about to scan the second + (we don't actually scan past it yet). We check under the operand on top of the stack and see the ·, which has higher precedence than +, so we reduce. This gives

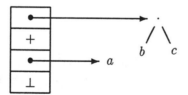

In this reduce step, we don't try to pop the (. Good thing, since it's not there. Left parentheses are popped only when they are there and when the symbol about to be scanned is a right parenthesis. Now we repeat the process. We still haven't scanned the second +, so we ask again whether the symbol immediately below the operand on top of the stack is of higher or equal precedence. In this case it is the +, which is of equal precedence, so we reduce.

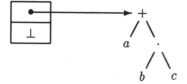

We are still looking at the + in the input string. Now we check again below the operand on top of the stack and find ⊥, which is of lower precedence, so we scan and push the +, then scan and push the d.

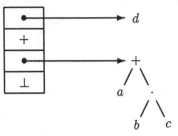

At this point we come to the end of the expression. We now reduce until no further reduce steps are possible. We are left with nothing on the stack but a pointer to the desired expression tree and the initial stack symbol.

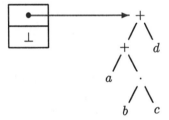

Historical Notes

An early paper on parsing is Knuth [71]. The theory is by now quite well developed, and we have only scratched the surface here. Good introductory texts are Aho and Ullman [2, 3, 4] and Lewis, Rosenkrantz, and Stearns [80].

Lecture 27

The Cocke–Kasami–Younger Algorithm

Given a CFL A and a string $x \in \Sigma^*$, how do we tell whether x is in A? If A is a deterministic CFL and we are given a deterministic PDA for it, we can easily write a program to simulate the PDA. In fact, this is a good way to do it in practice and is done frequently in compilers; we saw an example of this in Lecture 26.

What if A is not a deterministic CFL, or even if it is but we are not given a deterministic PDA for it? If A is given by a CFG G, we can first convert G to Chomsky normal form ($A \rightarrow BC$ or $A \rightarrow a$) so that each production either produces a terminal or increases the length of the sentential form, then try all derivations of length $2|x| - 1$ to see if any of them produce x. Unfortunately, there might be exponentially many such derivations, so this is rather inefficient. Alternatively, we might produce an equivalent NPDA and try all computation sequences, but again because of the nondeterminism there may be exponentially many to try.

Here is a cubic-time algorithm due to Cocke, Kasami, and Younger [65, 125]. It is an example of the technique of *dynamic programming*, a very useful technique in the design of efficient algorithms. It determines for each substring y of x the set of all nonterminals that generate y. This is done inductively on the length of y.

For simplicity, we will assume that the given grammar G is in Chomsky normal form. One can give a more general version of the algorithm that works for grammars not in this form.

We illustrate the algorithm with an example. Consider the following grammar for the set of all nonnull strings with equally many a's and b's:

$$S \to AB \mid BA \mid SS \mid AC \mid BD,$$
$$A \to a, \qquad B \to b,$$
$$C \to SB, \qquad D \to SA.$$

We'll run the algorithm on the input string $x = aabbab$. Let n be the length of the string (here $n = 6$). Draw $n + 1$ vertical lines separating the letters of x and number them 0 to n:

$$|a|a|b|b|a|b|$$
$$0\ 1\ 2\ 3\ 4\ 5\ 6$$

For $0 \le i < j \le n$, let x_{ij} denote the substring of x between lines i and j. In this example, $x_{1,4} = abb$ and $x_{2,6} = bbab$. The whole string x is $x_{0,n}$. Build a table T with $\binom{n}{2}$ entries, one for each pair i, j such that $0 \le i < j \le n$.

```
0
−   1
−   −   2
−   −   −   3
−   −   −   −   4
−   −   −   −   −   5
−   −   −   −   −   −   6
```

The i, jth entry of T, denoted T_{ij}, refers to the substring x_{ij}.

We will fill in each entry T_{ij} of T with the set of nonterminals of G that generate the substring x_{ij} of x. This information will be produced inductively, shorter substrings first.

We start with the substrings of length one. These are the substrings of x of the form $x_{i,i+1}$ for $0 \le i \le n - 1$ and correspond to the table entries along the top diagonal. For each such substring $c = x_{i,i+1}$, if there is a production $X \to c \in G$, we write the nonterminal X in the table at location $i, i + 1$.

```
0
A   1
−   A   2
−   −   B   3
−   −   −   B   4
−   −   −   −   A   5
−   −   −   −   −   B   6
```

In this example, B is written in $T_{3,4}$ because $x_{3,4} = b$ and $B \to b$ is a production of G. In general, $T_{i,i+1}$ may contain several nonterminals, because there may be several different productions with $c = x_{i,i+1}$ on the right-hand side. We write them all in the table at position $T_{i,i+1}$.

Now we proceed to the substrings of length two. These correspond to the diagonal in T immediately below the top diagonal we just filled in.

For each such substring $x_{i,i+2}$, we break the substring up into two non-null substrings $x_{i,i+1}$ and $x_{i+1,i+2}$ of length one and check the table entries $T_{i,i+1}$, $T_{i+1,i+2}$ corresponding to those substrings. These entries occur immediately above and to the right of $T_{i,i+2}$. We select a nonterminal from each of these locations (say X from $T_{i,i+1}$ and Y from $T_{i+1,i+2}$) and look to see if there are any productions $Z \to XY$ in G. For each such production we find, we label $T_{i,i+2}$ with Z. We do this for all possible choices of $X \in T_{i,i+1}$ and $Y \in T_{i+1,i+2}$.

In our example, for $x_{0,2} = aa$, we find only $A \in T_{0,1}$ and A in $T_{1,2}$, so we look for a production with AA on the right-hand side. There aren't any, so $T_{0,2}$ is the empty set. Let's write $\varnothing$ in the table to indicate this.

For $T_{1,3}$, we find A immediately above and B to the right, so we look for a production with AB on the right-hand side and find $S \to AB$, so we label $T_{1,3}$ with S. We continue in this fashion until all the $T_{i,i+2}$ are filled in.

```
0
A   1
Ø   A   2
–   S   B   3
–   –   Ø   B   4
–   –   –   S   A   5
–   –   –   –   S   B   6
```

Now we proceed to strings of length three. For each such string, there are two ways to break it up into two nonnull substrings. For example,

$$x_{0,3} = x_{0,1}x_{1,3} = x_{0,2}x_{2,3}.$$

We need to check both possibilities. For the first, we find $A \in T_{0,1}$ and $S \in T_{1,3}$, so we look for a production with right-hand side AS. There aren't any. Now we check $T_{0,2}$ and $T_{2,3}$. We find $\varnothing$ in $T_{0,2}$, so there is nothing more to check. We didn't find a nonterminal generating $x_{0,3}$, so we label $T_{0,3}$ with $\varnothing$.

For $x_{1,4} = x_{1,2}x_{2,4} = x_{1,3}x_{3,4}$, we find $A \in T_{1,2}$ and $\varnothing$ in $T_{2,4}$, so there is nothing here to check; and we find $S \subset T_{1,3}$ and $B \in T_{3,4}$, so we look for a production with right-hand side SB and find $C \to SB$; thus we label $T_{1,4}$

with C.

```
0
A    1
ø    A    2
ø    S    B    3
-    C    ø    B    4
-    -    -    S    A    5
-    -    -    -    S    B    6
```

We continue in this fashion, filling in the rest of the entries corresponding to strings of length three, then strings of length four, and so forth. For strings of length four, there are three ways to break them up, and all must be checked. The following is the final result:

```
0
A    1
ø    A    2
ø    S    B    3
S    C    ø    B    4
D    S    ø    S    A    5
S    C    ø    C    S    B    6
```

We see that $T_{0,6}$ contains S, the start symbol, indicating that

$$S \xrightarrow[G]{*} x_{0,6} = x,$$

so we conclude that x is generated by G.

In this example, there is at most one nonterminal in each location. This is because for this particular grammar, the nonterminals generate disjoint sets. In general, there may be more than one nonterminal in each location.

A formal description of the algorithm is given below. One can ascertain from the nested loop structure that the complexity of the algorithm is $O(pn^3)$, where $n = |x|$ and p is the number of productions of G.

```
for i := 0 to n − 1 do                    /* strings of length 1 first */
  begin
     T_{i,i+1} := ∅;                       /* initialize to ∅ */
     for A → a a production of G do
        if a = x_{i,i+1} then T_{i,i+1} := T_{i,i+1} ∪ {A}
  end;
for m := 2 to n do                        /* for each length m ≥ 2 */
  for i := 0 to n − m do                  /* for each substring */
    begin                                 /* of length m */
       T_{i,i+m} := ∅;                     /* initialize to ∅ */
       for j := i + 1 to i + m − 1 do     /* for all ways to break */
          for A → BC a production of G do /* up the string */
             if B ∈ T_{i,j} ∧ C ∈ T_{j,i+m}
                then T_{i,i+m} := T_{i,i+m} ∪ {A}
    end;
```

Closure Properties of CFLs

CFLs are closed under union: if A and B are CFLs, say generated by grammars G_1 and G_2 with start symbols S_1 and S_2, respectively, one can form a grammar generating $A \cup B$ by combining all productions of G_1 and G_2 along with a new start symbol S and new productions $S \to S_1$ and $S \to S_2$. Before combining the grammars, we must first make sure G_1 and G_2 have disjoint sets of nonterminals. If not, just rename the nonterminals in one of them.

Similarly, CFLs are closed under set concatenation: if A and B are CFLs generated by grammars G_1 and G_2 as above, one can form a grammar generating $AB = \{xy \mid x \in A,\ y \in B\}$ by combining G_1 and G_2 with a new start symbol S and new production $S \to S_1 S_2$.

CFLs are closed under asterate: if A is a CFL generated by a grammar with start symbol S_1, then A^* is generated by the same grammar but with new start symbol S and new productions $S \to S_1 S \mid \epsilon$.

CFLs are closed under intersection with regular sets: if A is a CFL and R is regular, then $A \cap R$ is a CFL (Homework 7, Exercise 2). This can be shown by a product construction involving a PDA for A and a DFA for R similar to the construction we used to show that the intersection of two regular sets is regular. This property is useful in simplifying proofs that certain sets are not context-free. For example, to show that the set

$$A = \{x \in \{a, b, c\}^* \mid \#a(x) = \#b(x) = \#c(x)\}$$

is not context-free, intersect it with $a^*b^*c^*$ to get

$$A \cap a^*b^*c^* = \{a^n b^n c^n \mid n \geq 0\},$$

which we have already shown is not context-free.

Techniques similar to those used in Lecture 10 to show that the regular sets are closed under homomorphic images and preimages can be used to show the same results for CFLs (Miscellaneous Exercise 79).

CFLs are *not* closed under intersection:

$$\{a^m b^m c^n \mid m, n \geq 0\} \cap \{a^m b^n c^n \mid m, n \geq 0\} = \{a^n b^n c^n \mid n \geq 0\}.$$

The product construction does not work for two CFLs; intuitively, there is no way to simulate two independent stacks with a single stack.

We have also shown in Lecture 22 that the family of CFLs is not closed under complement: the set $\{ww \mid w \in \{a,b\}^*\}$ is not a CFL, but its complement is.

Closure Properties of DCFLs

A *deterministic context-free language* (DCFL) is a language accepted by a deterministic PDA (DPDA). These automata were introduced in Supplementary Lecture F. A DPDA is like an NPDA, except that its transition relation is single-valued (i.e., is a function). We also need to include a special right endmarker ⊣ so that the machine can tell when it reaches the end of the input string. The endmarker is not necessary for an NPDA, because an NPDA can guess nondeterministically where the end of the input string is.

Most of the important examples of CFLs we have seen have been DCFLs. For example,

$$\{a^n b^n \mid n \geq 0\}$$

is a DCFL. The shift-reduce parser of Lecture 26 was also a DPDA.

Every DCFL is a CFL, but not vice versa. The set

$$\{a,b\}^* - \{ww \mid w \in \{a,b\}^*\}$$

is an example of a CFL that is not a DCFL. We showed in Lecture 22 that this set is a CFL, but its complement is not. This implies that neither set is accepted by any DPDA, since as we showed in Supplementary Lecture F, the family of DCFLs is closed under complement. Thus, unlike the case of finite automata, deterministic PDAs are strictly less powerful than nondeterministic ones.

DCFLs are not closed under union. For example, consider the union

$$\{a^m b^n c^k \mid m \neq n\} \cup \{a^m b^n c^k \mid n \neq k\}.$$

Each set is a DCFL. The union is a CFL—an NPDA could guess nondeterministically which condition to check for—but it is not a DCFL. If it were, then its complement

$$\sim\{a^m b^n c^k \mid m \neq n\} \cap \sim\{a^m b^n c^k \mid n \neq k\}$$

would be. But then intersecting with the regular set $a^* b^* c^*$ would give

$$\{a^n b^n c^n \mid n \geq 0\},$$

which is not even context-free.

Similarly, DCFLs are not closed under reversal, although proving this is a little harder. The set

$$\{b a^m b^n c^k \mid m \neq n\} \cup \{c a^m b^n c^k \mid n \neq k\}$$

over the alphabet $\{a, b, c\}$ is an example of a DCFL whose reversal is not a DCFL (Miscellaneous Exercise 93).

Historical Notes

The CKY algorithm first appeared in print in Kasami [65] and Younger [125], although Hopcroft and Ullman [60] credit the original idea to John Cocke.

Closure properties of CFLs were studied by Scheinberg [110], Ginsburg and Rose [46, 48], Bar-Hillel, Perles, and Shamir [8], and Ginsburg and Spanier [49].

See p. 180 for the history of DPDAs and DCFLs.

Supplementary Lecture G

The Chomsky–Schützenberger Theorem

Let PAREN_n denote the language consisting of all balanced strings of parentheses of n distinct types. This language is generated by the grammar

$$S \rightarrow [S]_1 \mid [S]_2 \mid \cdots \mid [S]_n \mid SS \mid \epsilon.$$

The languages PAREN_n are sometimes called *Dyck languages* in the literature.

The following theorem shows that the parenthesis languages PAREN_n play a special role in the theory of context-free languages: *every* CFL is essentially a parenthesis language modified in some relatively simple way. In a sense, balanced parentheses capture the essential structure of CFLs that differentiates them from the regular sets.

Theorem G.1 **(Chomsky–Schützenberger)** *Every context-free language is a homomorphic image of the intersection of a parenthesis language and a regular set. In other words, for every CFL A, there is an $n \geq 0$, a regular set R, and a homomorphism h such that*

$$A = h(\text{PAREN}_n \cap R).$$

Recall from Lecture 10 that a *homomorphism* is a map $h : \Gamma^* \rightarrow \Sigma^*$ such that $h(xy) = h(x)h(y)$ for all $x, y \in \Gamma^*$. It follows from this property that $h(\epsilon) = \epsilon$ and that h is completely determined by its values on Γ. The *homomorphic image* of a set $B \subseteq \Gamma^*$ under h is the set $\{h(x) \mid x \in B\} \subseteq \Sigma^*$, denoted $h(B)$.

Proof. Let $G = (N, \Sigma, P, S)$ be an arbitrary CFG in Chomsky normal form. Denote productions in P by $\pi, \rho, \sigma, \ldots$.

For $\pi \in P$, define

$$\pi' = \begin{cases} A \to \overset{1}{\underset{\pi}{[}} B \overset{12}{\underset{\pi\pi}{][}} C \overset{2}{\underset{\pi}{]}} & \text{if } \pi = A \to BC, \\[2mm] A \to \overset{1}{\underset{\pi}{[}} \overset{12}{\underset{\pi\pi}{][}} \overset{2}{\underset{\pi}{]}} & \text{if } \pi = A \to a; \end{cases}$$

and define the grammar $G' = (N, \Gamma, P', S)$ with

$$\Gamma = \{\overset{1}{\underset{\pi}{[}}, \overset{1}{\underset{\pi}{]}}, \overset{2}{\underset{\pi}{[}}, \overset{2}{\underset{\pi}{]}} \mid \pi \in P\},$$

$$P' = \{\pi' \mid \pi \in P\}.$$

The idea here is that a balanced string of parentheses generated by G' encodes a corresponding string generated by G along with its parse tree.

Let PAREN_Γ be the parenthesis language over parentheses Γ. Surely $L(G') \subseteq \mathrm{PAREN}_\Gamma$, since the productions of G' generate parentheses in well-nested matched pairs. However, not all strings in PAREN_Γ are generated by G'. Here are some properties satisfied by strings in $L(G')$ that are not satisfied by strings in PAREN_Γ in general:

(i) Every $\overset{1}{\underset{\pi}{]}}$ is immediately followed by a $\overset{2}{\underset{\pi}{[}}$.

(ii) No $\overset{2}{\underset{\pi}{]}}$ is immediately followed by a left parenthesis.

(iii) If $\pi = A \to BC$, then every $\overset{1}{\underset{\pi}{[}}$ is immediately followed by $\overset{1}{\underset{\rho}{[}}$ for some $\rho \in P$ with left-hand side B, and every $\overset{2}{\underset{\pi}{[}}$ is immediately followed by $\overset{1}{\underset{\sigma}{[}}$ for some $\sigma \in P$ with left-hand side C.

(iv) If $\pi = A \to a$, then every $\overset{1}{\underset{\pi}{[}}$ is immediately followed by $\overset{1}{\underset{\pi}{]}}$ and every $\overset{2}{\underset{\pi}{[}}$ is immediately followed by $\overset{2}{\underset{\pi}{]}}$.

In addition, all strings x such that $A \xrightarrow[G']{*} x$ satisfy the property

(v_A) The string x begins with $\overset{1}{\underset{\pi}{[}}$ for some $\pi \in P$ with left-hand side A.

Each of the properties (i) though (v_A) can be described by a regular expression; thus the sets

$$R_A = \{x \in \Gamma^* \mid x \text{ satisfies (i) through } (v_A)\}$$

are regular. We claim

Lemma G.2 $A \xrightarrow[G']{*} x \iff x \in \mathrm{PAREN}_\Gamma \cap R_A.$

Proof. The direction ($\Rightarrow$) is a straightforward proof by induction on the length of the derivation. For the direction ($\Leftarrow$), suppose $x \in \mathrm{PAREN}_\Gamma \cap R_A$. We proceed by induction on the length of x. It follows from properties (i) through (v_A) and the fact that x is a string of balanced parentheses that x is of the form

$$x = \overset{1}{\underset{\pi}{[}} y \overset{12}{\underset{\pi\pi}{]}\underset{}{[}} z \overset{2}{\underset{\pi}{]}}$$

for some $y, z \in \Gamma^*$ and π with left-hand side A. If $\pi = A \to BC$, then from property (iii), y satisfies (v_B) and z satisfies (v_C). Also, y and z satisfy (i) through (iv) and are balanced. Thus $y \in \mathrm{PAREN}_\Gamma \cap R_B$ and $z \in \mathrm{PAREN}_\Gamma \cap R_C$. By the induction hypothesis, $B \xrightarrow[G']{*} y$ and $C \xrightarrow[G']{*} z$; therefore,

$$A \xrightarrow[G']{1} \overset{1}{\underset{\pi}{[}} B \overset{12}{\underset{\pi\pi}{]}\underset{}{[}} C \overset{2}{\underset{\pi}{]}} \xrightarrow[G']{*} \overset{1}{\underset{\pi}{[}} y \overset{12}{\underset{\pi\pi}{]}\underset{}{[}} z \overset{2}{\underset{\pi}{]}} = x.$$

If $\pi = A \to a$, then from property (iv), $y = z = \epsilon$, and

$$A \xrightarrow[G']{1} \overset{1}{\underset{\pi}{[}} \overset{12}{\underset{\pi\pi}{]}\underset{}{[}} \overset{2}{\underset{\pi}{]}} = x. \qquad \square$$

It follows from Lemma G.2 that $L(G') = \mathrm{PAREN}_\Gamma \cap R_S$. Now define the homomorphism $h : \Gamma^* \to \Sigma^*$ as follows. For π of the form $A \to BC$, take

$$h\Big(\overset{1}{\underset{\pi}{[}}\Big) = h\Big(\overset{1}{\underset{\pi}{]}}\Big) = h\Big(\overset{2}{\underset{\pi}{[}}\Big) = h\Big(\overset{2}{\underset{\pi}{]}}\Big) = \epsilon.$$

For π of the form $A \to a$, take

$$h\Big(\overset{1}{\underset{\pi}{]}}\Big) = h\Big(\overset{2}{\underset{\pi}{[}}\Big) = h\Big(\overset{2}{\underset{\pi}{]}}\Big) = \epsilon,$$

$$h\Big(\overset{1}{\underset{\pi}{[}}\Big) = a.$$

Applying h to the production π' of P' gives the production π of P; thus $L(G) = h(L(G')) = h(\mathrm{PAREN}_\Gamma \cap R_S)$. This completes the proof of the Chomsky–Schützenberger theorem. $\qquad \square$

Historical Notes

The pivotal importance of balanced parentheses in the theory of context-free languages was recognized quite early on. The Chomsky–Schützenberger theorem is due to Chomsky and Schützenberger [19, 22].

Supplementary Lecture H

Parikh's Theorem

Here is a theorem that says a little more about the structure of CFLs. It says that for any CFL A, if we look only at the relative number of occurrences of terminal symbols in strings in A without regard to their order, then A is indistinguishable from a regular set.

Formally, let $\Sigma = \{a_1, \ldots, a_k\}$. The *Parikh map* is the function

$$\psi : \Sigma^* \to \mathbb{N}^k$$

defined by

$$\psi(x) \stackrel{\text{def}}{=} (\#a_1(x), \#a_2(x), \ldots, \#a_k(x)).$$

That is, $\psi(x)$ records the number of occurrences of each symbol in x. The structure Σ^* with binary operation $\cdot$ (concatenation) and constant ϵ forms a monoid,[1] as does the structure $\mathbb{N}^k$ with binary operation $+$ (componentwise addition) and identity $\bar{0} = (0, \ldots, 0)$, and ψ is a monoid homomorphism:

$$\psi(xy) = \psi(x) + \psi(y),$$
$$\psi(\epsilon) = \bar{0}.$$

---

[1] Recall from Lecture 2 that a *monoid* is an algebraic structure consisting of a set with an associative binary operation and an identity for that operation.

The main difference between the monoids Σ^* and $\mathbb{N}^k$ is that the latter is commutative,[2] whereas the former is not, except in the case $k = 1$. In fact, if $\equiv$ is the smallest monoid congruence[3] on Σ^* such that $a_i a_j \equiv a_j a_i$, $1 \leq i, j \leq k$, then $\mathbb{N}^k$ is isomorphic to the quotient[4] $\Sigma^*/\!\equiv$. The monoid Σ^* is sometimes called the *free monoid on k generators*, and $\mathbb{N}^k$ is sometimes called the *free commutative monoid on k generators*. The word "free" refers to the fact that the structures do not satisfy any equations besides the logical consequences of the monoid or commutative monoid axioms, respectively.

The *commutative image* of a set $A \subseteq \Sigma^*$ is its image under ψ:

$$\psi(A) \stackrel{\text{def}}{=} \{\psi(x) \mid x \in A\}.$$

If $u_1, \ldots, u_m \in \mathbb{N}^k$, the submonoid of $\mathbb{N}^k$ generated by $u_1, \ldots, u_m$ is denoted $\langle u_1, \ldots, u_m \rangle$. This is the smallest subset of $\mathbb{N}^k$ containing $u_1, \ldots, u_m$ and the monoid identity $\bar{0}$ and closed under $+$. Equivalently,

$$\langle u_1, \ldots, u_m \rangle = \{a_1 u_1 + \cdots + a_m u_m \mid a_1, \ldots, a_m \in \mathbb{N}\} \subseteq \mathbb{N}^k.$$

A subset of $\mathbb{N}^k$ is called *linear* if it is a coset of such a finitely generated submonoid; that is, if it is of the form

$$u_0 + \langle u_1, \ldots, u_m \rangle = \{u_0 + a_1 u_1 + \cdots + a_m u_m \mid a_1, \ldots, a_m \in \mathbb{N}\}.$$

A subset of $\mathbb{N}^k$ is called *semilinear* if it is a union of finitely many linear sets. For example,

$$\psi(\{a^n b^n \mid n \geq 0\}) = \psi(\{x \in \{a, b\}^* \mid \#a(x) = \#b(x)\})$$
$$= \{(n, n) \mid n \geq 0\}$$
$$= \langle (1, 1) \rangle$$

is a semilinear (in fact, linear) subset of $\mathbb{N}^2$, but $\{(n, n^2) \mid n \geq 0\}$ is not.

Theorem H.1   (Parikh)   *For any context-free language A, $\psi(A)$ is semilinear.*

The converse does not hold: the set $\{a^n b^n c^n \mid n \geq 0\}$ is not context-free but has a semilinear image under ψ. This is also the image of the CFL $\{(ab)^n c^n \mid n \geq 0\}$ and the regular set $(abc)^*$.

---

[2] A monoid is *commutative* if $xy = yx$ for all x and y.

[3] A *monoid congruence* is an equivalence relation $\equiv$ on the monoid that respects the monoid structure in the sense that if $x \equiv x'$ and $y \equiv y'$, then $xy \equiv x'y'$.

[4] The *quotient* of a monoid M by a congruence $\equiv$ is a monoid whose elements are the congruence classes $[x] \stackrel{\text{def}}{=} \{y \mid y \equiv x\}$, binary operation $[x] \cdot [y] \stackrel{\text{def}}{=} [xy]$, and constant $[1]$, where 1 is the identity of M. See Supplementary Lectures C and D for more information on these concepts.

For every semilinear set $S \subseteq \mathbb{N}^k$, it is not hard to construct a regular set $R \subseteq \Sigma^*$ such that $\psi(R) = S$. For example, $\{(n,n) \mid n \geq 0\} = \psi((ab)^*)$. For this reason, Parikh's theorem is sometimes stated as follows:

Every context-free language is letter-equivalent to a regular set,

where letter-equivalence means the sets have the same commutative image.

In order to prove Parikh's theorem, we need some definitions. Let $G = (N, \Sigma, P, S)$ be an arbitrary CFG in Chomsky normal form. Let $s, t, \ldots$ denote parse trees of G with a nonterminal at the root, nonterminals labeling the internal nodes, and terminals or nonterminals labeling the leaves. Define

$\mathbf{root}(s) \overset{\text{def}}{=}$ the nonterminal at the root of s;

$\mathbf{yield}(s) \overset{\text{def}}{=}$ the string of terminals and nonterminals at the leaves of s, reading left to right;

$\mathbf{depth}(s) \overset{\text{def}}{=}$ the length of the longest path in s from a leaf up to the root (the *length* of a path is the number of edges, or the number of nodes less one);

$N(s) \overset{\text{def}}{=}$ the set of nonterminals appearing in s.

Define a *pump* to be a parse tree s such that

(i) s contains at least two nodes; and

(ii) $\mathbf{yield}(s) = x \cdot \mathbf{root}(s) \cdot y$ for some $x, y \in \Sigma^*$; that is, all leaves are labeled with terminal symbols except one, and the nonterminal labeling that leaf is the same as the one labeling the root.

These objects arose in the proof of the pumping lemma for CFLs in Lecture 22: wherever a nonterminal A appears in a parse tree s, the tree can be split apart at that point and a pump u with $\mathbf{root}(u) = A$ inserted to get a larger parse tree t.

For parse trees s, t, define $s \lhd t$ if t can be obtained from s by splitting s at a node labeled with some nonterminal A and inserting a pump with root labeled A. The relation $\lhd$ is not a partial order (it is not reflexive or transitive), but it is *well founded* in the sense that there exists no infinite descending chain $s_0 \rhd s_1 \rhd s_2 \rhd \cdots$, because if $s \lhd t$, then s has strictly fewer nodes than t.

Define a pump t to be a *basic pump* if it is $\lhd$-minimal among all pumps; that is, if it does not properly contain another pump that could be cut out. In other words, a pump t is a *basic pump* if the only s such that $s \lhd t$ is the trivial one-node parse tree labeled with the nonterminal **root**(t). Basic pumps cannot be too big:

Lemma H.2   *If s is a basic pump, then* **depth**$(s) \leq 2n$, *where n is the number of nonterminals in N.*

Proof. Let π denote the path in s from the unique leaf with label **root**(s) up to the root. The path π can be no longer than n, because if it were, it would have a repeated nonterminal and would therefore contain a pump that could be removed, contradicting the $\lhd$-minimality of s. For any other leaf, the path from that leaf up to the first node on the path π can be no longer than $n + 1$ for the same reason. Thus the total length of any path from a leaf to the root can be no longer than $2n$. $\square$

It follows from Lemma H.2 and the fact that there are only finitely many productions in G that the number of basic pumps is finite, say p.

Lemma H.3   *Every parse tree t with* **yield**$(t) \in \Sigma^*$ *is either $\lhd$-minimal or contains a basic pump.*

Proof. If t is not $\lhd$-minimal, then by definition it contains a pump s. Let s be $\lhd$-minimal among all pumps contained in t. Then s is a basic pump, because if it were not, then it would contain a smaller pump u, and u would be a smaller pump contained in t, contradicting the minimality of s. $\square$

Define $s \leq t$ if t can be obtained from s by some finite sequence of insertions of basic pumps u such that $N(u) \subseteq N(s)$. In other words, starting from s, we are allowed to choose any occurrence of a nonterminal A in s and insert a basic pump u with **root**$(u) = A$ at that point, provided u contains no new nonterminals that are not already contained in s. If t can be obtained from s by a finite number of repetitions of this process, then $s \leq t$.

If $\alpha \in (N \cup \Sigma)^*$, define $\psi(\alpha) = \psi(x)$, where x is the string obtained from α by deleting all nonterminals. Let $\psi(t)$ abbreviate $\psi(\mathbf{yield}(t))$.

Lemma H.4   *The set $\{\psi(t) \mid s \leq t\}$ is linear.*

Proof.

$$\{\psi(t) \mid s \leq t\} = \psi(s) + <\{\psi(u) \mid u \text{ is a basic pump with } N(u) \subseteq N(s)\}>.$$

$\square$

Lemma H.5   *If s is $\leq$-minimal, then* **depth**$(s) \leq (p + 1)(n + 1)$, *where p is the number of distinct basic pumps and n is the size of N.*

Proof. If s had a path longer than **depth**$(s) \leq (p + 1)(n + 1)$, then that path could be broken up into $p + 1$ segments, each of length at least $n + 1$, and each segment would have a repeated nonterminal. Then there would be

$p + 1$ disjoint pumps. (Two pumps are considered *disjoint* if they have no nodes in common, or if the root of one is a leaf of the other.) Each of these $p + 1$ pumps either is basic or contains a basic pump by Lemma H.3; thus there would be $p + 1$ disjoint basic pumps. But there are only p distinct basic pumps in all, so by the pigeonhole principle there must be two disjoint occurrences of the same basic pump. But this contradicts the $\leq$-minimality of s, since one of these basic pumps could be deleted without changing the set of nonterminals contained in the tree.   □

Proof of Theorem H.1. Let

$$M = \{s \mid s \text{ is } \leq\text{-minimal}, \mathbf{root}(s) = S, \mathbf{yield}(s) \in \Sigma^*\}.$$

We show that

$$\psi(L(G)) = \bigcup_{s \in M} \{\psi(t) \mid s \leq t\}.$$

This set is semilinear by Lemma H.5, which implies that M is finite, and by Lemma H.4. Any t such that $s \leq t$ for some $s \in M$ has $\mathbf{root}(t) = S$ and $\mathbf{yield}(t) \in \Sigma^*$; thus $\mathbf{yield}(t) \in L(G)$ and $\psi(t) \in \psi(L(G))$. Conversely, any string $x \in L(G)$ has a parse tree t with $\mathbf{root}(t) = S$ and $\mathbf{yield}(t) = x$, and there must exist a $\leq$-minimal $s \leq t$. Then $s \in M$ and

$$\psi(x) \in \{\psi(t) \mid s \leq t\}.$$ □

Historical Notes

Parikh's theorem was first proved by Rohit Parikh [98]. Alternative proofs have been given by Goldstine [52], Harrison [55], and Kuich [75].

Lecture 28

Turing Machines and Effective Computability

In this lecture we introduce the most powerful of the automata we will study: Turing machines (TMs), named after Alan Turing, who invented them in 1936. Turing machines can compute any function normally considered computable; in fact, it is quite reasonable to define *computable* to mean computable by a TM.

TMs were invented in the 1930s, long before real computers appeared. They came at a time when mathematicians were trying to come to grips with the notion of *effective computation*. They knew various algorithms for computing things effectively, but they weren't quite sure how to define "effectively computable" in a general way that would allow them to distinguish between the computable and the noncomputable. Several alternative formalisms evolved, each with its own peculiarities, in the attempt to nail down this notion:

- Turing machines (Alan Turing [120]);

- Post systems (Emil Post [99, 100]);

- μ-recursive functions (Kurt Gödel [51], Jacques Herbrand);

- λ-calculus (Alonzo Church [23], Stephen C. Kleene [66]); and

- combinatory logic (Moses Schönfinkel [111], Haskell B. Curry [29]).

All of these systems embody the idea of *effective computation* in one form or another. They work on various types of data; for example, Turing machines manipulate strings over a finite alphabet, μ-recursive functions manipulate the natural numbers, the λ-calculus manipulates λ-terms, and combinatory logic manipulates terms built from combinator symbols.

However, there are natural translations between all these different types of data. For example, there is a simple one-to-one correspondence between strings in $\{0,1\}^*$ and natural numbers $\mathbb{N} = \{0, 1, 2, \ldots\}$ defined by

$$x \mapsto \#(1x) - 1, \tag{28.1}$$

where $\#y$ is the natural number represented by the binary string y. Conversely, it is easy to encode just about anything (natural numbers, λ-terms, strings in $\{0, 1, 2, \ldots, 9\}^*$, trees, graphs, ...) as strings in $\{0, 1\}^*$. Under these natural encodings of the data, it turns out that all the formalisms above can simulate one another, so despite their superficial differences they are all computationally equivalent.

Nowadays we can take unabashed advantage of our more modern perspective and add programming languages such as PASCAL or C (or idealized versions of them) to this list—a true luxury compared to what Church and Gödel had to struggle with.

Of the classical systems listed above, the one that most closely resembles a modern computer is the Turing machine. Besides the off-the-shelf model we will define below, there are also many custom variations (nondeterministic, multitape, multidimensional tape, two-way infinite tapes, and so on) that all turn out to be computationally equivalent in the sense that they can all simulate one another.

Church's Thesis

Because these vastly dissimilar formalisms are all computationally equivalent, the common notion of computability that they embody is extremely robust, which is to say that it is invariant under fairly radical perturbations in the model. All these mathematicians with their pet systems turned out to be looking at the same thing from different angles. This was too striking to be mere coincidence. They soon came to the realization that the commonality among all these systems must be the elusive notion of *effective computability* that they had sought for so long. Computability is not just Turing machines, nor the λ-calculus, nor the μ-recursive functions, nor the PASCAL programming language, but the common spirit embodied by them all.

Alonzo Church [25] gave voice to this thought, and it has since become known as *Church's thesis* (or the *Church–Turing thesis*). It is not a theorem, but rather a declaration that all these formalisms capture precisely our intuition about what it means to be effectively computable in principle, no more and no less. Church's thesis may not seem like such a big deal in retrospect, since by now we are thoroughly familiar with the capabilities of modern computers; but keep in mind that at the time it was first formulated, computers and programming languages had yet to be invented. Coming to this realization was an enormous intellectual leap.

Probably the most compelling development leading to the acceptance of Church's thesis was the Turing machine. It was the first model that could be considered readily programmable. If someone laid one of the other systems out in front of you and declared, "*This* system captures exactly what we mean by effectively computable," you might harbor some skepticism. But it is hard to argue with Turing machines. One can rightly challenge Church's thesis on the grounds that there are aspects of computation that are not addressed by Turing machines (for example, randomized or interactive computation), but no one could dispute that the notion of effective computability as captured by Turing machines is robust and important.

Universality and Self-Reference

One of the most intriguing aspects of these systems, and a pervasive theme in our study of them, is the idea of *programs as data*. Each of these programming systems is powerful enough that programs can be written that understand and manipulate other programs that are encoded as data in some reasonable way. For example, in the λ-calculus, λ-terms act as both programs and data; combinator symbols in combinatory logic manipulate other combinator symbols; there is a so-called Gödel numbering of the μ-recursive functions in which each function has a number that can be used as input to other μ-recursive functions; and Turing machines can interpret their input strings as descriptions of other Turing machines. It is not a far step from this idea to the notion of *universal simulation*, in which a universal program or machine U is constructed to take an encoded description of another program or machine M and a string x as input and perform a step-by-step simulation of M on input x. A modern-day example of this phenomenon would be a SCHEME interpreter written in SCHEME.

One far-reaching corollary of universality is the notion of *self-reference*. It is exactly this capability that led to the discovery of natural uncomputable problems. If you know some set theory, you can convince yourself that uncomputable problems must exist by a cardinality argument: there are uncountably many decision problems but only countably many Turing machines. However, self-reference allows us to construct very simple and natural examples of uncomputable problems. For example, there do not exist general procedures that can determine whether a given block of code in a given PASCAL program is ever going to be executed, or whether a given PASCAL program will ever halt. These are important problems that compiler builders would like to solve; unfortunately, one can give a formal proof that they are unsolvable.

Perhaps the most striking example of the power of self-reference is the incompleteness theorem of Kurt Gödel. Starting near the beginning of the twentieth century with Whitehead and Russell's *Principia Mathematica* [123], there was a movement to reduce all of mathematics to pure symbol manipulation, independent of semantics. This was in part to understand and avoid the set-theoretic paradoxes discovered by Russell and others. This movement was advocated by the mathematician David Hilbert and became known as the *formalist program*. It attracted a lot of followers and fed the development of formal logic as we know it today. Its proponents believed that all mathematical truths could be derived in some fixed formal system, just by starting with a few axioms and applying rules of inference in a purely mechanical way. This view of mathematical proof is highly computational. The formal deductive system most popular at the time for reasoning about the natural numbers, called *Peano arithmetic* (PA), was believed to be adequate for expressing and deriving mechanically all true statements of number theory. The incompleteness theorem showed that this was wrong: there exist even fairly simple statements of number theory that are true but not provable in PA. This holds not only for PA but for *any* reasonable extension of it. This revelation was a significant setback for the formalist program and sent shock waves throughout the mathematical world.

Gödel proved the incompleteness theorem using self-reference. The basic observation needed here is that the language of number theory is expressive enough to talk about itself and about proofs in PA. For example, one can write down a number-theoretic statement that says that a certain other number-theoretic statement has a proof in PA, and one can reason about such statements using PA itself. Now, by a tricky argument involving substitutions, one can actually construct statements that talk about whether they themselves are provable. Gödel actually constructed a sentence that said, "I am not provable." This construction is presented in detail in Supplementary Lecture K.

The consequences of universality are not only philosophical but also practical. Universality was in a sense the germ of the idea that led to the development of computers as we know them today: the notion of a *stored program*, a piece of software that can be read and executed by hardware. This programmability is what makes computers so versatile. Although it was only realized in physical form several years later, the notion was definitely present in Turing's theoretical work in the 1930s.

Informal Description of Turing Machines

We describe here a deterministic, one-tape Turing machine. This is the standard off-the-shelf model. There are many variations, apparently more powerful or less powerful but in reality not. We will consider some of these in Lecture 30.

A TM has a finite set of states Q, a semi-infinite tape that is delimited on the left end by an endmarker $\vdash$ and is infinite to the right, and a head that can move left and right over the tape, reading and writing symbols.

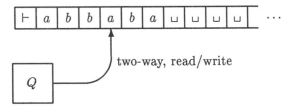

The input string is of finite length and is initially written on the tape in contiguous tape cells snug up against the left endmarker. The infinitely many cells to the right of the input all contain a special blank symbol $\sqcup$.

The machine starts in its start state s with its head scanning the left endmarker. In each step it reads the symbol on the tape under its head. Depending on that symbol and the current state, it writes a new symbol on that tape cell, moves its head either left or right one cell, and enters a new state. The action it takes in each situation is determined by a transition function δ. It *accepts* its input by entering a special accept state t and *rejects* by entering a special reject state r. On some inputs it may run infinitely without ever accepting or rejecting, in which case it is said to *loop* on that input.

Formal Definition of Turing Machines

Formally, a *deterministic one-tape Turing machine* is a 9-tuple

$$M = (Q, \Sigma, \Gamma, \vdash, \sqcup, \delta, s, t, r),$$

where

- Q is a finite set (the *states*);
- Σ is a finite set (the *input alphabet*);

- Γ is a finite set (the *tape alphabet*) containing Σ as a subset;

- $\sqcup \in \Gamma - \Sigma$, the *blank symbol*;

- $\vdash \in \Gamma - \Sigma$, the *left endmarker*;

- $\delta : Q \times \Gamma \to Q \times \Gamma \times \{L, R\}$, the *transition function*;

- $s \in Q$, the *start state*;

- $t \in Q$, the *accept state*; and

- $r \in Q$, the *reject state*, $r \neq t$.

Intuitively, $\delta(p, a) = (q, b, d)$ means, "When in state p scanning symbol a, write b on that tape cell, move the head in direction d, and enter state q." The symbols L and R stand for left and right, respectively.

We restrict TMs so that the left endmarker is never overwritten with another symbol and the machine never moves off the tape to the left of the endmarker; that is, we require that for all $p \in Q$ there exists $q \in Q$ such that

$$\delta(p, \vdash) = (q, \vdash, R). \tag{28.2}$$

We also require that once the machine enters its accept state, it never leaves it, and similarly for its reject state; that is, for all $b \in \Gamma$ there exist $c, c' \in \Gamma$ and $d, d' \in \{L, R\}$ such that

$$\begin{aligned} \delta(t, b) &= (t, c, d), \\ \delta(r, b) &= (r, c', d'). \end{aligned} \tag{28.3}$$

We sometimes refer to the state set and transition function collectively as the *finite control*.

Example 28.1   Here is a TM that accepts the non-context-free set $\{a^n b^n c^n \mid n \geq 0\}$. Informally, the machine starts in its start state s, then scans to the right over the input string, checking that it is of the form $a^* b^* c^*$. It doesn't write anything on the way across (formally, it writes the same symbol it reads). When it sees the first blank symbol $\sqcup$, it overwrites it with a right endmarker $\dashv$. Now it scans left, erasing the first c it sees, then the first b it sees, then the first a it sees, until it comes to the $\vdash$. It then scans right, erasing one a, one b, and one c. It continues to sweep left and right over the input, erasing one occurrence of each letter in each pass. If on some pass it sees at least one occurrence of one of the letters and no occurrences of another, it rejects. Otherwise, it eventually erases all the letters and makes one pass between $\vdash$ and $\dashv$ seeing only blanks, at which point it accepts.

Formally, this machine has

$$Q = \{s, q_1, \dots, q_{10}, t, r\},$$

$$\Sigma = \{a, b, c\},$$
$$\Gamma = \Sigma \cup \{\vdash, \sqcup, \dashv\}.$$

There is nothing special about $\dashv$; it is just an extra useful symbol in the tape alphabet. The transition function δ is specified by the following table:

	$\vdash$	a	b	c	$\sqcup$	$\dashv$
s	$(s, \vdash, R)$	(s, a, R)	(q_1, b, R)	(q_2, c, R)	$(q_3, \dashv, L)$	$-$
q_1	$-$	$(r, -, -)$	(q_1, b, R)	(q_2, c, R)	$(q_3, \dashv, L)$	$-$
q_2	$-$	$(r, -, -)$	$(r, -, -)$	(q_2, c, R)	$(q_3, \dashv, L)$	$-$
q_3	$(t, -, -)$	$(r, -, -)$	$(r, -, -)$	$(q_4, \sqcup, L)$	$(q_3, \sqcup, L)$	$-$
q_4	$(r, -, -)$	$(r, -, -)$	$(q_5, \sqcup, L)$	(q_4, c, L)	$(q_4, \sqcup, L)$	$-$
q_5	$(r, -, -)$	$(q_6, \sqcup, L)$	(q_5, b, L)	$-$	$(q_5, \sqcup, L)$	$-$
q_6	$(q_7, \vdash, R)$	(q_6, a, L)	$-$	$-$	$(q_6, \sqcup, L)$	$-$
q_7	$-$	$(q_8, \sqcup, R)$	$(r, -, -)$	$(r, -, -)$	$(q_7, \sqcup, R)$	$(t, -, -)$
q_8	$-$	(q_8, a, R)	$(q_9, \sqcup, R)$	$(r, -, -)$	$(q_8, \sqcup, R)$	$(r, -, -)$
q_9	$-$	$-$	(q_9, b, R)	$(q_{10}, \sqcup, R)$	$(q_9, \sqcup, R)$	$(r, -, -)$
q_{10}	$-$	$-$	$-$	(q_{10}, c, R)	$(q_{10}, \sqcup, R)$	$(q_3, \dashv, L)$

The symbol $-$ in the table above means "don't care." The transitions for t and r are not included in the table—just define them to be anything satisfying the restrictions (28.2) and (28.3). □

Configurations and Acceptance

At any point in time, the read/write tape of the Turing machine M contains a semi-infinite string of the form $y\sqcup^\omega$, where $y \in \Gamma^*$ (y is a finite-length string) and $\sqcup^\omega$ denotes the semi-infinite string

$$\sqcup \sqcup \sqcup \sqcup \sqcup \sqcup \sqcup \cdots.$$

(Here ω denotes the smallest infinite ordinal.) Although the string is infinite, it always has a finite representation, since all but finitely many of the symbols are the blank symbol $\sqcup$.

We define a *configuration* to be an element of $Q \times \{y\sqcup^\omega \mid y \in \Gamma^*\} \times \mathbb{N}$, where $\mathbb{N} = \{0, 1, 2, \ldots\}$. A configuration is a global state giving a snapshot of all relevant information about a TM computation at some instant in time. The configuration (p, z, n) specifies a current state p of the finite control, current tape contents z, and current position of the read/write head $n \geq 0$. We usually denote configurations by α, β, γ.

The *start configuration* on input $x \in \Sigma^*$ is the configuration

$$(s, \vdash x\sqcup^\omega, 0).$$

The last component 0 means that the machine is initially scanning the left endmarker $\vdash$.

One can define a *next configuration relation* $\xrightarrow[M]{1}$ as with PDAs. For a string $z \in \Gamma^\omega$, let z_n be the nth symbol of z (the leftmost symbol is z_0), and let $s_b^n(z)$ denote the string obtained from z by substituting b for z_n at position n. For example,

$$s_b^4(\vdash b\,a\,a\,a\,c\,a\,b\,c\,a\,\cdots) = \vdash b\,a\,a\,b\,c\,a\,b\,c\,a\,\cdots.$$

The relation $\xrightarrow[M]{1}$ is defined by

$$(p, z, n) \xrightarrow[M]{1} \begin{cases} (q, s_b^n(z), n - 1) & \text{if } \delta(p, z_n) = (q, b, L), \\ (q, s_b^n(z), n + 1) & \text{if } \delta(p, z_n) = (q, b, R). \end{cases}$$

Intuitively, if the tape contains z and if M is in state p scanning the nth tape cell, and δ says to print b, go left, and enter state q, then after that step the tape will contain $s_b^n(z)$, the head will be scanning the $n - 1$st tape cell, and the new state will be q.

We define the reflexive transitive closure $\xrightarrow[M]{*}$ of $\xrightarrow[M]{1}$ inductively, as usual:

- $\alpha \xrightarrow[M]{0} \alpha$,

- $\alpha \xrightarrow[M]{n+1} \beta$ if $\alpha \xrightarrow[M]{n} \gamma \xrightarrow[M]{1} \beta$ for some γ, and

- $\alpha \xrightarrow[M]{*} \beta$ if $\alpha \xrightarrow[M]{n} \beta$ for some $n \geq 0$.

The machine M is said to *accept* input $x \in \Sigma^*$ if

$$(s, \vdash x \sqcup^\omega, 0) \xrightarrow[M]{*} (t, y, n)$$

for some y and n, and *reject* x if

$$(s, \vdash x \sqcup^\omega, 0) \xrightarrow[M]{*} (r, y, n)$$

for some y and n. It is said to *halt* on input x if it either accepts x or rejects x. As with PDAs, this is just a mathematical definition; the machine doesn't really grind to a halt in the literal sense. It is possible that it neither accepts nor rejects, in which case it is said to *loop* on input x. A Turing machine is said to be *total* if it halts on all inputs; that is, if for all inputs it either accepts or rejects. The set $L(M)$ denotes the set of strings accepted by M.

We call a set of strings

- *recursively enumerable* (r.e.) if it is $L(M)$ for some Turing machine M,

- *co-r.e.* if its complement is r.e., and

- *recursive* if it is $L(M)$ for some *total* Turing machine M.

In common parlance, the term "recursive" usually refers to an algorithm that calls itself. The definition above has nothing to do with this usage. As used here, it is just a name for a set accepted by a Turing machine that always halts.

We will see lots of examples next time.

Historical Notes

Church's thesis is often referred to as the Church–Turing thesis, although Alonzo Church was the first to formulate it explicitly [25]. The thesis was based on Church and Kleene's observation that the λ-calculus and the μ-recursive functions of Gödel and Herbrand were computationally equivalent [25]. Church was apparently unaware of Turing's work at the time of the writing of [25], or if he was, he failed to mention it. Turing, on the other hand, cited Church's paper [25] explicitly in [120], and apparently considered his machines to be a much more compelling definition of computability. In an appendix to [120], Turing outlined a proof of the computational equivalence of Turing machines and the λ-calculus.

Lecture 29

More on Turing Machines

Last time we defined deterministic one-tape Turing machines:

$$M \quad = \quad (Q, \ \Sigma, \ \Gamma, \ \vdash, \ \sqcup, \ \delta, \ s, \ t, \ r)$$

states
input alphabet
tape alphabet
left endmarker
blank symbol
reject state
accept state
start state
transition function

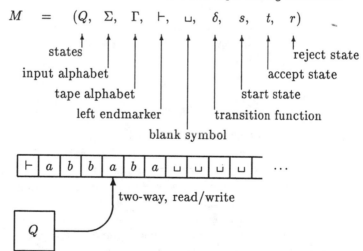

two-way, read/write

Q

In each step, based on the current tape symbol it is reading and its current state, it prints a new symbol on the tape, moves its head either left or right, and enters a new state. This action is specified formally by the transition function

$$\delta : Q \times \Gamma \to Q \times \Gamma \times \{L, R\}.$$

Intuitively, $\delta(p, a) = (q, b, d)$ means, "When in state p scanning symbol a, write b on that tape cell, move the head in direction d, and enter state q."

We defined a *configuration* to be a triple (p, z, n) where p is a state, z is a semi-infinite string of the form $y\sqcup^\omega$, $y \in \Sigma^*$, describing the contents of the tape, and n is a natural number denoting a tape head position.

The transition function δ was used to define the *next configuration relation* $\xrightarrow[M]{1}$ on configurations and its reflexive transitive closure $\xrightarrow[M]{*}$. The machine M *accepts* input $x \in \Sigma^*$ if

$$(s, \vdash x\sqcup^\omega, 0) \xrightarrow[M]{*} (t, y, n)$$

for some y and n, and *rejects* input x if

$$(s, \vdash x\sqcup^\omega, 0) \xrightarrow[M]{*} (r, y, n)$$

for some y and n. The left configuration above is the *start configuration* on input x. Recall that we restricted TMs so that once a TM enters its accept state, it may never leave it, and similarly for its reject state. If M never enters its accept or reject state on input x, it is said to *loop* on input x. It is said to *halt* on input x if it either accepts or rejects. A TM that halts on all inputs is called *total*.

Define the set

$$L(M) = \{x \in \Sigma^* \mid M \text{ accepts } x\}.$$

This is called the set *accepted by* M. A subset of Σ^* is called *recursively enumerable* (r.e.) if it is $L(M)$ for some M. A set is called *recursive* if it is $L(M)$ for some total M.

For now, the terms *r.e.* and *recursive* are just technical terms describing the sets accepted by TMs and total TMs, respectively; they have no other significance. We will discuss the origin of this terminology in Lecture 30.

Example 29.1 Consider the non-CFL $\{ww \mid w \in \{a, b\}^*\}$. It is a recursive set, because we can give a total TM M for it. The machine M works as follows. On input x, it scans out to the first blank symbol $\sqcup$, counting the number of symbols mod 2 to make sure x is of even length and rejecting immediately if not. It lays down a right endmarker $\dashv$, then repeatedly scans back and forth over the input. In each pass from right to left, it marks the first unmarked a or b it sees with $'$. In each pass from left to right, it marks the first unmarked a or b it sees with $`$. It continues this until all symbols are marked. For example, on input

$$a\,a\,b\,b\,a\,a\,a\,b\,b\,a$$

the initial tape contents are

$$\vdash a\,a\,b\,b\,a\,a\,a\,b\,b\,a\,\sqcup\sqcup\sqcup\cdots$$

and the following are the tape contents after the first few passes.

$\vdash a\,a\,b\,b\,a\,a\,a\,b\,b\,\acute{a}\dashv\sqcup\sqcup\sqcup\cdots$

$\vdash\grave{a}\,a\,b\,b\,a\,a\,a\,b\,b\,\acute{a}\dashv\sqcup\sqcup\sqcup\cdots$

$\vdash\grave{a}\,a\,b\,b\,a\,a\,a\,b\,\acute{b}\,\acute{a}\dashv\sqcup\sqcup\sqcup\cdots$

$\vdash\grave{a}\,\grave{a}\,b\,b\,a\,a\,a\,b\,\acute{b}\,\acute{a}\dashv\sqcup\sqcup\sqcup\cdots$

$\vdash\grave{a}\,\grave{a}\,b\,b\,a\,a\,a\,\acute{b}\,\acute{b}\,\acute{a}\dashv\sqcup\sqcup\sqcup\cdots$

Marking a with ` formally means writing the symbol $\grave{a}\in\Gamma$; thus

$$\Gamma=\{a,\,b,\,\vdash,\,\sqcup,\,\dashv,\,\grave{a},\,\grave{b},\,\acute{a},\,\acute{b}\}.$$

When all symbols are marked, we have the first half of the input string marked with ` and the second half marked with ´.

$\vdash\grave{a}\,\grave{a}\,\grave{b}\,\grave{b}\,\grave{a}\,\acute{a}\,\acute{a}\,\acute{b}\,\acute{b}\,\acute{a}\dashv\sqcup\sqcup\sqcup\cdots$

The reason we did this was to find the center of the input string.

The machine then repeatedly scans left to right over the input. In each pass it erases the first symbol it sees marked with ` but remembers that symbol in its finite control (to "erase" really means to write the blank symbol $\sqcup$). It then scans forward until it sees the first symbol marked with ´, checks that that symbol is the same, and erases it. If the two symbols are not the same, it rejects. Otherwise, when it has erased all the symbols, it accepts. In our example, the following would be the tape contents after each pass.

$\grave{a}\,\grave{a}\,\grave{b}\,\grave{b}\,\grave{a}\,\acute{a}\,\acute{a}\,\acute{b}\,\acute{b}\,\acute{a}\dashv\sqcup\sqcup\sqcup\cdots$

$\sqcup\,\grave{a}\,\grave{b}\,\grave{b}\,\grave{a}\,\sqcup\,\acute{a}\,\acute{b}\,\acute{b}\,\acute{a}\dashv\sqcup\sqcup\sqcup\cdots$

$\sqcup\,\sqcup\,\grave{b}\,\grave{b}\,\grave{a}\,\sqcup\,\sqcup\,\acute{b}\,\acute{b}\,\acute{a}\dashv\sqcup\sqcup\sqcup\cdots$

$\sqcup\,\sqcup\,\sqcup\,\grave{b}\,\grave{a}\,\sqcup\,\sqcup\,\sqcup\,\acute{b}\,\acute{a}\dashv\sqcup\sqcup\sqcup\cdots$

$\sqcup\,\sqcup\,\sqcup\,\sqcup\,\grave{a}\,\sqcup\,\sqcup\,\sqcup\,\sqcup\,\acute{a}\dashv\sqcup\sqcup\sqcup\cdots$

$\sqcup\,\sqcup\,\sqcup\,\sqcup\,\sqcup\,\sqcup\,\sqcup\,\sqcup\,\sqcup\,\sqcup\dashv\sqcup\sqcup\sqcup\cdots$ □

Example 29.2   We want to construct a total TM that accepts its input string if the length of the string is prime. This language is not regular or context-free. We will give a TM implementation of the *sieve of Eratosthenes*, which can be described informally as follows. Say we want to check whether n is prime. We write down all the numbers from 2 to n in order, then repeat the following: find the smallest number in the list, declare it prime, then cross off all multiples of that number. Repeat until each number in the list has been either declared prime or crossed off as a multiple of a smaller prime.

For example, to check whether 23 is prime, we would start with all the numbers from 2 to 23:

2   3   4   5   6   7   8   9   10   11   12   13   14   15   16   17   18   19   20   21   22   23

In the first pass, we cross off multiples of 2:

$\not{2}$ 3 $\not{4}$ 5 $\not{6}$ 7 $\not{8}$ 9 $\not{10}$ 11 $\not{12}$ 13 $\not{14}$ 15 $\not{16}$ 17 $\not{18}$ 19 $\not{20}$ 21 $\not{22}$ 23

The smallest number remaining is 3, and this is prime. In the second pass we cross off multiples of 3:

$\not{2}$ $\not{3}$ $\not{4}$ 5 $\not{6}$ 7 $\not{8}$ $\not{9}$ $\not{10}$ 11 $\not{12}$ 13 $\not{14}$ $\not{15}$ $\not{16}$ 17 $\not{18}$ 19 $\not{20}$ $\not{21}$ $\not{22}$ 23

Then 5 is the next prime, so we cross off multiples of 5; and so forth. Since 23 is prime, it will never be crossed off as a multiple of anything smaller, and eventually we will discover that fact when everything smaller has been crossed off.

Now we show how to implement this on a TM. Suppose we have a^p written on the tape. We illustrate the algorithm with $p = 23$.

$$\vdash a\,a\,a\,a\,a\,a\,a\,a\,a\,a\,a\,a\,a\,a\,a\,a\,a\,a\,a\,a\,a\,a\,a\,\sqcup\sqcup\sqcup\cdots$$

If $p = 0$ or $p = 1$, reject. We can determine this by looking at the first three cells of the tape. Otherwise, there are at least two a's. Erase the first a, scan right to the end of the input, and replace the last a in the input string with the symbol \$. We now have an a in positions $2, 3, 4, \ldots, p-1$ and \$ at position p.

$$\vdash \sqcup a\,a\,a\,a\,a\,a\,a\,a\,a\,a\,a\,a\,a\,a\,a\,a\,a\,a\,a\,a\,a\,a\,\$\,\sqcup\sqcup\sqcup\cdots$$

Now we repeat the following loop. Starting from the left endmarker $\vdash$, scan right and find the first nonblank symbol, say occurring at position m. Then m is prime (this is an invariant of the loop). If this symbol is the \$, we are done: $p = m$ is prime, so we halt and accept. Otherwise, the symbol is an a. Mark it with a $\hat{}$ and everything between there and the left endmarker with $\acute{}$.

$$\vdash \acute{\sqcup}\,\hat{a}\,a\,a\,a\,a\,a\,a\,a\,a\,a\,a\,a\,a\,a\,a\,a\,a\,a\,a\,a\,a\,\$\,\sqcup\sqcup\sqcup\cdots$$

We will now enter an inner loop to erase all the symbols occurring at positions that are multiples of m. First, erase the a under the $\hat{}$. (Formally, just write the symbol $\hat{\sqcup}$.)

$$\vdash \acute{\sqcup}\,\hat{\sqcup}\,a\,a\,a\,a\,a\,a\,a\,a\,a\,a\,a\,a\,a\,a\,a\,a\,a\,a\,a\,a\,\$\,\sqcup\sqcup\sqcup\cdots$$

Shift the marks to the right one at a time a distance equal to the number of marks. This can be done by shuttling back and forth, erasing marks on the left and writing them on the right. We know when we are done because the $\hat{}$ is the last mark moved.

$$\vdash \sqcup\sqcup\acute{a}\,\hat{a}\,a\,a\,a\,a\,a\,a\,a\,a\,a\,a\,a\,a\,a\,a\,a\,a\,a\,a\,a\,\$\,\sqcup\sqcup\sqcup\cdots$$

When this is done, erase the symbol under the $\hat{}$. This is the symbol occurring at position $2m$.

$$\vdash \sqcup\sqcup\acute{a}\,\hat{\sqcup}\,a\,a\,a\,a\,a\,a\,a\,a\,a\,a\,a\,a\,a\,a\,a\,a\,a\,a\,a\,\$\,\sqcup\sqcup\sqcup\cdots$$

Keep shifting the marks and erasing the symbol under the ˆ in this fashion until we reach the end.

$$\vdash \sqcup \sqcup a \sqcup a \sqcup a \sqcup a \sqcup a \sqcup a \sqcup a \sqcup a \sqcup a \sqcup a \sqcup \acute{\$} \hat{\sqcup} \sqcup \sqcup \cdots$$

If we find ourselves at the end of the string wanting to erase the $, reject—$p$ is a multiple of m but not equal to m. Otherwise, go back to the left and repeat. Find the first nonblank symbol and mark it and everything to its left.

$$\vdash \acute{u} \acute{u} \hat{a} \sqcup a \sqcup a \sqcup a \sqcup a \sqcup a \sqcup a \sqcup a \sqcup a \sqcup a \sqcup \$ \sqcup \sqcup \sqcup \cdots$$

Alternately erase the symbol under the ˆ and shift the marks until we reach the end of the string.

$$\vdash \sqcup \sqcup \sqcup a \sqcup a \sqcup \sqcup \sqcup a \sqcup a \sqcup \sqcup \sqcup a \sqcup a \sqcup \sqcup \acute{u} \acute{\$} \hat{\sqcup} \sqcup \sqcup \cdots$$

Go back to the left and repeat.

$$\vdash \acute{u} \acute{u} \acute{u} \acute{u} \hat{a} \sqcup a \sqcup \sqcup \sqcup a \sqcup a \sqcup \sqcup \sqcup a \sqcup a \sqcup \sqcup \sqcup \$ \sqcup \sqcup \sqcup \cdots$$

If we ever try to erase the $, reject—$p$ is not prime. If we manage to erase all the a's, accept. □

Recursive and R.E. Sets

Recall that a set A is *recursively enumerable* (r.e.) if it is accepted by a TM and *recursive* if it is accepted by a *total* TM (one that halts on all inputs).

The recursive sets are closed under complement. (The r.e. sets are not, as we will see later.) That is, if A is recursive, then so is $\sim A = \Sigma^* - A$. To see this, suppose A is recursive. Then there exists a total TM M such that $L(M) = A$. By switching the accept and reject states of M, we get a total machine M' such that $L(M') = \sim A$.

This construction does not give the complement if M is not total. This is because "rejecting" and "not accepting" are not synonymous for nontotal machines. To reject, a machine must enter its reject state. If M' is obtained from M by just switching the accept and reject states, then M' will accept the strings that M rejects and reject the strings that M accepts; but M' will still loop on the same strings that M loops on, so these strings are not accepted or rejected by either machine.

Every recursive set is r.e. but not necessarily vice versa. In other words, not every TM is equivalent to a total TM. We will prove this in Lecture 31. However, if both A and $\sim A$ are r.e., then A is recursive. To see this, suppose both A and $\sim A$ are r.e. Let M and M' be TMs such that $L(M) = A$ and $L(M') = \sim A$. Build a new machine N that on input x runs both M and

M' simultaneously on two different tracks of its tape. Formally, the tape alphabet of N contains symbols

| a |
| c |

| $\widehat{a}$ |
| c |

| a |
| $\widehat{c}$ |

| $\widehat{a}$ |
| $\widehat{c}$ |

where a is a tape symbol of M and c is a tape symbol of M'. Thus N's tape may contain a string of the form

b	$\widehat{a}$	b	a	b	a	b	a
c	c	c	d	d	c	$\widehat{c}$	d

$\ldots$

for example. The extra marks ^ are placed on the tape to indicate the current positions of the simulated read/write heads of M and M'. The machine N alternately performs a step of M and a step of M', shuttling back and forth between the two simulated tape head positions of M and M' and updating the tape. The current states and transition information of M and M' can be stored in N's finite control. If the machine M ever accepts, then N immediately accepts. If M' ever accepts, then N immediately rejects. Exactly one of those two events must eventually occur, depending on whether $x \in A$ or $x \in \sim A$, since $L(M) = A$ and $L(M') = \sim A$. Then N halts on all inputs and $L(N) = A$.

Decidability and Semidecidability

A property P of strings is said to be *decidable* if the set of all strings having property P is a recursive set; that is, if there is a total Turing machine that accepts input strings that have property P and rejects those that do not. A property P is said to be *semidecidable* if the set of strings having property P is an r.e. set; that is, if there is a Turing machine that on input x accepts if x has property P and rejects or loops if not. For example, it is decidable whether a given string x is of the form ww, because we can construct a Turing machine that halts on all inputs and accepts exactly the strings of this form.

Although you often hear them switched, the adjectives *recursive* and *r.e.* are best applied to sets and *decidable* and *semidecidable* to properties. The two notions are equivalent, since

$$P \text{ is decidable} \iff \{x \mid P(x)\} \text{ is recursive.}$$
$$A \text{ is recursive} \iff \text{``}x \in A\text{'' is decidable,}$$

$$P \text{ is semidecidable} \iff \{x \mid P(x)\} \text{ is r.e.,}$$
$$A \text{ is r.e.} \iff \text{``}x \in A\text{'' is semidecidable.}$$

Lecture 30

Equivalent Models

As mentioned, the concept of computability is remarkably robust. As evidence of this, we will present several different flavors of Turing machines that at first glance appear to be significantly more or less powerful than the basic model defined in Lecture 29 but in fact are computationally equivalent.

Multiple Tapes

First, we show how to simulate multitape Turing machines with single-tape Turing machines. Thus extra tapes don't add any power. A three-tape machine is similar to a one-tape TM except that it has three semi-infinite tapes and three independent read/write heads. Initially, the input occupies the first tape and the other two are blank. In each step, the machine reads the three symbols under its heads, and based on this information and the current state, it prints a symbol on each tape, moves the heads (they don't all have to move in the same direction), and enters a new state.

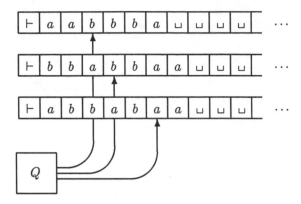

Its transition function is of type

$$\delta : Q \times \Gamma^3 \to Q \times \Gamma^3 \times \{L, R\}^3.$$

Say we have such a machine M. We build a single-tape machine N simulating M as follows. The machine N will have an expanded tape alphabet allowing us to think of its tape as divided into three tracks. Each track will contain the contents of one of M's tapes. We also mark exactly one symbol on each track to indicate that this is the symbol currently being scanned on the corresponding tape of M. The configuration of M illustrated above might be simulated by the following configuration of N.

$\vdash$	$\vdash$	a	a	$\widehat{b}$	b	b	a	$\sqcup$	$\sqcup$	$\sqcup$	$\sqcup$	
	$\vdash$	b	b	a	$\widehat{b}$	b	a	a	$\sqcup$	$\sqcup$	$\sqcup$	$\cdots$
	$\vdash$	a	b	b	a	b	$\widehat{a}$	a	$\sqcup$	$\sqcup$	$\sqcup$	

A tape symbol of N is either $\vdash$, an element of Σ, or a triple

c
d
e

where c, d, e are tape symbols of M, each either marked or unmarked. Formally, we might take the tape alphabet of N to be

$$\Sigma \cup \{\vdash\} \cup (\Gamma \cup \Gamma')^3,$$

where

$$\Gamma' \stackrel{\text{def}}{=} \{\widehat{c} \mid c \in \Gamma\}.$$

The three elements of $\Gamma \cup \Gamma'$ stand for the symbols in corresponding positions on the three tapes of M, either marked or unmarked, and is the blank symbol of N.

On input $x = a_1 a_2 \cdots a_n$, N starts with tape contents

$$\vdash a_1 \, a_2 \, a_3 \, \cdots \, a_n \, \sqcup \, \sqcup \, \sqcup \, \cdots,$$

It first copies the input to its top track and fills in the bottom two tracks with blanks. It also shifts everything right one cell so that it can fill in the leftmost cells on the three tracks with the simulated left endmarker of M, which it marks with $\widehat{}$ to indicate the position of the heads in the starting configuration of M.

	$\widehat{\vdash}$	a_1	a_2	a_3	a_4			a_n	$\sqcup$	$\sqcup$	
$\vdash$	$\widehat{\vdash}$	$\sqcup$	$\sqcup$	$\sqcup$	$\sqcup$	$\cdots$		$\sqcup$	$\sqcup$	$\sqcup$	$\cdots$
	$\widehat{\vdash}$	$\sqcup$	$\sqcup$	$\sqcup$	$\sqcup$			$\sqcup$	$\sqcup$	$\sqcup$	

Each step of M is simulated by several steps of N. To simulate one step of M, N starts at the left of the tape, then scans out until it sees all three marks, remembering the marked symbols in its finite control. When it has seen all three, it determines what to do according to M's transition function δ, which it has encoded in its finite control. Based on this information, it goes back to all three marks, rewriting the symbols on each track and moving the marks appropriately. It then returns to the left end of the tape to simulate the next step of M.

Two-Way Infinite Tapes

Two-way infinite tapes do not add any power. Just fold the tape someplace and simulate it on two tracks of a one-way infinite tape:

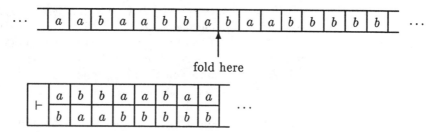

The bottom track is used to simulate the original machine when its head is to the right of the fold, and the top track is used to simulate the machine when its head is to the left of the fold, moving in the opposite direction.

Two Stacks

A machine with a two-way, *read-only* input head and two stacks is as powerful as a Turing machine. Intuitively, the computation of a one-tape TM can be simulated with two stacks by storing the tape contents to the left of the head on one stack and the tape contents to the right of the head on the other stack. The motion of the head is simulated by popping a symbol off one stack and pushing it onto the other. For example,

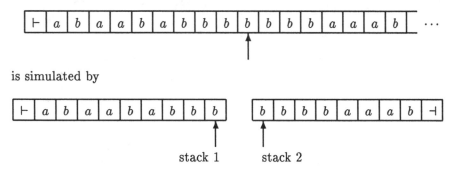

is simulated by

stack 1   stack 2

Counter Automata

A *k-counter automaton* is a machine equipped with a two-way read-only input head and k integer counters. Each counter can store an arbitrary nonnegative integer. In each step, the automaton can independently increment or decrement its counters and test them for 0 and can move its input head one cell in either direction. It cannot write on the tape.

A stack can be simulated with two counters as follows. We can assume without loss of generality that the stack alphabet of the stack to be simulated contains only two symbols, say 0 and 1. This is because we can encode finitely many stack symbols as binary numbers of fixed length, say m; then pushing or popping one stack symbol is simulated by pushing or popping m binary digits. Then the contents of the stack can be regarded as a binary number whose least significant bit is on top of the stack. The simulation maintains this number in the first of the two counters and uses the second to effect the stack operations. To simulate pushing a 0 onto the stack, we need to double the value in the first counter. This is done by entering a loop that repeatedly subtracts one from the first counter and adds two to the second until the first counter is 0. The value in the second counter is then twice the original value in the first counter. We can then transfer that value back to the first counter, or just switch the roles of the two counters. To push 1, the operation is the same, except the value of the second counter is incremented once at the end. To simulate popping, we need to divide the counter value by two; this is done by decrementing one counter while incrementing the other counter every second step. Testing the parity of the original counter contents tells whether a simulated 1 or 0 was popped.

Since a two-stack machine can simulate an arbitrary TM, and since two counters can simulate a stack, it follows that a four-counter automaton can simulate an arbitrary TM.

However, we can do even better: a two-counter automaton can simulate a four-counter automaton. When the four-counter automaton has the values i, j, k, ℓ in its counters, the two-counter automaton will have the value $2^i 3^j 5^k 7^\ell$ in its first counter. It uses its second counter to effect the counter operations of the four-counter automaton. For example, if the four-counter automaton wanted to add one to k (the value of the third counter), then the two-counter automaton would have to multiply the value in its first counter by 5. This is done in the same way as above, adding 5 to the second counter for every 1 we subtract from the first counter. To simulate a test for zero, the two-counter automaton has to determine whether the value in its first counter is divisible by 2, 3, 5, or 7, respectively, depending on which counter of the four-counter automaton is being tested.

Combining these simulations, we see that two-counter automata are as powerful as arbitrary Turing machines. However, as you can imagine, it takes an enormous number of steps of the two-counter automaton to simulate one step of the Turing machine.

One-counter automata are not as powerful as arbitrary TMs, although they can accept non-CFLs. For example, the set $\{a^n b^n c^n \mid n \geq 0\}$ can be accepted by a one-counter automaton.

Enumeration Machines

We defined the recursively enumerable (r.e.) sets to be those sets accepted by Turing machines. The term *recursively enumerable* comes from a different but equivalent formalism embodying the idea that the elements of an r.e. set can be enumerated one at a time in a mechanical fashion.

Define an *enumeration machine* as follows. It has a finite control and two tapes, a read/write *work tape* and a write-only *output tape*. The work tape head can move in either direction and can read and write any element of Γ. The output tape head moves right one cell when it writes a symbol, and it can only write symbols in Σ. There is no input and no accept or reject state. The machine starts in its start state with both tapes blank. It moves according to its transition function like a TM, occasionally writing symbols on the output tape as determined by the transition function. At some point it may enter a special *enumeration state*, which is just a distinguished state of its finite control. When that happens, the string currently written on the output tape is said to be *enumerated*. The output tape is then automatically erased and the output head moved back to the beginning of the tape (the work tape is left intact), and the machine continues from that point. The machine runs forever. The set $L(E)$ is defined to be the set of all strings in Σ^* that are ever enumerated by the enumeration machine E. The machine might never enter its enumeration state, in which case $L(E) = \varnothing$, or it might enumerate infinitely many strings. The same string may be enumerated more than once.

Enumeration machines and Turing machines are equivalent in computational power:

Theorem 30.1   *The family of sets enumerated by enumeration machines is exactly the family of r.e. sets. In other words, a set is $L(E)$ for some enumeration machine E if and only if it is $L(M)$ for some Turing machine M.*

Proof. We show first that given an enumeration machine E, we can construct a Turing machine M such that $L(M) = L(E)$. Let M on input x copy x to one of three tracks on its tape, then simulate E, using the other two tracks to record the contents of E's work tape and output tape. For every string enumerated by E, M compares this string to x and accepts if they match. Then M accepts its input x iff x is ever enumerated by E, so the set of strings accepted by M is exactly the set of strings enumerated by E.

Conversely, given a TM M, we can construct an enumeration machine E such that $L(E) = L(M)$. We would like E somehow to simulate M on all possible strings in Σ^* and enumerate those that are accepted.

Here is an approach that doesn't quite work. The enumeration machine E writes down the strings in Σ^* one by one on the bottom track of its work tape in some order. For every input string x, it simulates M on input x, using the top track of its work tape to do the simulation. If M accepts x, E copies x to its output tape and enters its enumeration state. It then goes on to the next string.

The problem with this procedure is that M might not halt on some input x, and then E would be stuck simulating M on x forever and would never move on to strings later in the list (and it is impossible to determine in general whether M will ever halt on x, as we will see in Lecture 31). Thus E should not just list the strings in Σ^* in some order and simulate M on those inputs one at a time, waiting for each simulation to halt before going on to the next, because the simulation might never halt.

The solution to this problem is *timesharing*. Instead of simulating M on the input strings one at a time, the enumeration machine E should run several simulations at once, working a few steps on each simulation and then moving on to the next. The work tape of E can be divided into segments separated by a special marker $\# \in \Gamma$, with a simulation of M on a different input string running in each segment. Between passes, E can move way out to the right, create a new segment, and start up a new simulation in that segment on the next input string. For example, we might have E simulate M on the first input for one step, then the first and second inputs for one step each, then the first, second, and third inputs for one step each, and so on. If any simulation needs more space than initially allocated in its segment, the entire contents of the tape to its right can be shifted to the right one cell. In this way M is eventually simulated on all input strings, even if some of the simulations never halt.   □

Historical Notes

Turing machines were invented by Alan Turing [120]. Originally they were presented in the form of enumeration machines, since Turing was interested in enumerating the decimal expansions of computable real numbers and values of real-valued functions. Turing also introduced the concept of nondeterminism in his original paper, although he did not develop the idea.

The basic properties of the r.e. sets were developed by Kleene [68] and Post [100, 101].

Counter automata were studied by Fischer [38], Fischer et al. [39], and Minsky [88].

Lecture 31

Universal Machines and Diagonalization

A Universal Turing Machine

Now we come to a crucial observation about the power of Turing machines: there exist Turing machines that can simulate other Turing machines whose descriptions are presented as part of the input. There is nothing mysterious about this; it is the same as writing a LISP interpreter in LISP.

First we need to fix a reasonable encoding scheme for Turing machines over the alphabet $\{0, 1\}$. This encoding scheme should be simple enough that all the data associated with a machine M—the set of states, the transition function, the input and tape alphabets, the endmarker, the blank symbol, and the start, accept, and reject states—can be determined easily by another machine reading the encoded description of M. For example, if the string begins with the prefix

$$0^n 10^m 10^k 10^s 10^t 10^r 10^u 10^v 1,$$

this might indicate that the machine has n states represented by the numbers 0 to $n - 1$; it has m tape symbols represented by the numbers 0 to $m - 1$, of which the first k represent input symbols; the start, accept, and reject states are s, t, and r, respectively; and the endmarker and blank symbol are u and v, respectively. The remainder of the string can consist of a sequence of substrings specifying the transitions in δ. For example, the substring

$$0^p 10^a 10^q 10^b 10$$

might indicate that δ contains the transition

$$((p, a), (q, b, L)),$$

the direction to move the head encoded by the final digit. The exact details of the encoding scheme are not important. The only requirements are that it should be easy to interpret and able to encode all Turing machines up to isomorphism.

Once we have a suitable encoding of Turing machines, we can construct a *universal Turing machine* U such that

$$L(U) \stackrel{\text{def}}{=} \{M \# x \mid x \in L(M)\}.$$

In other words, presented with (an encoding over $\{0, 1\}$ of) a Turing machine M and (an encoding over $\{0, 1\}$ of) a string x over M's input alphabet, the machine U accepts $M \# x$ iff M accepts x.[1] The symbol $\#$ is just a symbol in U's input alphabet other than 0 or 1 used to delimit M and x.

The machine U first checks its input $M \# x$ to make sure that M is a valid encoding of a Turing machine and x is a valid encoding of a string over M's input alphabet. If not, it immediately rejects.

If the encodings of M and x are valid, the machine U does a step-by-step simulation of M. This might work as follows. The tape of U is partitioned into three tracks. The description of M is copied to the top track and the string x to the middle track. The middle track will be used to hold the simulated contents of M's tape. The bottom track will be used to remember the current state of M and the current position of M's read/write head. The machine U then simulates M on input x one step at a time, shuttling back and forth between the description of M on its top track and the simulated contents of M's tape on the middle track. In each step, it updates M's state and simulated tape contents as dictated by M's transition function, which U can read from the description of M. If ever M halts and accepts or halts and rejects, then U does the same.

As we have observed, the string x over the input alphabet of M and its encoding over the input alphabet of U are two different things, since the two machines may have different input alphabets. If the input alphabet of

---

[1]Note that we are using the metasymbol M for both a Turing machine and its encoding over $\{0, 1\}$ and the metasymbol x for both a string over M's input alphabet and its encoding over $\{0, 1\}$. This is for notational convenience.

M is bigger than that of U, then each symbol of x must be encoded as a string of symbols over U's input alphabet. Also, the tape alphabet of M may be bigger than that of U, in which case each symbol of M's tape alphabet must be encoded as a string of symbols over U's tape alphabet. In general, each step of M may require many steps of U to simulate.

Diagonalization

We now show how to use a universal Turing machine in conjunction with a technique called *diagonalization* to prove that the halting and membership problems for Turing machines are undecidable. In other words, the sets

$$\mathrm{HP} \stackrel{\mathrm{def}}{=} \{M\#x \mid M \text{ halts on } x\},$$

$$\mathrm{MP} \stackrel{\mathrm{def}}{=} \{M\#x \mid x \in L(M)\}$$

are not recursive.

The technique of diagonalization was first used by Cantor at the end of the nineteenth century to show that there does not exist a one-to-one correspondence between the natural numbers $\mathbb{N}$ and its *power set*

$$2^{\mathbb{N}} = \{A \mid A \subseteq \mathbb{N}\},$$

the set of all subsets of $\mathbb{N}$. In fact, there does not even exist a function

$$f : \mathbb{N} \to 2^{\mathbb{N}}$$

that is onto. Here is how Cantor's argument went.

Suppose (for a contradiction) that such an onto function f did exist. Consider an infinite two-dimensional matrix indexed along the top by the natural numbers $0, 1, 2, \ldots$ and down the left by the sets $f(0), f(1), f(2), \ldots$. Fill in the matrix by placing a 1 in position i, j if j is in the set $f(i)$ and 0 if $j \notin f(i)$.

	0	1	2	3	4	5	6	7	8	9	$\cdots$
$f(0)$	1	0	0	1	1	0	1	0	1	1	
$f(1)$	0	0	1	1	0	1	1	0	0	1	
$f(2)$	0	1	1	0	0	0	1	1	0	1	
$f(3)$	0	1	0	1	1	0	1	1	0	0	
$f(4)$	1	0	1	0	0	1	0	0	1	1	$\cdots$
$f(5)$	1	0	1	1	0	1	1	1	0	1	
$f(6)$	0	0	1	0	1	1	0	0	1	1	
$f(7)$	1	1	1	0	1	1	1	0	1	0	
$f(8)$	0	0	1	0	0	0	0	1	1	0	
$f(9)$	1	1	0	0	1	0	0	1	0	0	
$\vdots$											$\ddots$

The ith row of the matrix is a bit string describing the set $f(i)$. For example, in the above picture, $f(0) = \{0, 3, 4, 6, 8, 9, \ldots\}$ and $f(1) = \{2, 3, 5, 6, 9, \ldots\}$. By our (soon to be proved fallacious) assumption that f is onto, every subset of $\mathbb{N}$ appears as a row of this matrix.

But we can construct a new set that does not appear in the list by complementing the main diagonal of the matrix (hence the term *diagonalization*). Look at the infinite bit string down the main diagonal (in this example, $1011010010\cdots$) and take its Boolean complement (in this example, $0100101101\cdots$). This new bit string represents a set B (in this example, $B = \{1, 4, 6, 7, 9, \ldots\}$). But the set B does not appear anywhere in the list down the left side of the matrix, since it differs from every $f(i)$ on at least one element, namely i. This is a contradiction, since every subset of $\mathbb{N}$ was supposed to occur as a row of the matrix, by our assumption that f was onto.

This argument works not only for the natural numbers $\mathbb{N}$, but for any set A whatsoever. Suppose (for a contradiction) there existed an onto function from A to its power set:

$$f : A \to 2^A.$$

Let

$$B = \{x \in A \mid x \notin f(x)\}$$

(this is the formal way of *complementing the diagonal*). Then $B \subseteq A$. Since f is onto, there must exist $y \in A$ such that $f(y) = B$. Now we ask whether $y \in f(y)$ and discover a contradiction:

$$y \in f(y) \iff y \in B \qquad \text{since } B = f(y)$$
$$\iff y \notin f(y) \quad \text{definition of } B.$$

Thus no such f can exist.

Undecidability of the Halting Problem

We have discussed how to encode descriptions of Turing machines as strings in $\{0, 1\}^*$ so that these descriptions can be read and simulated by a universal Turing machine U. The machine U takes as input an encoding of a Turing machine M and a string x and simulates M on input x, and

- halts and accepts if M halts and accepts x,
- halts and rejects if M halts and rejects x, and
- loops if M loops on x.

The machine U doesn't do any fancy analysis on the machine M to try to determine whether or not it will halt. It just blindly simulates M step by step. If M doesn't halt on x, then U will just go on happily simulating M forever.

It is natural to ask whether we can do better than just a blind simulation. Might there be some way to analyze M to determine in advance, before doing the simulation, whether M would eventually halt on x? If U could say for sure in advance that M would not halt on x, then it could skip the simulation and save itself a lot of useless work. On the other hand, if U could ascertain that M *would* eventually halt on x, then it could go ahead with the simulation to determine whether M accepts or rejects. We could then build a machine U' that takes as input an encoding of a Turing machine M and a string x, and

- halts and accepts if M halts and accepts x,

- halts and rejects if M halts and rejects x, and

- halts and rejects if M loops on x.

This would say that $L(U') = L(U) = \text{MP}$ is a recursive set.

Unfortunately, this is not possible in general. There are certainly machines for which it is possible to determine halting by some heuristic or other: machines for which the start state is the accept state, for example. However, there is no general method that gives the right answer for all machines.

We can prove this using Cantor's diagonalization technique. For $x \in \{0,1\}^*$, let M_x be the Turing machine with input alphabet $\{0,1\}$ whose encoding over $\{0,1\}^*$ is x. (If x is not a legal description of a TM with input alphabet $\{0,1\}^*$ according to our encoding scheme, we take M_x to be some arbitrary but fixed TM with input alphabet $\{0,1\}$, say a trivial TM with one state that immediately halts.) In this way we get a list

$$M_\epsilon, M_0, M_1, M_{00}, M_{01}, M_{10}, M_{11}, M_{100}, M_{101}, \ldots \tag{31.1}$$

containing all possible Turing machines with input alphabet $\{0,1\}$ indexed by strings in $\{0,1\}^*$. We make sure that the encoding scheme is simple enough that a universal machine can determine M_x from x for the purpose of simulation.

Now consider an infinite two-dimensional matrix indexed along the top by strings in $\{0,1\}^*$ and down the left by TMs in the list (31.1). The matrix contains an H in position x, y if M_x halts on input y and an L if M_x loops on input y.

	ϵ	0	1	00	01	10	11	000	001	010	$\cdots$
M_ϵ	H	L	L	H	H	L	H	L	H	H	
M_0	L	L	H	H	L	H	H	L	L	H	
M_1	L	II	H	L	L	L	H	H	L	H	
M_{00}	L	H	L	H	H	L	H	H	L	L	
M_{01}	H	L	H	L	L	H	L	L	H	H	$\cdots$
M_{10}	H	L	H	H	L	H	H	H	L	H	
M_{11}	L	L	H	L	H	H	L	L	H	H	
M_{000}	H	H	H	L	H	H	H	L	H	L	
M_{001}	L	L	H	L	L	L	L	H	H	L	
M_{010}	II	H	L	L	H	L	L	H	L	L	
$\vdots$											$\ddots$

The xth row of the matrix describes for each input string y whether or not M_x halts on y. For example, in the above picture, M_ϵ halts on inputs $\epsilon, 00, 01, 11, 001, 010, \ldots$ and does not halt on inputs $0, 1, 10, 000, \ldots$.

Suppose (for a contradiction) that there existed a *total* machine K accepting the set HP; that is, a machine that for any given x and y could determine the x, yth entry of the above table in finite time. Thus on input $M\#x$,

- K halts and accepts if M halts on x, and

- K halts and rejects if M loops on x.

Consider a machine N that on input $x \in \{0, 1\}^*$

(i) constructs M_x from x and writes $M_x\#x$ on its tape;

(ii) runs K on input $M_x\#x$, accepting if K rejects and going into a trivial loop if K accepts.

Note that N is essentially complementing the diagonal of the above matrix. Then for any $x \in \{0, 1\}^*$,

$$N \text{ halts on } x \Longleftrightarrow K \text{ rejects } M_x\#x \quad \text{definition of } N$$
$$\Longleftrightarrow M_x \text{ loops on } x \quad \text{assumption about } K.$$

This says that N's behavior is different from every M_x on at least one string, namely x. But the list (31.1) was supposed to contain all Turing machines over the input alphabet $\{0, 1\}$, including N. This is a contradiction.   □

The fallacious assumption that led to the contradiction was that it was possible to determine the entries of the matrix effectively; in other words, that there existed a Turing machine K that given M and x could determine in a finite time whether or not M halts on x.

One can always simulate a given machine on a given input. If the machine ever halts, then we will know this eventually, and we can stop the simulation and say that it halted; but if not, there is no way in general to stop after a finite time and say for certain that it will never halt.

Undecidability of the Membership Problem

The membership problem is also undecidable. We can show this by *reducing* the halting problem to it. In other words, we show that if there were a way to decide membership in general, we could use this as a subroutine to decide halting in general. But we just showed above that halting is undecidable, so membership must be undecidable too.

Here is how we would use a total TM that decides membership as a subroutine to decide halting. Given a machine M and input x, suppose we wanted to find out whether M halts on x. Build a new machine N that is exactly like M, except that it accepts whenever M would either accept or reject. The machine N can be constructed from M simply by adding a new accept state and making the old accept and reject states transfer to this new accept state. Then for all x, N accepts x iff M halts on x. The membership problem for N and x (asking whether $x \in L(N)$) is therefore the same as the halting problem for M and x (asking whether M halts on x). If the membership problem were decidable, then we could decide whether M halts on x by constructing N and asking whether $x \in L(N)$. But we have shown above that the halting problem is undecidable, therefore the membership problem must also be undecidable.

Lecture 32

Decidable and Undecidable Problems

Here are some examples of decision problems involving Turing machines. Is it decidable whether a given Turing machine

(a) has at least 481 states?

(b) takes more than 481 steps on input ϵ?

(c) takes more than 481 steps on *some* input?

(d) takes more than 481 steps on *all* inputs?

(e) ever moves its head more than 481 tape cells away from the left endmarker on input ϵ?

(f) accepts the null string ϵ?

(g) accepts any string at all?

(h) accepts every string?

(i) accepts a finite set?

(j) accepts a regular set?

(k) accepts a CFL?

(l) accepts a recursive set?

(m) is equivalent to a Turing machine with a shorter description?

Problems (a) through (e) are decidable and problems (f) through (m) are undecidable (proofs below). We will show that problems (f) through (l) are undecidable by showing that a decision procedure for one of these problems could be used to construct a decision procedure for the halting problem, which we know is impossible. Problem (m) is a little more difficult, and we will leave that as an exercise (Miscellaneous Exercise 131). Translated into modern terms, problem (m) is the same as determining whether there exists a shorter PASCAL program equivalent to a given one.

The best way to show that a problem is decidable is to give a total Turing machine that accepts exactly the "yes" instances. Because it must be total, it must also reject the "no" instances; in other words, it must not loop on any input.

Problem (a) is easily decidable, since the number of states of M can be read off from the encoding of M. We can build a Turing machine that, given the encoding of M written on its input tape, counts the number of states of M and accepts or rejects depending on whether the number is at least 481.

Problem (b) is decidable, since we can simulate M on input ϵ with a universal machine for 481 steps (counting up to 481 on a separate track) and accept or reject depending on whether M has halted by that time.

Problem (c) is decidable: we can just simulate M on all inputs of length at most 481 for 481 steps. If M takes more than 481 steps on some input, then it will take more than 481 steps on some input of length at most 481, since in 481 steps it can read at most the first 481 symbols of the input.

The argument for problem (d) is similar. If M takes more than 481 steps on all inputs of length at most 481, then it will take more than 481 steps on all inputs.

For problem (e), if M never moves more than 481 tape cells away from the left endmarker, then it will either halt or loop in such a way that we can detect the looping after a finite time. This is because if M has k states and m tape symbols, and never moves more than 481 tape cells away from the left endmarker, then there are only $482km^{481}$ configurations it could possibly ever be in, one for each choice of head position, state, and tape contents that fit within 481 tape cells. If it runs for any longer than that without moving more than 481 tape cells away from the left endmarker, then it must be in a loop, because it must have repeated a configuration. This can be detected by a machine that simulates M, counting the number of steps M takes on a separate track and declaring M to be in a loop if the bound of $482km^{481}$ steps is ever exceeded.

Problems (f) through (l) are undecidable. To show this, we show that the ability to decide any one of these problems could be used to decide the halting problem. Since we know that the halting problem is undecidable, these problems must be undecidable too. This is called a *reduction*.

Let's consider (f) first (although the same construction will take care of (g) through (i) as well). We will show that it is undecidable whether a given machine accepts ϵ, because the ability to decide this question would give the ability to decide the halting problem, which we know is impossible.

Suppose we could decide whether a given machine accepts ϵ. We could then decide the halting problem as follows. Say we are given a Turing machine M and string x, and we wish to determine whether M halts on x. Construct from M and x a new machine M' that does the following on input y:

(i) erases its input y;

(ii) writes x on its tape (M' has x hard-wired in its finite control);

(iii) runs M on input x (M' also has a description of M hard-wired in its finite control);

(iv) accepts if M halts on x.

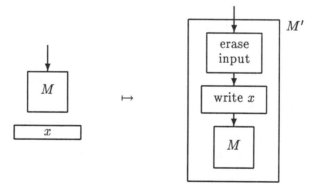

Note that M' does the same thing on all inputs y: if M halts on x, then M' accepts its input y; and if M does not halt on x, then M' does not halt on y, therefore does not accept y. Moreover, this is true for every y. Thus

$$L(M') = \begin{cases} \Sigma^* & \text{if } M \text{ halts on } x, \\ \varnothing & \text{if } M \text{ does not halt on } x. \end{cases}$$

Now if we could decide whether a given machine accepts the null string ϵ, we could apply this decision procedure to the M' just constructed, and this would tell whether M halts on x. In other words, we could obtain a decision procedure for halting as follows: given M and x, construct M', then ask whether M' accepts ϵ. The answer to the latter question is "yes" iff M halts on x. Since we know the halting problem is undecidable, it must also be undecidable whether a given machine accepts ϵ.

Similarly, if we could decide whether a given machine accepts any string at all, or whether it accepts every string, or whether the set of strings it accepts is finite, we could apply any of these decision procedures to M' and this would tell whether M halts on x. Since we know that the halting problem is undecidable, all of these problems must be undecidable too.

To show that (j), (k), and (l) are undecidable, pick your favorite r.e. but nonrecursive set A (HP or MP will do) and modify the above construction as follows. Given M and x, build a new machine M'' that does the following on input y:

(i) saves y on a separate track of its tape;

(ii) writes x on a different track (x is hard-wired in the finite control of M'');

(iii) runs M on input x (M is also hard-wired in the finite control of M'');

(iv) if M halts on x, then M'' runs a machine accepting A on its original input y, and accepts if that machine accepts.

Either M does not halt on x, in which case the simulation in step (iii) never halts and M'' never accepts any string; or M does halt on x, in which case M'' accepts its input y iff $y \in A$. Thus

$$L(M'') = \begin{cases} A & \text{if } M \text{ halts on } x, \\ \varnothing & \text{if } M \text{ does not halt on } x. \end{cases}$$

Since A is neither recursive, CFL, nor regular, and $\varnothing$ is all three of these things, if one could decide whether a given TM accepts a recursive, context-free, or regular set, then one could apply this decision procedure to M'' and this would tell whether M halts on x.

Lecture 33

Reduction

There are two main techniques for showing that problems are undecidable: *diagonalization* and *reduction*. We saw examples of diagonalization in Lecture 31 and reduction in Lecture 32.

Once we have established that a problem such as HP is undecidable, we can show that another problem B is undecidable by *reducing* HP to B. Intuitively, this means we can manipulate instances of HP to make them look like instances of the problem B in such a way that "yes" instances of HP become "yes" instances of B and "no" instances of HP become "no" instances of B. Although we cannot tell effectively whether a given instance of HP is a "yes" instance, the manipulation preserves "yes"-ness and "no"-ness. If there existed a decision procedure for B, then we could apply it to the disguised instances of HP to decide membership in HP. In other words, combining a decision procedure for B with the manipulation procedure would give a decision procedure for HP. Since we have already shown that no such decision procedure for HP can exist, we can conclude that no decision procedure for B can exist.

We can give an abstract definition of reduction and prove a general theorem that will save us a lot of work in undecidability proofs from now on.

Given sets $A \subseteq \Sigma^*$ and $B \subseteq \Delta^*$, a (many-one) *reduction* of A to B is a computable function

$$\sigma : \Sigma^* \to \Delta^*$$

such that for all $x \in \Sigma^*$,

$$x \in A \iff \sigma(x) \in B. \tag{33.1}$$

In other words, strings in A must go to strings in B under σ, and strings not in A must go to strings not in B under σ.

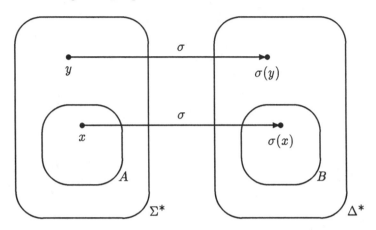

The function σ need not be one-to-one or onto. It must, however, be *total* and *effectively computable*. This means σ must be computable by a total Turing machine that on any input x halts with $\sigma(x)$ written on its tape. When such a reduction exists, we say that A is *reducible* to B via the map σ, and we write $A \leq_m B$. The subscript m, which stands for "many-one," is used to distinguish this relation from other types of reducibility relations.

The relation $\leq_m$ of reducibility between languages is transitive: if $A \leq_m B$ and $B \leq_m C$, then $A \leq_m C$. This is because if σ reduces A to B and τ reduces B to C, then $\tau \circ \sigma$, the composition of σ and τ, is computable and reduces A to C.

Although we have not mentioned it explicitly, we have used reductions in the last few lectures to show that various problems are undecidable.

Example 33.1   In showing that it is undecidable whether a given TM accepts the null string, we constructed from a given TM M and string x a TM M' that accepted the null string iff M halts on x. In this example,

$$A = \{M\#x \mid M \text{ halts on } x\} = \text{HP},$$
$$B = \{M \mid \epsilon \in L(M)\},$$

and σ is the computable map $M\#x \mapsto M'$. $\square$

Example 33.2   In showing that it is undecidable whether a given TM accepts a regular set, we constructed from a given TM M and string x a TM M'' such that

$L(M'')$ is a nonregular set if M halts on x and $\varnothing$ otherwise. In this example,

$$A = \{M\#x \mid M \text{ halts on } x\} = \text{HP},$$
$$B = \{M \mid L(M) \text{ is regular}\},$$

and σ is the computable map $M\#x \mapsto M''$.   □

Here is a general theorem that will save us some work.

Theorem 33.3   *(i) If $A \leq_m B$ and B is r.e., then so is A. Equivalently, if $A \leq_m B$ and A is not r e , then neither is B.*

(ii) If $A \leq_m B$ and B is recursive, then so is A. Equivalently, if $A \leq_m B$ and A is not recursive, then neither is B.

Proof. (i) Suppose $A \leq_m B$ via the map σ and B is r.e. Let M be a TM such that $B = L(M)$. Build a machine N for A as follows: on input x, first compute $\sigma(x)$, then run M on input $\sigma(x)$, accepting if M accepts. Then

$$\begin{aligned} N \text{ accepts } x &\Longleftrightarrow M \text{ accepts } \sigma(x) &&\text{definition of } N \\ &\Longleftrightarrow \sigma(x) \in B &&\text{definition of } M \\ &\Longleftrightarrow x \in A &&\text{by (33.1).} \end{aligned}$$

(ii) Recall from Lecture 29 that a set is recursive iff both it and its complement are r.e. Suppose $A \leq_m B$ via the map σ and B is recursive. Note that $\sim A \leq_m \sim B$ via the same σ (Check the definition!). If B is recursive, then both B and $\sim B$ are r.e. By (i), both A and $\sim A$ are r.e., thus A is recursive.   □

We can use Theorem 33.3(i) to show that certain sets are not r.e. and Theorem 33.3(ii) to show that certain sets are not recursive. To show that a set B is not r.e., we need only give a reduction from a set A we already know is not r.e. (such as $\sim$HP) to B. By Theorem 33.3(i), B cannot be r.e.

Example 33.4   Let's illustrate by showing that neither the set

$$\text{FIN} = \{M \mid L(M) \text{ is finite}\}$$

nor its complement is r.e. We show that neither of these sets is r.e. by reducing $\sim$HP to each of them, where

$$\sim \text{HP} = \{M\#x \mid M \text{ does not halt on } x\} :$$

(a) $\sim\text{HP} \leq_m \text{FIN}$,

(b) $\sim\text{HP} \leq_m \sim\text{FIN}$.

Since we already know that $\sim$HP is not r.e., it follows from Theorem 33.3(i) that neither FIN nor $\sim$FIN is r.e.

For (a), we want to give a computable map σ such that

$$M\#x \in {\sim}\mathrm{HP} \iff \sigma(M\#x) \in \mathrm{FIN}.$$

In other words, from $M\#x$ we want to construct a Turing machine $M' = \sigma(M\#x)$ such that

$$M \text{ does not halt on } x \iff L(M') \text{ is finite.} \qquad (33.2)$$

Note that the description of M' can depend on M and x. In particular, M' can have a description of M and the string x hard-wired in its finite control if desired.

We have actually already given a construction satisfying (33.2). Given $M\#x$, construct M' such that on all inputs y, M' takes the following actions:

 (i)   erases its input y;

 (ii) writes x on its tape (M' has x hard-wired in its finite control);

 (iii) runs M on input x (M' also has a description of M hard-wired in its finite control);

 (iv) accepts if M halts on x.

If M does not halt on input x, then the simulation in step (iii) never halts, and M' never reaches step (iv). In this case M' does not accept its input y. This happens the same way for all inputs y, therefore in this case, $L(M) = \varnothing$. On the other hand, if M does halt on x, then the simulation in step (iii) halts, and y is accepted in step (iv). Moreover, this is true for all y. In this case, $L(M) = \Sigma^*$. Thus

$$
\begin{aligned}
M \text{ halts on } x &\Rightarrow L(M') = \Sigma^* &\Rightarrow L(M') \text{ is infinite,}\\
M \text{ does not halt on } x &\Rightarrow L(M') = \varnothing &\Rightarrow L(M') \text{ is finite.}
\end{aligned}
$$

Thus (33.2) is satisfied. Note that this is all we have to do to show that FIN is not r.e.: we have given the reduction (a), so by Theorem 33.3(i) we are done.

There is a common pitfall here that we should be careful to avoid. It is important to observe that the computable map σ that produces a description of M' from M and x does not need to execute the program (i) through (iv). It only produces the description of a machine M' that does so. The computation of σ is quite simple—it does not involve the simulation of any other machines or anything complicated at all. It merely takes a description of a Turing machine M and string x and plugs them into a general description of a machine that executes (i) through (iv). This can be done quite easily by a total TM, so σ is total and effectively computable.

Now (b). By definition of reduction, a map reducing $\sim$HP to $\sim$FIN also reduces HP to FIN, so it suffices to give a computable map τ such that

$$M\#x \in \text{HP} \iff \tau(M\#x) \in \text{FIN}.$$

In other words, from M and x we want to construct a Turing machine $M'' = \tau(M\#x)$ such that

$$M \text{ halts on } x \iff L(M'') \text{ is finite.} \qquad (33.3)$$

Given $M\#x$, construct a machine M'' that on input y

(i) saves y on a separate track;

(ii) writes x on the tape;

(iii) simulates M on x for $|y|$ steps (it erases one symbol of y for each step of M on x that it simulates);

(iv) accepts if M has *not* halted within that time, otherwise rejects.

Now if M never halts on x, then M'' halts and accepts y in step (iv) after $|y|$ steps of the simulation, and this is true for all y. In this case $L(M'') = \Sigma^*$. On the other hand, if M does halt on x, then it does so after some finite number of steps, say n. Then M'' accepts y in (iv) if $|y| < n$ (since the simulation in (iii) has not finished by $|y|$ steps) and rejects y in (iv) if $|y| \geq n$ (since the simulation in (iii) does have time to complete). In this case M'' accepts all strings of length less than n and rejects all strings of length n or greater, so $L(M'')$ is a finite set. Thus

$$M \text{ halts on } x \Rightarrow L(M'') = \{y \mid |y| < \text{running time of } M \text{ on } x\}$$
$$\Rightarrow L(M'') \text{ is finite,}$$

$$M \text{ does not halt on } x \Rightarrow L(M'') = \Sigma^*$$
$$\Rightarrow L(M'') \text{ is infinite.}$$

Then (33.3) is satisfied.

It is important that the functions σ and τ in these two reductions can be computed by Turing machines that always halt. $\qquad \square$

Historical Notes

The technique of diagonalization was first used by Cantor [16] to show that there were fewer real algebraic numbers than real numbers.

Universal Turing machines and the application of Cantor's diagonalization technique to prove the undecidability of the halting problem appear in Turing's original paper [120].

Reducibility relations are discussed by Post [101]; see [106, 116].

Lecture 34

Rice's Theorem

Rice's theorem says that undecidability is the rule, not the exception. It is a very powerful theorem, subsuming many undecidability results that we have seen as special cases.

Theorem 34.1 **(Rice's theorem)** *Every nontrivial property of the r.e. sets is undecidable.*

Yes, you heard right: that's *every* nontrivial property of the r.e. sets. So as not to misinterpret this, let us clarify a few things.

First, fix a finite alphabet Σ. A *property of the r.e. sets* is a map

$$P : \{\text{r.e. subsets of } \Sigma^*\} \to \{\top, \bot\},$$

where $\top$ and $\bot$ represent truth and falsity, respectively. For example, the property of emptiness is represented by the map

$$P(A) = \begin{cases} \top & \text{if } A = \varnothing, \\ \bot & \text{if } A \neq \varnothing. \end{cases}$$

To ask whether such a property P is decidable, the set has to be presented in a finite form suitable for input to a TM. We assume that r.e. sets are presented by TMs that accept them. But keep in mind that the property is a property of *sets*, not of Turing machines; thus it must be true or false independent of the particular TM chosen to represent the set.

Here are some other examples of properties of r.e. sets: $L(M)$ is finite; $L(M)$ is regular; $L(M)$ is a CFL; M accepts 101001 (i.e., $101001 \in L(M)$); $L(M) = \Sigma^*$. Each of these properties is a property of the set accepted by the Turing machine.

Here are some examples of properties of Turing machines that are *not* properties of r.e. sets: M has at least 481 states; M halts on all inputs; M rejects 101001; there exists a smaller machine equivalent to M. These are not properties of sets, because in each case one can give two TMs that accept the same set, one of which satisfies the property and the other of which doesn't.

For Rice's theorem to apply, the property also has to be *nontrivial*. This just means that the property is neither universally true nor universally false; that is, there must be at least one r.e. set that satisfies the property and at least one that does not. There are only two trivial properties, and they are both trivially decidable.

Proof of Rice's theorem. Let P be a nontrivial property of the r.e. sets. Assume without loss of generality that $P(\varnothing) = \bot$ (the argument is symmetric if $P(\varnothing) = \top$). Since P is nontrivial, there must exist an r.e. set A such that $P(A) = \top$. Let K be a TM accepting A.

We reduce HP to the set $\{M \mid P(L(M)) = \top\}$, thereby showing that the latter is undecidable (Theorem 33.3(ii)). Given $M \# x$, construct a machine $M' = \sigma(M \# x)$ that on input y

(i) saves y on a separate track someplace;

(ii) writes x on its tape (x is hard-wired in the finite control of M');

(iii) runs M on input x (a description of M is also hard-wired in the finite control of M');

(iv) if M halts on x, M' runs K on y and accepts if K accepts.

Now either M halts on x or not. If M does not halt on x, then the simulation in (iii) will never halt, and the input y of M' will not be accepted. This is true for every y, so in this case $L(M') = \varnothing$. On the other hand, if M does halt on x, then M' always reaches step (iv), and the original input y of M' is accepted iff y is accepted by K; that is, if $y \in A$. Thus

$$M \text{ halts on } x \quad \Rightarrow \quad L(M') = A \quad \Rightarrow \quad P(L(M')) = P(A) = \top,$$
$$M \text{ does not halt on } x \quad \Rightarrow \quad L(M') = \varnothing \quad \Rightarrow \quad P(L(M')) = P(\varnothing) = \bot.$$

This constitutes a reduction from HP to the set $\{M \mid P(L(M)) = \top\}$. Since HP is not recursive, by Theorem 33.3, neither is the latter set; that is, it is undecidable whether $L(M)$ satisfies P.   □

Rice's Theorem, Part II

A property $P : \{\text{r.e. sets}\} \rightarrow \{\top, \bot\}$ of the r.e. sets is called *monotone* if for all r.e. sets A and B, if $A \subseteq B$, then $P(A) \leq P(B)$. Here $\leq$ means less than or equal to in the order $\bot \leq \top$. In other words, P is *monotone* if whenever a set has the property, then all supersets of that set have it as well. For example, the properties "$L(M)$ is infinite" and "$L(M) = \Sigma^*$" are monotone but "$L(M)$ is finite" and "$L(M) = \varnothing$" are not.

Theorem 34.2   **(Rice's theorem, part II)**   *No nonmonotone property of the r.e. sets is semidecidable. In other words, if P is a nonmonotone property of the r.e. sets, then the set $T_P = \{M \mid P(L(M)) = \top\}$ is not r.e.*

Proof. Since P is nonmonotone, there exist TMs M_0 and M_1 such that $L(M_0) \subseteq L(M_1)$, $P(M_0) = \top$, and $P(M_1) = \bot$.

We want to reduce $\sim\!\text{HP}$ to T_P, or equivalently, HP to $\sim\!T_P = \{M \mid P(L(M)) = \bot\}$. Since $\sim\!\text{HP}$ is not r.e., neither will be T_P. Given $M\#x$, we want to show how to construct a machine M' such that $P(M') = \bot$ iff M halts on x. Let M' be a machine that does the following on input y:

(i)   writes its input y on the top and middle tracks of its tape;

(ii) writes x on the bottom track (it has x hard-wired in its finite control);

(iii) simulates M_0 on input y on the top track, M_1 on input y on the middle track, and M on input x on the bottom track in a round-robin fashion; that is, it simulates one step of each of the three machines, then another step, and so on (descriptions of M_0, M_1, and M are all hard-wired in the finite control of M');

(iv) accepts its input y if either of the following two events occurs:

    (a) M_0 accepts y, or

    (b) M_1 accepts y and M halts on x.

Either M halts on x or not, independent of the input y to M'. If M does not halt on x, then event (b) in step (iv) will never occur, so M' will accept y iff event (a) occurs, thus in this case $L(M') = L(M_0)$. On the other hand, if M does halt on x, then y will be accepted iff it is accepted by either M_0 or M_1; that is, if $y \in L(M_0) \cup L(M_1)$. Since $L(M_0) \subseteq L(M_1)$, this is equivalent to saying that $y \in L(M_1)$, thus in this case $L(M') = L(M_1)$. We have shown

$$M \text{ halts on } x \Rightarrow L(M') = L(M_1)$$
$$\Rightarrow P(L(M')) = P(L(M_1)) = \bot,$$

$$M \text{ does not halt on } x \Rightarrow L(M') = L(M_0)$$
$$\Rightarrow P(L(M')) = P(L(M_0)) = \top.$$

The construction of M' from M and x constitutes a reduction from $\sim$HP to the set $T_P = \{M \mid P(L(M)) = \top\}$. By Theorem 33.3(i), the latter set is not r.e. $\qquad\square$

Historical Notes

Rice's theorem was proved by H. G. Rice [104, 105].

Lecture 35

Undecidable Problems About CFLs

In this lecture we show that a very simple problem about CFLs is undecidable, namely the problem of deciding whether a given CFG generates all strings.

It is decidable whether a given CFG generates any string at all, since we know by the pumping lemma that a CFG G that generates any string at all must generate a short string; and we can determine for all short strings x whether $x \in L(G)$ by the CKY algorithm.

This decision procedure is rather inefficient. Here is a better one. Let $G = (N, \Sigma, P, S)$ be the given CFG. To decide whether $L(G)$ is nonempty, we will execute an inductive procedure that marks a nonterminal when it is determined that that nonterminal generates some string in Σ^*—any string at all—and when we are done, ask whether the start symbol S is marked.

At stage 0, mark all the symbols of Σ. At each successive stage, mark a nonterminal $A \in N$ if there is a production $A \to \beta \in P$ and all symbols of β are marked. Quit when there are no more changes; that is, when for each production $A \to \beta$, either A is marked or there is an unmarked symbol of β. This must happen after a finite time, since there are only finitely many symbols to mark.

It can be shown that A is marked by this procedure if and only if there is a string $x \in \Sigma^*$ such that $A \xrightarrow[G]{*} x$. This can be proved by induction, the implication $\Rightarrow$ by induction on the stage that A is marked, and the implication $\Leftarrow$ by induction on the length of the derivation $A \xrightarrow[G]{*} x$.

Then $L(G)$ is nonempty iff there exists an $x \in \Sigma^*$ such that $S \xrightarrow[G]{*} x$ iff S is marked.

Believe it or not, this procedure can be implemented in linear time, so it is in fact quite easy to decide whether $L(G) = \varnothing$. See also Miscellaneous Exercise 134 for another approach.

The finiteness problem for CFLs is also decidable (Miscellaneous Exercise 135).

Valid Computation Histories

In contrast to the efficient algorithm just given, it is impossible to decide in general for a given CFG G whether $L(G) = \Sigma^*$. We will show this by a reduction from the halting problem.

The reduction will involve the set VALCOMPS(M, x) of *valid computation histories* of a Turing machine M on input x, defined below. This set is also useful in showing the undecidability of other problems involving CFLs, such as whether the intersection of two given CFLs is nonempty or whether the complement of a given CFL is a CFL.

Recall that a *configuration* α of a Turing machine M is a triple (q, y, n) where q is a state, y is a semi-infinite string describing the contents of the tape, and n is a nonnegative integer describing the head position.

We can encode configurations as finite strings over the alphabet

$$\Gamma \times (Q \cup \{-\}),$$

where Q is the set of states of M, Γ is the tape alphabet of M, and $-$ is a new symbol. A pair in $\Gamma \times (Q \cup \{-\})$ is written vertically with the element of Γ on top. A typical configuration (q, y, k) might be encoded as the string

$$\begin{array}{ccccccccc} \vdash & b_1 & b_2 & b_3 & \cdots & b_k & \cdots & b_m \\ - & - & - & - & \cdots & q & \cdots & - \end{array}$$

which shows the nonblank symbols of y on the top and indicates that the machine is in state q scanning the kth tape cell. Recall that the *start configuration* of M on input x is

$$\begin{array}{ccccc} \vdash & a_1 & a_2 & \cdots & a_n \\ s & - & - & \cdots & - \end{array}$$

where s is the start state of M and $x = a_1 a_2 \cdots a_n$.

A *valid computation history* of M on x is a list of such encodings of configurations of M separated by a special marker $\# \notin \Gamma \times (Q \cup \{-\})$; that is, a string

$$\#\alpha_0\#\alpha_1\#\alpha_2\# \cdots \#\alpha_N\#$$

such that

- α_0 is the start configuration of M on x;

- α_N is a halting configuration; that is, the state appearing in α_N is either the accept state t or the reject state r; and

- α_{i+1} follows in one step from α_i according to the transition function δ of M, for $0 \le i \le N - 1$; that is,

$$\alpha_i \xrightarrow[M]{1} \alpha_{i+1}, \quad 0 \le i \le N - 1,$$

    where $\xrightarrow[M]{1}$ is the next configuration relation of M.

In other words, the valid computation history describes a halting computation of the machine M on input x, if M does indeed halt. If M does not halt on x, then no such valid computation history exists.

Let $\Delta = \{\#\} \cup (\Gamma \times (Q \cup \{-\}))$. Then a valid computation history of M on x, if it exists, is a string in Δ^*. Define

$$\text{VALCOMPS}(M, x) \stackrel{\text{def}}{=} \{\text{valid computation histories of } M \text{ on } x\}.$$

Then $\text{VALCOMPS}(M, x) \subseteq \Delta^*$, and

$$\text{VALCOMPS}(M, x) = \varnothing \iff M \text{ does not halt on } x. \qquad (35.1)$$

Thus the complement of $\text{VALCOMPS}(M, x)$, namely

$$\sim \text{VALCOMPS}(M, x) = \Delta^* - \text{VALCOMPS}(M, x),$$

is equal to Δ^* iff M does not halt on x.

The key claim now is that $\sim \text{VALCOMPS}(M, x)$ is a CFL. Moreover, without knowing whether or not M halts on x, we can construct a CFG G for $\sim \text{VALCOMPS}(M, x)$ from a description of M and x. By (35.1), we will have

$$L(G) = \Delta^* \iff M \text{ does not halt on } x.$$

Since we can construct G effectively from M and x, this will constitute a reduction

$$\sim \text{HP} \le_{\text{m}} \{G \mid G \text{ is a CFG and } L(G) = \Delta^*\}.$$

By Theorem 33.3(i), the latter set is not r.e., which is what we want to show.

To show that $\sim\text{VALCOMPS}(M, x)$ is a CFL, let us carefully write down all the conditions for a string $z \in \Delta^*$ to be a valid computation history of M on x:

(1) z must begin and end with a #; that is, it must be of the form

$$\#\alpha_0\#\alpha_1\# \cdots \#\alpha_N\#,$$

where each α_i is in $(\Delta - \#)^*$;

(2) each α_i is a string of symbols of the form

$$\begin{array}{ccc} a & & a \\ - & \text{or} & q \end{array}$$

where exactly one symbol of α_i has an element of Q on the bottom and the others have $-$, and only the leftmost has a $\vdash$ on top;

(3) α_0 represents the start configuration of M on x;

(4) a halt state, either t or r, appears somewhere in z (by our convention that Turing machines always remain in a halt state once they enter it, this is equivalent to saying that α_N is a halt configuration); and

(5) $\alpha_i \xrightarrow[M]{1} \alpha_{i+1}$ for $0 \le i \le N - 1$.

Let

$$A_i = \{x \in \Delta^* \mid x \text{ satisfies condition } (i)\}, \quad 1 \le i \le 5.$$

A string in Δ^* is in $\text{VALCOMPS}(M, x)$ iff it satisfies all five conditions listed above; that is,

$$\text{VALCOMPS}(M, x) = \bigcap_{1 \le i \le 5} A_i.$$

A string is in $\sim\text{VALCOMPS}(M, x)$ iff it fails to satisfy at least one of conditions (1) through (5); that is, if it is in at least one of the $\sim A_i$, $1 \le i \le 5$. We show that each of the sets $\sim A_i$ is a CFL and show how to obtain a CFG G_i for it. Then $\sim\text{VALCOMPS}(M, x)$ is the union of the $\sim A_i$, and we know how to construct a grammar G for this union from the G_i.

The sets A_1, A_2, A_3, and A_4 are all regular sets, and we can easily construct right-linear CFGs for their complements from finite automata or regular expressions. The only difficult case will be A_5.

The set A_1 is the set of strings beginning and ending with a #. This is the regular set

$$\#\Delta^*\#.$$

To check that a string is in A_2, we need only check that between every two #'s there is exactly one symbol with a state q on the bottom, and $\vdash$ occurs on the top immediately after each # (except the last) and nowhere else. This can easily be checked with a finite automaton.

The set A_3 is the regular set

$$\# \;\vdash\; a_1\;\; a_2\;\; \cdots\;\; a_n\;\; \#\;\; \Delta^*$$
$$\quad\; s\;\; -\;\; -\;\; \cdots\;\; -$$

To check that a string is in A_4, we need only check that t or r appears someplace in the string. Again, this is easily checked by a finite automaton.

Finally, we are left with the task of showing that $\sim A_5$ is a CFL. Consider a substring $\cdots \#\alpha\#\beta\#\cdots$ of a string in Δ^* satisfying conditions (1) through (4). Note that if $\alpha \xrightarrow[M]{1} \beta$, then the two configurations must agree in most symbols except for a few near the position of the head; and the differences that can occur near the position of the head must be consistent with the action of δ. For example, the substring might look like

$$\cdots\; \#\;\; \vdash\;\; a\;\; b\;\; a\;\; a\;\; b\;\; a\;\; b\;\; b\;\; \#\;\; \vdash\;\; a\;\; b\;\; a\;\; b\;\; b\;\; a\;\; b\;\; b\;\; \#\;\; \cdots$$
$$\qquad\;\; -\;\; -\;\; -\;\; -\;\; q\;\; -\;\; -\;\; -\;\; -\qquad -\;\; -\;\; -\;\; p\;\; -\;\; -\;\; -\;\; -\;\; -$$

This would occur if $\delta(q,a) = (p,b,L)$. We can check that $\alpha \xrightarrow[M]{1} \beta$ by checking for all three-element substrings u of α that the corresponding three-element substring v of β differs from u in a way that is consistent with the operation of δ. *Corresponding* means occurring at the same distance from the closest # to its left. For example, the pair

$$a\;\; a\;\; b \qquad\quad a\;\; b\;\; b$$
$$-\;\; q\;\; - \qquad\quad p\;\; -\;\; -$$

occurring at a distance 4 from the closest # to their left in α and β, respectively, are consistent with δ, since $\delta(q,a) = (p,b,L)$. The pair

$$a\;\; b\;\; b \qquad\quad a\;\; b\;\; b$$
$$-\;\; -\;\; - \qquad\quad -\;\; -\;\; -$$

occurring at distance 7 are consistent (any two identical length-three substrings are consistent, since this would occur if the tape head were far away). The pair

$$a\;\; b\;\; a \qquad\quad a\;\; b\;\; a$$
$$-\;\; -\;\; - \qquad\quad -\;\; -\;\; p$$

occurring at distance 2 are consistent, because there exists a transition moving left and entering state p.

We can write down all consistent pairs of strings of length three over Δ. For any configurations α and β, if $\alpha \xrightarrow[M]{1} \beta$, then all corresponding substrings of length three of α and β are consistent. Conversely, if all corresponding substrings of length three of α and β are consistent, then $\alpha \xrightarrow[M]{1} \beta$. Thus, to check that $\alpha \xrightarrow[M]{1} \beta$ does *not* hold, we need only check that there exists a substring of α of length three such that the corresponding substring of β of length three is not consistent with the action of δ.

We now describe a nondeterministic PDA that accepts $\sim A_5$. We need to check that there exists i such that α_{i+1} does *not* follow from α_i according to δ. The PDA will scan across z and guess α_i nondeterministically. It then checks that α_{i+1} does not follow from α_i by guessing some length-three substring u of α_i, remembering it in its finite control, and checking that the corresponding length-three substring v of α_{i+1} is not consistent with u under the action of δ. It uses its stack to check that the distance of u from the last $\#$ is the same as the distance of v from the last $\#$. It does this by pushing the prefix of α_i in front of u onto the stack and then popping as it scans the prefix of α_{i+1} in front of v, checking that these two prefixes are the same length.

For example, suppose $\delta(q,a) = (p, b, R)$ and z contains the following substring:

$$\cdots \# \vdash a \quad b \quad a \quad a \quad b \quad a \quad b \quad b \quad \# \vdash a \quad b \quad a \quad a \quad b \quad b \quad b \quad b \quad \# \cdots$$
$$- \quad - \quad - \quad - \quad - \quad q \quad - \quad - \qquad - \quad - \quad - \quad - \quad p \quad - \quad - \quad -$$

Then z does not satisfy condition (5), because δ said to go right but z went left. We can check with a PDA that this condition is violated by guessing where the error is and checking that the corresponding length-three subsequences are not consistent with the action of δ. Scan right, pushing symbols from the $\#$ up to the substring

$$b \quad a \quad b$$
$$- \quad q \quad -$$

(we nondeterministically guess where this is). Scan these three symbols, remembering them in the finite control. Scan to the next $\#$ without altering the stack, then scan and pop the stack. When the stack is empty, we are about to scan the symbols

$$b \quad b \quad b$$
$$p \quad - \quad -$$

We scan these and compare them to the symbols from the first configuration we remembered in the finite control, and then we discover the error.

We have given a nondeterministic PDA accepting $\sim A_5$. From this and the finite automata for $\sim A_i$, $1 \leq i \leq 4$, we can construct a CFG G for their union $\sim \text{VALCOMPS}(M, x)$, and

$$L(G) = \Delta^* \iff M \text{ does not halt on } x.$$

If we could decide whether G generates all strings over its terminal alphabet, it would answer the question of whether M halts on x. We have thus reduced the halting problem to the question of whether a given grammar generates all strings. Since the halting problem is undecidable, we have shown:

Theorem 35.1 *It is undecidable for a given CFG G whether or not $L(G) = \Sigma^*$.*

Many other simple problems involving CFLs are undecidable: whether a given CFL is a DCFL, whether the intersection of two given CFLs is a CFL, whether the complement of a given CFL is a CFL, and so on. These problems can all be shown to be undecidable using valid computation histories. We leave these as exercises (Miscellaneous Exercise 121).

Historical Notes

Undecidable properties of context-free languages were established by Bar-Hillel et al. [8], Ginsburg and Rose [47], and Hartmanis and Hopcroft [56]. The idea of valid computation histories is essentially from Kleene [67, 68], where it is called the *T-predicate*.

Lecture 36

Other Formalisms

In this lecture and the next we take a brief look at some of the other traditional formalisms that are computationally equivalent to Turing machines. Each one of these formalisms embodies a notion of *computation* in one form or another, and each can simulate the others. In addition to Turing machines, we'll consider

- Post systems;
- type 0 grammars;
- μ-recursive functions (μ = "mu", Greek for m);
- λ-calculus (λ = "lambda", Greek for l);
- combinatory logic; and
- **while** programs.

Post Systems

By the 1920s, mathematicians had realized that much of formal logic was just symbol manipulation and strongly related to emerging notions of computability. Emil Post came up with a general formalism, now called *Post systems*, for talking about rearranging strings of symbols. A Post system consists of disjoint finite sets N and Σ of *nonterminal* and *terminal symbols*, respectively, a special *start symbol* $S \in N$, a set of *variables* $X_0, X_1, \ldots$ ranging over $(N \cup \Sigma)^*$, and a finite set of *productions* of the form

$$x_0 X_1 x_1 X_2 x_2 X_3 \cdots X_n x_n \rightarrow y_0 Y_1 y_1 Y_2 y_2 Y_3 \cdots Y_m y_m,$$

where the x_i and y_j are strings in $(N \cup \Sigma)^*$, and each Y_j is some X_i that occurs on the left-hand side. If a string in $(N \cup \Sigma)^*$ matches the left-hand side for some assignment of strings to the variables X_i, then that string can be rewritten as specified by the right-hand side. A string $x \in \Sigma^*$ is *generated* by the system if x can be derived from S by a finite sequence of such rewriting steps.

Post systems and Turing machines are equivalent in computational power. Any Post system can be simulated by a TM that writes the start symbol on a track of its tape, then does the pattern matching and string rewriting according to the productions of the Post system in all possible ways, accepting if its input x is ever generated. Conversely, given any TM M, a Post system P can be designed that mimics the action of M. The sentential forms of P encode configurations of M.

One of Post's main theorems was that Post systems in which all productions are of the more restricted form

$$xX \rightarrow Xy$$

are just as powerful as general Post systems. Productions of this form say, "Take the string x off the front of the sentential form if it's there, and put y on the back." If you did Miscellaneous Exercise 99 on queue machines, you may have already recognized that this is essentially the same result.

Type 0 Grammars

Grammars are a restricted class of Post systems that arose in formal language theory. There is a natural hierarchy of grammars, called the *Chomsky hierarchy*, which classifies grammars into four types named 0, 1, 2, and 3. The type 2 and type 3 grammars are just the context-free and right-linear grammars, respectively, which we have already seen. A more general class of grammars, called the *type 0* or *unrestricted* grammars, are much like CFGs, except that productions may be of the more general form

$$\alpha \rightarrow \beta, \tag{36.1}$$

where α and β are any strings of terminals and nonterminals whatsoever. A type 0 grammar consists of a finite set of such productions. If the left-hand side of a production matches a substring of a sentential form, then the substring can be replaced by the right-hand side of the production. A string x of terminal symbols is *generated* by G, that is, $x \in L(G)$, if x can be derived from the start symbol S by some finite number of such applications; in symbols, $S \xrightarrow[G]{*} x$.

Type 0 grammars are a special case of Post systems: the grammar production (36.1) corresponds to the Post production

$$X\alpha Y \rightarrow X\beta Y.$$

Type 0 grammars are the most powerful grammars in the Chomsky hierarchy of grammars and generate exactly the r.e. sets. One can easily build a Turing machine to simulate a given type 0 grammar. The machine saves its input x on a track of its tape. It then writes the start symbol S of the grammar on another track and applies productions nondeterministically, accepting if its input string x is ever generated.

Conversely, type 0 grammars can simulate Turing machines. Intuitively, sentential forms of the grammar encode configurations of the machine, and the productions simulate δ (Miscellaneous Exercise 104).

Type 1 grammars are the *context-sensitive grammars* (CSGs). These are like type 0 grammars with productions of the form (36.1), except that we impose the extra restriction that $|\alpha| \leq |\beta|$. Context-sensitive grammars are equivalent (except for a trivial glitch involving the null string) to *nondeterministic linear bounded automata* (LBAs), which are TMs that cannot write on the blank portion of the tape to the right of the input string (see Exercise 2 of Homework 8 and Exercise 2 of Homework 12). The bound on the tape in LBAs translates to the restriction $|\alpha| \leq |\beta|$ for CSGs.

The μ-Recursive Functions

Gödel defined a collection of number-theoretic functions $N^k \rightarrow N$ that, according to his intuition, represented all the computable functions. His definition was as follows:

(1) *Successor.* The function $s : N \rightarrow N$ given by $s(x) = x + 1$ is computable.

(2) *Zero.* The function $z : N^0 \rightarrow N$ given by $z(\ ) = 0$ is computable.

(3) *Projections.* The functions $\pi_k^n : N^n \rightarrow N$ given by $\pi_k^n(x_1, \ldots, x_n) = x_k$, $1 \leq k \leq n$, are computable.

(4) *Composition.* If $f : N^k \rightarrow N$ and $g_1, \ldots, g_k : N^n \rightarrow N$ are computable, then so is the function $f \circ (g_1, \ldots, g_k) : N^n \rightarrow N$ that on input $\overline{x} = x_1, \ldots, x_n$ gives

$$f(g_1(\overline{x}), \ldots, g_k(\overline{x})).$$

(5) *Primitive recursion.* If $h_i : \mathbb{N}^{n-1} \to \mathbb{N}$ and $g_i : \mathbb{N}^{n+k} \to \mathbb{N}$ are computable, $1 \leq i \leq k$, then so are the functions $f_i : \mathbb{N}^n \to \mathbb{N}$, $1 \leq i \leq k$, defined by mutual induction as follows:

$$f_i(0, \overline{x}) \overset{\text{def}}{=} h_i(\overline{x}),$$

$$f_i(x+1, \overline{x}) \overset{\text{def}}{=} g_i(x, \overline{x}, f_1(x, \overline{x}), \ldots, f_k(x, \overline{x})),$$

where $\overline{x} = x_2, \ldots, x_n$.

(6) *Unbounded minimization.* If $g : \mathbb{N}^{n+1} \to \mathbb{N}$ is computable, then so is the function $f : \mathbb{N}^n \to \mathbb{N}$ that on input $\overline{x} = x_1, \ldots, x_n$ gives the least y such that $g(z, \overline{x})$ is defined for all $z \leq y$ and $g(y, \overline{x}) = 0$ if such a y exists and is undefined otherwise. We denote this by

$$f(\overline{x}) = \mu y.(g(y, \overline{x}) = 0).$$

The functions defined by (1) through (6) are called the *μ-recursive functions.* The functions defined by (1) through (5) only are called the *primitive recursive functions.*

Example 36.1

- The constant functions $\mathbf{const}_n(\ ) = n$ are primitive recursive:

$$\mathbf{const}_n \overset{\text{def}}{=} \underbrace{\mathbf{s} \circ \cdots \circ \mathbf{s}}_{n} \mathbf{oz}.$$

- Addition is primitive recursive, since we can define

$$\mathbf{add}(0, y) \overset{\text{def}}{=} y,$$

$$\mathbf{add}(x+1, y) \overset{\text{def}}{=} \mathbf{s}(\mathbf{add}(x, y)).$$

This is a bona fide definition by primitive recursion: in rule (5) above, take $k = 1$, $n = 2$, $h = \pi_1^1$, and $g = \mathbf{s} \circ \pi_3^3$. Then

$$\mathbf{add}(0, y) = h(y) = y,$$

$$\mathbf{add}(x+1, y) = g(x, y, \mathbf{add}(x, y)) = \mathbf{s}(\mathbf{add}(x, y)).$$

- Multiplication is primitive recursive, since

$$\mathbf{mult}(0, y) \overset{\text{def}}{=} 0,$$

$$\mathbf{mult}(x+1, y) \overset{\text{def}}{=} \mathbf{add}(y, \mathbf{mult}(x, y)).$$

Note how we used the function $\mathbf{add}$ defined previously. We are allowed to build up primitive recursive functions inductively in this way.

- Exponentiation is primitive recursive, since

$$\mathbf{exp}(x, 0) \overset{\text{def}}{=} 1,$$

$$\mathbf{exp}(x, y+1) \overset{\text{def}}{=} \mathbf{mult}(x, \mathbf{exp}(x, y)).$$

- The predecessor function

$$x \doteq 1 = \begin{cases} x - 1 & \text{if } x > 0, \\ 0 & \text{if } x = 0 \end{cases}$$

is primitive recursive:

$$0 \doteq 1 \overset{\text{def}}{=} 0,$$
$$(x + 1) \doteq 1 \overset{\text{def}}{=} x.$$

- Proper subtraction

$$x \doteq y = \begin{cases} x - y & \text{if } x \geq y, \\ 0 & \text{if } x < y \end{cases}$$

is primitive recursive, and can be defined from predecessor in exactly the same way that addition is defined from successor.

- The sign function is primitive recursive:

$$\mathbf{sign}(x) \overset{\text{def}}{=} 1 \doteq (1 \doteq x)$$
$$= \begin{cases} 1 & \text{if } x > 0, \\ 0 & \text{if } x = 0. \end{cases}$$

- The relations $<, \leq, >, \geq, =$, and $\neq$, considered as $(0,1)$-valued functions, are all primitive recursive; for example,

$$\mathbf{compare}_\leq(x, y) \overset{\text{def}}{=} 1 \doteq \mathbf{sign}(x \doteq y)$$
$$= \begin{cases} 1 & \text{if } x \leq y, \\ 0 & \text{if } x > y. \end{cases}$$

- Functions can be defined by cases. For example,

$$g(x, y) = \begin{cases} x + 1 & \text{if } 2^x < y, \\ x & \text{if } 2^x \geq y \end{cases}$$

is primitive recursive:

$$g(x, y) \overset{\text{def}}{=} \mathbf{compare}_<(2^x, y) \cdot (x + 1) + \mathbf{compare}_\geq(2^x, y) \cdot x.$$

- Inverses of certain functions can be defined. For example, $\lceil \log_2 y \rceil$ is primitive recursive:[1] $\lceil \log_2 y \rceil = f(y, y)$, where

$$f(0, y) \overset{\text{def}}{=} 0,$$
$$f(x + 1, y) \overset{\text{def}}{=} g(f(x, y), y),$$

---

[1] $\lceil x \rceil$ = least integer not less than x; $\log_2$ = base 2 logarithm.

and g is from the previous example. The function f just continues to add 1 to its first argument x until the condition $2^x \geq y$ is satisfied. This must happen for some $x \leq y$. Inverses of other common functions, such as square root, can be defined similarly.   □

Observe that all the primitive recursive functions are total, whereas a μ-recursive function may not be. There exist total computable functions that are not primitive recursive; one example is *Ackermann's function*:

$$A(0, y) \overset{\text{def}}{=} y + 1,$$
$$A(x + 1, 0) \overset{\text{def}}{=} A(x, 1), \tag{36.2}$$
$$A(x + 1, y + 1) \overset{\text{def}}{=} A(x, A(x + 1, y)).$$

Lecture 37

The λ-Calculus

The λ-calculus (λ = "lambda," Greek for l) consists of a set of objects called λ-*terms* and some rules for manipulating them. It was originally designed to capture formally the notions of *functional abstraction* and *functional application* and their interaction.

The λ-calculus has had a profound impact on computing. One can see the basic principles of the λ-calculus at work in the functional programming language LISP and its more modern offspring SCHEME and DYLAN.

In mathematics, λ-notation is commonly used to represent functions. The expression $\lambda x.E(x)$ denotes a function that on input x computes $E(x)$. To apply this function to an input, one substitutes the input for the variable x in the body $E(x)$ and evaluates the resulting expression.

For example, the expression

$$\lambda x.(x+1)$$

might be used to denote the successor function on natural numbers. To apply this function to the input 7, we would substitute 7 for x in the body and evaluate:

$$(\lambda x.(x+1))7 \to 7+1 = 8.$$

In the programming language DYLAN, one would write

```
(method (x) (+ x 1))
```

for the same thing. The keyword method is really λ in disguise. If you typed

```
((method (x) (+ x 1)) 7)
```

at a DYLAN interpreter, it would print out 8.

For another example, the expression

$$\lambda x.f(gx)$$

denotes the composition of the functions f and g; that is, the function that on input x applies g to x, then applies f to the result. The expression

$$\lambda f.\lambda g.\lambda x.f(gx) \tag{37.1}$$

denotes the function that takes functions f and g as input and gives back their composition $\lambda x.f(gx)$. In DYLAN one would write

```
(method (f)
   (method (g)
      (method (x) (f (g x)))))
```

To see how this works, let's apply (37.1) to the successor function twice. We use different variables in the successor functions below for clarity. The symbol $\to$ denotes one substitution step.

$$
\begin{aligned}
&(\lambda f.\lambda g.\lambda x.(f(gx)))\,(\lambda y.(y+1))\,(\lambda z.(z+1)) &&\text{substitute } \lambda y.(y+1) \text{ for } f\\
&\to (\lambda g.\lambda x.((\lambda y.(y+1))(gx)))\,(\lambda z.(z+1)) &&\text{substitute } \lambda z.(z+1) \text{ for } g\\
&\to \lambda x.((\lambda y.(y+1))\,((\lambda z.(z+1))x)) &&\text{substitute } x \text{ for } z\\
&\to \lambda x.((\lambda y.(y+1))\,(x+1)) &&\text{substitute } x+1 \text{ for } y\\
&\to \lambda x.((x+1)+1)
\end{aligned}
$$

We could have substituted gx for y in the second step or $(\lambda z.(z+1))x$ for y in the third; we would have arrived at the same final result.

Functions represented by λ-terms have only one input. A function with two inputs x, y that returns a value M is modeled by a function with one input x that returns a function with one input y that returns a value M. The technical term for this trick is *currying* (after Haskell B. Curry).

The Pure λ-Calculus

In the *pure* λ-calculus, there are only variables $\{f, g, h, x, y, \ldots\}$ and operators for λ-abstraction and application. Syntactic objects called *λ-terms* are built inductively from these:

- any variable x is a λ-term;

- if M and N are λ-terms, then MN is a λ-term (functional application—think of M as a function that is about to be applied to input N); and

- if M is a λ-term and x is a variable, then $\lambda x.M$ is a λ-term (functional abstraction—think of $\lambda x.M$ as the function that on input x computes M).

The operation of application is not associative, and unparenthesized expressions are conventionally associated to the left; thus, MNP should be parsed $(MN)P$.

In the pure λ-calculus, λ-terms serve as both functions and data. There is nothing like "+1" as we used it informally above, unless we encode it somehow. We'll show how to do this below.

The substitution rule described informally above is called β-reduction. Formally, this works as follows. Whenever our λ-term contains a subterm of the form $(\lambda x.M)N$, we can replace this subterm by the term $\mathbf{s}_N^x(M)$, where $\mathbf{s}_N^x(M)$ denotes the term obtained by

(i) renaming the bound variables of M (those y occurring in the scope of some λy) as necessary so that neither x nor any variable of N occurs bound in M; and

(ii) substituting N for all occurrences of x in the resulting term.

Step (i) is necessary only to make sure that any free variables y of N will not be inadvertently captured by a λy occurring in M when the substitution is done in step (ii). This is the same problem that comes up in first-order logic. We can rename bound variables in λ-terms anytime, since their behavior as functions is not changed. For example, we can rewrite $\lambda y.xy$ as $\lambda z.xz$; intuitively, the function that on input y applies x to y is the same as the function that on input z applies x to z. The process of renaming bound variables is officially called α-reduction.

We denote α- and β-reduction by $\xrightarrow{\alpha}$ and $\xrightarrow{\beta}$, respectively. Thus

$$(\lambda x.M)N \xrightarrow{\beta} \mathbf{s}_N^x(M).$$

Computation in the λ-calculus is performed by β-reducing subterms whenever possible and for as long as possible. The order of the reductions doesn't matter, since there is a theorem that says that if you can reduce M to N_1 by some sequence of reduction steps and M to N_2 by some other sequence of reduction steps, then there exists a term P such that both N_1 and N_2 reduce to P.

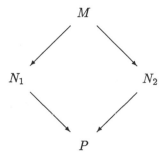

This is called the *Church–Rosser property* after Alonzo Church and J. Barkley Rosser.

A term is said to be in *normal form* if no β-reductions apply; that is, if it has no subterms of the form $(\lambda x.M)N$. A normal form corresponds roughly to a halting configuration of a Turing machine. By the Church–Rosser property, if a λ-term has a normal form, then that normal form is unique up to α-renaming.

There are terms with no normal form. These correspond to nonhalting computations of Turing machines. For example, the λ-term

$$(\lambda x.xx)(\lambda x.xx)$$

has no normal form—try to do a β-reduction and see what happens! The term $\lambda x.xx$ is analogous to a Turing machine that on input x runs M_x on x.

Church Numerals

To simulate the μ-recursive functions in the λ-calculus, we must first encode the natural numbers as λ-terms so they can be used in computations. Alonzo Church came up with a nice way to do this. His encoding is known as the *Church numerals*:

$$\overline{0} \overset{\text{def}}{=} \lambda f.\lambda x.x,$$

$$\overline{1} \overset{\text{def}}{=} \lambda f.\lambda x.fx,$$

$$\overline{2} \overset{\text{def}}{=} \lambda f.\lambda x.f(fx),$$

$$\overline{3} \overset{\text{def}}{=} \lambda f.\lambda x.f(f(fx)),$$

$$\vdots$$

$$\overline{n} \overset{\text{def}}{=} \lambda f.\lambda x.f^n x,$$

$$\vdots$$

where $f^n x$ is an abbreviation for the term

$$\underbrace{f(f(\cdots(f\,x)\cdots))}_{n}.$$

In other words, $\overline{n}$ represents a function that on input f returns the n-fold composition of f with itself. The $\overline{n}$ are all distinct and in normal form.

Using this representation of the natural numbers, the successor function can be defined as

$$s \overset{\text{def}}{=} \lambda m.\lambda f.\lambda x.f(mfx).$$

To see that this is correct, try applying it to any $\overline{n}$:

$$
\begin{aligned}
s\overline{n} &= (\lambda m.\lambda f.\lambda x.f(mfx))\,(\lambda f.\lambda x.f^n x) \\
&\overset{\alpha}{\longrightarrow} (\lambda m.\lambda g.\lambda y.g(mgy))\,(\lambda f.\lambda x.f^n x) \\
&\overset{\beta}{\longrightarrow} \lambda g.\lambda y.g((\lambda f.\lambda x.f^n x)gy) \\
&\overset{\beta}{\longrightarrow} \lambda g.\lambda y.g((\lambda x.g^n x)y) \\
&\overset{\beta}{\longrightarrow} \lambda g.\lambda y.g(g^n y) \\
&= \lambda g.\lambda y.g^{n+1}y \\
&\overset{\alpha}{\longrightarrow} \lambda f.\lambda x.f^{n+1}x \\
&= \overline{n+1}.
\end{aligned}
$$

One can likewise define addition, multiplication, and all the other μ-recursive functions.

Combinatory Logic

Combinatory logic is a form of variable-free λ-calculus. It was first invented to study the mathematics of symbol manipulation, especially substitution. The system consists of terms called *combinators* that are manipulated using *reduction rules*.

There are two primitive combinators S and K, which are just symbols, as well as a countable set of variables $\{X, Y, \dots\}$. More complicated combinators are formed inductively: S, K, and variables are combinators; and if M and N are combinators, then so is MN. Here MN is just a term, a syntactic object, but we can think of M as a function and N as its input; thus, MN represents the application of M to N. As with the λ-calculus, this operation is not associative, so we use parentheses to avoid ambiguity. By convention, a string of applications associates to the left; thus, XYZ should be parsed $(XY)Z$ and not $X(YZ)$.

Computation proceeds according to two reduction rules, one for S and one for K. For any terms M, N, and P,

$$SMNP \rightarrow MP(NP),$$
$$KMN \rightarrow M.$$

Computation in this system consists of a sequence of reduction steps applied to subterms of a term.

Other combinators can be built from S and K. For example, the combinator $I \stackrel{\text{def}}{=} SKK$ acts as the identity function: for any X,

$$IX = SKKX$$
$$ \rightarrow KX(KX) \quad \text{the } S \text{ rule}$$
$$ \rightarrow X \qquad\quad\ \text{the } K \text{ rule.}$$

Let $B = SK$. Whereas K picks out the first element of a pair, B picks out the second element:

$$BXY = SKXY \rightarrow KY(XY) \rightarrow Y.$$

One can construct fancy combinators from S and K that can rearrange symbols in every conceivable way. For example, to take two inputs and apply the second to the first, use the combinator $C = S(S(KS)B)K$:

$$CXY = S(S(KS)B)KXY$$
$$ \rightarrow S(KS)BX(KX)Y$$
$$ \rightarrow KSX(BX)(KX)Y$$
$$ \rightarrow S(BX)(KX)Y$$
$$ \rightarrow BXY(KXY)$$
$$ \rightarrow YX.$$

There is a theorem that says that no matter how you want to rearrange your inputs, there is a combinator built from S and K only that can do it. In other words, for any term M built from $X_1, \ldots, X_n$ and the application operator, there is a combinator D built from S and K only such that

$$DX_1 X_2 \cdots X_n \xrightarrow{\ *\ } M.$$

This theorem is called *combinatorial completeness*.

There is a *paradoxical combinator* $SII(SII)$, which corresponds to the λ-term $(\lambda x.xx)(\lambda x.xx)$. Like its counterpart, it has no normal form.

Like the λ-calculus, combinatory logic is powerful enough to simulate Turing machines.

Historical Notes

The late 1920s and 1930s were a hectic time. Turing machines (Turing [120]), Post systems (Post [99, 100]), μ-recursive functions (Gödel [51], Herbrand, Kleene [67]), the λ-calculus (Church [23, 24, 25, 26], Kleene [66], Rosser [107]), and combinatory logic (Schönfinkel [111], Curry [29]) were all developed around this time.

The λ-calculus is a topic unto itself. Barendregt's book [9] is an indispensable reference.

The μ-recursive functions were formulated by Gödel and presented in a series of lectures at Princeton in 1934. According to Church [25], Gödel acknowledged that he got the idea originally from Jacques Herbrand in conversation.

A proof of the equivalence of the μ-recursive functions and the λ-calculus first appeared in Church [25], although Church attributes the proof chiefly to Kleene. The equivalence of TMs and the λ-calculus was shown by Turing [120].

Various perspectives on this important period can be found in Kleene [69], Davis [31, 32], Rogers [106], Yasuhara [124], Jones [63], Brainerd and Landweber [15], Hennie [58], and Machtey and Young [81].

Chomsky [18] defined the Chomsky hierarchy and proved that the type 0 grammars generate exactly the r.e. sets.

The relationship between context-sensitive grammars and linear bounded automata was studied by Myhill [92], Landweber [78], and Kuroda [77].

Supplementary Lecture I

While Programs

We can relate the primitive and μ-recursive functions of Gödel to more modern concepts. Consider a simple programming language with variables $\mathbf{Var} = \{x, y, \ldots\}$ ranging over $\mathbb{N}$ containing the following constructs:

(i) *simple assignments* $x := 0$ $x := y + 1$ $x := y$

(ii) *sequential composition* $p \, ; q$

(iii) *conditional*   **if** $x < y$ **then** p **else** q

(iv) *for loop*   **for** y **do** p

(v) *while loop*   **while** $x < y$ **do** p

In (iii) and (v), the relation $<$ can be replaced by any one of $>$, $\geq$, $\leq$, $=$, or $\neq$. In (ii) we can parenthesize using **begin**. . . **end** if necessary.

Programs built inductively from these constructs are called **while** programs. Programs built without the **while** construct (v) are called **for** programs. We will show in Theorem I.1 that **while** programs compute exactly the μ-recursive functions and that **for** programs compute exactly the primitive recursive functions.

The intuitive operation of the **for** loop is as follows: upon entering the loop **for** y **do** p, the current value of variable y is determined, and the program

p is executed that many times. Assignment to the variable y within the body of the loop does not change the number of times the loop is executed, nor does execution of the body of the loop alone decrement y or change its value in any way except by explicit assignment.

The intuitive operation of the **while** loop is as follows: upon entering the loop **while** $x < y$ **do** p, the condition $x < y$ is tested with the current values of the variables x, y. If the condition is false, then the body of the loop is not executed, and control passes through to the statement following the **while** loop. If the condition is true, then the body p of the loop is executed once, and then the procedure is repeated with the new values of x, y. Thus the **while** loop repeatedly tests the condition $x < y$, and if true, executes the body p. The first time that the condition $x < y$ tests false (if ever), the body of the loop is not executed and control passes immediately to the statement following the loop. If the condition always tests true, then the **while** loop never halts, as for example with the program **while** $x = x$ **do** $x := x + 1$.

In the presence of the **while** loop, the **for** loop is redundant: **for** y **do** p is simulated by the **while** program

$$z := 0 \, ; w := y \, ; \textbf{while } z < w \textbf{ do begin } p \, ; z := z + 1 \textbf{ end}$$

where z and w are variables not occurring in p. However, note that **for** programs always halt. Thus the only source of potential nontermination is the **while** loop.

Semantics of While Programs

In order to prove the equivalence of **while** programs and the μ-recursive functions, we must give formal semantics for **while** programs.

A *state* or *environment* σ is an assignment of a nonnegative integer to each variable in **Var**; that is, $\sigma : \textbf{Var} \rightarrow \mathbb{N}$. The set of all such environments is denoted **Env**. If a program is started in an initial environment σ, then in the course of execution, the values of variables will be changed, so that if and when the program halts, the final environment will in general be different from σ. We thus interpret programs p as *partial* functions $\llbracket p \rrbracket : \textbf{Env} \rightarrow \textbf{Env}$. The value $\llbracket p \rrbracket(\sigma)$ is the final environment after executing the program p with initial environment σ, provided p halts. If p does not halt when started in initial environment σ, then $\llbracket p \rrbracket(\sigma)$ is undefined. Thus $\llbracket p \rrbracket : \textbf{Env} \rightarrow \textbf{Env}$ is a partial function; its domain is the set of σ causing p to halt. Note that whether or not p halts depends on the initial environment; for example, if $\sigma(x) = 0$, then the program **while** $x > 0$ **do** $x := x + 1$ halts on initial environment σ, whereas if $\sigma(x) = 1$, then it does not.

Formally, the meaning $[\![p]\!]$ of a **while** program p is defined inductively as follows. For $\sigma \in \mathbf{Env}$, $x \in \mathbf{Var}$, and $a \in \mathbb{N}$, let $\sigma[x \leftarrow a]$ denote the environment that is identical to σ except for the value of x, which is a. Formally,

$$\sigma[x \leftarrow a](y) \stackrel{\mathrm{def}}{=} \sigma(y), \quad \text{if } y \text{ is not } x,$$

$$\sigma[x \leftarrow a](x) \stackrel{\mathrm{def}}{=} a.$$

Let $[\![p]\!]^n$ denote the n-fold composition of the partial function $[\![p]\!]$:

$$[\![\nu]\!]^n = \underbrace{[\![\nu]\!] \circ \cdots \circ [\![p]\!]}_{n},$$

where $[\![p]\!]^0$ is the identity function on **Env**. Formally,

$$[\![p]\!]^0(\sigma) \stackrel{\mathrm{def}}{=} \sigma,$$

$$[\![p]\!]^{n+1}(\sigma) \stackrel{\mathrm{def}}{=} [\![p]\!]([\![p]\!]^n(\sigma)).$$

Now define

$$[\![x := 0]\!](\sigma) \stackrel{\mathrm{def}}{=} \sigma[x \leftarrow 0],$$

$$[\![x := y]\!](\sigma) \stackrel{\mathrm{def}}{=} \sigma[x \leftarrow \sigma(y)],$$

$$[\![x := y + 1]\!](\sigma) \stackrel{\mathrm{def}}{=} \sigma[x \leftarrow \sigma(y) + 1],$$

$$[\![p\,;q]\!](\sigma) \stackrel{\mathrm{def}}{=} [\![q]\!]([\![p]\!](\sigma)), \quad \text{or in other words,}$$

$$[\![p\,;q]\!] \stackrel{\mathrm{def}}{=} [\![q]\!] \circ [\![p]\!]$$

(here $[\![q]\!]([\![p]\!](\sigma))$ is undefined if $[\![p]\!](\sigma)$ is undefined),

$$[\![\mathbf{if}\ x < y\ \mathbf{then}\ p\ \mathbf{else}\ q]\!](\sigma)$$

$$\stackrel{\mathrm{def}}{=} \begin{cases} [\![p]\!](\sigma) & \text{if } \sigma(x) < \sigma(y), \\ [\![q]\!](\sigma) & \text{otherwise,} \end{cases}$$

$$[\![\mathbf{for}\ y\ \mathbf{do}\ p]\!](\sigma)$$

$$\stackrel{\mathrm{def}}{=} [\![p]\!]^{\sigma(y)}(\sigma),$$

$$[\![\mathbf{while}\ x < y\ \mathbf{do}\ p]\!](\sigma)$$

$$\stackrel{\mathrm{def}}{=} \begin{cases} [\![p]\!]^n(\sigma) & \text{if } n \text{ is the least number such} \\ & \text{that } [\![p]\!]^n(\sigma) \text{ is defined and} \\ & [\![p]\!]^n(\sigma)(x) \geq [\![p]\!]^n(\sigma)(y), \\ \text{undefined} & \text{if no such } n \text{ exists.} \end{cases}$$

We are now ready to give a formal statement of the equivalence of **while** programs and μ-recursive functions.

Theorem I.1   *(i) For every μ- (respectively, primitive) recursive function $f : \mathbb{N}^n \to \mathbb{N}$, there is a **while** (respectively, **for**) program p such that for any* *environment* σ, $[\![p]\!](\sigma)$ *is defined iff* $f(\sigma(x_1),\ldots,\sigma(x_n))$ *is defined; and if both are defined, then*

$$[\![p]\!](\sigma)(x_0) = f(\sigma(x_1),\ldots,\sigma(x_n)).$$

(ii) For every **while** *(respectively,* **for***) program p with variables* $x_1,\ldots,x_n$ *only, there are* μ- *(respectively, primitive) recursive functions* $f_i :$ $\mathbb{N}^n \to \mathbb{N}$, $1 \le i \le n$, *such that for any environment* σ, $[\![p]\!](\sigma)$ *is defined iff* $f_i(\sigma(x_1),\ldots,\sigma(x_n))$ *is defined,* $1 \le i \le n$; *and if all are defined, then*

$$f_i(\sigma(x_1),\ldots,\sigma(x_n)) = [\![p]\!](\sigma)(x_i), \quad 1 \le i \le n.$$

Once we have stated the theorem, the proof is quite straightforward and proceeds by induction on the structure of the program or μ-recursive function. We argue one case explicitly.

Suppose we are given a function $f : \mathbb{N}^n \to \mathbb{N}$ defined by primitive recursion. For simplicity, assume that the k in the primitive recursive definition of f is 1; then f is defined from $h : \mathbb{N}^{n-1} \to \mathbb{N}$ and $g : \mathbb{N}^{n+1} \to \mathbb{N}$ by

$$f(0,\overline{x}) = h(\overline{x}),$$
$$f(x+1,\overline{x}) = g(x,\overline{x},f(x,\overline{x})),$$

where $\overline{x} = x_2,\ldots,x_n$. We wish to give a program p that takes its inputs in variables x_1 and $\overline{x}$, computes f on these values, and leaves its result in x_0. By the induction hypothesis, g and h are computed by programs q and r, respectively. These programs expect their inputs in variables $x_1,\ldots,x_{n+1}$ and $x_2,\ldots,x_n$, respectively, and leave their outputs in x_0. Let $y_1,\ldots,y_n$ be new variables not occurring in either q or r. Then we can take p to be the following program:

```
y₁ := x₁ ; ··· ; yₙ := xₙ ;        /* save values of input variables */
r ;                                 /* set x₀ to h(x̄) */
x₁ := 0 ;                           /* initialize iteration count */
for y₁ do                           /* at this point x₀ contains f(x₁,x̄) */
  begin
    y₁ := x₁ ;                      /* save iteration count */
    x₂ := y₂ ; ··· ; xₙ := yₙ ;     /* restore values of other variables */
    xₙ₊₁ := x₀ ;                    /* output from previous iteration */
    q ;                            /* set x₀ to g(x₁,...,xₙ₊₁) */
    x₁ := y₁ + 1                    /* increment iteration count */
  end
```

Historical Notes

Gödel originally worked exclusively with the primitive recursive functions. Ackermann's [1] discovery of the non-primitive recursive yet intuitively computable total function (36.2) forced Gödel to rethink the foundations of his system and ultimately to include unbounded minimization, despite the fact that it led to partial functions. As we now know, this is inevitable: no r.e. list of total computable functions could contain all total computable functions, as can be shown by a straightforward diagonalization argument.

The relationship between the primitive recursive functions and **for** programs was observed by Meyer and Ritchie [86].

Supplementary Lecture J

Beyond Undecidability

Oracle Machines and Relative Computation

We know that virtually all interesting questions about Turing machines—whether a given TM halts on a given input, whether a given TM accepts a finite set, and so on—are undecidable. But are all these questions equally hard? For example, suppose by some magic we were given the power to decide the halting problem. Could we somehow use that power to decide if a given TM accepts a finite set? In other words, *relative to the halting problem*, is finiteness decidable?

Questions about relative computability can be formalized and studied using *oracle Turing machines*. Intuitively, an oracle TM is a TM equipped with an *oracle*, a set B to which the TM may pose membership questions and always receive correct answers after a finite time. The interesting thing about this definition is that it makes sense even if B is not recursive.

Formally, an *oracle Turing machine* is a TM that in addition to its ordinary read/write tape is equipped with a special one-way-infinite read-only input tape on which some infinite string is written. The extra tape is called the *oracle tape*, and the string written on it is called the *oracle*. The machine can move its oracle tape head one cell in either direction in each step and make decisions based on the symbols written on the oracle tape. Other than that, it behaves exactly like an ordinary Turing machine.

We usually think of the oracle as a specification of a set of strings. If the oracle is an infinite string over $\{0, 1\}$, then we can regard it as the characteristic function of a set $B \subseteq \mathbb{N}$, where the nth bit of the oracle string is 1 iff $n \in B$. In that way we can study computation relative to the set B.

There is nothing mysterious about oracle TMs. They operate exactly like ordinary TMs, the only difference being the oracle. Ordinary TMs are equivalent to oracle TMs with the null oracle $\varnothing$, whose characteristic function is $00000\cdots$; for such machines, the oracle gives no extra information that the TM doesn't already have.

For $A, B \subseteq \Sigma^*$, we say that A is *recursively enumerable (r.e.) in B* if there is an oracle TM M with oracle B such that $A = L(M)$. In addition, if M is total (i.e., halts on all inputs), we write $A \leq_T B$ and say that A is *recursive in B* or that A *Turing reduces to B*.

For example, the halting problem is recursive in the membership problem, since halting is decidable in the presence of an oracle for membership. Here's how: given a TM M and input x, first ask the oracle whether M accepts x. If the answer is yes, then M certainly halts on x. If the answer is no, switch accept and reject states of M to get the machine M', then ask the oracle whether M' accepts x. If the answer is yes, then M rejects x, therefore halts on x. If the answer is still no, then M neither accepts or rejects x, therefore loops on x. In all cases we can say definitively after a finite time whether M halts on x.

Likewise, the membership problem is recursive in the halting problem, since we can determine membership in the presence of an oracle for halting. Given a TM M and input x, modify M so as never to reject by making the reject state r into a nonreject state. You can add a new dummy inaccessible reject state if you like. Call this modified machine M'. Now on any input, M' accepts iff it halts, and $L(M) = L(M')$, so we can determine whether M accepts x by asking the oracle whether the modified machine M' halts on x.

It is not hard to show that the relation $\leq_T$ is transitive; that is, if A is recursive in B and B is recursive in C, then A is recursive in C. Moreover, the relation $\leq_m$ refines $\leq_T$; in other words, if $A \leq_m B$, then $A \leq_T B$ (Miscellaneous Exercise 141).

The relation $\leq_T$ is strictly coarser than $\leq_m$, since $\sim\!\text{HP} \not\leq_m \text{HP}$ but $\sim\!\text{HP} \leq_T \text{HP}$. In fact, any set A Turing reduces to its complement, since with an oracle for A, on input x one can simply ask the oracle whether $x \in A$, accepting if not and rejecting if so.

The Arithmetic Hierarchy

Once we have the notion of relative computation, we can define a hierarchy of classes as follows. Fix the alphabet $\{0,1\}$ and identify strings in $\{0,1\}^*$ with the natural numbers according to the one-to-one correspondence (28.1). Define

$$\Sigma_1^0 \stackrel{\text{def}}{=} \{\text{r.e. sets}\},$$

$$\Delta_1^0 \stackrel{\text{def}}{=} \{\text{recursive sets}\},$$

$$\Sigma_{n+1}^0 \stackrel{\text{def}}{=} \{\text{sets r.e. in some } B \in \Sigma_n^0\},$$

$$\Delta_{n+1}^0 \stackrel{\text{def}}{=} \{\text{sets recursive in some } B \in \Sigma_n^0\},$$

$$\Pi_n^0 \stackrel{\text{def}}{=} \{\text{complements of sets in } \Sigma_n^0\}.$$

Thus Π_1^0 is the class of co-r.e. sets. The classes Σ_n^0, Π_n^0, and Δ_n^0 comprise what is known as the *arithmetic hierarchy*.

Here is perhaps a more revealing characterization of the arithmetic hierarchy in terms of alternation of quantifiers. Recall from Exercise 1 of Homework 11 that a set A is r.e. iff there exists a decidable binary predicate R such that

$$A = \{x \mid \exists y \ R(x,y)\}. \tag{J.1}$$

For example,

$$\text{HP} = \{M \# x \mid \exists t \ M \text{ halts on } x \text{ in } t \text{ steps}\},$$

$$\text{MP} = \{M \# x \mid \exists t \ M \text{ accepts } x \text{ in } t \text{ steps}\}.$$

Note that the predicate "M halts on x" is not decidable, but the predicate "M halts on x in t steps" is, since we can just simulate M on input x with a universal machine for t steps and see if it halts within that time. Alternatively,

$$\text{HP} = \{M \# x \mid \exists v \ v \text{ is a halting computation history of } M \text{ on } x\},$$

$$\text{MP} = \{M \# x \mid \exists v \ v \text{ is an accepting computation history of } M \text{ on } x\}.$$

Thus the class Σ_1^0 is the family of all sets that can be expressed in the form (J.1).

Similarly, it follows from elementary logic that Π_1^0, the family of co-r.e. sets, is the class of all sets A for which there exists a decidable binary predicate R such that

$$A = \{x \mid \forall y \ R(x,y)\}. \tag{J.2}$$

We argued in Lecture 29 that a set is recursive iff it is both r.e. and co-r.e. In terms of our new notation,

$$\Delta_1^0 = \Sigma_1^0 \cap \Pi_1^0.$$

These results are special cases of the following theorem.

Theorem J.1   (i) A set A is in Σ_n^0 iff there exists a decidable $(n+1)$-ary predicate R such that

$$A = \{x \mid \exists y_1 \, \forall y_2 \, \exists y_3 \, \ldots \, Q y_n \, R(x, y_1, \ldots, y_n)\},$$

where $Q = \exists$ if n is odd, $\forall$ if n is even.

(ii) A set A is in Π_n^0 iff there exists a decidable $(n+1)$-ary predicate R such that

$$A = \{x \mid \forall y_1 \, \exists y_2 \, \forall y_3 \, \ldots \, Q y_n \, R(x, y_1, \ldots, y_n)\},$$

where $Q = \forall$ if n is odd, $\exists$ if n is even.

(iii) $\Delta_n^0 = \Sigma_n^0 \cap \Pi_n^0.$

Proof. Miscellaneous Exercise 137.   □

Example J.2   The set EMPTY $\overset{\text{def}}{=} \{M \mid L(M) = \varnothing\}$ is in Π_1^0, since

$$\text{EMPTY} = \{M \mid \forall x \, \forall t \, M \text{ does not accept } x \text{ in } t \text{ steps}\}.$$

The two universal quantifiers $\forall x \, \forall t$ can be combined into one using the computable one-to-one pairing function $\mathbb{N}^2 \to \mathbb{N}$ given by

$$(i, j) \mapsto \binom{i + j + 1}{2} + i. \tag{J.3}$$

		j				
	0	1	2	3	4	5
0	0	1	3	6	10	15
1	2	4	7	11	16	
2	5	8	12	17		
3	9	13	18			
4	14	19				
5	20					

i labels the rows.

□

Example J.3   The set TOTAL $\overset{\text{def}}{=} \{M \mid M \text{ is total}\}$ is in Π_2^0, since

$$\text{TOTAL} = \{M \mid \forall x \, \exists t \, M \text{ halts on } x \text{ in } t \text{ steps}\}.$$ □

Example J.4   The set FIN $\overset{\text{def}}{=} \{M \mid L(M) \text{ is finite}\}$ is in Σ_2^0, since

$$\text{FIN} = \{M \mid \exists n \; \forall x \text{ if } |x| > n \text{ then } x \notin L(M)\}$$
$$= \{M \mid \exists n \; \forall x \; \forall t \; |x| \leq n \text{ or } M \text{ does not accept } x \text{ in } t \text{ steps}\}.$$

Again, the two universal quantifiers $\forall x \; \forall t$ can be combined into one using (J.3). □

Example J.5   A set is *cofinite* if its complement is finite. The set

$$\text{COF} \overset{\text{def}}{=} \{M \mid L(M) \text{ is cofinite}\}$$

is in Σ_3^0, since

$$\text{COF} = \{M \mid \exists n \; \forall x \text{ if } |x| > n \text{ then } x \in L(M)\}$$
$$= \{M \mid \exists n \; \forall x \; \exists t \; |x| \leq n \text{ or } M \text{ accepts } x \text{ in } t \text{ steps}\}. \qquad □$$

Figure J.1 depicts the inclusions among the few lowest levels of the hierarchy. Each level of the hierarchy is strictly contained in the next; that is, $\Sigma_n^0 \cup \Pi_n^0 \subseteq \Delta_{n+1}^0$, but $\Sigma_n^0 \cup \Pi_n^0 \neq \Delta_{n+1}^0$. We have shown that there exist r.e. sets that are not co-r.e. (HP, for example) and co-r.e. sets that are not r.e. ($\sim$HP, for example). Thus Σ_1^0 and Π_1^0 are incomparable with respect to set inclusion. One can show in the same way that Σ_n^0 and Π_n^0 are incomparable with respect to set inclusion for any n (Miscellaneous Exercise 138).

Completeness

The membership problem MP $\overset{\text{def}}{=} \{M \# x \mid M \text{ accepts } x\}$ is not only undecidable but is in a sense a "hardest" r.e. set, since every other r.e. set $\leq_m$-reduces to it: for any Turing machine M, the map

$$x \mapsto M \# x \tag{J.4}$$

is a trivially computable map reducing $L(M)$ to MP.

We say that a set is *r.e.-hard* if every r.e. set $\leq_m$-reduces to it. In other words, the set B is *r.e.-hard* if for all r.e. sets A, $A \leq_m B$. As just observed, the membership problem MP is r.e.-hard. So is any other problem to which the membership problem $\leq_m$-reduces (e.g., the halting problem HP), because the relation $\leq_m$ is transitive.

A set B is said to be *r.e.-complete* if it is both an r.e. set and r.e.-hard. For example, both MP and HP are r.e.-complete.

More generally, if C is a class of sets, we say that a set B is $\leq_m$-*hard for C* (or just C-hard) if $A \leq_m B$ for all $A \in C$. We say that B is $\leq_m$-*complete for C* (or just C-complete) if B is $\leq_m$-hard for C and $B \in C$.

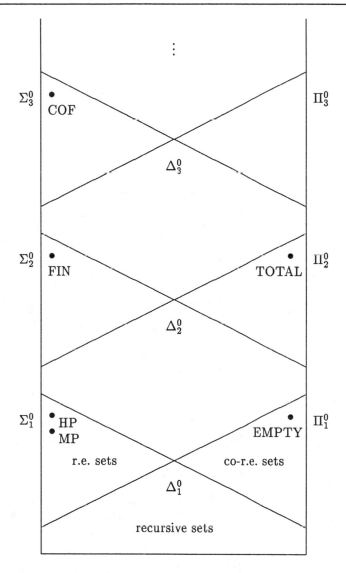

Figure J.1. The Arithmetic Hierarchy

One can prove a theorem corresponding to Theorem 33.3 that says that if $A \leq_m B$ and $B \in \Sigma_n^0$, then $A \in \Sigma_n^0$, and if $A \leq_m B$ and $B \in \Delta_n^0$, then $A \in \Delta_n^0$. Since we know that the hierarchy is strict (each level is properly contained in the next), if B is $\leq_m$-complete for Σ_n^0, then $B \notin \Pi_n^0$ (or Δ_n^0 or Σ_{n-1}^0).

It turns out that each of the problems mentioned above is $\leq_m$-complete for the level of the hierarchy in which it naturally falls:

(i) HP is $\leq_m$-complete for Σ_1^0,

(ii) MP is $\leq_m$-complete for Σ_1^0,

(iii) EMPTY is $\leq_m$-complete for Π_1^0,

(iv) TOTAL is $\leq_m$-complete for Π_2^0,

(v) FIN is $\leq_m$-complete for Σ_2^0, and

(vi) COF is $\leq_m$-complete for Σ_3^0.

Since the hierarchy is strict, none of these problems is contained in any class lower in the hierarchy or $\leq_T$-reduces to any problem complete for any class lower in the hierarchy. If it did, then the hierarchy would collapse at that level. For example, EMPTY does not reduce to HP and COF does not reduce to FIN.

We prove (v); the others we leave as exercises (Miscellaneous Exercise 142). We have already argued that FIN $\in \Sigma_2^0$. To show that it is $\leq_m$-hard for Σ_2^0, we need to show that any set in Σ_2^0 reduces to it. We use the characterization of Theorem J.1. Let

$$A = \{x \mid \exists y \, \forall z \, R(x,y,z)\}$$

be an arbitrary set in Σ_2^0, where $R(x,y,z)$ is a decidable ternary predicate. Let M be a total machine that decides R. We need to construct a machine N effectively from a given x such that $N \in$ FIN iff $x \in A$; in other words, N accepts a finite set iff $\exists y \, \forall z \, R(x,y,z)$. Let N on input w

(i) write down all strings y of length at most $|w|$;

(ii) for each such y, try to find a z such that $\neg R(x,y,z)$ (i.e., such that M rejects $x\#y\#z$), and accept if all these trials are successful. The machine N has x and a description of M hard-wired in its finite control.

In step (ii), for each y of length at most $|w|$, N can just enumerate strings z in some order and run M on $x\#y\#z$ until some z is found causing M to reject. Since M is total, N need not worry about timesharing. If no such z is ever found, N just goes on forever. Surely such an N can be built effectively from M and x.

Now if $x \in A$, then there exists y such that for all z, $R(x,y,z)$ (i.e., for all z, M accepts $x\#y\#z$); thus step (ii) fails whenever $|w| \geq |y|$. In this case N accepts a finite set. On the other hand, if $x \notin A$, then for all y there exists a z such that $\neg R(x,y,z)$, and these are all found in step (ii). In this case, N accepts Σ^*.

We have shown that the machine N accepts a finite set iff $x \in A$, therefore the map $x \mapsto N$ constitutes a $\leq_m$-reduction from A to FIN. Since A was an arbitrary element of Σ_2^0, FIN is $\leq_m$-hard for Σ_2^0.

The Analytic Hierarchy and Π_1^1

The arithmetic hierarchy is defined in terms of *first-order quantification*, or quantification over natural numbers or strings. But it doesn't stop there: if we consider *second-order quantification*—quantification over functions and relations—we get the so-called *analytic hierarchy* consisting of classes Σ_n^1, Π_n^1, Δ_n^1. The entire arithmetic hierarchy is strictly contained in Δ_1^1, the lowest class in the analytic hierarchy. Elements of Δ_1^1 are called *hyperarithmetic sets*.

A remarkable theorem due to Kleene says that the sets of natural numbers definable by one universal second-order quantifier (i.e., the Π_1^1 sets) are exactly the sets definable by first-order induction.

The class Π_1^1 also has natural complete problems. For example, suppose we are given a recursive binary relation $\prec$ on $\mathbb{N}$; that is, a recursive subset of $\mathbb{N}^2$. A natural question to ask is whether the relation is *well founded*; that is, whether there exists no infinite descending chain

$$n_0 \succ n_1 \succ n_2 \succ \cdots.$$

This decision problem is $\leq_m$-complete for Π_1^1.

These results are getting a bit beyond our scope, so we'll stop here.

Historical Notes

Oracle Turing machines were first defined by Turing [121]. The arithmetic and analytic hierarchies were studied by Kleene [68]; see also Rogers [106], Shoenfield [115], Kleene [69], and Soare [116].

Modern-day complexity theory has its roots in the theory of recursive functions and effective computability. The $\leq_T$- and $\leq_m$-reducibility relations, the concepts of completeness and hardness, and the arithmetic hierarchy all have their subrecursive counterparts; see Karp [64], Cook [28], and Stockmeyer [118]. For an introduction to complexity theory, see Hartmanis and Stearns [57], Garey and Johnson [40], or Papadimitriou [97].

Lecture 38

Gödel's Incompleteness Theorem

In 1931 Kurt Gödel [50, 51] proved a momentous theorem with far-reaching philosophical consequences: he showed that *no* reasonable formal proof system for number theory can prove all true sentences. This result set the logic community on its ear and left Hilbert's formalist program in shambles. This result is widely regarded as one of the greatest intellectual achievements of twentieth-century mathematics.

With our understanding of reductions and r.e. sets, we are in a position to understand this theorem and give a complete proof. It is thus a fitting note on which to end the course.

The Language of Number Theory

The first-order language of number theory L is a formal language for expressing properties of the natural numbers

$$\mathbb{N} = \{0, 1, 2, \ldots\}.$$

The language is built from the following symbols:

- variables $x, y, z, \ldots$ ranging over $\mathbb{N}$;

- operator symbols $+$ (addition) and $\cdot$ (multiplication);

- constant symbols 0 (additive identity) and 1 (multiplicative identity);

- relation symbol = (other relation symbols $<$, $\leq$, $>$, and $\geq$ are definable);

- quantifiers $\forall$ (for all) and $\exists$ (there exists);

- propositional operators $\vee$ (or), $\wedge$ (and), $\neg$ (not), $\rightarrow$ (if-then), and $\leftrightarrow$ (if and only if); and

- parentheses.

Rather than give a formal definition of the well-formed formulas of this language (which we could easily do with a CFG), let's give some examples of formulas and their interpretations.

We can define other comparison relations besides =; for example,

$$x \leq y \stackrel{\text{def}}{=} \exists z \; x + z = y,$$
$$x < y \stackrel{\text{def}}{=} \exists z \; x + z = y \wedge \neg(z = 0).$$

Many useful number-theoretic concepts can be formalized in this language. For example:

- "q is the quotient and r the remainder obtained when dividing x by y using integer division":

$$\text{INTDIV}(x, y, q, r) \stackrel{\text{def}}{=} x = qy + r \; \wedge \; r < y$$

- "y divides x":

$$\text{DIV}(y, x) \stackrel{\text{def}}{=} \exists q \; \text{INTDIV}(x, y, q, 0)$$

- "x is even":

$$\text{EVEN}(x) \stackrel{\text{def}}{=} \text{DIV}(2, x)$$

Here 2 is an abbreviation for 1+1.

- "x is odd":

$$\text{ODD}(x) \stackrel{\text{def}}{=} \neg\text{EVEN}(x)$$

- "x is prime":

$$\text{PRIME}(x) \stackrel{\text{def}}{=} x \geq 2 \; \wedge \; \forall y \; (\text{DIV}(y, x) \rightarrow (y = 1 \vee y = x))$$

- "x is a power of two":

$$\text{POWER}_2(x) \stackrel{\text{def}}{=} \forall y \; (\text{DIV}(y, x) \wedge \text{PRIME}(y)) \rightarrow y = 2$$

- "y is a power of two, say 2^k, and the kth bit of the binary representation of x is 1":

$$\text{BIT}(x,y) \stackrel{\text{def}}{=} \text{POWER}_2(y) \ \wedge \ \forall q \ \forall r \ (\text{INTDIV}(x,y,q,r) \to \text{ODD}(q))$$

Here is an explanation of the formula $\text{BIT}(x,y)$. Suppose x and y are numbers satisfying $\text{BIT}(x,y)$. Since y is a power of two, its binary representation consists of a 1 followed by a string of zeros. The formula $\text{BIT}(x,y)$ is true precisely when x's bit in the same position as the 1 in y is 1. We get hold of this bit in x by dividing x by y using integer division; the quotient q and remainder r are the binary numbers illustrated. The bit we are interested in is 1 iff q is odd.

$$
\begin{aligned}
y \ &= \ \ \ \ \ \ \ \ \ \ \ \ \ \ \ \ \ 1\,0\,0\,0\,0\,0\,0\,0\,0\,0\,0\,0 \\
x \ &= \ \ \underbrace{1\,1\,0\,1\,1\,0\,0\,1}_{q}\underbrace{0\,1\,0\,0\,0\,1\,0\,1\,1\,0\,1\,1}_{r}
\end{aligned}
$$

This formula is useful for treating numbers as bit strings and indexing into them with other numbers to extract bits. We will use this power below to write formulas that talk about valid computation histories of Turing machines.

If there are no free (unquantified) variables, then the formula is called a *sentence*. Every sentence has a well-defined truth value under its natural interpretation in $\mathbb{N}$. Examples are

$$\forall x \ \exists y \ y = x + 1 \qquad \text{"Every number has a successor."}$$
$$\forall x \ \exists y \ x = y + 1 \qquad \text{"Every number has a predecessor."}$$

Of these two sentences, the first is true and the second is false (0 has no predecessor in $\mathbb{N}$).

The set of true sentences in this language is called *(first-order) number theory* and is denoted $\text{Th}(\mathbb{N})$. The *decision problem* for number theory is to decide whether a given sentence is true; that is, whether a given sentence is in $\text{Th}(\mathbb{N})$.

Peano Arithmetic

The most popular proof system for number theory is called *Peano arithmetic* (PA). This system consists of some basic assumptions called *axioms*, which are asserted to be true, and some *rules of inference*, which can be applied in a mechanical way to derive further theorems from the axioms.

Among the axioms of PA, there are axioms that apply to first-order logic in general and are not particular to number theory, such as axioms for manipulating

- propositional formulas, such as $(\varphi \wedge \psi) \rightarrow \varphi$;

- quantifiers, such as $(\forall x \; \varphi(x)) \rightarrow \varphi(17)$; and

- equality, such as $\forall x \; \forall y \; \forall z \; (x = y \wedge y = z \rightarrow x = z)$.

In addition, PA has the following axioms particular to number theory:

$\forall x \; \neg(0 = x + 1)$	0 is not a successor
$\forall x \; \forall y \; (x + 1 = y + 1 \rightarrow x = y)$	successor is one-to-one
$\forall x \; x + 0 = x$	0 is an identity for $+$
$\forall x \; \forall y \; x + (y + 1) = (x + y) + 1$	$+$ is associative
$\forall x \; x \cdot 0 = 0$	0 is an annihilator for $\cdot$
$\forall x \; \forall y \; x \cdot (y + 1) = (x \cdot y) + x$	$\cdot$ distributes over $+$
$(\varphi(0) \wedge \forall x \; (\varphi(x) \rightarrow \varphi(x + 1))) \rightarrow \forall x \; \varphi(x)$	induction axiom

where $\varphi(x)$ denotes any formula with one free variable x. The last axiom is called the *induction axiom*. It is actually an axiom *scheme* because it represents infinitely many axioms, one for each $\varphi(x)$. It is really the induction principle on $\mathbb{N}$ as you know it: in words,

- if φ is true of 0 (basis), and

- if for any x, from the assumption that φ is true of x, it follows that φ is true of $x + 1$ (induction step),

then we can conclude that φ is true of all x.

There are also two *rules of inference* for deriving new theorems from old:

$$\frac{\varphi \quad \varphi \rightarrow \psi}{\psi}, \qquad \frac{\varphi}{\forall x \; \varphi}.$$

These two rules are called *modus ponens* and *generalization*, respectively.

A *proof* of φ_n is a sequence $\varphi_0, \varphi_1, \varphi_2, \ldots, \varphi_n$ of formulas such that each φ_i either is an axiom or follows from formulas occurring earlier in the list by a rule of inference. A sentence of the language is a *theorem* of the system if it has a proof.

A proof system is said to be *sound* if all theorems are true; that is, if it is not possible to prove a false sentence. This is a basic requirement of all reasonable proof systems; a proof system wouldn't be much good if its theorems were false. The system PA is sound, as one can show by induction on the length of proofs: all the axioms are true, and any conclusion derived by a rule of inference from true premises is true. Soundness means that the following set inclusions hold:

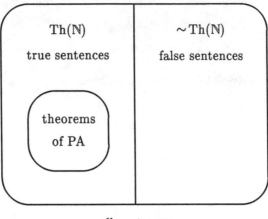

all sentences

A proof system is said to be *complete* if all true statements are theorems of the system; that is, if the set of theorems coincides with $\text{Th}(\mathbb{N})$.

Lecture 39

Proof of the Incompleteness Theorem

Gödel proved the incompleteness theorem by constructing, for any reasonable proof system, a sentence of number theory φ that asserts its own unprovability in that system:

$$\varphi \text{ is true} \iff \varphi \text{ is not provable.} \tag{39.1}$$

Any reasonable proof system, including PA, is sound; this means that for any sentence ψ,

$$\psi \text{ is provable} \Rightarrow \psi \text{ is true} \tag{39.2}$$

(a proof system would not be worth much if some of its theorems were false). Then φ must be true, because otherwise

$$
\begin{aligned}
\varphi \text{ is false} &\Rightarrow \varphi \text{ is provable} &&\text{by (39.1)} \\
&\Rightarrow \varphi \text{ is true} &&\text{by (39.2),}
\end{aligned}
$$

a contradiction. Since φ is true, by (39.1) φ is not provable.

The construction of φ is quite interesting by itself, since it captures in no uncertain terms the notion of self-reference. The power that one needs to construct such a self-referential sentence is present in Turing machines and all modern programming languages. For example, the following is a C program that prints itself:

```
char *s="char *s=%c%s%c;%cmain(){printf(s,34,s,34,10,10);}%c";
main(){printf(s,34,s,34,10,10);}
```

Here 34 and 10 are the ASCII codes for double quote (") and newline, respectively. Although it's a mind-bender to try to figure out what this program does, it's worth the attempt, because once you understand this you have understood the main idea behind Gödel's construction.

We'll construct Gödel's self-referential sentence in Supplementary Lecture K. For now we take a simpler approach that still retains the most important consequences. We will argue that in PA or any other reasonable proof system for number theory,

  (i) the set of theorems (provable sentences) is r.e., but

 (ii) the set $Th(\mathbb{N})$ of true sentences is not,

therefore the two sets cannot be equal, and the proof system cannot be complete. This approach is due to Turing [120].

The set of theorems of PA is certainly r.e.: one can enumerate the theorems by enumerating all the axioms and systematically applying the rules of inference in all possible ways, emitting every sentence that is ever derived. This is true for any reasonable proof system.

The crux then is to show:

Lemma 39.1   *$Th(\mathbb{N})$ is not r.e.*

Proof. We prove this by a reduction $\sim\!HP \leq_m Th(\mathbb{N})$. The result will then follow from Theorem 33.3(i) and the fact that $\sim\!HP$ is not r.e. Recall that

$$HP = \{M\#x \mid M \text{ halts on input } x\}.$$

Given $M\#x$, we show how to produce a sentence γ in the language of number theory such that

$$M\#x \in \sim\!HP \iff \gamma \in Th(\mathbb{N});$$

that is,

M does not halt on $x \iff \gamma$ is true.

In other words, given M and x, we want to construct a sentence γ in the language of number theory that says, "M does not halt on x." This will be possible because the language of number theory is strong enough to talk about Turing machines and whether or not they halt.

Recall the formula $\text{BIT}(y, x)$ constructed in Lecture 38, which allows us to think of numbers as bit strings and extract bits from them. Using this as a starting point, we will be able to construct a series of formulas culminating in a formula $\text{VALCOMP}_{M,x}(y)$ that says that y represents a valid computation history of M on input x; that is, y represents a sequence of configurations $\alpha_0, \alpha_1, \ldots, \alpha_N$ of M, encoded over some alphabet Δ, such that

(i) α_0 is the start configuration of M on x,

(ii) α_{i+1} follows from α_i according to the transition function δ of M, and

(iii) α_N is a halt configuration.

These are the same valid computation histories we saw in Lecture 34. Once we have the formula $\text{VALCOMP}_{M,x}(y)$, we can say that M does not halt on x by saying that there does not exist a valid computation history:

$$\gamma \overset{\text{def}}{=} \neg \exists y \; \text{VALCOMP}_{M,x}(y).$$

This constitutes a reduction from $\sim \text{HP}$ to $\text{Th}(\mathbb{N})$.

It remains only to provide the gory details of the construction of γ from M and x. Here they are. Assume that configurations of M are encoded over a finite alphabet Δ of size p, where p is prime. Every number has a unique p-ary representation. We use this representation instead of the binary representation for convenience.

Let the symbols of the start configuration of M on $x = a_1 a_2 \cdots a_n$ be encoded by the p-ary digits $k_0, \ldots, k_n$ as shown:

$$
\begin{array}{ccccccc}
\vdash & a_1 & a_2 & a_3 & a_4 & \cdots & a_n \\
s & - & - & - & - & \cdots & - \\
\\
k_0 & k_1 & k_2 & k_3 & k_4 & \cdots & k_n
\end{array}
$$

Let the blank symbol $\sqcup$ be encoded by the p-ary digit k.

Let C be the set of all sextuples (a, b, c, d, e, f) of p-ary digits such that if the three elements of Δ represented by a, b, and c occur consecutively in a configuration α_i, and if d, e, and f occur in the corresponding locations in α_{i+1}, then this would be consistent with the transition function δ. For example, if

$$\delta(q, a) = (p, b, R),$$

then the sextuple

$$
\begin{array}{ccccc}
a \quad a \quad b & & a \quad b \quad b \\
- \quad q \quad - & & - \quad - \quad p
\end{array}
$$

would be in C.

Now it's time to define some formulas.

- "The number y is a power of p." Here p is a fixed prime that depends on M.

$$\text{POWER}_p(y) \overset{\text{def}}{=} \forall z \ (\text{DIV}(z,y) \wedge \text{PRIME}(z) \rightarrow z = p)$$

- "The number d is a power of p and specifies the length of v as a string over Δ."

$$\text{LENGTH}(v,d) \overset{\text{def}}{=} \text{POWER}_p(d) \ \wedge \ v < d$$

- "The p-ary digit of v at position y is b" (assuming y is a power of p).

$$\text{DIGIT}(v,y,b) \overset{\text{def}}{=} \exists u \ \exists a \ (v = a + by + upy \ \wedge \ a < y \ \wedge \ b < p)$$

- "The three p-ary digits of v at position y are b, c, and d" (assuming y is a power of p).

$$3\text{DIGIT}(v,y,b,c,d) \overset{\text{def}}{=} \exists u \ \exists a \ (v = a + by + cpy + dppy + upppy$$
$$\wedge \ a < y \ \wedge \ b < p \ \wedge \ c < p \ \wedge \ d < p)$$

- "The three p-ary digits of v at position y match the three p-ary digits of v at z according to δ" (assuming y and z are powers of p).

$$\text{MATCH}(v,y,z)$$
$$\overset{\text{def}}{=} \bigvee_{(a,b,c,d,e,f) \in C} 3\text{DIGIT}(v,y,a,b,c) \ \wedge \ 3\text{DIGIT}(v,z,d,e,f)$$

- "The string v represents a string of successive configurations of M of length c up to d" = "All pairs of three-digit sequences exactly c apart in v match according to δ" (assuming c and d are powers of p).

$$\text{MOVE}(v,c,d) \overset{\text{def}}{=} \forall y \ (\text{POWER}_p(y) \ \wedge \ yppc < d) \rightarrow \text{MATCH}(v,y,yc)$$

- "The string v starts with the start configuration of M on input $x = a_1 a_2 \ldots a_n$ padded with blanks out to length c" (assuming c is a power of p; n and p^i, $0 \leq i \leq n$, are fixed constants depending only on M).

$$\text{START}(v,c) \overset{\text{def}}{=} \bigwedge_{i=0}^{n} \text{DIGIT}(v,p^i,k_i) \ \wedge \ p^n < c$$
$$\wedge \ \forall y \ (\text{POWER}_p(y) \ \wedge \ p^n < y < c \rightarrow \text{DIGIT}(v,y,k))$$

- "The string v has a halt state in it somewhere."

$$\text{HALT}(v,d) \overset{\text{def}}{=} \exists y \ (\text{POWER}_p(y) \ \wedge \ y < d \ \wedge \ \bigvee_{a \in H} \text{DIGIT}(v,y,a))$$

Here H is the set of all p-ary digits corresponding to symbols of Δ containing halt states.

- "The string v is a valid computation history of M on x."

$$\text{VALCOMP}_{M,x}(v) \stackrel{\text{def}}{=} \exists c\, \exists d\ (\text{POWER}_p(c)\ \wedge\ c < d\ \wedge\ \text{LENGTH}(v,d)$$
$$\wedge\ \text{START}(v,c)\ \wedge\ \text{MOVE}(v,c,d)\ \wedge\ \text{HALT}(v,d))$$

- "The machine M does not halt on x."

$$\neg \exists v\ \text{VALCOMP}_{M,x}(v)$$

This concludes the proof of the incompleteness theorem. $\square$

Supplementary Lecture K

Gödel's Proof

Gödel proved the incompleteness theorem by constructing, for any reasonable proof system, a sentence of number theory that asserts its own unprovability. Here is the essence of Gödel's construction.

We use the symbols $\vdash$ and $\vDash$ for provability in Peano arithmetic (PA) and truth, respectively. That is,

$$\vDash \varphi \overset{\text{def}}{\Longleftrightarrow} \text{sentence } \varphi \text{ is true in } \mathbb{N},$$

$$\vdash \varphi \overset{\text{def}}{\Longleftrightarrow} \text{sentence } \varphi \text{ is provable in PA}.$$

To say that PA is *sound* says that every theorem of PA is true; in other words, for any sentence φ, if $\vdash \varphi$, then $\vDash \varphi$. The soundness of PA can be established by induction on the length of proofs, using the fact that all axioms of PA are true and the induction rules preserve truth. (We haven't defined *truth*, but we'll come back to this later.)

Let formulas of number theory be coded as natural numbers in some reasonable way. Fix this coding and let $\ulcorner \varphi \urcorner$ denote the code of the formula φ. First we prove a lemma due to Gödel that is a kind of fixpoint theorem.

Lemma K.1   **(Gödel's fixpoint lemma)**   *For any formula $\psi(x)$ with one free variable x, there exists a sentence τ such that*

$$\vdash \quad \tau \leftrightarrow \psi(\ulcorner\tau\urcorner);$$

that is, the sentences τ and $\psi(\ulcorner\tau\urcorner)$ are provably equivalent in PA.

Note that τ is heavily self-referential. It asserts that its own code satisfies the property ψ.

Proof. Let x_0 be a fixed variable. One can construct a formula

$$\text{SUBST}(x, y, z)$$

with free variables x, y, z asserting the following:

> The number z is the code of the formula obtained by substituting the constant whose value is x for all free occurrences of the variable x_0 in the formula whose code is y.

For example, if $\varphi(x_0)$ is a formula possibly containing a free occurrence of x_0 but no other free variables, then the sentence

$$\text{SUBST}(7, \ulcorner\varphi(x_0)\urcorner, 312)$$

is true iff $312 = \ulcorner\varphi(7)\urcorner$.

We omit the details of the construction of SUBST, but the crucial insight is that given a sufficiently nice encoding of formulas as numbers, the logical machinery is powerful enough to talk about formulas and substitution. One would presumably think of numbers as bit strings and use the formula $\text{BIT}(x, y)$ constructed in Lecture 37 for this purpose.

Now define

$$\sigma(x) \overset{\text{def}}{=} \forall y \ \text{SUBST}(x, x, y) \to \psi(y),$$
$$\tau \overset{\text{def}}{=} \sigma(\ulcorner\sigma(x_0)\urcorner).$$

Then τ is the desired fixpoint of ψ:

$$
\begin{aligned}
\tau \ &= \ \sigma(\ulcorner\sigma(x_0)\urcorner) \\
&= \ \forall y \ \text{SUBST}(\ulcorner\sigma(x_0)\urcorner, \ulcorner\sigma(x_0)\urcorner, y) \to \psi(y) \\
&\Longleftrightarrow \ \forall y \ y = \ulcorner\sigma(\ulcorner\sigma(x_0)\urcorner)\urcorner \to \psi(y) \\
&= \ \forall y \ y = \ulcorner\tau\urcorner \to \psi(y) \\
&\Longleftrightarrow \ \psi(\ulcorner\tau\urcorner).
\end{aligned}
$$

We have argued informally that τ and $\psi(\ulcorner\tau\urcorner)$ are equivalent, but the entire argument can be formalized in PA. $\square$

Now we observe that the language of number theory is also strong enough to talk about provability in Peano arithmetic. In particular, it is possible to code sequences of formulas as numbers and write down a formula

$$\text{PROOF}(x, y)$$

that asserts that the sequence of formulas whose code is given by x is a legal proof in PA and constitutes a proof of the formula whose code is given by y. That is, for any sequence π of formulas and formula φ,

$$\vdash \text{PROOF}(\ulcorner\pi\urcorner, \ulcorner\varphi\urcorner) \iff \pi \text{ is a proof in PA of } \varphi.$$

Provability in PA is then encoded by the formula

$$\text{PROVABLE}(y) \overset{\text{def}}{=} \exists x \; \text{PROOF}(x, y).$$

Then for any sentence φ of L,

$$\vdash \varphi \iff \; \vDash \text{PROVABLE}(\ulcorner\varphi\urcorner). \tag{K.1}$$

Moreover,

$$\vdash \varphi \iff \; \vdash \text{PROVABLE}(\ulcorner\varphi\urcorner). \tag{K.2}$$

This says, "φ is provable iff it is provable that φ is provable." The direction $(\Rightarrow)$ holds because if φ is provable, then there exists a proof π of φ, and PA is clever enough to recognize that π is a proof of φ (i.e., that $\text{PROOF}(\ulcorner\pi\urcorner, \ulcorner\varphi\urcorner)$) and use this fact in a proof that such a proof exists. The direction $(\Leftarrow)$ follows from (K.1) and the soundness of PA.

Applying the fixpoint lemma (Lemma K.1) to the predicate $\neg\text{PROVABLE}(x)$, we obtain a sentence ρ that asserts its own unprovability:

$$\vdash \quad \rho \leftrightarrow \neg\text{PROVABLE}(\ulcorner\rho\urcorner); \tag{K.3}$$

in other words, ρ is true iff it is not provable in PA. By the soundness of PA, we have

$$\vDash \quad \rho \leftrightarrow \neg\text{PROVABLE}(\ulcorner\rho\urcorner). \tag{K.4}$$

Then the sentence ρ must be true, since if not, then

$$\begin{aligned}
\vDash \neg\rho &\Rightarrow \; \vDash \text{PROVABLE}(\ulcorner\rho\urcorner) &&\text{by (K.4)} \\
&\Rightarrow \; \vdash \rho &&\text{by (K.1)} \\
&\Rightarrow \; \vDash \rho &&\text{by the soundness of PA,}
\end{aligned}$$

a contradiction. Therefore $\vDash \rho$. But again,

$$\begin{aligned}
\vDash \rho &\Rightarrow \; \vDash \neg\text{PROVABLE}(\ulcorner\rho\urcorner) &&\text{by (K.4)} \\
&\Rightarrow \; \nvDash \text{PROVABLE}(\ulcorner\rho\urcorner) &&\text{by the definition of truth} \\
&\Rightarrow \; \nvdash \rho &&\text{by (K.1).}
\end{aligned}$$

Thus ρ is true but not provable.

The Second Incompleteness Theorem

In the last section we constructed a sentence ρ such that

(i) ρ is true, but

(ii) ρ is not provable in PA.

Now in a weak moment, we might reason as follows. If PA is so all-powerful, why can't we just encode the whole argument of the previous section in PA as well? Then (i) and (ii) should be provable in PA. But this would say that ρ is provable in PA, yet provably not provable in PA. We would appear to have a paradox on our hands. Thinking about this is enough to make your head swim.

To sort this out, observe that there is logic going on at two levels here. The object of our study is a logical system, namely the language of number theory L and its deductive system PA; but we are reasoning about it using another logical system, which we will call the *metasystem*. The symbols $\vdash$, $\vDash$, $\Rightarrow$, and $\Longleftrightarrow$ that we used in the previous section are not symbols of L, but *metasymbols*, or symbols of the metasystem. The statements we made about truth and provability of sentences of L are *metastatements*.

For example, let φ be a sentence of L. The statement $\vdash \varphi$ is not a sentence of L but a metastatement that says, "φ is provable in PA." Similarly, $\vDash \varphi$ is a metastatement that says, "φ is true."

Now certain metastatements about L and PA can be encoded in L using the coding scheme $\ulcorner \varphi \urcorner$ and reasoned about in PA. For example, the metastatement $\vdash \varphi$ is encoded as the sentence $\text{PROVABLE}(\ulcorner \varphi \urcorner)$ of L. The metastatement (K.1) expresses the correctness of this encoding.

Other metastatements cannot be expressed in L. For example, the metastatement "φ is true" cannot be expressed in L. You might think that the sentence φ itself does this, but it doesn't, at least not in the way we want to use it: to encode meta-arguments in PA, we have to work with the code $\ulcorner \varphi \urcorner$ of φ, so there would have to be a formula $\text{TRUE}(x)$ of L such that for all sentences φ of L,

$$\vDash \varphi \Longleftrightarrow \ \vDash \text{TRUE}(\ulcorner \varphi \urcorner). \tag{K.5}$$

But it follows from the fixpoint lemma (Lemma K.1) that no such formula can exist. If it did, then there would exist a sentence σ such that

$$\vDash \sigma \Longleftrightarrow \ \vDash \neg\text{TRUE}(\ulcorner \sigma \urcorner);$$

but by (K.5),

$$\models \sigma \iff \ \models \text{TRUE}(\ulcorner \sigma \urcorner),$$

a contradiction.

The language L is not powerful enough to express the *truth* of sentences of L or the *soundness* of PA (which refers to truth). These are external concepts, and we must deal with them in the metasystem. However, L and PA are powerful enough to express and reason about *provability* and *consistency*, which are the internal analogs of truth and soundness, respectively. *Consistency* just means that no contradiction can be derived; in other words, $\perp$ (falsity) is not a theorem. The consistency of PA is expressed in L as follows:

$$\text{CONSIS} \stackrel{\text{def}}{=} \neg\text{PROVABLE}(\ulcorner \perp \urcorner).$$

Meta-arguments involving only the concepts of provability and consistency can typically be mapped down into PA. For example, the argument we gave in the last section for (K.2) can be mapped down into PA, giving

$$\vdash \quad \text{PROVABLE}(\ulcorner \varphi \urcorner) \leftrightarrow \text{PROVABLE}(\ulcorner \text{PROVABLE}(\ulcorner \varphi \urcorner) \urcorner). \tag{K.6}$$

With this in mind, we can try to recreate the argument of the previous section without reference to truth or soundness. This leads to the following amazing consequence.

Theorem K.2   **(Gödel's second incompleteness theorem)**   *No sufficiently powerful deductive system can prove its own consistency, unless it is inconsistent.*

Of course, if the system is inconsistent (i.e., if it can prove $\perp$), then it can prove anything, including its own consistency.

We prove the second incompleteness theorem for PA. But it actually holds for any sufficiently powerful deductive system, where "sufficiently powerful" just means strong enough to encode and reason about certain simple metastatements involving provability and consistency such as those discussed above.

Proof. Let ρ be the formula of (K.3). If $\vdash \rho$, then $\vdash \text{PROVABLE}(\ulcorner \rho \urcorner)$ by (K.2), but also $\vdash \neg\text{PROVABLE}(\ulcorner \rho \urcorner)$ by (K.3), so PA would be inconsistent. Furthermore, this argument can be mapped down into PA using (K.6), giving

$$\vdash \quad \text{PROVABLE}(\ulcorner \rho \urcorner) \rightarrow \neg\text{CONSIS},$$

or in contrapositive form,

$$\vdash \quad \text{CONSIS} \rightarrow \neg\text{PROVABLE}(\ulcorner \rho \urcorner). \tag{K.7}$$

Now suppose that consistency were provable; that is, ⊢ CONSIS. By (K.7), we would have ⊢ ¬PROVABLE($\ulcorner \rho \urcorner$). Then by (K.3), we would have ⊢ ρ. But we have just shown that this implies that PA is inconsistent.

Thus if PA is consistent, then ⊬ CONSIS.   □

The Consistency of Mathematics

The *metasystem* we have been talking about so glibly is *Zermelo–Fraenkel set theory* (ZF), a modification of Cantor's original set theory that evolved after Russell discovered an inconsistency.

In Cantor's system one could form the set of all elements satisfying any given property. But consider the property $x \notin x$. If you could form the set

$$b \stackrel{\text{def}}{=} \{x \mid x \notin x\},$$

then $b \in b$ iff $b \notin b$, a contradiction. This is known as Russell's paradox. (Notice any similarities to anything in Lecture 31?)

Over the years, mathematicians and logicians have come to fairly universal agreement that ZF forms a reasonable foundation for most of classical mathematics (type theory and intuitionism excluded). Pure ZF set theory is a first-order theory that deals with nothing but sets, sets of sets, sets of sets of sets, and so on. There is an "element of" relation $\in$, a basic set $\varnothing$, and ways of constructing more complicated sets inductively. The natural numbers are defined inductively as certain sets:

$$0 \stackrel{\text{def}}{=} \varnothing,$$
$$1 \stackrel{\text{def}}{=} \{0\},$$
$$2 \stackrel{\text{def}}{=} \{0,1\},$$
$$3 \stackrel{\text{def}}{=} \{0,1,2\},$$

and so on. There are axioms and proof rules for manipulating sets, and the Peano axioms for number theory can be derived from them.

In ZF one can give formal semantics for the language L of number theory, including a definition of *truth*. One can then prove that relative to that semantics, PA is sound, therefore consistent. But is ZF consistent? No one knows. And Gödel's theorem says that no one can *ever* know, short of discovering an inconsistency. As far as we can tell, a new Russell's paradox could be discovered tomorrow, and much of the structure of mathematics that has been built over the last century would come crashing down.

Gödel's theorem says that we cannot prove the consistency of ZF in ZF any more than we can prove the consistency of PA in PA. In order to prove the consistency of ZF, we would have to go outside of ZF to an even larger metasystem. But then we would be faced with the same question about the consistency of that metasystem. At some point, we just have to stop and take consistency as a matter of faith. Most mathematicians would agree that ZF is just as good a place as any to do this. But the only assurance we have that the ice is solid under our feet is that no one has broken through yet—at least not since Cantor!

Exercises

Homework 1

1. Design deterministic finite automata for each of the following sets:

   (a) the set of strings in $\{4, 8, 1\}^*$ containing the substring 481;

   (b) the set of strings in $\{a\}^*$ whose length is divisible by either 2 or 7;

   (c) the set of strings $x \in \{0, 1\}^*$ such that $\#0(x)$ is even and $\#1(x)$ is a multiple of three;

   (d) the set of strings over the alphabet $\{a, b\}$ containing at least three occurrences of three consecutive b's, overlapping permitted (e.g., the string $bbbbb$ should be accepted);

   (e) the set of strings in $\{0, 1, 2\}^*$ that are ternary (base 3) representations, leading zeros permitted, of numbers that are not multiples of four. (Consider the null string a representation of zero.)

2. Consider the following two deterministic finite automata.

		a	b
$\rightarrow$	1	1	2
	2F	2	1

		a	b
$\rightarrow$	1	2	3
	2	3	1
	3F	1	2

   Use the product construction to produce deterministic automata accepting (a) the intersection and (b) the union of the two sets accepted by these automata.

3. Let $M = (Q, \Sigma, \delta, s, F)$ be an arbitrary DFA. Prove by induction on $|y|$ that for all strings $x, y \in \Sigma^*$ and $q \in Q$,

   $$\widehat{\delta}(q, xy) = \widehat{\delta}(\widehat{\delta}(q, x), y),$$

   where $\widehat{\delta}$ is the extended version of δ defined on all strings described in Lecture 3.

4. For $k \geq 1$ and $p \geq 2$, let

   $$A_{k,p} \stackrel{\text{def}}{=} \{x \in \{0, 1, \ldots, p-1\}^* \mid x \text{ is a } p\text{-ary representation of a multiple of } k\}.$$

   In Lecture 4 we gave a DFA for the set $A_{3,2}$, the multiples of three in binary, and proved it correct. Generalize the construction and proof to arbitrary k and p.

Homework 2

1. The following nondeterministic automaton accepts the set of strings in $\{a, b\}^*$ ending in aaa. Convert this automaton to an equivalent deterministic one using the subset construction. Show clearly which subset of $\{s, t, u, v\}$ corresponds to each state of the deterministic automaton. Omit inaccessible states.

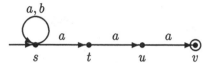

2. The *reverse* of a string x, denoted **rev** x, is x written backwards. Formally,

$$\mathbf{rev}\ \epsilon \overset{\text{def}}{=} \epsilon, \qquad \mathbf{rev}\ xa \overset{\text{def}}{=} a\,\mathbf{rev}\ x.$$

For example, **rev** $abbaaab = baaabba$. For $A \subseteq \Sigma^*$, define

$$\mathbf{rev}\ A \overset{\text{def}}{=} \{\mathbf{rev}\ x \mid x \in A\}.$$

For example, **rev** $\{a, ab, aab, aaab\} = \{a, ba, baa, baaa\}$. Show that for any $A \subseteq \Sigma^*$, if A is regular, then so is **rev** A.

3. The *Hamming distance* between two bit strings x and y (notation: $H(x, y)$) is the number of places at which they differ. For example, $H(011, 110) = 2$. (If $|x| \neq |y|$, then their Hamming distance is infinite.) If x is a string and A is a set of strings, the Hamming distance between x and A is the distance from x to the closest string in A:

$$H(x, A) \overset{\text{def}}{=} \min_{y \in A} H(x, y).$$

For any set $A \subseteq \{0, 1\}^*$ and $k \geq 0$, define

$$N_k(A) \overset{\text{def}}{=} \{x \mid H(x, A) \leq k\},$$

the set of strings of Hamming distance at most k from A. For example, $N_0(\{000\}) = \{000\}$, $N_1(\{000\}) = \{000, 001, 010, 100\}$, and $N_2(\{000\}) = \{0, 1\}^3 - \{111\}$.

Prove that if $A \subseteq \{0, 1\}^*$ is regular, then so is $N_2(A)$. (*Hint:* If A is accepted by a machine with states Q, build a machine for $N_2(A)$ with states $Q \times \{0, 1, 2\}$. The second component tells how many errors you have seen so far. Use nondeterminism to guess the string $y \in A$ that the input string x is similar to and where the errors are.)

Homework 3

1. Give regular expressions for each of the following subsets of $\{a, b\}^*$.

    (a) $\{x \mid x$ contains an even number of a's$\}$

    (b) $\{x \mid x$ contains an odd number of b's$\}$

    (c) $\{x \mid x$ contains an even number of a's or an odd number of b's$\}$

    (d) $\{x \mid x$ contains an even number of a's and an odd number of b's$\}$

    Try to simplify the expressions as much as possible using the algebraic laws of Lecture 9. Recall that regular expressions over $\{a, b\}$ may use ϵ, $\emptyset$, a, b, and operators $+$, $*$, and $\cdot$ only; the other pattern operators are not allowed.

2. Give deterministic finite automata accepting the sets of strings matching the following regular expressions.

    (a) $(000^* + 111^*)^*$

    (b) $(01 + 10)(01 + 10)(01 + 10)$

    (c) $(0 + 1(01^*0)^*1)^*$

    Try to simplify as much as possible.

3. For any set of strings A, define the set

$$\text{MiddleThirds } A = \{y \mid \exists x, z \; |x| = |y| = |z| \text{ and } xyz \in A\}.$$

    For example, $\text{MiddleThirds}\{\epsilon, a, ab, bab, bbab, aabbab\} = \{\epsilon, a, bb\}$. Show that if A is regular, then so is MiddleThirds A.

Homework 4

1. Show that the following sets are not regular.

   (a) $\{a^n b^m \mid n = 2m\}$

   (b) $\{x \in \{a, b, c\}^* \mid x \text{ is a palindrome; i.e., } x = \mathbf{rev}(x)\}$

   (c) $\{x \in \{a, b, c\}^* \mid \text{the length of } x \text{ is a square}\}$

   (d) The set PAREN of balanced strings of parentheses ( ). For example, the string $((()()))(()) $ is in PAREN, but the string $)(()$ is not.

2. The operation of *shuffle* is important in the theory of concurrent systems. If $x, y \in \Sigma^*$, we write $x \parallel y$ for the set of all strings that can be obtained by shuffling strings x and y together like a deck of cards; for example,

   $$ab \parallel cd = \{abcd, acbd, acdb, cabd, cadb, cdab\}.$$

   The set $x \parallel y$ can be defined formally by induction:

   $$\epsilon \parallel y \overset{\text{def}}{=} \{y\},$$
   $$x \parallel \epsilon \overset{\text{def}}{=} \{x\},$$
   $$xa \parallel yb \overset{\text{def}}{=} (x \parallel yb) \cdot \{a\} \cup (xa \parallel y) \cdot \{b\}.$$

   The shuffle of two languages A and B, denoted $A \parallel B$, is the set of all strings obtained by shuffling a string from A with a string from B:

   $$A \parallel B \overset{\text{def}}{=} \bigcup_{\substack{x \in A \\ y \in B}} x \parallel y.$$

   For example,

   $$\{ab\} \parallel \{cd, e\} = \{abe, aeb, eab, abcd, acbd, acdb, cabd, cadb, cdab\}.$$

   (a) What is $(01)^* \parallel (10)^*$?

   (b) Show that if A and B are regular sets, then so is $A \parallel B$. (*Hint:* Put a pebble on a machine for A and one on a machine for B. Guess nondeterministically which pebble to move. Accept if both pebbles occupy accept states.)

3. For each of the two automata

		a	b
→	1	1	4
	2	3	1
	3F	4	2
	4F	3	5
	5	4	6
	6	6	3
	7	2	4
	8	3	1

		a	b
→	1F	3	5
	2F	8	7
	3	7	2
	4	6	2
	5	1	8
	6	2	3
	7	1	4
	8	5	1

(a) say which states are accessible and which are not;

(b) list the equivalence classes of the collapsing relation $\approx$ defined in Lecture 13:

$$p \approx q \stackrel{\text{def}}{\Longleftrightarrow} \forall x \in \Sigma^* \ (\widehat{\delta}(p, x) \in F \Longleftrightarrow \widehat{\delta}(q, x) \in F);$$

(c) give the automaton obtained by collapsing equivalent states and removing inaccessible states.

Homework 5

1. The following table defines four special types of CFGs obtained by restricting productions to the form shown, where A, B represent nonterminals, a a single terminal symbol, and x a string of terminals:

Grammar type	Form of productions
right-linear	$A \to xB$ or $A \to x$
strongly right-linear	$A \to aB$ or $A \to \epsilon$
left-linear	$A \to Bx$ or $A \to x$
strongly left-linear	$A \to Ba$ or $A \to \epsilon$

   Prove that each of these four types of grammars generates exactly the regular sets. Conclude that every regular set is a CFL.

2. Prove that the CFG

   $$S \to aSb \mid bSa \mid SS \mid \epsilon$$

   generates the set of all strings over $\{a, b\}$ with equally many a's and b's. (*Hint*: Characterize elements of the set in terms of the graph of the function $\#b(y) - \#a(y)$ as y ranges over prefixes of x, as we did in Lecture 20 with balanced parentheses.)

3. Give a CFG for the set PAREN_2 of balanced strings of parentheses of two types ( ) and [ ]. For example, ([( ) [ ]] ([ ])) is in PAREN_2, but [( ]) is not. Prove that your grammar is correct. Use the following inductive definition: PAREN_2 is the smallest set of strings such that

   (i) $\epsilon \in \mathrm{PAREN}_2$;

   (ii) if $x \in \mathrm{PAREN}_2$, then so are (x) and $[x]$; and

   (iii) if x and y are both in PAREN_2, then so is xy.

   (*Hint*: Your grammar should closely model the inductive definition of the set. For one direction of the proof of correctness, use induction on the length of the derivation. For the other direction, use induction on stages of the inductive definition of PAREN_2. The basis is (i), and there will be two cases of the induction step corresponding to (ii) and (iii).)

4. Give a PDA for the set PAREN_2 of Exercise 3 that accepts by empty stack. Specify all transitions.

Homework 6

1. Prove that the following CFG G in Greibach normal form generates exactly the set of nonnull strings over $\{a, b\}$ with equally many a's and b's:

   $$S \rightarrow aB \mid bA,$$
   $$A \rightarrow aS \mid bAA \mid a,$$
   $$B \rightarrow bS \mid aBB \mid b.$$

   (*Hint*: Strengthen your induction hypothesis to describe the sets of strings generated by the nonterminals A and B: for $x \neq \epsilon$,

   $$S \xrightarrow[G]{*} x \iff \#a(x) = \#b(x),$$

   $$A \xrightarrow[G]{*} x \iff ???,$$

   $$B \xrightarrow[G]{*} x \iff ???.)$$

2. Construct a pushdown automaton that accepts the set of strings in $\{a, b\}^*$ with equally many a's and b's. Specify all transitions.

3. Let $b(n)$ denote the binary representation of $n \geq 1$, leading zeros omitted. For example, $b(5) = 101$ and $b(12) = 1100$. Let $\$$ be another symbol not in $\{0, 1\}$.

   (a) Show that the set

   $$\{b(n)\$b(n+1) \mid n \geq 1\}$$

   is not a CFL.

   (b) Suppose we reverse the first numeral; that is, consider the set

   $$\{\mathbf{rev}\, b(n)\$b(n+1) \mid n \geq 1\}.$$

   Show that this set is a CFL.

4. Recall from Exercise 3 of Homework 5 the set $PAREN_2$ of balanced strings of parentheses of two types, ( ) and [ ]. Give CFGs in Chomsky and Greibach normal form generating the set $PAREN_2 - \{\epsilon\}$, and prove that they are correct.

Homework 7

1. Describe a parser to parse regular expressions according to the precedence relation

   $$* > \cdot > +$$

   Here $>$ means "has higher precedence than." The main differences you will have to account for between regular expressions and the arithmetic expressions discussed in Lecture 26 are: (i) the unary operator $*$ comes *after* its operand, not before it as with unary minus; and (ii) the concatenation operator $\cdot$ can be omitted. Illustrate the action of your parser on the expression

   $$(a + b)^* + ab^* a.$$

2. Prove that if A is a CFL and R is a regular set, then $A \cap R$ is a CFL. (*Hint*: Use a product construction.)

3. Recall the shuffle operator $\|$ from Homework 4. Show that the shuffle of two CFLs is not necessarily a CFL. (*Hint*: Use the previous exercise to simplify the argument.)

4. Let A be any regular set. Show that the set

   $$\{x \mid \exists y \ |y| = 2^{|x|} \text{ and } xy \in A\}$$

   is regular.

Homework 8

1. Describe a TM that accepts the set $\{a^n \mid n$ is a power of 2$\}$. Your description should be at the level of the descriptions in Lecture 29 of the TM that accepts $\{ww \mid w \in \Sigma^*\}$ and the TM that implements the sieve of Eratosthenes. In particular, do not give a list of transitions.

2. A *linear bounded automaton* (LBA) is exactly like a one-tape Turing machine, except that the input string $x \in \Sigma^*$ is enclosed in left and right endmarkers ⊢ and ⊣ which may not be overwritten, and the machine is constrained never to move left of the ⊢ nor right of the ⊣. It may read and write all it wants between the endmarkers.

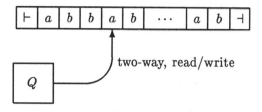

(a) Give a rigorous formal definition of deterministic linearly bounded automata, including a definition of configurations and acceptance. Your definition should begin as follows: "A *deterministic linearly bounded automaton (LBA)* is a 9-tuple

$$M = (Q,\ \Sigma,\ \Gamma,\ \vdash,\ \dashv,\ \delta,\ s,\ t,\ r),$$

where Q is a finite set of *states*, ... "

(b) Let M be a linear bounded automaton with state set Q of size k and tape alphabet Γ of size m. How many possible configurations are there on input x, $|x| = n$?

(c) Argue that the halting problem for deterministic linear bounded automata is decidable. (*Hint:* You need to be able to detect after a finite time if the machine is in an infinite loop. Presumably the result of part (b) would be useful here.)

(d) Prove by diagonalization that there exists a recursive set that is not accepted by any LBA.

3. Let A be any regular set. Show that the set

$$\{x \mid \exists y\ |y| = |x|^2 \text{ and } xy \in A\}$$

is regular.

Homework 9

1. Prove that the following question is undecidable. Given a Turing machine M and state q of M, does M ever enter state q on some input? (This problem is analogous to the problem of identifying *dead code*: given a PASCAL program containing a designated block of code, will that block of code ever be executed?)

2. Prove that it is undecidable whether two given Turing machines accept the same set. (This problem is analogous to determining whether two given PASCAL programs are equivalent.)

3. Prove that the emptiness problem for deterministic linearly bounded automata (i.e., whether $L(M) = \varnothing$) is undecidable. (*Hint*: Think VALCOMPS.)

4. Prove that an r.e. set is recursive iff there exists an enumeration machine that enumerates it in increasing order.

5. For $A, B \subseteq \Sigma^*$, define

$$A/B \stackrel{\text{def}}{=} \{x \mid \exists y \in B \; xy \in A\},$$
$$A \leftarrow B \stackrel{\text{def}}{=} \{x \mid \forall y \in B \; xy \in A\}.$$

   (a) Show that if A is regular and B is any set whatsoever, then A/B and $A \leftarrow B$ are regular.

   (b) Show that even if we are given a finite automaton for A and a Turing machine for B, we cannot necessarily construct an automaton for A/B or $A \leftarrow B$ effectively.

Homework 10

1. Show that neither the set

   $$\text{TOTAL} \stackrel{\text{def}}{=} \{M \mid M \text{ halts on all inputs}\}$$

   nor its complement is r.e.

2. Consider one-tape Turing machines that are constrained not to over-write the input string. They may write all they want on the blank portion of the tape to the right of the input string.

   (a) Show that these machines accept only regular sets. (If you're thinking, "Hey, why not just copy the input string out to the blank portion of the tape," think again ...)

   (b) Show that, despite (a), it is impossible to construct an equivalent finite automaton effectively from such a machine.

3. Show that it is undecidable whether the intersection of two CFLs is nonempty. (*Hint:* Use a variant of VALCOMPS in which every other configuration is reversed:

   $$\alpha_0 \# \mathbf{rev}\ \alpha_1 \# \alpha_2 \# \mathbf{rev}\ \alpha_3 \# \cdots \# \alpha_n.$$

   Express this set as the intersection of two CFLs.)

Homework 11

1. Recursive enumerability is intimately linked with the idea of *unbounded existential search*. Often an algorithm for accepting an r.e. set can be characterized in terms of searching for a *witness* or *proof* that a given input x is in the set.

   A binary relation R on strings over $\{0,1\}$ is called *recursive* if the set

   $$\{x\#y \mid R(x,y)\}$$

   is a recursive set. Here $\#$ is just another input symbol different from 0 or 1.

   Show that a set $A \subseteq \{0,1\}^*$ is r.e. if and only if there exists a recursive binary relation R such that

   $$A = \{x \in \{0,1\}^* \mid \exists y \ R(x,y)\}.$$

2. Show that it is undecidable whether the intersection of two given CFLs is again a CFL. (*Hint*: Use Homework 10, Exercise 3.)

Homework 12

1. A *context-sensitive grammar* (CSG) or *type 1 grammar* is a type 0 grammar that obeys the following additional restriction: all productions $\alpha \rightarrow \beta$ satisfy $|\alpha| \le |\beta|$. Give CSGs for the following sets.

   (a) $\{x \in \{a, b, c\}^+ \mid \#a(x) = \#b(x) = \#c(x)\}$

   (b) $\{a^{n^2} \mid n \ge 1\}$

2. Show that context-sensitive grammars and nondeterministic linearly bounded automata are equivalent in the following sense:

   (a) for every context-sensitive grammar G, there is a nondeterministic LBA M such that $L(M) = L(G)$; and

   (b) for every nondeterministic LBA M, there is a context-sensitive grammar G such that $L(G) = L(M) - \{\epsilon\}$.

3. Give constructions showing that the following number-theoretic functions are primitive recursive.

   (a) **quotient**(x, y) = quotient when dividing x by y using integer division; for example, **quotient**$(7, 2) = 3$.

   (b) **remainder**(x, y) = remainder when dividing x by y using integer division; for example, **remainder**$(7, 2) = 1$.

   (c) **prime**(x) = 1 if x is prime, 0 otherwise.

Miscellaneous Exercises

Finite Automata and Regular Sets

1. Let B be a set of strings over a fixed finite alphabet. We say B is *transitive* if $BB \subseteq B$ and *reflexive* if $\epsilon \in B$. Prove that for any set of strings A, A^* is the smallest reflexive and transitive set containing A. That is, show that A^* is a reflexive and transitive set containing A, and if B is any other reflexive and transitive set containing A, then $A^* \subseteq B$.

2. Consider the following pairs of deterministic finite automata. Use the product construction to produce deterministic automata accepting (i) the intersection and (ii) the union of the sets accepted by these automata.

    (a)

	a	b
$\rightarrow$ 1	2	2
2F	1	1

	a	b
$\rightarrow$ 1	1	2
2F	2	1

    (b)

	a	b
$\rightarrow$ 1	2	3
2F	3	1
3F	1	2

	a	b
$\rightarrow$ 1F	3	2
2	1	3
3F	2	1

(c)

$$\begin{array}{c|cc} & a & b \\ \rightarrow \quad 1 & 2 & 2 \\ 2F & 1 & 1 \end{array} \qquad \begin{array}{c|cc} & a & b \\ \rightarrow \quad 1 & 2 & 1 \\ 2F & 1 & 2 \end{array}$$

3. Consider the following nondeterministic finite automaton.

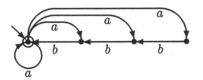

(a) Give a string beginning with a that is *not* accepted.

(b) Construct an equivalent deterministic automaton using the subset construction. Assuming the states are named s, t, u, v from left to right, show clearly which subset of $\{s, t, u, v\}$ corresponds to each state of the deterministic automaton. Omit inaccessible states.

4. Consider the following NFA.

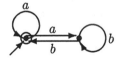

(a) Construct an equivalent DFA using the subset construction. Omit inaccessible states.

(b) Give an equivalent regular expression.

5. Convert the following nondeterministic finite automata to equivalent deterministic ones using the subset construction. Show clearly which subset of $\{s, t, u, v\}$ corresponds to each state of the deterministic automaton. Omit inaccessible states.

(a)

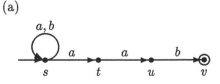

(b)

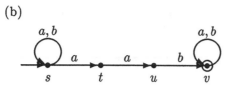

^{H}6. Prove that NFAs are exponentially more succinct than DFAs: for any m, there exists an NFA with m states such that any equivalent DFA has at least 2^{m-1} states.

7. A convenient way of specifying automata is in terms of *transition matrices*. If the automaton has n states, the transition function δ can be specified by an $n \times n$ matrix G, indexed by states, whose u, vth entry gives the set of input symbols taking state u to state v; in symbols,

$$G_{uv} = \{a \in \Sigma \mid \delta(u, a) = v\}.$$

For example, the transition function of the automaton of Example 3.1 of Lecture 3 could be represented by the 4×4 matrix

$$\begin{bmatrix} \{b\} & \{a\} & \varnothing & \varnothing \\ \varnothing & \{b\} & \{a\} & \varnothing \\ \varnothing & \varnothing & \{b\} & \{a\} \\ \varnothing & \varnothing & \varnothing & \{a, b\} \end{bmatrix}.$$

Consider the collection of square matrices indexed by Q whose entries are subsets of Σ^*. We can define addition and multiplication on such matrices in a natural way as follows:

$$(A + B)_{uv} \overset{\text{def}}{=} A_{uv} \cup B_{uv},$$
$$(AB)_{uv} \overset{\text{def}}{=} \bigcup_{w \in Q} A_{uw} B_{wv}.$$

Let us also define the identity matrix I:

$$I_{uv} \overset{\text{def}}{=} \begin{cases} \{\epsilon\} & \text{if } u = v, \\ \varnothing & \text{otherwise.} \end{cases}$$

The powers of a matrix are defined inductively:

$$A^0 \overset{\text{def}}{=} I,$$
$$A^{n+1} \overset{\text{def}}{=} A^n A.$$

^{*S}(a) Prove that

$$(A^n)_{uv} = \{x \in \Sigma^* \mid |x| = n \text{ and } \widehat{\delta}(u, x) = v\}.$$

(b) Define the asterate A^* of the matrix A to be the componentwise union of all the powers of A:

$$(A^*)_{uv} \overset{\text{def}}{=} \bigcup_{n \geq 0} (A^n)_{uv}.$$

Let s be the start state of the automaton and F the set of accept states. Prove that

$$L(M) = \bigcup_{t \in F} (A^*)_{st}.$$

8. Generalize Homework 2, Exercise 3 to arbitrary distance k. That is, prove that if $A \subseteq \{0,1\}^*$ is regular, then so is $N_k(A)$, the set of strings of Hamming distance at most k from some string in A.

9. (a) Show that if an NFA with k states accepts any string at all, then it accepts a string of length $k - 1$ or less.

   [H](b) Give an NFA over a single letter alphabet that rejects some string, but the length of the shortest rejected string is strictly more than the number of states.

   [**H](c) Give a construction for arbitrarily large NFAs showing that the length of the shortest rejected string can be exponential in the number of states.

10. Recall from Lecture 10 that an *NFA with ϵ-transitions* is a structure

$$M = (Q,\ \Sigma,\ \epsilon,\ \Delta,\ S,\ F)$$

such that ϵ is a special symbol not in Σ and

$$M_\epsilon = (Q,\ \Sigma \cup \{\epsilon\},\ \Delta,\ S,\ F)$$

is an ordinary NFA over the alphabet $\Sigma \cup \{\epsilon\}$.

Define the ϵ-closure $C_\epsilon(A)$ of a set $A \subseteq Q$ to be the set of all states reachable from some state in A under a sequence of zero or more ϵ-transitions:

$$C_\epsilon(A) \overset{\text{def}}{=} \bigcup_{x \in \{\epsilon\}^*} \widehat{\Delta}(A, x).$$

(a) Using ϵ-closure, define formally acceptance for NFAs with ϵ-transitions in a way that captures the intuitive description given in Lecture 6.

(b) Prove that under your definition, NFAs with ϵ-transitions accept only regular sets.

(c) Prove that the two definitions of acceptance—the one given in part (a) involving ϵ-closure and the one given in Lecture 10 involving homomorphisms—are equivalent.

11. Give regular expressions for each of the following subsets of $\{a, b\}^*$. Recall that regular expressions over $\{a, b\}$ may use ϵ, $\emptyset$, a, b, and operators $+$, *, and $\cdot$ only.

   (a) $\{x \mid x$ does not contain the substring $a\}$

   (b) $\{x \mid x$ does not contain the substring $ab\}$

   **(c) $\{x \mid x$ does not contain the substring $aba\}$

   Try to simplify the expressions as much as possible using the algebraic laws of Lecture 9.

12. Match each NFA with an equivalent regular expression.

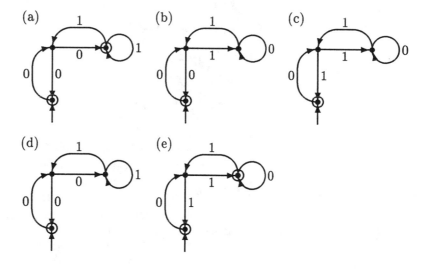

   (i) $\epsilon + 0(01^*1 + 00)^*01^*$

   (ii) $\epsilon + 0(10^*1 + 10)^*10^*$

   (iii) $\epsilon + 0(10^*1 + 00)^*0$

   (iv) $\epsilon + 0(01^*1 + 00)^*0$

   (v) $\epsilon + 0(10^*1 + 10)^*1$

13. Match each NFA with an equivalent regular expression.

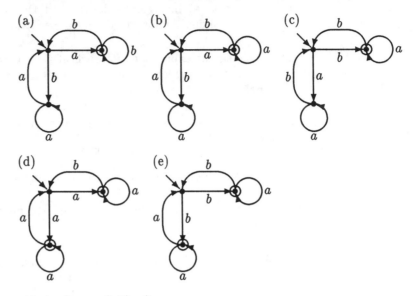

(i) $(aa^*b + ba^*b)^* ba^*$

(ii) $(aa^*a + aa^*b)^* aa^*$

(iii) $(ba^*a + ab^*b)^* ab^*$

(iv) $(ba^*a + aa^*b)^* aa^*$

(v) $(ba^*a + ba^*b)^* ba^*$

14. Give an NFA with four states equivalent to the regular expression

$(01 + 011 + 0111)^*.$

Convert this automaton to an equivalent deterministic one using the subset construction. Name the states of your NFA, and show clearly which set of states corresponds to each state of the DFA. Omit inaccessible states.

15. Give a regular expression equivalent to the following automaton.

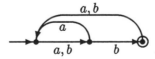

16. Give deterministic finite automata equivalent to the following regular expressions.

(a) $(00 + 11)^* (01 + 10) (00 + 11)^*$

(b) $(000)^*1 + (00)^*1$

(c) $(0(01)^*(1 + 00) + 1(10)^*(0 + 11))^*$

17. Give a regular expression equivalent to the following DFA.

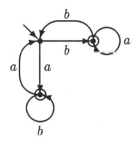

18. Consider the regular sets denoted by the following pairs of regular expressions. For each pair, say whether the two sets are equal. If so, give a proof using the algebraic laws of Lecture 9; if not, give an example of a string in one that is not in the other.

(i) $(0 + 1)^*$ $0^* + 1^*$

(ii) $0(120)^*12$ $01(201)^*2$

(iii) $\emptyset^*$ ϵ^*

(iv) $(0^*1^*)^*$ $(0^*1)^*$

(v) $(01 + 0)^*0$ $0(10 + 0)^*$

19. Let $\alpha = (a + b)^*ab(a + b)^*)$. Give a regular expression equivalent to the pattern $\sim\alpha$ when

(a) $\Sigma = \{a, b\}$,

(b) $\Sigma = \{a, b, c\}$.

Simplify the expressions as much as possible.

20. Prove the following theorems of Kleene algebra. Reason equationally using axioms (A.1) through (A.15) only.

[S](a) $a^*a^* = a^*$

(b) $a^*a = aa^*$

(c) $u^{**} = u^*$

(d) $(a^*b)^*a^* = (a + b)^*$

(e) $a(ba)^* = (ab)^*a$

(f) $a^* = (aa)^* + a(aa)^*$

21. Prove Lemma A.1.

*22. Prove that in the presence of Kleene algebra axioms (A.1) through (A.11), axioms (A.12) and (A.14) are equivalent (and by symmetry, so are (A.13) and (A.15)).

*23. Here is a purely algebraic version of Miscellaneous Exercise 1. An element c of a Kleene algebra $\mathcal{K}$ is said to be *reflexive* if $1 \leq c$ and *transitive* if $cc \leq c$. We say that c *contains* a if $a \leq c$. Prove that for any $a \in \mathcal{K}$,

(a) a^* is reflexive and transitive and contains a; and

(b) a^* is the least element of $\mathcal{K}$ satisfying these properties. That is, if c is any element of $\mathcal{K}$ that is reflexive and transitive and contains a, then $a^* \leq c$.

This justifies the terminology *reflexive transitive closure*.

**24. Prove Lemma A.2: the family $\mathcal{M}(n, \mathcal{K})$ of $n \times n$ matrices over a Kleene algebra $\mathcal{K}$ with the matrix operations defined as in Supplementary Lecture A again forms a Kleene algebra.

^{S}25. Prove Theorem A.3.

^{HS}26. For any set of strings A, define the set

$$\text{FirstHalves } A = \{x \mid \exists y \ |y| = |x| \text{ and } xy \in A\}.$$

For example, FirstHalves $\{a, ab, bab, bbab\} = \{a, bb\}$. Show that if A is regular, then so is FirstHalves A.

27. For any set of strings A, define the set

$$\text{FirstThirds } A = \{x \mid \exists y \ |y| = 2|x| \text{ and } xy \in A\}.$$

For example, FirstThirds $\{\epsilon, a, ab, bab, bbab\} = \{\epsilon, b\}$. Show that if A is regular, then so is FirstThirds A.

28. Given a set $A \subseteq \{0, 1\}^*$, let

$$A' = \{xy \mid x1y \in A\}.$$

That is, A' consists of all strings obtained from a string in A by deleting exactly one 1. Show that if A is regular, then so is A'.

29. For A a set of natural numbers, define

binary $A = \{$binary representations of numbers in $A\} \subseteq (0+1)^*$,

unary $A = \{0^n \mid n \in A\} \subseteq 0^*$.

For example, if $A = \{2, 3, 5\}$, then

binary $A = \{10, 11, 101\}$,

unary $A = \{00, 000, 00000\}$.

Consider the following two propositions:

(i) For all A, if **binary** A is regular, then so is **unary** A.

(ii) For all A, if **unary** A is regular, then so is **binary** A.

One of (i) and (ii) is true and the other is false. Which is which? Give a proof and a counterexample.

*30. Let A be a regular set. Consider the two sets

$$\{x \mid \exists n \geq 0 \; \exists y \in A \; y = x^n\},$$
$$\{x \mid \exists n \geq 0 \; \exists y \in A \; x = y^n\}.$$

One is necessarily regular and one is not. Which is which? Give a proof and a counterexample.

*^{H}31. One of the following subsets of $\{a, b, \$\}^*$ is regular and the other is not. Which is which? Give proofs.

$$\{xy \mid x, y \in \{a, b\}^*, \; \#a(x) = \#b(y)\}$$
$$\{x\$y \mid x, y \in \{a, b\}^*, \; \#a(x) = \#b(y)\}$$

***^{H}32. Two of the following three sets are always regular for any regular set A. Which are they? Give two proofs and a counterexample.

(a) $\{x \mid x^{|x|} \in A\}$

(b) $\{x \mid \exists y \; |y| = 2^{2^{|x|}} \text{ and } xy \in A\}$

(c) $\{x \mid \exists y \; |y| = \log |x| \text{ and } xy \in A\}$

**^{HS}33. Let p be any polynomial of degree d with nonnegative integer coefficients. Show that if A is a regular set, then so is the set

$$A' = \{x \mid \exists y \; |y| = p(|x|) \text{ and } y \in A\}.$$

***34. (Seiferas and McNaughton [113])   Let $f : \mathbb{N} \to \mathbb{N}$ be a function. Call
f *regularity preserving* if the set

$$\{x \mid \exists y \; |y| = f(|x|) \text{ and } xy \in A\}$$

is regular whenever A is. Call f *weakly regularity preserving* if the set

$$\{x \mid \exists y \; |y| = f(|x|) \text{ and } y \in A\}$$

is regular whenever A is. Prove that the following statements are
equivalent:

(a) f is regularity preserving;

(b) f is weakly regularity preserving;

(c) for any ultimately periodic set $U \subseteq \mathbb{N}$, the set

$$f^{-1}(U) = \{m \mid f(m) \in U\}$$

is also ultimately periodic; and

(d) for any $n \in \mathbb{N}$, the set $\{m \mid f(m) = n\}$ is ultimately periodic,
and f is ultimately periodic mod p for any $p \geq 1$ in the sense
that

$$\forall p \geq 1 \; \exists q \geq 1 \; \overset{\infty}{\forall} n \; f(n) \equiv f(n+q) \bmod p.$$

Here $\overset{\infty}{\forall}$ means "for almost all" or "for all but finitely many."
Formally,

$$\overset{\infty}{\forall} n \; \varphi(n) \overset{\text{def}}{\Longleftrightarrow} \exists m \geq 0 \; \forall n \geq m \; \varphi(n).$$

^{S}35. Show that the set $\{ww \mid w \in \{0,1\}^*\}$ is not regular.

^{S}36. Show that the set

$$\text{PRIMES} \overset{\text{def}}{=} \{a^p \mid p \text{ is prime}\}$$

is not regular.

37. Which of the following sets are regular and which are not? Give justification.

(a) $\{a^n b^{2m} \mid n \geq 0 \text{ and } m \geq 0\}$

(b) $\{a^n b^m \mid n = 2m\}$

(c) $\{a^n b^m \mid n \neq m\}$

(d) $\{a^{p-1} \mid p \text{ is prime}\}$

(e) $\{xcx \mid x \in \{a,b\}^*\}$

(f) $\{xcy \mid x,y \in \{a,b\}^*\}$

(g) $\{a^n b^{n+481} \mid n \geq 0\}$

(h) $\{a^n b^m \mid n - m \leq 481\}$

(i) $\{a^n b^m \mid n \geq m \text{ and } m \leq 481\}$

(j) $\{a^n b^m \mid n \geq m \text{ and } m \geq 481\}$

(k) $L((a^*b)^* a^*)$

(l) $\{a^n b^n c^n \mid n \geq 0\}$

(m) {syntactically correct PASCAL programs}

38. For each of the following subsets of $\{0,1\}^*$, tell whether or not it is regular. Give proof.

    (a) $\{x \mid \#1(x) = 2 \cdot \#0(x)\}$

    (b) $\{x \mid \#1(x) - \#0(x) < 10\}$

    (c) $\{x \mid \#1(x) \cdot \#0(x) \text{ is even}\}$

39. Prove that the set $\{a^n b^m c^k \mid n, m, k \geq 0, \ n + m = k\}$ is not regular.

40. Prove that the set $\{a^i b^j \mid i \text{ is even or } j < i\}$ is not regular.

41. Prove that no infinite subset of $\{a^n b^n \mid n \geq 0\}$ is regular.

**42. Give a set $A \subseteq \{a,b\}^*$ such that neither A nor $\{a,b\}^* - A$ contains an infinite regular subset. Prove that this is true of your set.

**H43. Give a nonregular set that satisfies condition (P) of the pumping lemma for regular sets (Lecture 11); that is, such that the demon has a winning strategy. Thus (P) is a necessary but not a sufficient condition for a set to be regular.

44. Prove the following stronger versions of the pumping lemma for regular sets that give necessary and sufficient conditions for a set to be regular.

    *S(a) (Jaffe [62])   A set $A \subseteq \Sigma^*$ is regular if and only if there exists $k \geq 0$ such that for all $y \in \Sigma^*$ with $|y| = k$, there exist $u, v, w \in \Sigma^*$ such that $y = uvw$, $v \neq \epsilon$, and for all $z \in \Sigma^*$ and $i \geq 0$,

    $$yz \in A \iff uv^i wz \in A.$$

*(b) (Stanat and Weiss [117])   A set $A \subseteq \Sigma^*$ is regular if and only if there exists $k \geq 0$ such that for all $y \in \Sigma^*$ with $|y| \geq k$, there exist $u, v, w \in \Sigma^*$ such that $y = uvw$, $v \neq \epsilon$, and for all $x, z \in \Sigma^*$ and $i \geq 0$,

$$xuz \in A \Longleftrightarrow xuv^i z \in A.$$

45. Let A be any subset of $\{a\}^*$ whatsoever.

*H(a) Show that A^* is regular.

**S(b) Show that

$$A^* = \{a^{np} \mid n \geq 0\} - G,$$

where G is some finite set and p is the greatest common divisor of all elements of the set $\{m \mid a^m \in A\}$. This is a generalization of the so-called postage stamp problem: any amount of postage over 7 cents can be made with some combination of 3 and 5 cent stamps.

46. Prove that the DFA with 15 states shown in Lecture 5 for the set (5.1) is minimal.

47. Minimize the following DFAs. Indicate clearly which equivalence class corresponds to each state of the new automaton.

(a)

		a	b
→	1	6	3
	2	5	6
	3F	4	5
	4F	3	2
	5	2	1
	6	1	4

(b)

		a	b
→	1	2	3
	2	5	6
	3F	1	4
	4F	6	3
	5	2	1
	6	5	4

(c)

		a	b
→	0F	3	2
	1F	3	5
	2	2	6
	3	2	1
	4	5	4
	5	5	3
	6	5	0

(d)

		a	b
→	0	3	5
	1	2	4
	2	6	3
	3	6	6
	4F	0	2
	5F	1	6
	6	2	6

(e)

	a	b
→ 0	3	5
1	6	3
2	6	4
3	6	6
4F	0	5
5F	2	4
6	1	6

(f)

	a	b
→ 0	2	5
1	6	2
2	6	6
3	6	4
4F	5	0
5F	4	3
6	1	6

(g)

	a	b
→ 1F	6	4
2F	7	5
3	2	8
4	1	8
5	2	6
6	3	1
7	5	2
8	4	2

(h)

	a	b
→ 1	6	2
2	3	6
3F	2	4
4F	5	3
5	4	1
6	1	5
7	1	8
8	8	7

48. Consider the DFA with states $\mathbb{Z}_5 = \{0, 1, 2, 3, 4\}$, input alphabet $\{0, 1\}$, start state 0, final state 0, and transition function

$$\delta(q, i) = (q^2 - i) \bmod 5, \quad q \in \mathbb{Z}_5, \ i \in \{0, 1\}.$$

Prove that this DFA accepts exactly the set of binary strings containing an even number of 1's.

HS 49. Prove the correctness of the collapsing algorithm of Lecture 14 (Theorem 14.3).

50. Let $\Sigma = \{a, b\}$. For any $x \in \Sigma^*$, define

suf $x = \{ux \mid u \in \Sigma^*\}$,

the set of strings ending with x. The set **suf** x is accepted by a nondeterministic finite automaton with $|x| + 1$ states. For example, here is a nondeterministic finite automaton for **suf** $abbaba$:

a, b

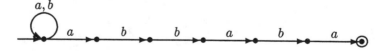

(a) Draw the minimal *deterministic* finite automaton for **suf** $abbaba$.

H(b) Argue that for any x, the minimal deterministic finite automaton for **suf x has exactly $|x| + 1$ states.

**H51. (Greibach) Let M be an NFA, $A = L(M)$. Starting with M, do the following:

(a) reverse the transitions and interchange start and final states to get an NFA for **rev** A;

(b) determinize the resulting NFA by the subset construction, omitting inaccessible states;

(c) do the above two steps again.

Prove that the resulting automaton is the minimal DFA for A.

52. For each of the following finite automata:

(i) Give an equivalent minimal deterministic finite automaton. Don't forget to remove inaccessible states.

(ii) Give an equivalent regular expression.

(a)

	a	b
→ 1F	2	5
2F	1	4
3	7	2
4	5	7
5	4	3
6	3	6
7	3	1

(b)

	a	b
→ 1F	2	6
2F	1	7
3	5	2
4	2	3
5	3	1
6	7	3
7	6	5

(c)

	a	b
→ 1	1	3
2F	6	3
3	5	7
4F	6	1
5	1	7
6F	2	7
7	5	3

(d)

	a	b
→ 1F	2	5
2F	1	6
3	4	3
4	7	1
5	6	7
6	5	4
7	4	2

53. Consider the DFA with states $\mathbb{Z}_5 = \{0, 1, 2, 3, 4\}$, input alphabet $\{0, 1\}$, start state 0, final state 0, and transition function

$$\delta(q, i) = (q^2 + i) \bmod 5, \quad q \in \mathbb{Z}_5, \ i \in \{0, 1\}.$$

Give an equivalent minimal DFA.

54. Let $\equiv$ be any right congruence of finite index on Σ^*. Prove that any equivalence class of $\equiv$ is a regular subset of Σ^*.

55. Consider the regular set R represented by the regular expression

$$a^* b^* + b^* a^*.$$

   (a) Draw the minimal DFA for R.

   [H](b) Give a regular expression describing each of the equivalence classes of the Myhill–Nerode relation $\equiv_R$ defined in Lecture 16.

56. Let PAREN be the set of balanced strings of parentheses [ ]. Describe the equivalence classes of the relation $\equiv_{\text{PAREN}}$ defined in Lecture 16.

[**S]57. For strings x and y over a finite alphabet Σ, define $x \sqsubseteq y$ if x is a (not necessarily contiguous) substring of y; that is, if x can be obtained from y by deleting zero or more letters. For example,

$$abc \sqsubseteq ababac \sqsubseteq cabacbaac.$$

A subset $A \subseteq \Sigma^*$ is said to be *closed downward under* $\sqsubseteq$ if $x \in A$ whenever $x \sqsubseteq y$ and $y \in A$. Show that any subset of Σ^* closed downward under $\sqsubseteq$ is regular.

You may use *Higman's lemma*: any subset of Σ^* has a finite $\sqsubseteq$-base. A $\sqsubseteq$-*base* of a set X is a subset $X_0 \subseteq X$ such that for all $y \in X$ there exists an $x \in X_0$ such that $x \sqsubseteq y$. Higman's lemma is equivalent to saying that the set of $\sqsubseteq$-minimal elements of any $X \subseteq \Sigma^*$ is finite. You need not prove Higman's lemma.

58. (Kapur)   Allow a concise representation of strings by using exponents to denote repeated substrings. For example,

$$0101010101000 = (01)^5 0^3 = 0(10)^5 0^2.$$

Denote by $/x/$ the length of the most concise representation of string x (exponents are given in binary). Let $|x|$ denote the ordinary length of x. Let R be a regular set.

*(a) Show that there exist constants c and d depending only on R such that for all $x \in R$, there exists another string $y \in R$ such that $|y| - |x| \leq d$ and $/y/ \leq c \log |y|$.

**(b) Answer the same question with the condition $|y| - |x| \leq d$ replaced by the condition $|y| = |x|$.

***^{S}59. Here is a generalization of nondeterminism. An *alternating finite automaton* (AFA) is a 5-tuple

$$M = (Q, \Sigma, \delta, F, \alpha)$$

where Q is a finite set of *states*, Σ is a finite *input alphabet*, $F : Q \to \{0, 1\}$ is the characteristic function of a set of *final states*, that is,

$$F(q) = \begin{cases} 1 & \text{if } q \text{ is a final state,} \\ 0 & \text{otherwise,} \end{cases}$$

δ is the *transition function*

$$\delta : (Q \times \Sigma) \to ((Q \to \{0, 1\}) \to \{0, 1\}),$$

and α is the *acceptance condition*

$$\alpha : (Q \to \{0, 1\}) \to \{0, 1\}.$$

Intuitively, a computation of M generates a computation tree whose depth is the length of the input string. The function F gives a labeling of 0 or 1 to the leaves of this computation tree. For all $q \in Q$ and $a \in \Sigma$, the Boolean function

$$\delta(q, a) : (Q \to \{0, 1\}) \to \{0, 1\}$$

takes a Boolean labeling on states at level i and computes a new labeling at level $i - 1$; this is used to pass Boolean labels 0 or 1 back up the computation tree. The machine accepts if the labeling at level 0 satisfies α. An NFA is just an AFA in which the Boolean functions α and $\delta(q, a)$ compute the Boolean "or" of some subset of the inputs.

Formally, the transition function δ uniquely determines a map

$$\widehat{\delta} : (Q \times \Sigma^*) \to ((Q \to \{0, 1\}) \to \{0, 1\}),$$

defined inductively as follows: for $q \in Q$, $a \in \Sigma$, and $x \in \Sigma^*$,

$$\widehat{\delta}(q, \epsilon)(u) = u(q),$$
$$\widehat{\delta}(q, ax)(u) = \delta(q, a)(\lambda p.(\widehat{\delta}(p, x)(u))).$$

(Here "$\lambda p \dots$" means "the function which on input p computes $\dots$;" see Lecture 37.) The machine is said to *accept* $x \in \Sigma^*$ if

$$\alpha(\lambda p.(\widehat{\delta}(p, x)(F))) = 1.$$

Prove that a set $A \subseteq \Sigma^*$ is accepted by a k-state alternating finite automaton if and only if its reverse **rev** A is accepted by a 2^k-state deterministic finite automaton.

[H]60. Show that minimal-state NFAs are not necessarily unique.

61. (Vardi [122])   In this exercise we show that two-way nondeterministic finite automata accept only regular sets. Let M be a 2NFA with states Q, start states S, accept state t, and transition function

$$\Delta : Q \times (\Sigma \cup \{\vdash, \dashv\}) \to 2^{Q \times (\{L, R\})}.$$

Assume without loss of generality that whenever M accepts, it moves its head all the way to the right endmarker $\dashv$ and enters its accept state t.

(a) Let $x = a_1 a_2 \cdots a_n \in \Sigma^*$, $a_i \in \Sigma$, $1 \le i \le n$. Let $a_0 = \vdash$ and $a_{n+1} = \dashv$. Argue that x is *not* accepted by M iff there exist sets $W_i \subseteq Q$, $0 \le i \le n + 1$, such that

- $S \subseteq W_0$;

- if $u \in W_i$, $0 \le i \le n$, and $(v, R) \in \Delta(u, a_i)$, then $v \in W_{i+1}$;

- if $u \in W_i$, $1 \le i \le n+1$, and $(v, L) \in \Delta(u, a_i)$, then $v \in W_{i-1}$; and

- $t \notin W_{n+1}$.

[H](b) Using (a), show that $\sim L(M)$, hence $L(M)$, is regular.

62. Prove Lemma B.8.

63. Prove that if a bisimulation between two NFAs is a one-to-one correspondence on the states, then it is an isomorphism.

64. Prove that if NFAs M and N are bisimilar, then the relation (B.1) of Supplementary Lecture B gives a bisimulation between the deterministic automata obtained from M and N by the subset construction.

65. Prove that two DFAs are bisimilar if and only if they accept the same set.

66. Prove Lemma C.11.

67. Prove Lemma D.2.

68. Prove that the relation $\equiv_A$ defined in the statement of the Myhill–Nerode theorem for term automata (Theorem D.3) is a congruence on the term algebra $T_\Sigma(A)$.

Miscellaneous Exercises

Pushdown Automata and Context-Free Languages

69. Consider the following context-free grammar G:

$$S \to ABS \mid AB,$$
$$A \to aA \mid a,$$
$$B \to bA.$$

Which of the following strings are in $L(G)$ and which are not? Provide derivations for those that are in $L(G)$ and reasons for those that are not.

(a) *aabaab*

(b) *aaaaba*

(c) *aabbaa*

(d) *abaaba*

*H70. Consider the context-free grammar G with start symbol S and productions

$$S \to aAB \mid aBA \mid bAA \mid \epsilon,$$
$$A \to aS \mid bAAA,$$
$$B \to aABB \mid aBAB \mid aBBA \mid bS.$$

Prove that $L(G)$ is the language consisting of all words that have exactly twice as many a's as b's.

71. Give a grammar with no ϵ- or unit productions generating the set $L(G) - \{\epsilon\}$, where G is the grammar

$$S \to aSbb \mid T,$$
$$T \to bTaa \mid S \mid \epsilon.$$

72. Give grammars in Chomsky and Greibach normal form for the following context-free languages.

   (a) $\{a^n b^{2n} c^k \mid k, n \geq 1\}$

   (b) $\{a^n b^k a^n \mid k, n \geq 1\}$

   (c) $\{a^k b^m c^n \mid k, m, n \geq 1, \ 2k \geq n\}$

   (d) $\{a, b\}^* - \{\text{palindromes}\}$

73. Let $\Sigma = \{0, 1\}$. Let $\bar{x}$ denote the Boolean complement of x; that is, the string obtained from x by changing all 0's to 1's and 1's to 0's. Let **rev** x denote the reverse of x; that is, the string x written backwards. Consider the set

$$A = \{x \mid \textbf{rev } x = \bar{x}\}.$$

For instance, the strings 011001 and 010101 are in A but 101101 is not.

   (a) Give a CFG for this set.

   (b) Give grammars in Chomsky and Griebach normal form for $A - \{\epsilon\}$.

*74. Consider the set of all strings over $\{a, b\}$ with no more than twice as many a's as b's:

$$\{x \in \{a, b\}^* \mid \#a(x) \leq 2\#b(x)\}.$$

   (a) Give a CFG for this set, and prove that it is correct.

   (b) Give a pushdown automaton for this set. Specify completely all data (states, transitions, etc.) and whether your machine accepts by final state or empty stack. Show sample runs on the input strings $aabbaa$, $aaabbb$, and $aaabaa$.

75. Our definition of patterns and regular expressions in Lecture 7 was a little imprecise since it did not mention parentheses. Make this definition precise by using a CFG to specify the set of regular expressions over an alphabet Σ. The grammar you come up with should have terminal symbols $\Sigma \cup \{\epsilon, \emptyset, +, \cdot, (,), *\}$.

76. Consider the set

$$a^* b^* c^* - \{a^n b^n c^n \mid n \geq 0\},$$

the set of all strings of a's followed by b's followed by c's such that the number of a's, b's, and c's are not all equal.

   (a) Give a CFG for the set, and prove that your grammar is correct.

   (b) Give an equivalent PDA.

*S77. What set is generated by the following grammar?

$$S \rightarrow bS \mid Sa \mid aSb \mid \epsilon$$

Give proof.

S78. For $A, B \subseteq \Sigma^*$, define

$$A/B \stackrel{\text{def}}{=} \{x \in \Sigma^* \mid \exists y \in B \ xy \in A\}.$$

Prove that if L is a CFL and R is a regular set, then L/R is CFL.

H79. Show that the context-free languages are closed under homomorphic images and preimages.

H80. (Ginsburg and Rice [45])   Show that any context-free subset of $\{a\}^*$ is regular.

81. The specification of **while** programs at the beginning of Supplementary Lecture I is rather imprecise. Give a rigorous context-free specification.

82. Prove that the set

$$\text{PRIMES} \stackrel{\text{def}}{=} \{a^p \mid p \text{ is prime}\}$$

is not context-free.

**H83. Show that $\{a, b\}^* - \{a^n b^{n^2} \mid n \geq 0\}$ is not context-free.

84. Which of the following sets are context-free and which are not? Give grammars for those that are context-free and proof for those that are not.

(a) $\{a^n b^m c^k \mid n, m, k \geq 1 \text{ and } (2n = 3k \text{ or } 5k = 7m)\}$

(b) $\{a^n b^m c^k \mid n, m, k \geq 1 \text{ and } (2n = 3k \text{ and } 5k = 7m)\}$

(c) $\{a^n b^m c^k \mid n, m, k \geq 1 \text{ and } (n \neq 3m \text{ or } n \neq 5k)\}$

(d) $\{a^n b^m c^k \mid n, m, k \geq 1 \text{ and } (n \neq 3m \text{ and } n \neq 5k)\}$

(e) $\{a^n b^m c^k \mid n, m, k \geq 1 \text{ and } n + k = m\}$

(f) $\{a^i b^j c^k d^\ell \mid i, j, k, \ell \geq 1, \ i = j, \ k = \ell\}$

(g) $\{a^i b^j c^k d^\ell \mid i, j, k, \ell \geq 1, \ i = k, \ j = \ell\}$

(h) $\{a^i b^j c^k d^\ell \mid i, j, k, \ell \geq 1, \ i = \ell, \ j = k\}$

85. Say whether the following sets are (i) regular, (ii) context-free but not regular, or (iii) not context-free. Give justification.

(a) $\{x \in \{a, b, c\}^* \mid \#a(x) = \#b(x) = \#c(x)\}$

(b) $\{a^j \mid j \text{ is a power of } 2\}$

(c) $\{x \in \{0, 1\}^* \mid x \text{ represents a power of 2 in binary}\}$

(d) $L(a^* b^* c^*)$

(e) the set of all balanced strings of parentheses of three types,
( ) [ ] { }

(f) $\{a^n b^m \mid n \neq m\}$

(g) $\{a^n b^m c^k d^\ell \mid 2n = 3k \text{ or } 5m = 7\ell\}$

(h) $\{a^n b^m c^k d^\ell \mid 2n = 3k \text{ and } 5m = 7\ell\}$

(i) $\{a^n b^m c^k d^\ell \mid 2n = 3m \text{ and } 5k = 7\ell\}$

(j) $\{a^n b^m c^k d^\ell \mid 2n = 3\ell \text{ and } 5k = 7m\}$

(k) $\{a^i b^j c^k \mid i, j, k \geq 0 \text{ and } i > j \text{ and } j > k\}$

(l) $\{a^i b^j c^k \mid i, j, k \geq 0 \text{ and } (i > j \text{ or } j > k)\}$

(m) $\{x \in \{a, b\}^* \mid \#a(x) > \#b(x)\}$

(n) $\{a^m b^n \mid m, n \geq 0, \ 5m + 3n = 24\}$

(o) $\{a^m b^n \mid m, n \geq 0, \ 5m - 3n = 24\}$

[^{**H}**]86.** Give a non-context-free set that satisfies the condition of the pumping lemma for CFLs given in Lecture 22; that is, such that the demon has a winning strategy.

87. Let Σ be a finite alphabet. For a set $A \subseteq \Sigma^*$, define

$$\textbf{cycle } A = \{yx \mid xy \in A\},$$
$$\textbf{permute } A = \{y \mid \exists x \in A \;\forall a \in \Sigma \; \#a(x) = \#a(y)\}.$$

For example, if $\Sigma = \{a, b, c\}$ and $A = \{aaabc\}$, then

$$\textbf{cycle } A = \{aaabc, aabca, abcaa, bcaaa, caaab\},$$
$$\textbf{permute } A = \{aaabc, aabca, abcaa, bcaaa, caaab,$$
$$aabac, abaca, bacaa, acaab, caaba,$$
$$abaac, baaca, aacab, acaba, cabaa,$$
$$baaac, aaacb, aacba, acbaa, cbaaa\}.$$

Which of the following propositions are true and which are false? Give proof.

(a) For all $A \subseteq \Sigma^*$, if A is regular, then so is **cycle** A.

(b) For all $A \subseteq \Sigma^*$, if A is regular, then so is **permute** A.

[^{**H}**]**(c) For all $A \subseteq \Sigma^*$, if A is context-free, then so is **cycle** A.

(d) For all $A \subseteq \Sigma^*$, if A is context-free, then so is **permute** A.

88. Recall the shuffle operator $\|$ from Homework 4.

(a) Show that if L is context-free and R is regular, then $L \| R$ is context-free.

*(b) If L is a DCFL, is $L \| R$ necessarily a DCFL? Give proof.

*89. For $A, B \subseteq \Sigma^*$, define

$$A/B \stackrel{\text{def}}{=} \{x \mid \exists y \in B \; xy \in A\}$$
$$A \leftarrow B \stackrel{\text{def}}{=} \{x \mid \forall y \in B \; xy \in A\}.$$

Exactly one of the following two statements is true.

(a) If L is context-free, then so is L/Σ^*.

(b) If L is context-free, then so is $L \leftarrow \Sigma^*$.

Which is true? Give a proof and a counterexample.

90. Let $\Sigma = \{a, b, c\}$. Exactly one of the following four statements is true.

(a) For any $A \subseteq \Sigma^*$, if A is regular, then so is $\{xx \mid x \in A\}$.

(b) For any $A \subseteq \Sigma^*$, if A is regular, then so is $\{x \mid xx \in A\}$.

(c) For any $A \subseteq \Sigma^*$, if A is context-free, then so is $\{xx \mid x \in A\}$.

*H(d) For any $A \subseteq \Sigma^*$, if A is context-free, then so is $\{x \mid xx \in A\}$.

Which is true? Give a proof and three counterexamples.

91. Using the grammar

$$S \to AB, \qquad A \to a, \qquad B \to AB \mid b,$$

run the CKY algorithm on the string aab. Draw a table like the following one and fill it in completely.

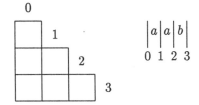

92. (a) Modify the CKY algorithm to count the number of parse trees of a given string and to construct one if the number is nonzero.

(b) Test your algorithm of part (a) on the grammar

$$S \to ST \mid a,$$
$$T \to BS,$$
$$B \to +$$

and string

$$a + a + a + a.$$

(Sanity check: the string has five parse trees.)

***H93. Let $D \subseteq \Sigma^*$ be a DCFL. One of the following sets is always a DCFL, the other is not necessarily. Which is which? Give proof for both.

(a) $\{x \mid \exists a \in \Sigma \; xa \in D\}$

(b) $\{x \mid \exists a \in \Sigma \; ax \in D\}$

Conclude that the family of DCFLs is not closed under reversal.

94. Let Σ be a fixed finite signature as described in Supplementary Lecture C. Give an unambiguous context-free grammar for the set of ground terms over Σ. *Unambiguous* means that there is exactly one parse tree for each ground term. Prove that your grammar is correct and that it is unambiguous.

**95. The context-free language $\{a^n b^n \mid n \geq 0\}$ is the unique $\subseteq$-minimal solution of the equation

$$\mathbf{X} = a\mathbf{X}b + \epsilon.$$

In general, let Σ be a finite alphabet. Consider finite systems of equations of the form

$$\mathbf{X}_1 = \mathcal{E}_1(\mathbf{X}_1, \dots, \mathbf{X}_n),$$
$$\vdots$$
$$\mathbf{X}_n = \mathcal{E}_n(\mathbf{X}_1, \dots, \mathbf{X}_n),$$

where the $\mathbf{X}_i$ are variables ranging over subsets of Σ^* and the $\mathcal{E}_i$ are regular expressions over $\mathbf{X}_1, \dots, \mathbf{X}_n$ and Σ.

(a) Argue that any such system has a unique minimal solution

$$X_1, \dots, X_n \in (2^{\Sigma^*})^n.$$

You may want to use the *Knaster–Tarski theorem*: any monotone map on a complete partial order has a unique least fixpoint. A map f on a partially ordered set is *monotone* if $x \leq y \rightarrow f(x) \leq f(y)$. A partially ordered set is *complete* if every subset of that set has a least upper bound.

(b) For the $X_1, \dots, X_n$ of part (a), show that X_1 is a context-free language.

(c) Show that all context-free languages arise in this way.

Miscellaneous Exercises

Turing Machines and Effective Computability

96. Give a Turing machine with input alphabet $\{a\}$ that on input a^m halts with a^{m^2} written on its tape. Describe the operation of the machine both informally and formally. Be sure to specify all data.

97. The Euclidean algorithm computes the greatest common divisor (GCD) of two nonnegative integers:

    ```
    procedure gcd(m,n):
    if n = 0 then return(m)
                else return(gcd(n,m mod n))
    ```

    Give a Turing machine with input alphabet $\{a, \#\}$ that on input $a^m \# a^n$ halts with $a^{\gcd(m,n)}$ written on its tape. Describe the operation of the machine both informally and formally. Be sure to specify all data.

98. Prove that the class of r.e. sets is closed under union and intersection.

99. A *queue machine* is like a Turing machine, except that it has a queue instead of a tape. It has a finite queue alphabet Γ and a finite input alphabet $\Sigma \subseteq \Gamma$. If $x \in \Sigma^*$ is the input, the machine starts in its start state s with $x\$$ in the queue, where $\$$ is a special symbol in $\Gamma - \Sigma$. In each step, it removes a symbol from the front of the queue. Based on

that symbol and the current state, it pushes a string $z \in \Gamma^*$ onto the back of the queue and enters a new state according to the transition function δ. It accepts by emptying its queue.

^S(a) Give a rigorous formal definition of these machines, including a definition of configurations and acceptance. Your definition should begin as follows: "A *queue machine* is a sextuple

$$M = (Q, \Sigma, \Gamma, \$, \delta, s),$$

where ..."

***^{HS}(b) Prove that queue machines and Turing machines are equivalent in power.

100. A *one-counter automaton* is an automaton with a finite set of states Q, a two-way read-only input head, and a separate counter that can hold any nonnegative integer. The input $x \in \Sigma^*$ is enclosed in endmarkers $\vdash, \dashv \notin \Sigma$, and the input head may not go outside the endmarkers. The machine starts in its start state s with its counter empty and with its input head pointing to the left endmarker $\vdash$. In each step, it can test its counter for zero. Based on this information, its current state, and the symbol its input head is currently reading, it can either add one to its counter or subtract one, move its input head either left or right, and enter a new state. It accepts by entering a distinguished final state t.

(a) Give a rigorous formal definition of these machines, including a definition of acceptance. Your definition should begin as follows: "A *one-counter automaton* is a septuple

$$M = (Q, \Sigma, \vdash, \dashv, s, t, \delta),$$

where ..."

*(b) Prove that the membership problem for deterministic one-counter automata is decidable: given M and x, does M accept x?

^H(c) Prove that the emptiness problem is undecidable: given a one-counter automaton M, is $L(M) = \varnothing$?

101. A *ray automaton* consists of an infinite number of deterministic finite automata $A_0, A_1, A_2, \ldots$ arranged in a line. The automata all have the same set of states Q, the same start state s, and the same transition function δ except A_0, which has a different transition function δ_0 since it has no left neighbor. They all start simultaneously in their initial state s and execute synchronously. In each step, each A_i moves to a new state, depending on its own current state and the current states of its

immediate left and right neighbors, according to its transition function. The ray automaton is said to *halt* if A_0 ever enters a distinguished final state t. There is no input alphabet.

(a) Give a rigorous formal definition of ray automata, including a definition of execution and halting. Your definition should begin as follows: "A *ray automaton* is a quintuple

$$\mathcal{A} = (Q, \ s, \ t, \ \delta_0, \ \delta),$$

where Q is a finite set of *states*, ... "

(b) Prove that the halting problem for ray automata is undecidable.

(c) Is the halting problem for ray automata semidecidable? Why or why not?

102. A *deterministic two-dimensional Turing machine* is like a Turing machine except that instead of a one-dimensional tape it has a two-dimensional tape that is like a chessboard, infinite in all directions. It has a finite input alphabet Σ and a finite tape alphabet Γ containing Σ as a subset. If $x \in \Sigma^*$ is the input, $|x| = n$, the machine starts in its start state s with x written in tape cells $(0,1)$, $(0,2)$, ..., $(0,n)$, the origin $(0,0)$ containing a special symbol $O \in \Gamma - \Sigma$, and all other cells (i,j) containing a special blank symbol $\sqcup \in \Gamma - \Sigma$. It has a read/write head initially pointing to the origin. In each step, it reads the symbol of Γ currently occupying the cell it is scanning. Depending on that symbol and the current state of the finite control, it writes a symbol of Γ on that cell, moves one cell either north, south, east, or west, and enters a new state, according to its transition function δ. It accepts its input by erasing the entire board; that is, filling all cells with $\sqcup$.

[H](a) Give a rigorous formal definition of these machines, including a definition of configurations, the next configuration relation, and acceptance. Try to be as precise as possible. Your definition should begin as follows: "A *two-dimensional Turing machine* is a 7-tuple

$$M = (Q, \ \Sigma, \ \Gamma, \ \sqcup, \ O, \ s, \ \delta),$$

where Q is a finite set of *states*, ... "

(b) Argue that two-dimensional Turing machines and ordinary Turing machines are equivalent in the sense that each can simulate the other. Describe the simulations *informally* (i.e., no transitions) but in sufficient detail that transitions implementing your description could readily be written down.

103. A nondeterministic Turing machine is one with a multiple-valued transition relation. Give a formal definition of these machines. Argue that every nondeterministic TM can be simulated by a deterministic TM.

104. Show that the type 0 grammars (see Lecture 36) generate exactly the r.e. sets.

105. For $A, B \subseteq \Sigma^*$, define

$$A/B \stackrel{\text{def}}{=} \{x \in \Sigma^* \mid \exists y \in B \ xy \in A\}.$$

   (a) Show that if A and B are r.e., then so is A/B.

   *H(b) Show that every r.e. set can be represented as A/B with A and B CFLs.

106. Is it decidable, given $M\#y$, whether the Turing machine M ever writes a nonblank symbol on its tape on input y? Why or why not?

107. Is it decidable for TMs M whether $L(M) = \text{rev } L(M)$? Give proof.

108. Tell whether the following problems are decidable or undecidable. Give proof.

   (a) Given a TM M and a string y, does M ever write the symbol $\#$ on its tape on input y?

   (b) Given a CFG G, does G generate all strings except ϵ?

   (c) Given an LBA M, does M accept a string of even length?

   (d) Given a TM M, are there infinitely many TMs equivalent to M?

109. Tell whether or not the following sets are r.e. Give proof.

   (a) $\{(M, N) \mid M$ takes fewer steps than N on input $\epsilon\}$

   (b) $\{M \mid M$ takes fewer than 481^{481} steps on some input$\}$

   (c) $\{M \mid M$ takes fewer than 481^{481} steps on at least 481^{481} different inputs$\}$

   (d) $\{M \mid M$ takes fewer than 481^{481} steps on all inputs$\}$

110. Show that the set $\{M \mid M$ accepts at least 481 strings$\}$ is r.e. but not co-r.e.

111. One of the following sets is r.e. and the other is not. Which is which? Give proof for both.

    (a) $\{M \mid L(M) \text{ contains at least 481 elements}\}$

    (b) $\{M \mid L(M) \text{ contains at most 481 elements}\}$

112. Show that the set

    $$\{M \mid M \text{ halts on all inputs of length less than 481}\}$$

    is r.e., but its complement is not.

^{S}113. Let M range over Turing machine descriptions. Show that neither the set

    $$\text{REG} \stackrel{\text{def}}{=} \{M \mid L(M) \text{ is a regular set}\}$$

    nor its complement is recursively enumerable.

114. Let $|M|$ denote the length of the description of the Turing machine M. Are the following problems decidable? Give proof.

    (a) Does a given Turing machine M take at least $|M|$ steps on some input?

    (b) ... on all inputs?

115. Tell whether the following problems are decidable or undecidable, and give proof:

    (a) whether a given TM runs for at least 481^{481} steps on input a^{481};

    (b) whether a given TM ever reenters its start state on any input;

    *(c) whether a given Turing machine will ever move its head left more than ten times on input a^{481};

    *(d) whether a given Turing machine will ever print more than 481 nonblank symbols on input a^{481}.

116. Think for two minutes about why the following problems are undecidable, but don't write anything down:

    (a) whether two given C++ programs compute the same function;

    (b) whether a given C++ program will ever get into an infinite loop on some input;

(c) whether a given μ-recursive function is total;

(d) whether a given λ-term reduces to normal form.

117. Show that the following problems of pairs of Turing machines are undecidable:

(a) whether $L(M) = L(N)$;

(b) whether $L(M) \subseteq L(N)$;

(c) whether $L(M) \cap L(N) = \emptyset$;

(d) whether $L(M) \cap L(N)$ is a recursive set;

(e) whether $L(M) \cap L(N)$ is finite.

**118. Formalize and prove the following extension of Rice's theorem that has the results of Exercise 117 as special cases: every nontrivial property of *pairs* of r.e. sets is undecidable.

119. Let G and G' denote context-free grammars over $\{a, b\}$. Prove that the following problems are undecidable:

H(a) whether $L(G) = L(G')$;

(b) whether $L(G) \subseteq L(G')$;

*(c) whether $L(G) = L(G)L(G)$.

120. One of the following problems is decidable and the other is not. Which is which? Give proof for both.

(a) Given a CFL L and a regular set R, is $L \subseteq R$?

(b) Given a CFL L and a regular set R, is $R \subseteq L$?

H121. Prove that the following problems are undecidable:

(a) whether a given CFL is a DCFL;

(b) whether the intersection of two given CFLs is a CFL;

(c) whether the complement of a given CFL is a CFL;

**(d) whether the union of two given DCFLs is a DCFL.

122. Prove that it is undecidable whether a given LBA halts on all inputs.

^{H}123. Show that the finiteness problem for Turing machines reduces to the finiteness problem for LBAs.

124. Prove that it is undecidable whether a given LBA accepts a regular set.

125. Consider the following context-sensitive productions.

$$S \rightarrow bSb,$$
$$S \rightarrow AcA,$$
$$Ab \rightarrow A,$$
$$Ab \rightarrow b,$$
$$bA \rightarrow b,$$
$$bA \rightarrow A.$$

Let G be the grammar given by all the rules except for the last, and let G' the grammar given by all the rules including the last. One of $L(G)$ and $L(G')$ is regular, and the other is context-free but not regular. Which is which, and why?

126. Give a set over a *single letter alphabet* in each of the following classes, or explain why such a set does not exist:

   (a) regular;

   (b) DCFL but not regular;

   (c) CFL but not DCFL;

   (d) recursive but not CFL;

   (e) r.e. but not recursive;

   (f) not r.e.

127. Prove that every infinite regular set contains a non-r.e. subset.

^{*H}128. Prove that every infinite r.e. set contains an infinite recursive subset.

*129. In this exercise we will prove a kind of fixpoint theorem for Turing machines known as the *recursion theorem*.

   If M is a TM, let $M(x)$ denote the contents of M's tape at the point that M halts on input x, provided M does indeed halt on input x. If M does not halt on input x, then $M(x)$ is undefined.

A partial function $\sigma : \Sigma^* \to \Sigma^*$ is said to be a *computable function* if $\sigma(x) = M(x)$ for some Turing machine M. In addition, σ is a *total computable function* if M is total.

Let M_x be the TM whose encoding over Σ^* is x.

Theorem **(Recursion theorem)**   *Let $\sigma : \Sigma^* \to \Sigma^*$ be any total computable function. Then there exists a string u such that*

$$L(M_u) = L(M_{\sigma(u)}).$$

(a) Let $\sigma : \Sigma^* \to \Sigma^*$ be a given total computable function, say computable by a total TM K. Let N be a TM that on input x computes a *description* of a machine that does the following on input y:

- constructs M_x;

- runs M_x on input x;

- if it halts, runs K on $M_x(x)$;

- interprets the result of that computation, $K(M_x(x))$, as the description of a TM, and simulates that TM on the original input y, accepting or rejecting as that machine accepts or rejects, respectively.

Argue that N is total and that

$$L(M_{N(x)}) = L(M_{\sigma(M_x(x))}).$$

(b) Let v be a description of the machine N; that is, $N = M_v$. Argue that $N(v)$ is the desired fixpoint of σ.

^{H}130. Give a short proof of Rice's theorem using the recursion theorem (see Miscellaneous Exercise 129).

^{**H}131. A TM is *minimal* if it has the fewest states among all TMs that accept the same set. Prove that there does not exist an infinite r.e. set of minimal TMs.

132. ^{H}(a) Show that there does not exist an r.e. list of Turing machines such that every machine on the list is total (i.e., halts on all inputs) and every recursive set is represented by some machine on the list.

^{**H}(b) Show that there exists an r.e. list of Turing machines such that every machine on the list accepts a recursive set and every recursive set is represented by some machine on the list.

133. In addition to the usual constructs of **while programs (simple assignment, conditional, while loop, sequential composition), add a print statement

> **print** x **and halt**

that prints the current value of a variable and halts. Call two programs *equivalent* if for all initial values of the variables, one program halts iff the other does, and whenever they both halt, they print the same value.

One of the following problems is decidable and the other is undecidable. Which is which? Justify your answers.

(a) Given a program, does there exist an equivalent program with at most one **while** loop?

(b) Given a program, does there exist an equivalent program with no **while** loops?

134. This question is for those who know something about propositional logic. A *propositional Horn clause* is a disjunction of literals with at most one positive literal. The clause

$$\neg P_1 \vee \neg P_2 \vee \cdots \vee \neg P_n \vee Q$$

is often written as

$$P_1 \wedge P_2 \wedge \cdots \wedge P_n \rightarrow Q,$$

and the clause

$$\neg P_1 \vee \neg P_2 \vee \cdots \vee \neg P_n$$

can be written as

$$P_1 \wedge P_2 \wedge \cdots \wedge P_n \rightarrow \bot,$$

where $\bot$ denotes falsity. Any single positive literal Q is also a Horn clause.

(a) Show that the emptiness problem for context-free languages (i.e., given a context-free grammar G, deciding whether $L(G) = \varnothing$) reduces to the satisfiability problem for finite conjunctions of Horn clauses, and vice versa.

(b) Since the satisfiability of propositional formulas is decidable, what can we conclude about the decidability of the emptiness problem for CFLs?

[H]135. Show that the finiteness problem for regular sets and context-free languages (i.e., whether a given machine/grammar accepts/generates a finite set) is decidable.

136. Show that FIN $\leq_T$ REG. In other words, suppose you are given an oracle that will always answer questions of the form "Is $L(M)$ a regular set?" truthfully. Show how to use such an oracle to decide questions of the form "Is $L(M)$ finite?"

**137. Prove Theorem J.1.

*[H]138. Let $\mathrm{HP}_1 \stackrel{\text{def}}{=} \mathrm{HP}$, and let HP_{n+1} be the halting problem for oracle Turing machines with oracle HP_n, $n \geq 1$; that is,

$$\mathrm{HP}_{n+1} \stackrel{\text{def}}{=} \{M \# x \mid M \text{ is an oracle TM with oracle } \mathrm{HP}_n,$$
$$M \text{ halts on input } x\}.$$

The oracle need not be represented in the description of the oracle machine M. Show that $\mathrm{HP}_n \in \Sigma_n^0 - \Pi_n^0$.

139. Show that the integer square root function is primitive recursive. On input n, the function should return the greatest integer less than or equal to the square root of n.

[H]140. A language B is said to be *computable in linear time* if there exists a deterministic Turing machine M and a constant $c > 0$ such that $L(M) = B$ and M always halts within cn steps on inputs of length n. Show that there exists a recursive set that is not computable in linear time.

141. Show that the Turing reducibility relation $\leq_T$ is reflexive and transitive and that $\leq_m$ refines $\leq_T$.

142. Prove that the following sets are $\leq_m$-complete for the given classes:

   (a) EMPTY is $\leq_m$-complete for Π_1^0;

   *(b) TOTAL is $\leq_m$-complete for Π_2^0;

   **(c) COF is $\leq_m$-complete for Σ_3^0;

   **(d) the set

   $$\mathrm{REG} \stackrel{\text{def}}{=} \{M \mid L(M) \text{ is a regular set}\}$$

   is $\leq_m$-complete for Σ_3^0.

*[H]143. Prove that there exists a total computable function $f : \mathrm{N} \to \mathrm{N}$ that is not provably total in Peano arithmetic.

Hints for Selected Miscellaneous Exercises

6. Look for a clue in Lecture 5.

9. (b) Build an NFA with seven states arranged in loops of length two and five. Assign start and final states so that the shortest rejected string is of length $9 = 2 \cdot 5 - 1$.

   (c) The product of a set of distinct primes is exponential in their sum.

26. Given a DFA M for A, build an NFA M' for FirstHalves A that implements the following idea: put a white pebble on the start state of M and green and blue pebbles on an arbitrary guessed state of M. Never move the green pebble. Move the white pebble forward in response to input symbols and move the blue pebble forward according to some nondeterministically guessed input symbol. Accept if the white and green pebbles occupy the same state and the blue pebble occupies an accept state when the input string is exhausted. Describe M' formally and prove that it accepts the set FirstHalves A. Presumably the set of states of M' will be the set $Q \times Q \times Q$ encoding the positions of the three pebbles.

   In general, you will see several problems of the form

   show that if A is a regular set, then so is A',

where A' is some set formed by massaging A in some way. Exercise 2 of Homework 2 about **rev** A and Exercise 3 of Homework 3 about MiddleThirds A are of this type. Most of these problems can be solved by applying the following five-step protocol:

Step 1   Assume we are given a deterministic finite automaton

$$M = (Q, \Sigma, \delta, s, F)$$

accepting A. We want to build a nondeterministic automaton

$$M' = (Q', \Sigma, \Delta', S', F')$$

accepting A'. Come up with an intuitive design of M' in terms of moving pebbles around on the states of M. Think about the initial configuration of pebbles, how the pebbles should move in response to each input symbol, and what the accepting configurations should be.

Step 2   Write down a formal description of $Q', \Sigma, \Delta', S',$ and F' that formally captures your intuition about moving the pebbles developed in step 1. The first thing to think about is what the states Q' should be. You need to figure out how to encode formally the information that the new machine needs to remember at each step. Make sure the types are right; for example, whatever you decide the set of states Q' should be, the start state should be an element of Q' and the set of accept states F' should be a subset of Q'. If you are designing a deterministic machine M', then δ' should be a function $Q' \times \Sigma \to Q'$. If M' is to be nondeterministic, then you should have $\Delta' : Q' \times \Sigma \to 2^{Q'}$.

Step 3   In step 2 you defined a transition function Δ' of M'. Most likely, Δ' was defined in terms of the transition function δ of M. State a lemma extending this relationship to a relationship between $\widehat{\Delta}$ and $\widehat{\Delta}'$.

Step 4   Prove the lemma stated in step 3 by induction on $|x|$. The proof will most likely use the standard inductive definitions of $\widehat{\delta}$ and $\widehat{\Delta}'$, as well as the definition you gave in step 2 of Δ' in terms of δ.

Step 5   Prove that $L(M') = A'$. The proof will generally use the lemma proved in step 4 and the definitions of S' and F'.

Step 1 is usually not much of a problem, since it is usually easy to see how to move the pebbles. Steps 2 and 3 typically give the most trouble. If the lemma in step 3 is formulated correctly, the proofs in 4 and 5 should be fairly routine.

An example of an application of this protocol is given in the solution to this exercise on p. 358.

31. One of the sets is $\{a, b\}^*$.

32. Use the matrix representation of Miscellaneous Exercise 7.

33. Use the fact that

$$p(n+1) = \sum_{i=0}^{d} \frac{p^{(i)}(n)}{i!},$$

where $p^{(i)}$ denotes the ith derivative of p.

43. Try

$$\bigcup_{n \geq 0} (a^+ c)^n (b^+ c)^n + (a+b+c)^* cc(a+b+c)^*$$

with $k = 3$.

45. (a) By Theorem 12.3, it suffices to show that A^* is ultimately periodic. You can take as period the length of the smallest nonnull
element of A. This is not necessarily the smallest period, but it
will do.

49. For the direction ($\Rightarrow$), use induction on the stages of the algorithm.
For the direction ($\Leftarrow$), use induction on $|x|$.

50. (b) Consider the relation

$$y \equiv z \overset{\text{def}}{\Longleftrightarrow} \text{overlap}(y, x) = \text{overlap}(z, x),$$

where $\text{overlap}(y, x)$ is the longest string that is both a suffix of y
and a prefix of x. Use the Myhill–Nerode theorem.

51. Suppose that you start with a DFA for B with no inaccessible states,
reverse the transitions and exchange the start and final states to get
an NFA for **rev** B, then construct an equivalent DFA using the subset construction, omitting inaccessible states. Prove that the resulting
automaton is the minimal DFA for **rev** B.

55. (b) Two of them are ϵ and aa^*.

60. $aa^* \equiv a^* a$.

61. (b) Build an NFA whose states are subsets of Q. Let the machine
guess the sets W_i.

70. Prove inductively that

$$S \xrightarrow[G]{*} x \iff \#a(x) = 2\#b(x),$$

$$A \xrightarrow[G]{*} x \iff \#a(x) = 2\#b(x) + 1,$$

$$B \xrightarrow[G]{*} x \iff \#a(x) = 2\#b(x) - 2.$$

Think about the graph of the function $\#a(y) - 2\#b(y)$ for prefixes y of x.

79. Everything you need can be found in Lecture 10.

80. Use Parikh's theorem (Theorem H.1) and the theorem on ultimate periodicity (Theorem 12.3).

83. Use Parikh's theorem (Theorem H.1) and the fact that the complement of a semilinear subset of $\mathbb{N}^k$ is semilinear.

86. Show that the condition (P) of the pumping lemma for regular sets given in Lecture 11 implies the condition of the pumping lemma for context-free languages given in Lecture 22. Give a non-context-free set satisfying (P). A slightly modified version of the hint for Miscellaneous Exercise 43 should do.

87. (c) Build a PDA that pushes and pops antimatter.

90. (d) Consider the set

$$A = \{a^n b^n c^m a^m b^k c^k \mid n, m, k \geq 1\}.$$

93. (a) Let

$$M = (Q, \Sigma, \Gamma, \delta, \bot, \dashv, s, \varnothing)$$

be a DPDA for D that accepts by empty stack. Prove that for $p, q \in Q$ and $a \in \Sigma$,

$$\{\gamma \in \Gamma^* \mid (p, a, \gamma) \xrightarrow[M]{*} (q, \epsilon, \epsilon)\}$$

is a regular set.

(b) See the end of Lecture 27.

99. (b) Simulating a queue machine with a Turing machine is easy. The other direction is tricky. Make the queue of the queue machine contain a representation of the configuration of the Turing ma-

chine. The hard part is simulating a left move of the Turing machine. You need to go all the way around the queue.

You might try breaking your solution into two steps:

(i) First invent a new kind of Turing machine, a *one-way* Turing machine. These machines can only move right on the tape. When they see the right endmarker, they magically jump back to the left endmarker. Show that one-way machines can simulate ordinary TMs. Simulate a left move of the ordinary TM by pushing a marker all the way around to the right.

(ii) Simulate one-way machines with queue machines.

100. (c) Think VALCOMPS.

102. (a) The infinite checkerboard should be $\mathbb{Z} \times \mathbb{Z}$, where $\mathbb{Z}$ is the set of integers $\{\ldots, -2, -1, 0, 1, 2, 3, \ldots\}$. Tape contents should be modeled by functions $f : \mathbb{Z} \times \mathbb{Z} \to \Gamma$, which assign a tape symbol in Γ to each cell $(i, j) \in \mathbb{Z} \times \mathbb{Z}$.

105. (b) Think VALCOMPS.

119. (a) Take G to be $S \to aS \mid bS \mid \epsilon$.

121. Think VALCOMPS.

123. Think VALCOMPS.

128. Use Exercise 4 of Homework 9.

130. Let P be a nontrivial property of the r.e. sets. Then there exist TMs $M_\top$ and $M_\perp$ such that $P(L(M_\top)) = \top$ and $P(L(M_\perp)) = \perp$. Show that if it were decidable for TMs M whether $P(L(M)) = \top$, then we could construct a total computable map σ with no fixpoint, contradicting the recursion theorem (see Miscellaneous Exercise 129).

131. Use the recursion theorem (see Miscellaneous Exercise 129).

132. (a) Diagonalize.

(b) Let $\leq$ be an arbitrary computable linear order on the set of input strings. Given M, let M' be a machine that on input x simulates M on all $y \leq x$.

135. Use the pumping lemma.

138. Diagonalize.

140. Construct a list of total Turing machines that run in linear time such that every set computable in linear time is accepted by some machine on the list. Build a machine that diagonalizes over this list.

143. Diagonalize.

Solutions to Selected Miscellaneous Exercises

7. (a) By induction on n.

Basis

$$(A^0)_{uv} = I_{uv}$$
$$= \begin{cases} \{\epsilon\} & \text{if } u = v, \\ \varnothing & \text{otherwise} \end{cases}$$
$$= \{x \in \Sigma^* \mid |x| = 0 \text{ and } \widehat{\delta}(u, x) = v\}.$$

Induction step

$$(A^{n+1})_{uv}$$
$$= (A^n A)_{uv}$$
$$= \bigcup_{w \in Q} (A^n)_{uw} A_{wv}$$
$$= \bigcup_{w \in Q} \{x \in \Sigma^* \mid |x| = n \text{ and } \widehat{\delta}(u, x) = w\} \cdot \{a \in \Sigma \mid \delta(w, a) = v\}$$
$$= \{xa \in \Sigma^* \mid |x| = n \text{ and } \exists w \ \widehat{\delta}(u, x) = w \text{ and } \delta(w, a) = v\}$$
$$= \{xa \in \Sigma^* \mid |x| = n \text{ and } \widehat{\delta}(u, xa) = v\}$$
$$= \{y \in \Sigma^* \mid |y| = n + 1 \text{ and } \widehat{\delta}(u, y) = v\}.$$

20. (a) We'll show the inequality in both directions using the axioms (A.1) through (A.15).

Since $a^* = 1 + aa^*$ by (A.10), we have $aa^* \le a^*$ by the definition of $\le$. Then $a^*a^* \le a^*$ follows from (A.14).

Conversely,

$$a^*a^* = a^*(1 + aa^*) \quad \text{by (A.10)}$$
$$= a^* + a^*aa^* \quad \text{by (A.8);}$$

therefore, $a^* \le a^*a^*$ by the definition of $\le$.

25. We show first that A^*b is a solution of $x = Ax + b$. By Lemma A.2, we have that $A^* = AA^* + I$; this is just axiom (A.10) of Kleene algebra. Multiplying both sides by b and distributing, we get $A^*b = AA^*b + b$, which is just $x = Ax + b$ with A^*b substituted for x.

Now we wish to show that A^*b is the least solution. Let c be any other solution; then $c = Ac + b$. The array c is a vector of length n over the Kleene algebra $\mathcal{K}$. Form a square matrix C by juxtaposing n copies of c. Form the matrix B from b similarly. Then $C = AC + B$. By Lemma A.2 and axiom (A.12) of Kleene algebra, $A^*B \le C$, therefore $A^*b \le c$.

26. We show that if A is regular, then so is FirstHalves A using the five-step protocol given in the hint for this exercise on p. 351.

Step 1   Let

$$M = (Q, \Sigma, \delta, s, F)$$

be a DFA for A. Here is an informal description of an NFA M' for FirstHalves A in terms of pebbles. There will be a white pebble, a green pebble, and a blue pebble on the automaton at any point in time. We start with the white pebble on the start state of M and the blue and green pebbles together on a nondeterministically chosen state of M. The initial position of the blue and green pebbles is a guess as to where M will be after scanning x. In each step, we move the white pebble forward according to the input symbol and move the blue pebble forward according to some nondeterministically chosen symbol. The green pebble never moves. When the end of the input x is reached, we accept iff the white pebble and green pebble occupy the same state and the blue pebble occupies an accept state. The white pebble will occupy the state $\widehat{\delta}(s, x)$, since we moved it according to the input x. The blue pebble will occupy some state q reachable from the position of the green pebble under some string y such that $|y| = |x|$. If the white and green pebbles occupy the same state and the blue pebble occupies an accept state, then we can concatenate x and y to get a string twice as long as x accepted by M.

Step 2   Now let's do this formally. Define the NFA

$$M' = (Q', \Sigma, \Delta', S', F')$$

as follows. We take the states of M' to be $Q' \stackrel{\text{def}}{=} Q^3$, the set of ordered triples of elements of Q. For $(p, q, r) \in Q'$, the first component models the position of the white pebble, the second models the position of the green pebble, and the third models the position of the blue pebble.

The transition function Δ' must be a function

$$\Delta' : Q' \times \Sigma \to 2^{Q'}.$$

For any $p, q, r \in Q$ and $a \in \Sigma$, we define

$$\Delta'((p,q,r),a) \stackrel{\text{def}}{=} \{(\delta(p,a), q, \delta(r,b)) \mid b \in \Sigma\}.$$

These are the possible next pebble positions after (p,q,r) on input $a \in \Sigma$. The first component $\delta(p,a)$ says that we move the white pebble according to the input symbol a; the second component q says that we leave the green pebble where it is; and the third component $\delta(r,b)$ says that we move the blue pebble according to $b \in \Sigma$. All possible b are included, which reflects the idea that M' is guessing the next symbol of the string y.

We define the start states of M' to be

$$S' \stackrel{\text{def}}{=} \{(s,t,t) \mid t \in Q\},$$

modeling all possible initial configurations of pebbles. The white pebble initially occupies the start state of M and the green and blue pebbles occupy an arbitrary nondeterministically chosen state of M.

Finally, we take the accept states of M' to be

$$F' \stackrel{\text{def}}{=} \{(u,u,v) \mid u \in Q, v \in F\},$$

indicating that we accept provided the white and green pebbles occupy the same state and the blue pebble occupies an accept state.

Step 3   Our formal definition specifies a relationship between δ and Δ'. Now let's try to extend it to a relationship between $\widehat{\delta}$ and $\widehat{\Delta}'$. Intuitively, after scanning a string x of length n starting in some start state (s,q,q), the machine M' can be in any state of the form $(\widehat{\delta}(s,x), q, \widehat{\delta}(q,y))$ for some $y \in \Sigma^n$.

Lemma   *For any $x \in \Sigma^*$,*

$$\widehat{\Delta}'(S', x) = \{(\widehat{\delta}(s,x), q, \widehat{\delta}(q,y)) \mid q \in Q, y \in \Sigma^{|x|}\}.$$

Step 4   We prove the lemma of step 3 by induction on $|x|$. For the basis $x = \epsilon$, we use the base clauses (3.1) and (6.1) in the inductive definitions of $\widehat{\delta}$ and $\widehat{\Delta}'$ and the definition of S':

$$\widehat{\Delta}'(S', \epsilon) = S'$$
$$= \{(s, q, q) \mid q \in Q\}$$
$$= \{(\widehat{\delta}(s, \epsilon), q, \widehat{\delta}(q, \epsilon)) \mid q \in Q\}$$
$$= \{(\widehat{\delta}(s, \epsilon), q, \widehat{\delta}(q, y)) \mid q \in Q, \ y \in \Sigma^0\}.$$

For the induction step, assume that the lemma is true for x; that is,

$$\widehat{\Delta}'(S', x) = \{(\widehat{\delta}(s, x), q, \widehat{\delta}(q, y)) \mid q \in Q, \ y \in \Sigma^{|x|}\}.$$

We want to show that it is true for xa; that is,

$$\widehat{\Delta}'(S', xa) = \{(\widehat{\delta}(s, xa), q, \widehat{\delta}(q, yb)) \mid q \in Q, \ y \in \Sigma^{|x|}, \ b \in \Sigma\},$$

where $a \in \Sigma$. The argument uses the inductive definitions of $\widehat{\Delta}'$ and $\widehat{\delta}$, the induction hypothesis, and the definition of Δ' in terms of δ given in step 2:

$\widehat{\Delta}'(S', xa)$

$$= \bigcup_{(p,q,r) \in \widehat{\Delta}'(S',x)} \Delta'((p, q, r), a) \qquad \text{by (6.2)}$$

$$= \bigcup_{q \in Q, \ y \in \Sigma^{|x|}} \Delta'((\widehat{\delta}(s, x), q, \widehat{\delta}(q, y)), a) \qquad \text{induction hypothesis}$$

$$= \bigcup_{q \in Q, \ y \in \Sigma^{|x|}} \{(\delta(\widehat{\delta}(s, x), a), q, \delta(\widehat{\delta}(q, y), b)) \mid b \in \Sigma\}$$

$$\qquad\qquad\qquad\qquad\qquad\qquad\qquad \text{definition of } \Delta'$$

$$= \bigcup_{q \in Q, \ y \in \Sigma^{|x|}} \{(\widehat{\delta}(s, xa), q, \widehat{\delta}(q, yb)) \mid b \in \Sigma\} \qquad \text{by (3.2)}$$

$$= \{(\widehat{\delta}(s, xa), q, \widehat{\delta}(q, yb)) \mid q \in Q, \ y \in \Sigma^{|x|}, \ b \in \Sigma\}. \qquad \square$$

Step 5   Finally, we prove $L(M') = \text{FirstHalves } L(M)$. For any $x \in \Sigma^*$,

$x \in L(M')$

$\iff \widehat{\Delta}'(S', x) \cap F' \neq \varnothing$

$\iff \{(\widehat{\delta}(s, x), q, \widehat{\delta}(q, y)) \mid q \in Q, \ y \in \Sigma^{|x|}\}$ the lemma of step 3
$\qquad \cap \{(u, u, v) \mid u \in Q, \ v \in F\} \neq \varnothing$ definition of F'

$\iff \exists y \in \Sigma^{|x|} \ \exists q \in Q \ \widehat{\delta}(s, x) = q \text{ and } \widehat{\delta}(q, y) \in F$

$\iff \exists y \in \Sigma^{|x|} \ \widehat{\delta}(\widehat{\delta}(s, x), y) \in F$

$\iff \exists y \in \Sigma^{|x|} \ \widehat{\delta}(s, xy) \in F$ Homework 2, Exercise 3

$$\Longleftrightarrow \exists y \in \Sigma^{|x|} \ xy \in L(M)$$
$$\Longleftrightarrow x \in \text{FirstHalves } L(M). \qquad \Box$$

33. Using the fact that

$$p(n+1) = \sum_{i=0}^{d} \frac{p^{(i)}(n)}{i!},$$

where $p^{(i)}$ denotes the ith derivative of p, we have

$$p^{(j)}(n+1) = \sum_{i=0}^{d-j} \frac{p^{(i+j)}(n)}{i!} = \sum_{k=j}^{d} \frac{p^{(k)}(n)}{(k-j)!},$$

therefore

$$\frac{p^{(j)}(n+1)}{j!} = \sum_{k=j}^{d} \binom{k}{j} \frac{p^{(k)}(n)}{k!}. \tag{1}$$

Also,

$$\frac{p^{(j)}(0)}{j!} = a_j, \tag{2}$$

where a_j is the coefficient of n^j in $p(n)$. Let $M = (Q, \Sigma, \Delta, s, F)$ be an NFA for A. We will build a DFA $M' = (Q', \Sigma, \delta', s', F')$ for A'. Let B be the square Boolean matrix indexed by states of M such that

$$B_{uv} \overset{\text{def}}{=} \begin{cases} 1 & \text{if } \exists a \in \Sigma \ v \in \Delta(u,a), \\ 0 & \text{otherwise.} \end{cases}$$

Let B^n be the nth Boolean power of B, B^0 the identity matrix. One can show by induction on n that

$$(B^n)_{uv} = \begin{cases} 1 & \text{if } \exists y \in \Sigma^n \ v \in \widehat{\Delta}(\{u\}, y), \\ 0 & \text{otherwise.} \end{cases} \tag{3}$$

In other words, $(B^n)_{uv} = 1$ iff there exists a path of length n from u to v in the graph representation of the automaton.

Now consider the set of all square Boolean matrices indexed by the states of M. The states Q' of M' will be the set of all sequences $(C_0, C_1, \ldots, C_d)$ of $d+1$ such matrices, which we denote by $(C_i \mid 0 \le i \le d)$. Define

$$\delta'((C_i \mid 0 \le i \le d), a) = (\prod_{k=j}^{d} C_k^{\binom{k}{j}} \mid 0 \le j \le d),$$

$$s' = (B^{a_i} \mid 0 \le i \le d),$$

$$F' = \{(C_i \mid 0 \le i \le d) \mid \exists q \in F \ (C_0)_{sq} = 1\}.$$

Lemma *Let $x \in \Sigma^*$. Then*
$$\widehat{\delta}'(s', x) = (B^{p^{(i)}(|x|)/i!} \mid 0 \le i \le d).$$

Proof. By induction on $|x|$.

Basis

$$
\begin{aligned}
\widehat{\delta}'(s', \epsilon) &= s' && \text{definition of } \widehat{\delta}' \\
&= (B^{a_i} \mid 0 \le i \le d) && \text{definition of } s' \\
&= (B^{p^{(i)}(0)/i!} \mid 0 \le i \le d) && \text{by (2)} \\
&= (B^{p^{(i)}(|\epsilon|)/i!} \mid 0 \le i \le d).
\end{aligned}
$$

Induction step

Assume true for x. Then

$$
\begin{aligned}
\widehat{\delta}'(s', xa) &= \delta'(\widehat{\delta}'(s', x), a) && \text{definition of } \widehat{\delta}' \\
&= \delta'((B^{p^{(i)}(|x|)/i!} \mid 0 \le i \le d), a) && \text{induction hypothesis} \\
&= (\prod_{k=j}^{d} (B^{p^{(k)}(|x|)/k!})^{\binom{k}{j}} \mid 0 \le j \le d) && \text{definition of } \delta' \\
&= (B^{\sum_{k=j}^{d} \binom{k}{j} p^{(k)}(|x|)/k!} \mid 0 \le j \le d) \\
&= (B^{p^{(i)}(|x|+1)/i!} \mid 0 \le i \le d) && \text{by (1)} \\
&= (B^{p^{(i)}(|xa|)/i!} \mid 0 \le i \le d). && \square
\end{aligned}
$$

Theorem $L(M') = A'$.

Proof.

$$
\begin{aligned}
&x \in L(M') \\
\iff& \widehat{\delta}'(s', x) \in F' && \text{definition of acceptance} \\
\iff& (B^{p^{(i)}(|x|)/i!} \mid 0 \le i \le d) \in F' && \text{by the lemma} \\
\iff& \exists q \in F \ B^{p(|x|)}(s, q) = 1 && \text{definition of } F' \\
\iff& \exists y \in \Sigma^{p(|x|)} \ F \cap \widehat{\Delta}(\{s\}, y) \ne \varnothing && \text{by (3)} \\
\iff& \exists y \in \Sigma^{p(|x|)} \ y \in L(M) && \text{definition of acceptance} \\
\iff& x \in A' && \text{definition of } A' \qquad \square
\end{aligned}
$$

35. Let
$$A = \{ww \mid w \in \{0,1\}^*\}.$$

Note that $\{ww \mid w \in \{0\}^*\}$ is regular—it is just the set of strings of 0's of even length.

To show that A is nonregular, we will show that we have a winning strategy in the demon game. The demon picks some k. Now we take $x = 0$, $y = 1^k$, and $z = 01^k$. Then $xyz = 01^k01^k$, which is in A, and $|y| = k$. The demon must now choose u, v, w such that $y = uvw$ and $v \neq \epsilon$. Say the demon picks u, v, w of lengths j, m, n, respectively. Then $k = j + m + n$ and $m > 0$. But whatever the demon picks, we can win by taking $i = 0$:

$$xuv^0wz = xuwz = 01^{k-m}01^k,$$

which is not in A because it is not of the form ww for any w.

36. Recall that a number is *prime* if it is greater than 1 and has no divisors other than 1 and itself. PRIMES is an example of a single letter alphabet set that is not regular because the elements of the set do not appear with any predictable pattern.

Suppose the demon chooses k. You choose $x = z = \epsilon$ and $y = a^p$, where p is the smallest prime greater than k (Euclid proved that there exist infinitely many primes, so p exists). Then $xyz = a^p \in$ PRIMES and $|y| = p > k$. The demon must now choose u, v, w such that $y = uvw$ and $v \neq \epsilon$. Say the lengths of u, v, w are j, m, n, respectively. Then $k = j + m + n$ and $m > 0$. You now need to find i such that $xuv^iwz \notin$ PRIMES (i.e., $|xuv^iwz|$ is not prime). But

$$|xuv^iwz| = j + im + n = p + (i - 1)m,$$

so we need to find i such that $p + (i-1)m$ is not prime. Take $i = p+1$. Then

$$p + (i - 1)m = p + pm = p(1 + m),$$

which is not prime since it has factors p and $1 + m$. You win.

44. (a) First we show that the given condition is necessary for regularity. Let $A \subseteq \Sigma^*$ be a regular set, and let k be the number of states of a DFA for A. Then for all $y \in \Sigma^*$ with $|y| = k$, the automaton repeats a state while scanning y. Let v be a nonnull substring of y such that the automaton is in the same state just before and just after scanning v, and let $y = uvw$. Then for all $z \in \Sigma^*$ and $i \geq 0$, the automaton is in the same state after scanning $yz = uvwz$ as after scanning uv^iwz; therefore,

$$yz \in A \iff uv^iwz \in A.$$

Now we show that the given condition is sufficient for regularity. Let $A \subseteq \Sigma^*$ such that A satisfies the given condition. For any $x \in \Sigma^*$ with $|x| \geq k$, by applying the condition with $i = 0$

as many times as necessary, we can repeatedly delete nonnull substrings of x until we obtain a string x' of length $k - 1$ or less such that for all $z \in \Sigma^*$,

$$xz \in A \iff x'z \in A.$$

This says that $x \equiv_A x'$, where $\equiv_A$ is the relation (16.1). Since every $\equiv_A$-class contains a string of length $k-1$ or less, the relation $\equiv_A$ is of finite index. By the Myhill–Nerode theorem, A is regular.

45.   (b)   Equivalently, if $A \subseteq \mathbb{N}$ and $\widehat{A}$ is the smallest subset of $\mathbb{N}$ containing A and 0 and closed under addition, then A^* consists of all but finitely many multiples of gcd A.

First we consider the case $|A| = 2$. Let $m\mathbb{N}$ denote the set of all nonnegative multiples of m, and let $m\mathbb{N} + n\mathbb{N}$ denote the set of all sums $am + bn$ for $a, b \geq 0$. Write $A \sim B$ if A and B differ by a finite set; that is, if the set $(A - B) \cup (B - A)$ is finite.

Lemma   *Let m and n be positive integers, $g = \gcd(m, n)$. Then*

$$m\mathbb{N} + n\mathbb{N} \sim g\mathbb{N}.$$

Moreover, $\operatorname{lcm}(m, n) - m - n$ is the largest multiple of g not expressible in the form $am + bn$ with $a, b \geq 0$.

Proof. We first show a special case: if m and n are relatively prime, then $m\mathbb{N} + n\mathbb{N} \sim \mathbb{N}$. Moreover, the largest number not expressible in the form $am + bn$ with $a, b \geq 0$ is $mn - m - n$.

Suppose $mn - m - n$ were so expressible, say $am + bn = mn - m - n$. Then $(a + 1)m + (b + 1)n = mn$. Since m and n are relatively prime, m must divide $b + 1$ and n must divide $a + 1$. The smallest values of a and b for which this is true would be $a = n - 1$ and $b = m - 1$, which are already too big:

$$(n - 1)m + (m - 1)n = 2mn - m - n > mn - m - n.$$

Now let's show that $mn - m - n + 1$ is expressible. Let $u < n$ and $v < m$ such that $vn - um = 1$. (The numbers u and v can be produced by an extended version of the Euclidean GCD algorithm.) Take $a = n - u - 1$ and $b = v - 1$. Then

$$am + bn = (n - u - 1)m + (v - 1)n$$
$$= mn - um - m + vn - n$$
$$= mn - m - n + 1.$$

Now we proceed by induction. Suppose we have some $am + bn \geq mn - m - n + 1$. Since

$$(u - 1)m + (m - v - 1)n = um - m + mn - vn - n$$

$$= mn - m - n - 1,$$

we must have either $a \geq u$ or $b \geq m - v$. If the former, take $a' = a - u$ and $b' = b + v$ to get

$$a'm + b'n = (a - u)m + (b + v)n$$
$$= am - um + bn + vn$$
$$= am + bn + 1.$$

If the latter, take $a' = a + n - u$ and $b' = b - m + v$, and again

$$a'm + b'n = (a + n - u)m + (b - m + v)n$$
$$= am + mn - um + bn - mn + vn$$
$$= am + bn + 1.$$

If m and n are not relatively prime, say $g = \gcd(m, n)$, then everything is scaled by g. Any $am + bn$ is a multiple of g since g divides m and n, and the largest multiple of g not so expressible is

$$((m/g)(n/g) - m/g - n/g)g = \operatorname{lcm}(m, n) - m - n.$$

Now we use this to show that for any $A \subseteq \mathbb{N}$, $\widehat{A}$ consists of all but finitely many multiples of $g = \gcd A$. This follows from the observation that $\gcd A = \gcd X$ for some finite subset $X \subseteq A$ and from applying the lemma iteratively to obtain

$$\sum_{m \in X} \sum m\mathbb{N} \sim g\mathbb{N}. \qquad \square$$

49. Suppose first that $\{p, q\}$ is marked. We proceed by induction on the stages of the algorithm. If $\{p, q\}$ is marked in step 2, then either $p \in F$ and $q \notin F$ or vice versa, therefore $p \not\approx q$ (take $x = \epsilon$ in the definition of $\approx$). If it is marked in step 3, then for some $a \in \Sigma$, $\{\delta(p, a), \delta(q, a)\}$ was marked at some earlier stage. By the induction hypothesis, $\delta(p, a) \not\approx \delta(q, a)$, therefore $p \not\approx q$ by Lemma 13.5.

Conversely, suppose $p \not\approx q$. By definition, there exists an $x \in \Sigma^*$ such that either $\widehat{\delta}(p, x) \in F$ and $\widehat{\delta}(q, x) \notin F$ or vice versa. We proceed by induction on the length of x. If $x = \epsilon$, then either $p \in F$ and $q \notin F$ or vice versa, so $\{p, q\}$ is marked in step 2. If $x = ay$, then either $\widehat{\delta}(\delta(p, a), y) \in F$ and $\widehat{\delta}(\delta(q, a), y) \notin F$ or vice versa. By the induction hypothesis, $\{\delta(p, a), \delta(q, a)\}$ is eventually marked by the algorithm, and $\{p, q\}$ will be marked in the following step.

57. A subset of Σ^* is closed downward under $\sqsubseteq$ iff its complement is closed upward under $\sqsubseteq$. Since the complement of any regular set is regular, it suffices to show that all upward-closed sets are regular.

Let $\min X$ denote the set of $\sqsubseteq$-minimal elements of X, and let

$$y\!\uparrow \; = \{x \in \Sigma^* \mid y \sqsubseteq x\}.$$

Then X is upward-closed iff

$$X = \{x \in \Sigma^* \mid \exists y \in \min X \; y \sqsubseteq x\}$$
$$= \bigcup_{y \in \min X} y\!\uparrow .$$

By Higman's lemma, this is a finite union of sets of the form $y\!\uparrow$. Since a finite union of regular sets is regular, it suffices to show that any $y\!\uparrow$ is regular. But

$$a_1 a_2 \cdots a_n\!\uparrow \; = L(\Sigma^* a_1 \Sigma^* a_2 \Sigma^* \cdots \Sigma^* a_n \Sigma^*).$$

59. To construct a DFA from an AFA, let

$$A = (Q_A, \; \Sigma, \; \delta_A, \; F_A, \; \alpha_A)$$

be the given AFA, $|Q_A| = k$. Let Q_D be the set of all functions $Q_A \rightarrow \{0,1\}$. Define the DFA

$$D = (Q_D, \; \Sigma, \; \delta_D, \; F_D, \; s_D),$$

where

$$\delta_D(u,a)(q) = \delta_A(q,a)(u), \tag{4}$$
$$F_D = \alpha_A, \tag{5}$$
$$s_D = F_A. \tag{6}$$

To construct an AFA from a DFA, let

$$D = (Q_D, \; \Sigma, \; \delta_D, \; F_D, \; s_D)$$

be the given DFA, $|Q_D| = k$. Let Q_A be any set of size $\lceil \log k \rceil$ and identify each element of Q_D with a distinct function $Q_A \rightarrow \{0,1\}$. Define the AFA

$$A = (Q_A, \; \Sigma, \; \delta_A, \; F_A, \; \alpha_A),$$

where δ_A, F_A, and α_A are defined such that (4), (5), and (6) hold. (For $u \notin Q_D$, define $\delta_A(q,a)(u)$ arbitrarily.)

In both reductions, one can show by induction on $|x|$ that for any $q \in Q_A$, $u \in Q_D$, and $x \in \Sigma^*$,

$$\widehat{\delta}_D(u,x)(q) = \widehat{\delta}_A(q, \mathbf{rev}\, x)(u).$$

In particular,

$$x \in L(D) \iff F_D(\widehat{\delta}_D(s_D, x)) = 1$$

$$\Longleftrightarrow \alpha_A(\hat{\delta}_D(F_A, x)) = 1$$
$$\Longleftrightarrow \alpha_A(\lambda q.(\hat{\delta}_D(F_A, x)(q))) = 1$$
$$\Longleftrightarrow \alpha_A(\lambda q.(\hat{\delta}_A(q, \mathbf{rev}\, x)(F_A))) = 1$$
$$\Longleftrightarrow \mathbf{rev}\, x \in L(A).$$

77. The set generated is $\{a, b\}^*$. We can prove this by induction on string length. The null string is generated in one step. For nonnull strings, either the string begins with b, in which case we use the first production; or ends with a, in which case we use the second production; or neither, in which case we use the third production. In any case the induction hypothesis implies that the rest of the string can be generated.

78. Let P be a PDA for L and M a DFA for R. Build a PDA for L/R that on input x scans x and simulates P, then when it comes to the end of the input x, guesses the string y and continues to simulate P (from the same configuration where it left off) but also runs M simultaneously on the guessed y starting from the start state. It accepts if both L and M accept. Thus it accepts its original input x if it was successfully able to guess a string y such that $xy \in L(P)$ and $y \in L(M)$; that is, if there exists y such that $xy \in L$ and $y \in R$.

Here is an alternative proof using homomorphisms. Suppose the alphabet is $\{a, b\}$. Let $\{a', b'\}$ be another copy of the alphabet disjoint from $\{a, b\}$. Let h be the homomorphism that erases marks; that is, $h(a) = h(a') = a$ and $h(b) = h(b') = b$. Let g be the homomorphism that erases the unmarked symbols and erases the marks on the marked symbols; that is, $g(a) = g(b) = \epsilon$, $g(a') = a$, $g(b') = b$. Then

$$L/R = g(h^{-1}(L) \cap \{a', b'\}^* R). \tag{7}$$

This is a CFL, since CFLs are closed under homomorphic preimage, intersection with regular set, and homomorphic image.

To see (7), first consider the set $h^{-1}(L)$. This is the set of all strings that look like strings in L, except that some of the symbols are marked. Now intersect with the regular set $\{a', b'\}^* R$. This gives the set of strings of the form $x'y$ such that the symbols of x' are marked, those of y are unmarked, $xy \in L$, and $y \in R$. Now apply g to this set of strings. Applied to a string $x'y$ as described above, we would get x. Therefore, the resulting set is the set of all x such that there exists y such that $x'y \in h^{-1}(L) \cap \{a', b'\}^* R$; in other words, such that $xy \in L$ and $y \in R$. This is L/R.

99. (a) A *queue machine* is a sextuple

$$M = (Q, \Sigma, \Gamma, \$, s, \delta),$$

where

- Q is a finite set of *states,*

- Σ is a finite *input alphabet,*

- Γ is a finite *queue alphabet,*

- $\$ \in \Gamma - \Sigma$ is the *initial queue symbol,*

- $s \in Q$ is the *start state,* and

- $\delta : Q \times \Gamma \to Q \times \Gamma^*$ is the *transition function.*

A *configuration* is a pair $(q, \gamma) \in Q \times \Gamma^*$ giving the current state and current contents of the queue. The *start configuration* on input x is the pair $(s, x\$)$. The *next configuration relation* $\xrightarrow[M]{1}$ is defined as follows: if

$$\delta(p, A) = (q, \gamma),$$

then

$$(p, A\alpha) \xrightarrow[M]{1} (q, \alpha\gamma).$$

The relation $\xrightarrow[M]{*}$ is the reflexive transitive closure of $\xrightarrow[M]{1}$. An *accept configuration* is any configuration of the form (q, ϵ), where $q \in Q$ and ϵ is the null string. The queue machine M is said to *accept* $x \in \Sigma^*$ if

$$(s, x\$) \xrightarrow[M]{*} (q, \epsilon) \qquad \text{for some } q \in Q.$$

(b) To simulate a queue machine U on a Turing machine T, let T maintain the contents of U's queue on its tape and simulate the action of U, shuttling back and forth from the front to the back of the simulated queue. Each simulated step of U consists of T moving to the front of the simulated queue, erasing the first symbol and remembering it in the finite control, then moving to the back of the simulated queue to write symbols. The simulated queue migrates to the right on T's tape, but that's okay, because there's plenty of room. The machine T accepts if its tape ever becomes completely blank, which indicates that the simulated queue of U is empty.

The simulation in the other direction is much harder. Given a Turing machine T, we build a queue machine U that simulates moves of T, using the queue to maintain a description of T's current configuration. We will represent configurations by strings such as

$\vdash a\ b\ a\ a\ b\ a\ q\ b\ b\ a\ \$$

for example; exactly one of the symbols is a state of T (q in this example), and its position in the string indicates the position of the tape head of T, which is immediately to the right of the state. If the state is just before the $, this models T scanning a blank cell to the right of the portion of its tape represented in the configuration.

The queue machine U will also have an "internal queue" that will hold two symbols of this configuration; since this is only a finite amount of information, the internal queue can be encoded in the finite control of U. The remaining portion of the configuration will be held in the external queue. Since configurations have at least three symbols (state, left endmarker, $), even if the tape is blank, the external queue will never be prematurely emptied.

Let x be the input string. The queue machine U starts with $x\$$ in its external queue. It enters a state representing an internal queue of

$s\ \vdash$

The internal and external queues concatenated together represent the start configuration of T on input x:

$s\ \vdash x\ \$$

A **rotate** operation consists of rotating the symbols on the internal and external queues as follows:

internal queue   external queue

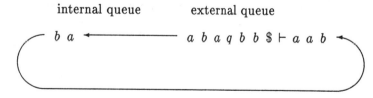

Formally, this is done by popping the first element off the front of the external queue and pushing the front element of the internal queue onto the back of the external queue, then changing state to reflect the new contents of the internal queue. In this example, after one rotation we would have

$a\ a$ $b\ a\ q\ b\ b\ \$ \vdash a\ a\ b\ b$

on the internal and external queues, respectively.

We simulate a step of T as follows. If the rightmost symbol of the internal queue is not a state of T, we **rotate** until this becomes true. In this example, after three more steps we would have

$$a \; q \qquad\qquad\qquad b \; b \; \$ \vdash a \; a \; b \; b \; a \; a \; b$$

Now we have the symbol that T is scanning (say b) at the head of the external queue and the current state of T (say q) rightmost on the internal queue. We read b at the head of the queue. If b is not $\$$, we simulate a move of T as follows.

- If $\delta_T(q, b) = (p, c, R)$ and the leftmost symbol of the internal queue is d, we push d onto the back of the external queue and make $(c \, p)$ the new internal queue.

- If $\delta_T(q, b) = (p, c, L)$ and the leftmost symbol of the internal queue is d, we push p onto the back of the external queue and make $(d \, c)$ the new internal queue.

In the example above, this would give

$$a \; p \qquad\qquad\qquad b \; \$ \vdash a \; a \; b \; b \; a \; a \; b \; a$$

if $\delta_T(q, b) = (p, a, R)$, and

$$a \; a \qquad\qquad\qquad b \; \$ \vdash a \; a \; b \; b \; a \; a \; b \; q$$

if $\delta_T(q, b) = (p, a, L)$. If the symbol at the head of the external queue is $\$$, then this indicates that the tape head of T is scanning a blank symbol to the right of the portion of the tape represented in the configuration. For example,

$$b \; q \qquad\qquad\qquad \$ \vdash a \; a \; b \; b \; b \; a \; a \; b \; a \; b$$

In this case, when we pop $\$$ we don't simulate a move of T immediately; first we insert an extra blank symbol $\sqcup$ between the state and the $\$$. We do this by pushing both symbols in the internal queue onto the back of the external queue and making the new internal queue $(\sqcup \, \$)$. In this example, the resulting queue contents would be

$$\sqcup \; \$ \qquad\qquad\qquad \vdash a \; a \; b \; b \; b \; a \; a \; b \; a \; b \; b \; q$$

We continue to simulate moves of T. If T ever enters its accept state, then U goes into a little subroutine that just empties its external queue, thereby accepting.

113. Let

$$\mathrm{REG} = \{M \mid L(M) \text{ is regular}\}.$$

A corollary of Rice's theorem for r.e. sets (Theorem 34.2) is that any semidecidable property of the r.e. sets is monotone. That is, if P is a property of r.e. sets such that $\{M \mid P(L(M))\}$ is r.e., A and B are r.e. sets, $A \subseteq B$, and $P(A)$, then $P(B)$. Applying this corollary with $P(C)$ = "C is regular," $A = \varnothing$, and $B = \{a^n b^n \mid n \geq 0\}$ gives immediately that REG is not r.e. Similarly, applying the corollary with $P(C) =$ "C is not regular," $A = \{a^n b^n \mid n \geq 0\}$, and $B = \Sigma^*$ gives immediately that REG is not co-r.e.

References

[1] W. ACKERMANN, Zum Hilbertschen Aufbau der reellen Zahlen, *Math. Annalen*, 99 (1928), pp. 118–133.

[2] A.V. AHO AND J.D. ULLMAN, *The Theory of Parsing, Translation, and Compiling, Vol. I: Parsing*, Prentice Hall, Englewood Cliffs, NJ, 1972.

[3] ——, *The Theory of Parsing, Translation, and Compiling, Vol. II: Compiling*, Prentice Hall, Englewood Cliffs, NJ, 1973.

[4] ——, *Principles of Compiler Design*, Addison-Wesley, Reading, MA, 1977.

[5] M.A. ARBIB AND Y. GIVE'ON, Algebra automata I: Parallel programming as a prolegomenon to the categorical approach, *Information and Control*, 12 (1968), pp. 331–345.

[6] R.C. BACKHOUSE, *Closure Algorithms and the Star-Height Problem of Regular Languages*, Ph.D. thesis, Imperial College, London, 1975.

[7] J.W. BACKUS, The syntax and semantics of the proposed international algebraic language of the Zürich ACM-GAMM conference, in *Proc. Intl. Conf. Information Processing*, UNESCO, 1959, pp. 125–132.

[8] Y. BAR-HILLEL, M. PERLES, AND E. SHAMIR, On formal properties of simple phrase structure grammars, *Z. Phonetik. Sprachwiss. Kommunikationsforsch.*, 14 (1961), pp. 143–172.

[9] H.P. BARENDREGT, *The Lambda Calculus*, North-Holland, Amsterdam, 1984.

[10] S.L. BLOOM AND Z. ÉSIK, Equational axioms for regular sets, *Mathematical Structures in Computer Science*, 3 (1993), pp. 1–24.

[11] M. BOFFA, Une remarque sur les systèmes complets d'identités rationnelles, *Informatique Théoretique et Applications/Theoretical Informatics and Applications*, 24 (1990), pp. 419–423.

[12] ——, Une condition impliquant toutes les identités rationnelles, *Informatique Théoretique et Applications/Theoretical Informatics and Applications*, 29 (1995), pp. 515–518.

[13] W.S. BRAINERD, *Tree Generating Systems and Tree Automata*, Ph.D. thesis, Purdue University, Indiana, 1967.

[14] ——, The minimalization of tree automata, *Information and Control*, 13 (1968), pp. 484–491.

[15] W.S. BRAINERD AND L.H. LANDWEBER, *Theory of Computation*, John Wiley, New York, 1974.

[16] G. CANTOR, Über eine Eigenschaft des Inbegriffes aller reellen algebraischen Zahlen, *J. für die reine und angewandte Mathematik*, 77 (1874), pp. 258–262. Reprinted in *Georg Cantor Gesammelte Abhandlungen*, Berlin, Springer-Verlag, 1932, pp. 115–118.

[17] N. CHOMSKY, Three models for the description of languages, *IRE Trans. Information Theory*, 2 (1956), pp. 113–124.

[18] ——, On certain formal properties of grammars, *Information and Control*, 2 (1959), pp. 137–167.

[19] ——, Context-free grammars and pushdown storage, Tech. Rep., MIT Research Lab. in Electronics, Cambridge, MA, 1962.

[20] ——, Formal properties of grammars, *Handbook of Math. Psych.*, 2 (1963), pp. 323–418.

[21] N. CHOMSKY AND G.A. MILLER, Finite state languages, *Information and Control*, 1 (1958), pp. 91–112.

[22] N. CHOMSKY AND M.P. SCHÜTZENBERGER, The algebraic theory of context free languages, in *Computer Programming and Formal Systems*, P. Braffort and D. Hirschberg, eds., North-Holland, Amsterdam, 1963, pp. 118–161.

[23] A. CHURCH, A set of postulates for the foundation of logic, *Ann. Math.*, 33–34 (1933), pp. 346–366, 839–864.

[24] ——, A note on the Entscheidungsproblem, *J. Symbolic Logic*, 58 (1936), pp. 345–363.

[25] ——, An unsolvable problem of elementary number theory, *Amer. J. Math.*, 58 (1936), pp. 345–363.

[26] ——, The calculi of lambda-conversion, *Ann. Math. Studies*, 6 (1941).

[27] J.H. CONWAY, *Regular Algebra and Finite Machines*, Chapman and Hall, London, 1971.

[28] S.A. COOK, The complexity of theorem proving procedures, in *Proc. Third Symp. Theory of Computing*, Assoc. Comput. Mach., New York, 1971, pp. 151–158.

[29] H.B. CURRY, An analysis of logical substitution, *Amer. J. Math.*, 51 (1929), pp. 363–384.

[30] N.J. CUTLAND, *Computability*, Cambridge University, Cambridge, 1980.

[31] M. DAVIS, *Computability and Unsolvability*, McGraw-Hill, New York, 1958.

[32] ———, *The Undecidable*, Raven Press, Hewlitt, NY, 1965.

[33] A. EHRENFEUCHT, R. PARIKH, AND G. ROZENBERG, Pumping lemmas and regular sets, *SIAM J. Computing*, 10 (1981), pp. 536–541.

[34] S. EILENBERG AND J.B. WRIGHT, Automata in general algebra, *Information and Control*, 11 (1967), pp. 452–470.

[35] J. ENGELFRIET, Tree automata and tree grammars, Tech. Rep. DAIMI FN-10, Aarhus University, Aarhus, Denmark, 1975.

[36] J. EVEY, Application of pushdown store machines, in *Proc. Fall Joint Computer Conf.*, AFIPS Press, Montvale, NJ, 1963, pp. 215–227.

[37] P.C. FISCHER, On computability by certain classes of restricted Turing machines, in *Proc. Fourth Symp. Switching Circuit Theory and Logical Design*, 1963, pp. 23–32.

[38] ———, Turing machines with restricted memory access, *Information and Control*, 9 (1966), pp. 364–379.

[39] P.C. FISCHER, A.R. MEYER, AND A.L. ROSENBERG, Counter machines and counter languages, *Math. Systems Theory*, 2 (1968), pp. 265–283.

[40] M.R. GAREY AND D.S. JOHNSON, *Computers and Intractibility: A Guide to the Theory of NP-Completeness*, W.H. Freeman, New York, 1979.

[41] F. GÉCSEG AND I. PEÁK, *Algebraic Theory of Automata*, Akadémiai Kiadó, Budapest, 1972.

[42] F. GÉCSEG AND M. STEINBY, *Tree Automata*, Akadémiai Kiadó, Budapest, 1984.

[43] S. GINSBURG, *The Mathematical Theory of Context-Free Languages*, McGraw-Hill, New York, 1966.

[44] S. GINSBURG AND S.A. GREIBACH, Deterministic context-free languages, *Information and Control*, 9 (1966), pp. 563–582.

[45] S. GINSBURG AND H.G. RICE, Two families of languages related to ALGOL, *J. Assoc. Comput. Mach.*, 9 (1962), pp. 350–371.

[46] S. GINSBURG AND G.F. ROSE, Operations which preserve definability in languages, *J. Assoc. Comput. Mach.*, 10 (1963), pp. 175–195.

[47] ———, Some recursively unsolvable problems in ALGOL-like languages, *J. Assoc. Comput. Mach.*, 10 (1963), pp. 29–47.

[48] ———, Preservation of languages by transducers, *Information and Control*, 9 (1966), pp. 153–176.

[49] S. GINSBURG AND E.H. SPANIER, Quotients of context-free languages, *J. Assoc. Comput. Mach.*, 10 (1963), pp. 487–492.

[50] K. GÖDEL, Über formal unentscheidbare Sätze der Principia Mathematica und verwandter Systeme I, *Monatshefte für Mathematik und Physik*, 38 (1931), pp. 173–198.

[51] ——, On undecidable propositions of formal mathematical systems, in *The Undecidable*, M. Davis, ed., Raven Press, Hewlitt, NY, 1965, pp. 5–38.

[52] J. GOLDSTINE, A simplified proof of Parikh's theorem, *Discrete Math.*, 19 (1977), pp. 235–240.

[53] S.A. GREIBACH, A new normal form theorem for context-free phrase structure grammars, *J. Assoc. Comput. Mach.*, 12 (1965), pp. 42–52.

[54] L. HAINES, *Generation and recognition of formal languages*, Ph.D. thesis, MIT, Cambridge, MA, 1965.

[55] M.A. HARRISON, *Introduction to Formal Language Theory*, Addison-Wesley, Reading, MA, 1978.

[56] J. HARTMANIS AND J.E. HOPCROFT, Structure of undecidable problems in automata theory, in *Proc. Ninth Symp. Switching and Automata Theory*, IEEE, 1968, pp. 327–333.

[57] J. HARTMANIS AND R.E. STEARNS, On the complexity of algorithms, *Trans. Amer. Math. Soc.*, 117 (1965), pp. 285–306.

[58] F.C. HENNIE, *Introduction to Computability*, Addison-Wesley, Reading, MA, 1977.

[59] J.E. HOPCROFT, An $n \log n$ algorithm for minimizing the states in a finite automaton, in *The Theory of Machines and Computation*, Z. Kohavi, ed., Academic Press, New York, 1971, pp. 189–196.

[60] J.E. HOPCROFT AND J.D. ULLMAN, *Introduction to Automata Theory, Languages, and Computation*, Addison-Wesley, Reading, MA, 1979.

[61] D.A. HUFFMAN, The synthesis of sequential switching circuits, *J. Franklin Institute*, 257 (1954), pp. 161–190, 275–303.

[62] J. JAFFE, A necessary and sufficient pumping lemma for regular languages, *SIGACT News*, 10 (1978), pp. 48–49.

[63] N.D. JONES, *Computability Theory: An Introduction*, Academic Press, New York, 1973.

[64] R.M. KARP, Reducibility among combinatorial problems, in *Complexity of Computer Computations*, R.E. Miller and J.W. Thatcher, eds., Plenum Press, New York, 1972, pp. 85–103.

[65] T. KASAMI, An efficient recognition and syntax algorithm for context-free languages, Tech. Rep. AFCRL-65-758, Air Force Cambridge Research Lab, Bedford, MA, 1965.

[66] S.C. KLEENE, A theory of positive integers in formal logic, *Amer. J. Math.*, 57 (1935), pp. 153–173, 219–244.

[67] ——, General recursive functions of natural numbers, *Math. Annalen*, 112 (1936), pp. 727–742.

[68] ——, Recursive predicates and quantifiers, *Trans. Amer. Math. Soc.*, 53 (1943), pp. 41–74.

[69] ——, *Introduction to Metamathematics*, D. van Nostrand, Princeton, NJ, 1952.

[70] ——, Representation of events in nerve nets and finite automata, in *Automata Studies*, C.E. Shannon and J. McCarthy, eds., Princeton University Press, Princeton, NJ, 1956, pp. 3–41.

[71] D.E. KNUTH, On the translation of languages from left to right, *Information and Control*, 8 (1965), pp. 607–639.

[72] D.C. KOZEN, *The Design and Analysis of Algorithms*, Springer-Verlag, New York, 1991.

[73] ——, A completeness theorem for Kleene algebras and the algebra of regular events, *Infor. and Comput.*, 110 (1994), pp. 366–390.

[74] D. KROB, A complete system of B-rational identities, *Theoretical Computer Science*, 89 (1991), pp. 207–343.

[75] W. KUICH, The Kleene and Parikh theorem in complete semirings, in *Proc. 14th Colloq. Automata, Languages, and Programming*, T. Ottmann, ed., vol. 267 of *Lect. Notes in Comput. Sci.*, EATCS, Springer-Verlag, New York, 1987, pp. 212–225.

[76] W. KUICH AND A. SALOMAA, *Semirings, Automata, and Languages*, Springer-Verlag, Berlin, 1986.

[77] S.Y. KURODA, Classes of languages and linear bounded automata, *Information and Control*, 7 (1964), pp. 207–223.

[78] P.S. LANDWEBER, Three theorems on phrase structure grammars of type 1, *Information and Control*, 6 (1963), pp. 131–136.

[79] H.R. LEWIS AND C.H. PAPADIMITRIOU, *Elements of the Theory of Computation*, Prentice Hall, Englewood Cliffs, NJ, 1981.

[80] P.M. LEWIS, D.J. ROSENKRANTZ, AND R.E. STEARNS, *Compiler Design Theory*, Addison-Wesley, Reading, MA, 1976.

[81] M. MACHTEY AND P. YOUNG, *An Introduction to the General Theory of Algorithms*, North-Holland, Amsterdam, 1978.

[82] Z. MANNA, *Mathematical Theory of Computation*, McGraw-Hill, New York, 1974.

[83] A.A. MARKOV, *The Theory of Algorithms*, vol. 42, Trudy Math. Steklov Inst., 1954. English translation, National Science Foundation, Washington, DC, 1961.

[84] W.S. McCULLOCH AND W. PITTS, A logical calculus of the ideas immanent in nervous activity, *Bull. Math. Biophysics*, 5 (1943), pp. 115–143.

[85] R. McNAUGHTON AND H. YAMADA, Regular expressions and state graphs for automata, *IEEE Trans. Electronic Computers*, 9 (1960), pp. 39–47.

[86] A.R. MEYER AND D.M. RITCHIE, The complexity of loop programs, in *Proc. ACM Natl. Meeting*, 1967, pp. 465–469.

[87] R. MILNER, Operational and algebraic semantics of concurrent processes, in *Handbook of Theoretical Computer Science*, J. van Leeuwen, ed., vol. B, North-Holland, Amsterdam, 1990, pp. 1201–1242.

[88] M.L. MINSKY, Recursive unsolvability of Post's problem of 'tag' and other topics in the theory of Turing machines, *Ann. Math.*, 74 (1961), pp. 437–455.

[89] M.L. MINSKY AND S. PAPERT, Unrecognizable sets of numbers, *J. Assoc. Comput. Mach.*, 13 (1966), pp. 281–286.

[90] E.F. MOORE, Gedanken experiments on sequential machines, *Automata Studies*, (1956), pp. 129–153.

[91] J. MYHILL, Finite automata and the representation of events, Technical Note WADD 57-624, Wright Patterson AFB, Dayton, Ohio, 1957.

[92] ———, Linear bounded automata, Technical Note WADD 60-165, Wright Patterson AFB, Dayton, Ohio, 1960.

[93] P. NAUR, Revised report on the algorithmic language ALGOL 60, *Comm. Assoc. Comput. Mach.*, 6 (1963), pp. 1–17.

[94] A. NERODE, Linear automaton transformations, *Proc. Amer. Math. Soc.*, 9 (1958), pp. 541–544.

[95] A.G. OETTINGER, Automatic syntactic analysis and the pushdown store, *Proc. Symposia on Applied Math.*, 12 (1961).

[96] W. OGDEN, A helpful result for proving inherent ambiguity, *Math. Systems Theory*, 2 (1968), pp. 191–194.

[97] C.H. PAPADIMITRIOU, *Computational Complexity*, Addison-Wesley, Reading, MA, 1994.

[98] R. PARIKH, On context-free languages, *J. Assoc. Comput. Mach.*, 13 (1966), pp. 570–581.

[99] E. POST, Finite combinatory processes-formulation, I, *J. Symbolic Logic*, 1 (1936), pp. 103–105.

[100] ———, Formal reductions of the general combinatorial decision problem, *Amer. J. Math.*, 65 (1943), pp. 197–215.

[101] ———, Recursively enumerable sets of positive natural numbers and their decision problems, *Bull. Amer. Math. Soc.*, 50 (1944), pp. 284–316.

[102] M.O. RABIN AND D.S. SCOTT, Finite automata and their decision problems, *IBM J. Res. Develop.*, 3 (1959), pp. 115–125.

[103] V.N. REDKO, On defining relations for the algebra of regular events, *Ukrain. Mat. Z.*, 16 (1964), pp. 120–126. In Russian.

[104] H.G. RICE, Classes of recursively enumerable sets and their decision problems, *Trans. Amer. Math. Soc.*, 89 (1953), pp. 25–59.

[105] ———, On completely recursively enumerable classes and their key arrays, *J. Symbolic Logic*, 21 (1956), pp. 304–341.

[106] H. ROGERS, JR., *Theory of Recursive Functions and Effective Computability*, McGraw-Hill, New York, 1967.

[107] J.B. ROSSER, A mathematical logic without variables, *Ann. Math.*, 36 (1935), pp. 127–150.

[108] A. SALOMAA, Two complete axiom systems for the algebra of regular events, *J. Assoc. Comput. Mach.*, 13 (1966), pp. 158–169.

[109] A. SALOMAA AND M. SOITTOLA, *Automata Theoretic Aspects of Formal Power Series*, Springer-Verlag, New York, 1978.

[110] S. SCHEINBERG, Note on the Boolean properties of context-free languages, *Information and Control*, 3 (1960), pp. 372–375.

[111] M. SCHÖNFINKEL, Über die Bausteine der mathematischen Logik, *Math. Annalen*, 92 (1924), pp. 305–316.

[112] M.P. SCHÜTZENBERGER, On context-free languages and pushdown automata, *Information and Control*, 6 (1963), pp. 246–264.

[113] J.I. SEIFERAS AND R. MCNAUGHTON, Regularity-preserving relations, *Theor. Comput. Sci.*, 2 (1976), pp. 147–154.

[114] J.C. SHEPHERDSON, The reduction of two-way automata to one-way automata, *IBM J. Res. Develop.*, 3 (1959), pp. 198–200.

[115] J.R. SHOENFIELD, *Degrees of Unsolvability*, North-Holland, Amsterdam, 1971.

[116] R.I. SOARE, *Recursively Enumerable Sets and Degrees*, Springer-Verlag, Berlin, 1987.

[117] D. STANAT AND S. WEISS, A pumping theorem for regular languages, *SIGACT News*, 14 (1982), pp. 36–37.

[118] L.J. STOCKMEYER, The polynomial-time hierarchy, *Theor. Comput. Sci.*, 3 (1976), pp. 1–22.

[119] J.W. THATCHER AND J.B. WRIGHT, Generalized finite automata theory with an application to a decision problem of second order logic, *Math. Syst. Theory*, 2 (1968), pp. 57–81.

[120] A.M. TURING, On computable numbers with an application to the Entscheidungsproblem, *Proc. London Math. Soc.*, 42 (1936), pp. 230–265. Erratum: Ibid., 43 (1937), pp. 544–546.

[121] ———, Systems of logic based on ordinals, *Proc. London Math. Soc.*, 42 (1939), pp. 230–265.

[122] M.Y. VARDI, A note on the reduction of two-way automata to one-way automata, *Information Processing Letters*, 30 (1989), pp. 261–264.

[123] A.N. WHITEHEAD AND B. RUSSELL, *Principia Mathematica*, Cambridge University Press, Cambridge, 1910–1913. Three volumes.

[124] A. YASUHARA, *Recursive Function Theory and Logic*, Academic Press, New York, 1971.

[125] D.H. YOUNGER, Recognition and parsing of context-free languages in time n^3, *Information and Control*, 10 (1967), pp. 189–208.

Notation and Abbreviations

Index